CREATING
CAREER
SUCCESS

A Flexible Plan for the World of Work

CREATING
CAREER
SUCCESS

A Flexible Plan for the World of Work

FRANCINE FABRICANT

JENNIFER PETERS

**Fashion Institute of Technology,
State University of New York**

DEBRA J. STARK

Ramapo College of New Jersey

WADSWORTH
CENGAGE Learning·

Australia • Brazil • Canada • Mexico • Singapore • Spain • United Kingdom • United States

WADSWORTH
CENGAGE Learning·

Creating Career Success: A Flexible Plan for the World of Work
Fabricant, Peters, Stark

Director, Developmental Studies: Annie Todd

Executive Editor: Shani Fisher

Senior Development Editor: Julia Giannotti

Assistant Editor: Angela Hodge

Media Editor: Amy Gibbons

Content Project Manager: Jessica Rasile

Senior Art Director: Pam Galbreath

Rights Acquisition Specialist:
   Shalice Shah-Caldwell

Manufacturing Planner: Sandee Milewski

Senior Marketing Manager: Elinor Gregory

Marketing Communications Manager: Linda Yip

Production Service/Compositor: S4Carlisle

Cover and Text Design: Lisa Buckley Design

Library of Congress Control Number: 2012945125

ISBN-13: 978-1-133-31390-8

ISBN-10: 1-133-31390-6

Wadsworth
20 Channel Center Street
Boston, MA 02210
USA

Cengage Learning is a leading provider of customized learning solutions with office locations around the globe, including Singapore, the United Kingdom, Australia, Mexico, Brazil, and Japan. Locate your local office at: **international.cengage.com/region**

Cengage Learning products are represented in Canada by Nelson Education, Ltd.

For your course and learning solutions, visit **www.cengage.com.**

Purchase any of our products at your local college store or at our preferred online store **www.cengagebrain.com**

Printed in the United States of America
3 4 5 6 19 18 17 16

Brief Contents

SECTION 1 Know Yourself

Gaining self-awareness about your skills, preferences, and values will lay the groundwork for your career development.

CHAPTER 1 Prepare

Begin your journey by learning how careers develop and identifying resources available to you.

CHAPTER 2 Skills

Reflect on your past experiences and activities to begin assessing the skills you have and the ones you need to build for your career.

CHAPTER 3 Preferences

Discover the role your interests and personality have in developing your career. By exploring what you like and don't like, you'll identify careers that are consistent with your preferences.

CHAPTER 4 Values

Increase your chances of being satisfied and successful in your career by assessing what is important to you and what motivates you.

SECTION 2 Explore Your Options

Building your research, communication, and decision-making skills will help you make career-related decisions and prepare to market your assets in the world of work.

CHAPTER 5 Explore

Learn about careers that interest you and open up new career possibilities by developing research skills, learning how to use current technology, and taking advantage of internships and other forms of exploration.

CHAPTER 6 Relationships

Build your social network and develop meaningful connections to find information, gain support, and learn about opportunities and positions that may never be formally posted.

CHAPTER 7 Decision Making

Learn strategies for making decisions and moving into action while adopting an open-minded approach that will help you succeed in an unpredictable world of work.

SECTION 3 Market Yourself

Marketing yourself successfully in the world of work is a skill to use throughout your career.

CHAPTER 8 Tools

Build your personal brand by creating powerful tools such as targeted résumés, cover letters, and a strong online presence.

CHAPTER 9 Launch

Begin your job search by building skills for interviewing, networking, and evaluating future job offers.

CHAPTER 10 Career Management

Prepare for your transition into the workplace and build the necessarily skills that will demonstrate your professionalism.

Contents

iStockphoto.com/Christopher Futcher

CHAPTER 2

Skills 24

What Have You Done? 25

Career Journal: Motivated Skills   26

Skills for Career Success 27

Masterfile (Royalty-Free Div.)

Assess Your Skills 33

Evidence of Skills 38

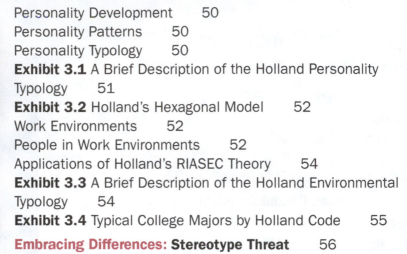

CHAPTER 4

Values 73

iStockphoto.com/Steve Debenport

CHAPTER 6

Relationships   125

StockLite/Shutterstock.com

iStockphoto.com/Aldo Murillo

West Coast Surfer/age fotostock

Résumés for the Real World   180

Just Say It! Action Verbs   187

Prepare Winning Cover Letters   189

Additional Job Search Tools   192

CHAPTER 9

Launch   225

AP Photo/Republican-Herald, Nick Meyer

iStockphoto.com/kristian sekulic

Quick Guide to Key Themes in This Text

Creating Career Success will help students:

- Build a self-directed, flexible, and adaptable career plan

- Create a network of meaningful connections

- Build and promote a personal brand

- Write a résumé and cover letter that will get through the initial screening process

- Take advantage of unplanned events

- Use technology to benefit all aspects of career development

For more information, continue reading the preface!

In the past few years, so much has changed in the world of

work. It used to be possible to make decisions about one's future and plan a career and a future path. Now, in an economy where job security is a thing of the past, layoffs are common, and people change jobs and careers frequently, planning a career may seem overwhelming. We believe it is possible to look at an unpredictable world and feel confident about career potential. The skills for building career success are different than before, and that is why we wrote this text.

Today, a whole new approach is needed. When we began exploring how to take the experience in our courses and bring it to life in the pages of a book, we hoped to bring to students the excitement, curiosity, and structure that is critical for proactive career development.

Helping students develop careers in an unpredictable economy is a recent challenge. As instructors and career counselors, we know that the job market changes rapidly due to innovation and globalization, and that job security no longer exists. Many of us have shifted our focus away from helping students make one-time career decisions and toward learning to be open-minded and to create opportunity.

We wrote this book because we believe that the traditional tools of career development, namely, assessment, exploration, and decision making are more important than ever. Students need to be prepared to manage the unexpected twists and turns they face. *Creating Career Success* offers students a foundation for understanding how their assets are relevant in the economy and how to build a future that meets their personal goals.

Creating Career Success helps students develop a self-directed, flexible plan to launch and manage their careers over the years to come, using the latest technological resources and job-search strategies. Through a process of self-assessment, students identify their skills, interests, and values and then learn to connect their strengths with knowledge they acquire about the world of work. Most importantly, students are encouraged to keep their minds and options open, and to engage themselves fully in their own career development.

> "Designed for students who are ready to take action and control of their own career management, this textbook promotes not only development and exploration, but also the need to be adaptable and proactive when achieving career decision-making success."
>
> **Sally Dingee,**
> **Monroe Community College**

> "These real-world snapshots of employee and employer are indispensable. Outstanding!"
>
> **Doris Haugen,**
> **Judson University**

We look forward to being part of the journey!

The tools in this text are designed to help students learn about themselves and the world around them, make better decisions, and create their own personal version of career success. Read on to see how this book can answer common questions we hear from students.

How will this text help me build a career?

Preparing for a career and the job search is exciting—students are embarking on a path that is up to them to construct. However, career development can also seem overwhelming because there is so much that is unknown or that might change. Students may be concerned about their decisions, the job search, the impact of the economy, and more.

Creating Career Success helps students build a *flexible* and *adaptable* plan for self-management in an unpredictable environment. Self-awareness, global awareness, and self-marketing skills will help students navigate their careers throughout their lifespan.

Readers are introduced to real people and fictional students throughout the text, allowing them to connect their experiences to real and possible situations.

> "This text addresses the current need for students to take responsibility, be flexible and adaptable, and be engaged in every step of their career."
>
> **James Rubin,**
> **Paradise Valley**
> **Community College**

- **Career Profile.** Organized in a question and answer format, the Career Profile feature highlights success stories of real people in the workplace and their employers, coworkers, or mentors. Readers will see firsthand what it takes to be successful in today's workplace and be prompted to think critically about skills, values, and strategies they can apply to their own career development.
- **Career Profile Case Studies.** Case studies highlight common issues, questions, and challenges that many students will face when building a career. To help these case studies come alive, **Chapter 8: Tools** includes examples of job-search materials such as résumés, cover letters, and target jobs or internships related to each case study. For example, students are introduced to Alex Moreno in **Chapter 4: Values.** Alex has decided to postpone medical school and find an interim job that would help him explore his interests while gaining experience in the field of medical research. In **Chapter 8, Tools,** readers see examples of a job listing that he is applying to, his targeted résumé, a networking-style cover letter, and a curriculum vitae or CV for those positions that request one.

rubberball/Jupiterimages

CAREER PROFILE ● Noemi S., Print and Web Publishing

Name: Noemi S.
College Degree: BA in Hispanic Studies
Current Position: Associate Editor
Employer: Manhattan Bride

Tell us a little about your academic experience and career preparation.
I worked for a year and a half to save money before college. I went to one four-year college first and then transferred to another with a full scholarship for the rest of my education. Even though the scholarship covered my tuition, I needed money for expenses, and so I started a full-time job while I was in school. It was hard to leave work for my classes, and I got a lower grade in one class and was off the dean's list for the first time. This motivated me to start my own business as a personal trainer while I was still in school, to set my own hours.

What led you to your current position?
When I graduated, I kept working as a personal trainer while I figured out what I wanted to do. One day, I was looking online at a celebrity wedding and I told my sister what I liked and what I would do differently for the wedding. She said, "You

should be in that industry. You love weddings." I went to the From Noemi's Employer
Name: Rick Bard
Title: Editor/Publisher, Manhattan Bride

How do you approach the hiring process?
Our approach to hiring is closely tied to our organizational values. Over 25 years ago, while publishing a different magazine, I started a foundation to raise money for homeless children in New York and to help fund breast cancer research. The first event was at the Plaza Hotel, and it felt like a large, important wedding. I turned to the bridal magazines and realized that a lot of my questions about planning this event were not being answered. Fifteen years later, after throwing more than 40 major charitable events, I started Manhattan Bride. Our touchstone is the generous spirit and ambiance we tried to create for each of those charitable events. We want to offer our clients that same spirit of generosity, always giving more quality and service than they expect. We want our new hires to appreciate this spirit of generosity and to be aligned with that purpose. We want to train people, so we're looking for people with a certain amount

When students learn more about careers that connect to their current interests, it allows them to remain flexible and open-minded as they become exposed to information about the world of work. **Career Journal**, found throughout the text, encourages readers to personalize the chapter content to their own lives.

Understanding the relationship between careers and preferences can help students identify patterns of interest and personality types and how these relate to career fields. **Chapter 3: Preferences** will help students understand the career paths and occupations that are typically chosen by people with similar interests and preferences, and help them consider how they want to connect their own preferences with the world of work. Special tools include:

"My favorite feature is the Journaling exercise. It teaches students how to creatively write and view their lives and allows them to think outside the box, which often leads to new career discoveries! In my experience, students often keep journals even when they are done with the class. Some have obtained jobs through journaling."

Pam Zuckerman, Fashion Institute of Technology

- **Career Journal: What Do You Like?** Students are guided to reflect on their interests and assess the areas that energize them most. Assessing preferences early on will help students identify themes and learning opportunities that they want to pursue.
- **Holland's Personality Types.** Students will learn about Holland's RIASEC Theory and explore Realistic, Investigative, Artistic, Social, Enterprising, and Conventional themes. Students are given the opportunity to see how their own RIASEC Code connects with occupations and majors to help them identify careers they want to explore.
- **Myers-Briggs Type Indicator.** Students learn to explore their preferences along each of the four dimensions of the MBTI® instrument: how they get energized, gather information, make decisions, and act on that information (Briggs Myers, Kirby, and Myers 1998). Students will learn how their preferences are related to occupations and majors and how understanding preferences can help them succeed in the workplace.

© Wavebreak Media ltd./Corbis

>>CAREER JOURNAL • Motivated Skills

Use the space below to write about your thoughts and feelings.

Describe an experience in which you used or developed a skill that was so enjoyable that you would like to continue developing it. What was the experience? What did you do?

What skill(s) did you use?

What made this skill enjoyable for you to use? Did any aspects of this skill feel like it came naturally for you? Did any aspects pose a challenge for you?

How will I find a job in today's economy?

It used to be possible to create a long-term, reliable plan for one's career within a fairly predictable global economy. Now, it is up to students to adapt and respond to a rapidly changing world. Mastering job-search skills is a valuable, lifelong asset in a global economy where people change jobs and careers frequently and job security no longer exists. Features in this text that help students understand the reality of today's world include:

- **Career Portfolio.** The online **FolioTek** portfolio tool will help students develop career-management skills by providing a format for organizing job-search materials, storing key tools for assessment, and providing a resource for tracking accomplishments and identifying career-building needs.
- **Embracing Differences**. This feature, found in each chapter, will help students learn about how the workplace is becoming more diverse, understand their rights as they apply to disabilities, and see the need for individuals to work together, find common themes, and manage differences effectively.
- **Work with Awareness**. In each chapter, students will consider how they wish to connect their values with their career and learn strategies to apply socially-aware concepts to their career plan.
- **Tech Savvy.** As technology continues to evolve, the way we work changes. Readers will learn ways to effectively and responsibly use technology to find information and promote their personal brand.

Ana Blazic/Shutterstock.com

⟫ WORK WITH AWARENESS ● Sustainability and Green Careers

A growing segment in the job market is represented by green careers. Green careers involve jobs that preserve and restore the quality of the environment. There may be many reasons for the growing trend for green careers, including such issues as long-term cost savings, an interest in preserving the environment, or a desire for companies to appeal to environmentally conscious consumers. Regardless of the determining factors, green careers are expanding significantly.

In fact, the growth of green careers has far exceeded growth in other areas. Between 1987 and 1997, green careers grew at almost triple the rate of traditional jobs (3.7% vs. 9.1%)

(Coulter, 2011). Furthermore, green careers are not only for sc[ientists] and white-collar managers. For instance, 69 percent of a[ll] green careers are in manufacturing, compared to 43 percent o[f] all U.S. jobs (Kuang, 2011). In addition, many opportunities are[e] opening for green jobs in a wide range of industries including [ ] traditional fields, such as banking, consumer products, marketin[g] or the law, in ways that are indirectly related to the green mov[e]ment, environmental issues, or sustainability. An example is a[ ] consumer-goods company aiming to reduce the plastic involve[d] in packaging for their products.

⟫ TECH SAVVY ● Use Social Media To Become an Information Magnet

Social media has added a new spin on career exploration. Now you can filter the news, search easily for information in your industry, and have current events and employer updates sent to your e-mail or social media accounts. Here are some of the most common social media resources and how they can help you stay up-to-date.

Facebook. On Facebook, anytime you "like" a company or professional organization, updates will show up in your newsfeed. To have industry-specific information come to you, consider "liking" a news source or informational site for your industry. Some suggestions include Mashable for techies, MediaBistro for media-related fields, or Stylesight for fashion trends.

Twitter. Twitter allows you to "follow" companies or people in the fields that interest you. With Twitter, you stay on top of your industry by reading brief entries that are 140 character or less, may include links to helpful articles or blogs, and are connected by an archival system using hashtags (e.g. #education). To find

people and organizations for your professional interests, choose "#discover" on the top bar, then "browse categories" on the far left, and type the name of any topic that interests you.

Pinterest. Pinterest is a great resource for learning more about people's interests and sources for inspiration, from products to images. By looking up the Pinterest pages of organizations, people in your industry, and bloggers who comment on your industry, you can search images that impact their ideas. These may also include comments and links to related blogs or websites. Although Pinterest has gained in popularity, you may find more professional activity on Pinterest in visual fields, such as fashion, design, art, and architecture.

LinkedIn. LinkedIn allows you to join groups related to your career interests and follow companies of interest. When you join a group, you will be prompted to decide the frequency with which you want to receive updates and how you wish to be contacted. Searching directly for companies and looking to see if any of your connections work there is a great way to find

---

"Students have heard much on globalization, but, for many, it is just another word. What is contained in the chapters I read reveals applicable information that discusses pertinent issues of diversity and its place in the larger world of work."

**Jeanne Kempiak,
College of DuPage**

As students prepare to market themselves and develop job-search tools, they need to consider their assets and how others perceive them. Students will learn how to connect their experiences, skills, interests, activities, and achievements with the world of work, and *build their very own personal brand*.

Résumés and cover letters are two key elements of students' personal branding tools. *Creating Career Success* shows readers how to build effective résumés that present a story of their experiences, skills, and assets, set up in an easy-to-read format, and targeted for a specific position. Most recruiters will spend *20–30 seconds or less* reviewing résumés in the initial screening process. Students will be guided to create documents that make it past this half-minute review. Specific coverage includes:

"I love the details that you have written in the cover letters and résumés. I really like the idea that you included several examples that would cover the wide range of students (ages 16–61) that I have in my classes. In the past, I have always shown them an example of my CV so they would know what one looks like. You have provided that in the text. This is an excellent, well-done chapter. BRAVO!"

**Victoria Basnett,
St. John's River State College**

- **Complete Package of Sample Job Search Tools.** Résumés and cover letters in **Chapter 8: Tools** correspond with the case study students highlighted in each chapter. These résumés and cover letters are prepared to answer a specific job or internship opportunity, also included in the text. This unique approach allows readers to see targeted résumés, cover letters, thank you notes, and other job search tools for each of the case study students.
- **Step-by-Step Approach to Creating a Targeted Résumé.** A targeted résumé is designed to highlight the assets and accomplishments that are most relevant to the needs of the reader. A successful targeted résumé makes the employer think, "Wow! These are exactly the requirements that meet our needs!"
- **Techniques for Submitting Résumés and Cover Letters Online.** Understanding the basics will help students prepare a résumé that is compatible with current technology and develop an approach that is responsive to the evolving demands of employers.

》》EXHIBIT 8.13 ● Reverse Chronological Résumé/Leticia Beason/ Event Coordinator

Leticia Beason
15544 South Hidden Springs Drive
Oro Valley, Arizona 54859
(520) 555-8792 • leticiajbeason@gmail.com

OBJECTIVE	Event Coordinator
EDUCATION	**University of Arizona**, Tucson, AZ
Bachelor of Arts in Sociology, Expected May 2013

University of Westminster, London, United Kingdom
Study Abroad: British Theatre, Literature, and Women Studies, Fall 2011 |
| **EXPERIENCE** | **Marriot International**, Tucson, AZ
Intern, Event Planning, Summer 2012
• Assisted with coordination of corporate meetings and events.
• Acted as point person between Events Coordinator and hourly associates, ensuring that associates understood expectations and parameters for event.
• Provided administrative support for staff of 10 senior event planners.
• Worked with social media tools to distribute weekly newsletter.
• Scheduled new clients and participated in customer meetings to plan details for events.
• Performed post-event follow-up with clients.

YMCA, Tucson, AZ
Lifeguard and Swim Instructor, Summers 2009, 2010, 2011
• Maintained certifications and supervised pool area.
• Taught weekly swim lessons; assisted with special-needs children. |
| **ACTIVITIES** | **Public Relations Student Society of America**, Member, Spring 2012 - Present

University Dance Team, Member, Fall 2010 - Present
Captain, Spring 2012 - Present

Alpha Epsilon Phi, Member, Fall 2010 - Present
Public Relations Representative, Spring 2012 - Present |
| **SKILLS** | **Computer:** Microsoft Office (Word, Excel, Outlook, PowerPoint), FileMaker Pro, InDesign, HTML, and Photoshop.
Social Media: Facebook, LinkedIn, Twitter.
Language: Working knowledge of French. |

How do I set career goals and make important decisions?

Throughout their careers, students will need to face big decisions, such as choosing a major or a career direction, as well as small steps, like selecting activities and courses that will help them build skills and credentials. There are specific ways *Creating Career Success* will guide students in improving their career decision-making skills:

- **Using the Your Flexible Plan Feature.** In this end-of-chapter feature, students will be presented with a Plan of Analysis or Plan of Action to assist with short-term decision making and to serve as a reference tool for the future. Students will learn to identify and address challenges so they can take steps to move ahead.

- **Dealing with Information Overload.** In today's world, choosing an occupation, job, or major is complicated by an array of choices. There are far more specialty areas for academic study, numerous choices for higher learning including brick-and-mortar and online settings, seemingly endless options for gathering career information, and millions of online resources for job openings. Students are given strategies for wading through all this helpful, but sometimes overwhelming, information.

- **Taking Advantage of Unplanned Events.** Many people attribute some of their greatest career opportunities to luck. Chance meetings, unexpected job offers, and pivotal project assignments are often described "lucky breaks," "perfect timing," or "being in the right place at the right time." Students will learn how to create a strategy to increase their likelihood of encountering unplanned events. They also will learn to make decisions even while remaining open-minded about future opportunities. This realistic and positive approach will help students engage more fully in career development at every stage of the process, and can be especially helpful for students who are undecided about their career interests.

- **Decision-Making Skills Can Also Be Practiced by Using Additional Chapter Support Material.** This includes the following:
  - **Exhibits.** For students who learn best by seeing tables, charts, graphic illustrations, and sample materials (e.g., résumés and cover letters), these will offer examples and data regarding key aspects of career development.
  - **Performance Appraisal.** The end-of-chapter Quiz and Thought Questions allow students to test their knowledge of key chapter themes.
  - **Tasks.** End-of-chapter exercises are designed to help students explore and personalize chapter content.
  - **Update Your Portfolio.** Students are directed to the online Career Portfolio, which will help them develop career-management skills by providing a format for organizing their job-search materials, storing key tools for assessment, and providing a resource for tracking their accomplishments and identifying career-building needs.

"My students struggle with trying to decide on what type of career/job in that it provides concrete strategies on how they can better make decisions related to their career."

Satya Patel, LIM College

Lane Oatey/blue jean images/Jupiterimages

Students will learn early on that relationships are a critical component of their ongoing career development. Throughout our work and life, many of our most interesting and rewarding opportunities develop out of relationships. Building and nurturing genuine relationships can help gain support, information, and access throughout one's career. *Creating Career Success* will help students:

> I really like the Networking aspect, and I always tell my students that the three most important parts of career development are: networking, networking, networking!"
>
> **Gary John**
>
> **Richland College**

- **Build a Network.** Making meaningful connections will take some strategy, a bit of effort, and it may take a dose of courage to talk to new people; but it offers a lot of benefits as well. Students will read about concrete ways to turn connections into relationships.
- **Use Social Media to Make Connections**. Students will learn to use LinkedIn, Google+, Facebook, and Pinterest to expand their career network.
- **Go on Informational Interviews.** Students will learn what an informational interview is and a step-by-step approach to make the most out of informational interview opportunities.
- **Navigate the Hidden Job Market.** Most estimates suggest that more than 75 percent of jobs are not advertised. Learning how to network for both internships and jobs is important and requires proactive behavior, follow up, and the ability to self-manage. These skills will help students prepare for the way jobs are typically found.

Kurhan/Shutterstock.com

EXHIBIT 6.4 ● LinkedIn Request

LinkedIn generates an automatic request to request a connection, shown here. Note that it does not help the recipient understand the context of the request, nor remind the recipient of any details about the sender.

LinkedIn

Leticia Beason requested to add you as a connection on LinkedIn:

I'd like to add you to my professional network on LinkedIn.

-Leticia

Accept　View Invitation from Leticia Beason

…modifying your request on LinkedIn, as shown here, you can be more specific and personal when you request a connection on …In. LinkedIn restricts the number of characters allowed per message. Note that although this is short, the note offers enough …ation to inform the recipient of details about the sender. Use a formal greeting, such as Mr. or Ms., unless you are certain that …sing your contact by a first name is appropriate.

LinkedIn

Leticia Beason requested to add you as a connection on LinkedIn

Dear Ryan,

It was great to speak with you yesterday. I really enjoyed our conversation regarding my interest in a career in event planning, and would like to add you to my network. Thank you.

Best Regards,

Leticia Beason

Accept　View Invitation from Leticia Beason

…also possible to send a personalized message on LinkedIn to be introduced to someone you have never met, shown here. …the category "expertise request," and the subject can be written "informational interview." …r message to Donna O'Grady:　　　　Include a brief note for Ryan Donald:

de others on this message
To: Donna O'Grady
Subject: Informational Interview

Ms. O'Grady,

…ave a mutual connection, Ryan Donald, who is an alumnus from my …ge, University of Arizona. I am interested in a career in event planning, and …ng to learn more about the field. I was impressed by your profile, and would …o schedule a brief conversation or informational interview.

…Regards,

…ia Beason

…I Message　or Cancel

Include others on this message
To: Ryan Donald
Subject: Informational Interview

Dear Ryan,

Thank you again for our meeting. I was reviewing your profile, and noticed you have a connection, Donna O'Grady, at Jones Event Productions in Phoenix. I was hoping you would forward her this message exploring the possibility of scheduling a brief conversation or informational interview. Thank you very much.

Best Regards,

Leticia Beason

Send Message　or Cancel

>> EXHIBIT 6.3 ● Informational Interview Request

 Here is an example of a request from a student with no experience in the field.

To:　rkdonald@donaldgorhamevents.com
Cc:
Bcc:
Subject:　Student Referred by Professor David Wheeler

Dear Mr. Donald,

I am a junior at University of Arizona and am writing at the suggestion Professor David Wheeler. After discussing my interest in exploring a career in event planning, Professor Wheeler recommended I contact you. He spoke very highly of your success as an event planner, and I was hoping you might be available for an informational interview. I have researched the field online and am trying to decide if event planning would be a good fit for me. I hope to learn more about your experiences, as well as the skills and abilities that you think are essential. I would also like to learn more about what I can do now as a college student to prepare myself for this field.

I would greatly appreciate it if I could meet with you for a short informational interview. I will call you next week to set up an appointment. In addition, I can be reached at 702.555.5555 or at this e-mail address. I would like to thank you in advance for your assistance.

Best regards,

Leticia Beason

» Support Materials

Creating Career Success comes with a full package of support material to help you teach this course.

For Faculty

The Instructor Website offers:

- **Instructor's Resource Manual.** Designed to help you make the most out of the text, the IRM will cover the following material:
  - **Chapter by Chapter Guide.** In each chapter, the following topics will be addressed:
    - *Prepare:* How to prepare and set goals for the class session
    - *Engage:* Suggested icebreakers and group activities
    - *Personalize:* How to develop relevant examples
    - *Assign:* Suggested assignments for homework, midterms, and final exams
  - **General Resources.** Suggestions for connecting the content of the textbook with some of the specific needs of the following groups will be included:
    - New to the workforce
    - Changing careers
    - Returning to the workforce
    - Military to civilian
    - Specific majors (liberal arts, business, art and design, STEM majors)
  - **Additional Topics.**
    - Developing and using a Career Portfolio including self-management of the Career Portfolio after the course
    - Integrating Career Assessments (including the MBTI® assessment, MBTI®Complete, SDS, Strong Interest Inventory® assessment, and the iStartStrong™ Report)
    - Facilitating discussion boards (oriented toward online or hybrid courses, but can be used for in-person courses as well)
    - Helping students develop, manage, and use social media in their career
    - Working with guest speakers
    - Providing support or referral for individuals on an as-needed basis
- **Test Bank**
- **Sample Syllabi.** Sample syllabi will be included for the following courses:
  - 3-credit course
  - 3-credit course (online or hybrid)
  - 1-credit course
  - Suggestions for abbreviated courses and courses that focus on specific topics, such as the internship or job search.
- **PowerPoint Presentations**

For Students

Creating Career Success includes College Success CourseMate, which helps you make the grade. College Success CourseMate includes:

- An interactive eBook, with highlighting, note taking, and search capabilities
- Interactive learning tools including:
  - Quizzes
  - Flashcards
  - Videos
  - Direct access into **Career Transitions**, a self-paced application that provides hands-on guidance with all aspects of job-seeking and career exploration (Use **Career Transitions** to do the following: discover your career interests; identify new opportunities based on your work and/or military experience; research growing career paths, including green and new economy jobs; find relevant education and training; create résumés and cover letters; locate and apply for jobs; prepare for interviews.)
  - A link to an up-to-date career blog written by the authors on current and relevant events relating to career development
- Engagement Tracker, a first-of-its-kind tool that monitors student engagement in the course

Go to http://www.cengagebrain.com to access these resources, and look for this icon to find resources related to your text in College Success CourseMate.

FolioTek

Give your students the ability to organize and manage resources in an easy to use on-line repository! Cengage's FolioTek portfolio solution allows students to easily store, organize and share resources – from classroom assignments to professional employment tools – in a secure, streamlined environment. Using a simple navigation menu, students can upload and customize their portfolio to their specifications. Faculty can easily create and moderate "Communities" for their classes. Contact your Cengage Learning representative for more information about bundling FolioTek access for your students.

Career Portfolio samples using the FolioTek portfolio solution are available in CourseMate. With tasks, sample job search tools, and exercises straight from the book, these samples build on the text's Career Profile—Case Studies to give students an example of how to create a Career Portfolio as a tool for learning and a place to store materials for the job search.

MBTI® Instrument

The MBTI®Complete is a one-stop, online offering that combines the world's most trusted and widely used personality instrument with a basic interpretation. Instructors are not required to be certified to administer MBTI®Complete. Students take the assessment on their own, participate in an interactive learning session, and automatically receive a three-page type description based on their results. Instructor materials include *16 Paths to Student Success,* a lesson planner detailing how to incorporate MBTI® personality styles into your instruction on time management, communication, learning styles, and study skills.

Acknowledgments

It is with great appreciation that we would like to thank everyone who helped us create this textbook. We would like to thank the amazing team at Cengage Learning, with special thanks to Shani Fisher, our Senior Sponsoring Editor. This project would not have happened without her encouragement, direction, and insight. We would like to thank Julia Giannotti, our Development Editor, whose clear and helpful comments improved the entire writing and editing process. We would also like to thank Angela Hodge, Amy Gibbons, Elinor Gregory, Robert White, and Jessica Rasile. Numerous others at Cengage Learning also assisted in bringing the textbook and ancillaries to you, and we would like to thank everyone on this enthusiastic and knowledgeable team. We would like to thank Wendy Granger at Q2A/Bill Smith for helping us visually represent our ideas through her photo sourcing for the textbook. We would like to thank Kannan Poojli Vadivelu and everyone at S4Carlisle Publishing Services for their attention to detail and collaboration during the copyediting process. We would like to thank Dick Knowdell for sharing his valuable tools for assessing motivated skills and career values. We would like to thank CPP, Inc. and PAR. We also would like to thank Rick Bard, for taking our author photographs. We are especially grateful to all of the people we interviewed for the Career Profiles, who serve as real-world inspiration for those reading this book.

We would like to thank all of the reviewers, whose thoughtful feedback and suggestions helped shape the text, including:

Benjamin Alexander, South Plains College

Susan Aufderheide, Purdue University

Patricia Avila, Riverside City College

Victoria Basnett, St. Johns River State College

Kara Becker, LIM College

Phyllis Bickers, Auburn University

Lynn Brysacz, Glendale CC

Christine Daves, Minneapolis College of Art and Design

Carrie DeLeon, Columbia Basin College

Sally Dingee, Monroe Community College

Linda Dunham, Central Piedmont Community College

Laura Emerick, St. Cloud State University

Tamekca Faria, Delaware State University

Celeste Fenton, Hillsborough Community College

Dawn Forrester, Mt. Hood Community College

Gladys Green, State College of Florida

Doris Haugen, Judson University

Christina Havlin, ECPI University

Kathryn Jackson, Loyola University Chicago

La-Dana Jenkins, Borough of Manhattan Community College

Gary John, Richland College

Elvira Johnson, Central Piedmont Community College

Deb Kelly, The College of New Jersey

Jennifer Kelly, Nassau Community College

Jeanne Kempiak, College of DuPage

Cheryll LeMay, Diablo Valley College

Robert Lewallen, Iowa Western Community College

Jana Lithgow, Loyola University Chicago

Sabrina Marschall, Shippensburg University

Mary Mazuk, Mount St. Joseph

Satya Patel, LIM College

Dorali Pichardo-Diaz, Rio Hondo College

Cynthia Prehar, Framingham State University

Tami Prichard, Texas Tech University

Eileen Quaglino, Ramapo College of New Jersey

Emily Reabe, Triton College

Ricky Riley, City College

Barbara Rodriguez, Florida National College

Lisa Romain, Palomar College

Lynn Rosen, University of Pittsburgh

Shirley Rowe, University of Texas at San Antonio

James Rubin, Paradise Valley Community College

Debra Schultz, Carroll University

Lisa L. Sharp, Heartland Community College

Joe Spence, Broome Community College

Belen Torres-Gil, Rio Hondo College

Melody Vaught, Santiago Canyon College

Dan Wilcox, Kansas State University

Pam Zuckerman, Fashion Institute of Technology

We would like to specifically thank Shirley Rowe and Belen Torres-Gil for their contribution to the ancillaries. We would like to thank the Fashion Institute of Technology for providing Jennifer Peters with a sabbatical that allowed her to work full-time on this textbook. All of us would like to thank our departments and colleagues for their support and insight. Finally, we would like to thank the librarians and desk staff at The Bryant Library and the libraries at Hofstra University for their extensive resources and assistance. And, of course, we would like to thank our students and clients, who have been our greatest source of inspiration, and for whom this book is dedicated.

Additionally, we would like to thank those who helped us in more ways than we can list:

Thank you, Ken, Lindsay, Rebecca, Sabrina, and Dad, for your support and love, throughout this project and always!—Francine Fabricant

I want to thank my children Jonah and Sara. You are the inspiration in my life, and this book is for you! I would also like to thank my parents, Joe and Gloria, for always believing in me, and Phil, for sharing my joy in this project.—Jennifer Peters

Thank you to my daughter, Julia, for her support during this project, and to my mom, Kay, for loving me unconditionally. My endless gratitude to my family, friends and colleagues.—Debra J. Stark

» About the Authors

The authors welcome you to connect on LinkedIn and join their network.

Francine Fabricant

Photo by Rick Bard © 2012

Francine Fabricant, MA, EdM is a career counselor in private practice with over 12 years experience. She is a Lecturer at Hofstra University Continuing Education, an Adjunct Instructor at NYIT Extended Education, and a frequent speaker on career topics. She also has developed and delivered numerous career and job search programs in partnership with not-for-profit organizations. Through her courses and workshops, she provides support for those in career fields as varied as education, politics, media, finance, entrepreneurial paths, medicine, engineering, not-for-profit, fashion, and the arts. Her community-based workshops have been profiled in *The New York Times*. Formerly, she served as a career counselor at the Columbia University Center for Career Education and as a career counselor and part-time faculty member at the Fashion Institute of Technology (FIT). She holds a Bachelor of Arts degree cum laude from Barnard College, Columbia University, as well as a Master of Arts in Organizational Psychology and a Master of Education in Psychological Counseling, both from Teachers College, Columbia University. She is a National Certified Counselor (NCC), a Master Career Counselor (MCC), and a Board Certified Coach (BCC). Before entering the field of career development, she held positions in magazine editorial, public relations, and marketing.

Jennifer Peters

Fashion Institute of Technology,
State University of New York

Jennifer Peters, MBA, MSED is an Associate Professor and Counselor in the Career and Internship Center at the Fashion Institute of Technology (FIT) with over 11 years of experience in Career Counseling focusing on the fashion and related industries. She is very knowledgeable and passionate about sustainability and social media. In addition to counseling she taught Career Planning for several years and is currently teaching an internship course on Career Exploration. She is very active on her campus serving on numerous faculty, union and college-wide committees. She has been on the Executive Board of MNYCCPOA, a New York area college career counselors' organization, for the past five years serving as Treasurer, Second Vice President and is currently the Historian. In addition, she is an active member of numerous career counseling focused professional organizations. Prior to working in career development she was the Director of Student Services at the French Culinary Institute in New York City for four years. She holds a Bachelor of Arts degree from Binghamton University in Binghamton, New York and she has two masters degrees; one in Guidance and Counseling from Hunter College in New York City, and one in Business Administration from Binghamton University.

Photo by Rick Bard © 2012

Debra J. Stark, MA, is the Assistant Director of Employer Relations and Alumni Career Advisor at Ramapo College of New Jersey, where she has worked since 1996. In this role she advises both students and alumni, connects with corporate and agency recruiters, maintains the order and collection development of the Career Resource Center, administers and creates career development instruction modules, teaches the upper level Career Achievement Program, and oversees the center's online career management system. Debra has made significant contributions through service on several college-wide committees including the Middle States Steering Committee and Institutional Effectiveness. Debra has presented nationally and internationally for student and professional audiences on a variety of career topics. She is also an adjunct professor in the School of American and International Studies. Prior to her work with the Career Center, she was the Freshman Advisement and Registration Program Coordinator. Her experience outside of higher education includes international business, customer relations, and corporate training and development. Debra is associated with the following relevant associations: EACE, MNYCCPOA, NJACE, CRMA, and MACCA. Debra earned a Bachelor of Arts in history and a Master of Arts in Liberal Studies at Ramapo College of New Jersey.

Debra J. Stark
Ramapo College of New Jersey

Photo by Rick Bard © 2012

Know Yourself

iStockphoto.com/Christopher Futcher

Prepare

> For tomorrow belongs to the people who prepare for it today.
> —*African Proverb*

What's Inside

Prepare to . . .

- Lay the groundwork for your career education
- Explore trends in the world of work
- Become familiar with the field of career development
- Set up a Career Portfolio and learn about its purpose
- Learn about resources that can be useful for your career development

This is the time to start thinking about your future and all the possibilities life has to offer. To get the most out of your career education, prepare by laying the groundwork for your self-assessment.

» Where Should I Start?

The career you develop will impact all aspects of your life. Where you live, how you spend your day, and the people you meet are all influenced by your career. Your career determines your lifestyle, influences how others perceive you, and impacts your daily schedule and long-term planning.

With so many aspects of your life involved, you may be wondering where to start. The good news is—you've already started. Just by living your life, you have already accumulated a great deal of information toward developing a worthwhile and satisfying career. The activities and exercises in this text are designed to help you organize and assess what you already know, discover additional information about yourself and the world of work, and become more articulate about your goals and the opportunities that interest you.

Whether you want to make a career decision, choose a major, prepare for a future job search, or change careers, these tips will help you get the most out of your career education.

Prepare for Your Lifetime, Not Just for Your Next Job

By fully engaging in the process of career development, rather than the single one-time event of "getting a job," you will lay the groundwork for greater opportunities in the future. This involves an introspective assessment of yourself, an exploration of the world of work, and the development of a thoughtful and strategic approach to self-marketing and career management. This will prepare you to make informed decisions and reach your personal goals. As you begin to develop a clearer understanding of yourself and the world of work, you will start to notice themes and recognize career possibilities.

Be Honest with Yourself

It can be hard to be honest about what you want. In this text you will be asked many questions that are designed to help you become more aware of your thoughts and feelings, biases and preconceptions, as well as fears and aspirations. Then, you will look for concrete ways to gather helpful information and make decisions.

Here are a few of the thoughts or concerns other people have had about careers. As you review this list, think about the concerns or questions you have.

- The more I learn about career options, the more I feel there is no good choice—or too many good choices—for me.
- My biggest career concern is how to make money.
- To do what I really want, I need further education, but I don't know if I'm ready to make that commitment.

Being honest with yourself about what is important to you is the first step in preparing for career development.

r-bit co Ltd/A.collection/Getty Images

- My career interests are different from my family's expectations, and I'm not sure they will support me.
- I know what I like, but I don't think I can make a living doing it.
- I want to have time for my family and a career.

Enjoy the Learning

The subject of your career education is you. What you like, what you value, and what you want to do are some of the things you will be studying as you read this textbook. Sometimes it will be great fun, as you meet people you like and learn about things you would love to do. However, there might be times when you have to step back, because an experience was not what you expected, or you learned something that made a direction seem like a poor fit. Career development is self-directed, and the decisions for your future are up to you. Take notice of the careers and examples in this course, and in your research, that you enjoy most.

Enlist the Help of Others

Getting support can make difficult times much more manageable. When you seek out support, you may find that when you mention the word "career" to others, you are quickly engaged in a conversation about available jobs, such as where to find them, who's hiring, or how to get one. However, that may not be what you want right now. You may want feedback on particular career questions, insight about someone's chosen profession, or information about the job market. Figuring out exactly how others can be helpful and preparing your questions in advance can be the key to getting the support you need. Your support network can be an invaluable resource during your self-assessment and career exploration. Identify people in your network and how they can help.

Expect Change, and Aim for a Flexible and Responsive Career

A flexible and responsive career allows you to grow and develop as a person, because your interests, skills, and values will also evolve. Realizing early that you will want different things at different times in your life can make it easier to accept and embrace the change that lies ahead. Furthermore, as you change internally in the years to come, so will the environment around you. You can't always control events that will impact your career, but you can develop career resilience and a flexible career plan.

Your ability to adapt to a shifting marketplace can help you seek out a match for your assets regardless of the economy, technological advances, or other changes that are likely to occur. This may lead you to seek out new responsibilities on the job, change jobs, or seek additional education or training as your career progresses.

Use the space below to write about your thoughts and feelings.

Career Journals give you an opportunity to connect your thoughts and feelings to chapter topics. Although these journals have directed questions, and limited write-in space, feel free to continue your thoughts in the margins or on another page. If writing about your thoughts is unfamiliar to you, try a technique called freewriting, in which you write the first thoughts that come to mind, unedited and without using proper grammar. This can help you identify your thoughts and ideas, without stopping yourself to focus on writing skills.

Think of a career you have considered recently, wanted to pursue when you were a child, or a fantasy career that you would like if there were no obstacles.

What career are you picturing?

Describe as much as you can about the environment, the people, and the activities you are picturing. What do you think an average day might be like for this person? With whom does he or she interact? What is he or she wearing, doing, saying, or thinking? What is the scenery—is it outdoors or indoors, in an office or a field setting? What types of materials help this person do his or her job (e.g., animals, medical equipment, computers, laboratory equipment, a sewing machine, a paintbrush)?

What makes this career appealing to you?

Do you imagine yourself taking the steps to pursue this career? Why or why not?

Journal Feedback . . . The answers to these questions will begin to offer insight into your skills, personal preferences, values, and sources for motivation.

» Prepare for the World of Work

The changing landscape of today's workplace is dominated by themes of diversity, multigenerational issues, technology, and globalization. Here are some of the ways the world of work is evolving.

Diversity

A wide range of racial, ethnic, and religious groups now make up our society and the workplace. Women now comprise almost half the workforce. There has been a decrease in gendered occupations and an ==increase in the number of women and people of color in leadership roles.== The number of workers with both hidden and visible disabilities has increased, and employers have made accommodations to physical structures and removed other barriers, such as adding wheelchair accessible ramps to entryways, and incorporating technology that allows for greater accessibility.

Here are just a few of the ways diversity impacts our society.

- Schools adapt to address the needs of people with different languages, cultures, experiences, and educational needs.
- Products and services are developed for, and marketed to, a more diverse audience.
- Many businesses have learned to value diversity in their employees.
- Employers have made changes to their methods of training and motivating employees.
- Government policies shift with the changing needs of the population.
- Individuals must learn to improve their ability to work with others.

Learning about the world of work will help you prepare for trends that will impact your career.

Jon Feingersh/Blend/Jupiterimages

Learning more about diversity and improving your ability to succeed in a diverse work environment are the focus of the Embracing Differences feature throughout this textbook. This will give you the opportunity to reflect on your ideas and experiences, as you develop strategies to succeed in diverse work environments.

Multigenerational Issues

Diversity in the workforce is also represented by differences between generations. The workforce now includes individuals from four generations, since the lifespan has increased and workers are retiring later or not retiring at all. Working in a multigenerational environment requires individuals to find common goals and manage differences. According to Lancaster and Stillman, authors of *When Generations Collide* (2002), these are some of the defining characteristics of the generations and also ways they may clash.

Traditionalists (Born 1900–1945). This generation was influenced by the presence of numerous significant events, such as World War I, the Roaring Twenties, the Great Depression, the New Deal, World War II, the Korean War, and the GI Bill. Over 50 percent of Traditionalist men were in the military. This generation is known as hardworking and patriotic, and often believes that partnering with powerful institutions and a top-down approach to authority are methods for success. Lancaster and Stillman identify Traditionalists as having a belief in the power of a "chain of command" (p. 20, 2002). A key word for this generation is "loyal."

Baby Boomers (Born 1946–1964). This generation was influenced by the increase in consumerism, the invention of the television, and the availability of jobs and the GI Bill. In addition, with 80 million peers, this generation is called the "Me Generation," and is also marked by competition. Lancaster and Stillman suggest that Boomers may clash with other generations because of their belief in "change of command," since they are apt to notice flaws in leadership and feel empowered to make necessary changes (p. 22, 2002). A key word for this generation is "optimistic."

Generation X (Born 1965–1980). This small generation of 46 million grew up during the introduction of numerous technological developments, including cable TV, VCRs, video games, microwaves, pagers, cell phones, and personal computers. Their childhood was also marked by a message of violence, AIDS, drug abuse, kidnappings, and drunk drivers. Divorce increased, and they received the message that the world was changing and no longer safe or secure. They may be willing to work long and hard, but prefer their own schedule or flexibility for family or other needs. Lancaster and Stillman argue that Generation Xers clash with other generations because of their belief in "self-command" (p. 26, 2002). A key word for this generation is "skepticism."

Millennials (Born 1981–1999). With 76 million members, this generation has also been called the "Echo Boom," "Generation Y," the "Baby Busters," "Generation Next." Recently another moniker has emerged, "Generation R," to reflect the impact of entering the labor force during a recession (Taylor and Keeter, 2010). Millennials have come of age in a world of diversity and advanced technology, layoffs, and a downturn economy. Unlike Gen Xers, who were concerned about safety in their

Working effectively with members of many generations is an important skill in the current world of work.

John Lund/Marc Romanelli/Getty Images

communities, this generation is concerned about safety on an individual level due to such incidences as school shootings. The parenting style of Boomers has also impacted this generation, who, in turn, speak up to authority, feel empowered, and value collaboration. Lancaster and Stillman suggest that Millennials may clash with other generations because their approach may be "Don't command—collaborate!" (2002, p. 31). A key word for this generation is "realistic."

Here are some of the ways generational differences may influence your assumptions.

- Do you expect older workers to lack technological skills?
- Do you look down on workers who prefer to make their own hours, even when they excel?
- Do you find it disrespectful when others speak up in meetings, especially when they have little or no experience dealing with the topic?
- Do you feel that your opinion should be valued, regardless of your position within an organization?

You will have an opportunity to explore your assumptions about generational differences in **Task 1.2**. Becoming aware of your assumptions and becoming open to different points of view can help you demonstrate respect for various approaches to work tasks and styles, making it easier for you to build relationships and be successful with others in your career.

Technology and Globalization

Each generation in the workforce today has needed to adapt to significant technological changes. These developments impact the world of work in many ways, bringing people closer together, shifting the traditional top-down power structure, and increasing the need for lifelong learning.

A Hierarchical Global Economy. In the twentieth century, developments such as cars, trains, airplanes, telephones, and personal computers impacted travel, information, and communication. This enabled businesses to buy and sell across far distances, and led to global competition and a global economy. In fact, in 1964, Marshall McLuhan first coined the term, "global village" (1994). Businesses sold all over the world, and global skills became increasingly relevant.

A "Flat" Global Economy. The late twentieth century and early twenty-first century have been marked by technological advances that connect individuals directly. These include the Internet, social media, cell phones, smart phones, and more. In *The World Is Flat*, Thomas Friedman (2005) argues that power used to exist vertically, with corporate and political leaders on top, but it has become flat, giving everyone a chance to connect directly. For example, with a personal website, anyone can buy and sell goods directly with customers anywhere in the world.

To compete in the global economy, entrepreneurial skills, technological skills, creativity, broad areas of knowledge, and an understanding of the horizontal power structure will be critical. Issues relating to technology and your career will be addressed throughout the text through **Tech Savvy** features, and topics that help you become socially aware and prepare for the global economy will be addressed in the **Work with Awareness** feature.

Attitudes and Behaviors for Career Development

In the world of work, the majority of success stories are not sports figures, celebrities, or public figures. Most working Americans who are leading fulfilled careers have found a way to connect their skills, preferences, and values with the world around them. They have not built their careers on bad behavior or outrageous acts, like some of the breakout stars of reality television shows. Nor do most people turn a successful work history into superstardom like today's well-known celebrity chefs. Nevertheless, these are often the success stories that dominate the media.

Throughout this book, you will be introduced to real people in the **Career Profiles**, whose careers reflect themes of educational attainment, professionalism, creativity, commitment, engagement, and a willingness to learn. They are in industries including business, talent management, publishing, fashion, information services, health care, education, and more. You will learn how their choices and actions have helped them expand their options and increase their employability.

» What Is Career Development?

Career development involves learning about yourself, connecting your self-awareness with the world of work, making decisions, and taking action. Learning about these topics will help you make informed, thoughtful decisions throughout your lifetime. The goal of career development is not only to create a successful career, but to develop a life that is personally meaningful and rewarding, given your own priorities and goals.

Name: Thomas Cain
Associate Degree: AAS in General Studies
Field of Interest: Computer Science
Bachelor Degree: BS in Computer Science (currently enrolled)
Internship/Co-op: UPS Information Services

Courtesy of Thomas Cain

Can you describe your position?

I'm in a co-op program [a paid, year-round internship], and I work several days a week, mostly testing hardware and software, and contributing to projects. UPS has really helped me expand my skills. This is the first experience I've had in my career field. A lot of what I do involves making sure the devices that the drivers use are working properly. I've even had the chance to write some programs for automated testing. It's a lot of fun.

Can you describe your career preparation and academic experience?

I always thought I'd go to a four-year school, but when I graduated high school, I wasn't sure what I wanted to do. I went to community college first, while working full-time for the Army and Air Force Exchange, a retail business serving military personnel, for which I also served in Operation Enduring Freedom in Afghanistan for six months. I actually considered three or four majors. I took several computer science classes, which I knew would count toward my degree. I liked them, but I realized how much I really liked programming after a more advanced programming class. When I transferred to a bachelor's program it was a major step. I'm hoping I can do this forever. It feels like a career for me.

How did you find your current position?

A friend from school referred me to UPS. We met in a calculus class, and he mentioned he was having a hard time. I ended up tutoring him, and we both did well in the class and became good friends. He was working at UPS, told me about the opportunity and recommended me. Now we share a cubicle. I believe that if you want help in the future, you have to help other people. It's all give and take. Building a network is important in college so that you have people to talk with and to rely on.

From Thomas's Employer

Courtesy of Amy McGuigan

Name: Amy McGuigan
Title: Area HR Representative, UPS Information Services

What strengths made Thomas a strong contributor to your organization?

In my conversations with Thomas, it's clear that he has a passion for the career field that he has chosen, which is a coveted attribute in our corporate culture. With passion comes innovation. Technology changes quickly, and we need people who can bring us their new ideas, who can recognize where we need to go, and who have the talent to take us there. We've been around for more than a century, and I think the reason for that is our people—people who recognize when change is necessary and in turn bring their ideas and experiences to the table to ensure we position ourselves for the next century.

What qualities and experience do you look for in your summer interns and co-op students?

It's always desirable for our interns to have some prior work experience. The preference is for the work to be in IT; however, any work experience can be an indicator that the student has initiative. Although each department has a definite skill set that they're seeking, we also look for students who have a diverse skill base that would help them to succeed in the current position as well as future opportunities throughout the organization. We have limitless opportunities available—at all levels—to those who want them and have the drive and determination to go after them. We look for individuals who want to be developed through training and job rotation so that we can prepare for the long-range vision of the organization.

What steps did Thomas take that helped him prepare for his career?

_____

_____

_____

What actions did Thomas take that helped him find and secure his current position?

_____

_____

_____

For additional questions, visit CourseMate.

Careers and Life

In the United States, we often refer to a career as a series of jobs. While a job is a paid position with a set of required skills and tasks, a career evolves over time, reflects broad themes, and involves an accumulation of skills and talents. Your career is more than your paid employment. It is how you spend your time and what you do throughout your lifespan. Career development also involves preparing for the many twists and turns your life can take. This may involve managing periods where you do not work, or when you are changing jobs or careers.

The Origins of Career Development

In the early twentieth century, the American landscape was transforming and there was a desire to help people find meaningful and satisfying work. This period was marked by a shift from rural to urban living and from farming to factory life. At the same time, psychology was growing as a field and a helping profession. This helped launch the connected disciplines of vocational psychology, career development, and career counseling.

Career Development Theory

There are numerous theories and models to assist in all aspects of your career development, including self-assessment, career exploration, and decision making. By integrating theory into your career education, you will learn to apply various tools and approaches to help you resolve some of your more challenging questions and prepare for your future.

Connecting Interests and Occupations. One approach to understanding careers involves understanding the connections between our interests and the jobs we choose. Frank Parsons, who is credited as the founder of the field of vocational psychology, aimed to understand who we are, what the world of work has to offer, and

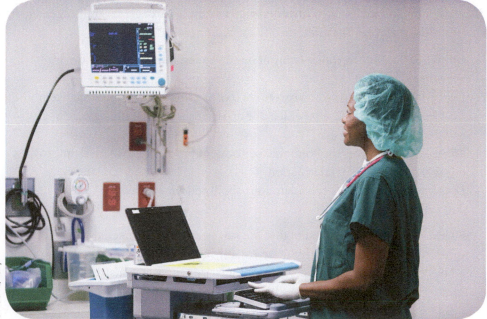

Career theories help us make sense of the relationship between people and careers in the changing landscape of work.

© PhotoAlto/Alamy

how we can best match our skills to an occupation (1909). His work formed the foundation for those who believed that satisfying work could be found in matching a person's attributes to a particular function.

One notable theorist who built on Parsons's work is John Holland, whose theory of personality type is explored in **Chapter 3: Preferences**. Holland's framework is the foundation for many resources currently used by career counselors and coaches.

Developmental Theories. In addition to considering the relationship between interests and occupations, theorists have built on developmental theories to explain career development. These theories look at stages of growth throughout the lifespan to understand the connection between people and careers.

Donald Super made significant contributions to the field of career development as a developmental theorist. He suggested that one's self-concept evolved through the combination of life roles and life stages (1980). According to Super, your self-concept—your understanding of who you are—is influenced by many factors, including your capabilities, your experiences, and your interactions with others (1957). His developmental theory suggests that careers evolve over time, rather than being chosen in a one-time decision.

Super identified nine life roles (1980). These life roles are characterized by activities, experiences, and relationships with others.

- Child
- Student
- Leisurite (he used this term to describe a person engaged in leisure activities)
- Citizen
- Worker (including unemployed worker)
- Spouse (or partner)
- Homemaker
- Parent
- Pensioner (or retiree)

He also identified five life stages (1990). He believed that we move through these stages throughout our lifetime, and also may cycle through the stages repeatedly. For instance, a person exploring a career change will cycle through several stages again, within the larger cycle. These are the life stages Super identified:

- *Growth* is the time in which many of our attitudes, interests, and skills are developed.
- *Exploration* is the stage when career choices are narrowed but not finalized.
- *Establishment* is the stage in which our experiences help us clarify our interests and career choices.
- *Maintenance* involves the continual adjustment process that involves improving our working position and situation.
- *Disengagement* involves considerations about retirement, reduced work output, and eventual retirement.

Furthermore, Super suggested that life stages are interconnected with life roles. For example, a young person may be establishing his or her career at the same time he is becoming a spouse, a parent, or a citizen, and may also still be a son or daughter.

Name: Carlos Rivas
Degree: BA in Government and Spanish (*currently enrolled*)
Internships: Marketing Intern, Teach For America Career Services Intern, Career Services Center

Courtesy of Carlos Rivas

Can you describe your internships and work experience?

Since my first semester in college, I have worked as an intern in the Career Services Center. I learned about the importance of summer internships, and I recognized how influential my experiences have been on my career interests and goals. Since I was 10 years old, I have been involved with the Block Club Federation, a not-for-profit organization in Chicago. This organization is really important to me, and I've been able to become very close to the executive director. When I go home, she's one of the first people I see, and I really want to give back to the organization. Since eighth grade, I had the opportunity to start helping out, and have been working with them all through college, developing my grant-writing and program-development skills. Many of my other work experiences were in education. In college, I spent a semester in Washington, D.C., working full-time as an intern in the Department of Education. I also was a summer intern in the Chicago Public Schools. Most recently, I served as a summer marketing intern for Teach For America, and next year I will start working with Teach For America, teaching high school Spanish and starting an MA program in teaching.

What have you done as a student to build your professional reputation?

At the Career Services Center, I want people to know that I'm dependable, and that they can count on me. I do what's expected of me, and I realize there's always room for growth. I'll tell people to give me extra work and that I'll get it done. My first year, I offered to redo the flyers to post throughout campus; then I became the person who does flyers. Then I was given the opportunity to start doing our brochure for industry night [a career fair], and that's how I ended up getting involved in marketing projects. In my junior year, I realized I was becoming education or education-policy focused, and I needed to get involved in more activities that reflected my interest in not-for-profit management. That was actually why I was so interested in the marketing internship at Teach For America. Then I made sure to use the skills I learned there, such as improving my e-mail communication by using their strategies. I also try to use my technology skills to help, so I'll set someone up on Skype, help with a presentation, or fix a copier, and when I help other people, it builds trust. I can become more involved in projects, and learn from others.

From Carlos's Project Supervisor
Name: Beth Ricca
Title: Associate Director, Career Services Center

Courtesy of Beth Ricca

Can you describe Carlos's approach to career planning?

From the time he arrived on campus, Carlos saw an on-campus position as a way to have a meaningful learning opportunity. He became a member of our student staff, and worked with students, staff, and alumni. He was interested in the many constituencies we worked with, and also in learning about employers and the internships that were available. He took advantage of the Sponsored Summer Internship Program, receiving funding to work over the summer in an unpaid internship. He also planned early so he could take advantage of the program to work in Washington, D.C., for a semester and also study abroad in Argentina another semester. He was actually away from school for a full year, building skills that related directly to his interests. This took a lot of planning on his part.

What qualities help Carlos make a strong contribution as an employee?

What strikes me most about Carlos is his ability to read a situation. He's easy to talk with, and was always asking for extra work and taking on new responsibilities. He likes keeping busy. One thing that I noticed was that he had a special ability to connect with people from different backgrounds and ages. That makes him likeable. He's also very willing to accept feedback. If he's working on a project, he'll ask for feedback and take it, but he also shares his point of view.

What steps did Carlos take that helped him prepare for his career?

_____

_____

_____

What has Carlos done to expand his career opportunities?

_____

_____

_____

For additional questions, visit CourseMate.

» Create a Career Portfolio

The purpose of creating a Career Portfolio throughout this text is to enhance your career development. Organizing your job search materials is a great way to start your career education, but a Career Portfolio does more than help you keep track of the materials you need for a job search. A Career Portfolio can actually help you improve your career by raising your awareness of your assets and areas for growth.

Portfolio Thinking

The concept of "Portfolio Thinking" involves reviewing past successes to highlight skills, abilities, interests, and values, and then using these insights to see skills gaps and develop appropriate plans (Borgen and Amundson, 2001). Developing a Career Portfolio also has been shown to help people recognize personal accomplishments, enhance career resilience, and lead people to consider an expanded range of career options (Borgen, Amundson, and Reuter, 2004).

By seeing your materials organized together, you can learn how employers will view you, and identify skill areas you want to develop. Your Career Portfolio will help you make decisions and take appropriate steps to build your career.

Career Portfolios and the Job Search

At this time, most employers still want only the basics: a résumé, cover letter, and a page of references if requested. However, in some cases, they may request a writing sample or some other exhibit of your work. Knowing what employers expect and how to apply for jobs and internships is part of the process of career development, and is likely to change with technological developments. Plan to use your Career Portfolio to store all of your career development materials in one place, so that they are available when you need them. When you are ready for a job or internship search, you may want to separate personal development materials from job search tools within your portfolio, or create a personal website or online portfolio consisting only of job search tools specifically for employers to access during your job search.

Although the Career Portfolio will involve collecting, organizing, and storing materials, you may never send it out in its entirety or bring it in full to interviews, like an artist's portfolio. Nor should you plan to send a link to employers for your complete Career Portfolio during a job search. However, you may want to share a link with someone who will examine your full body of work, such as a mentor or someone who will serve as a reference for you. Your Career Portfolio is not intended solely for a job search. The primary purpose of the Career Portfolio you create in this text is to enhance your career development, by increasing your self-awareness, helping you stay organized, and laying the groundwork for a job or internship search.

Get Started

It is fine to start this process with few, if any, of the materials for your Career Portfolio. By starting a Career Portfolio early on in your career development, you will be able to choose skill-building experiences, courses, and activities that will give you content for your résumé. You will also learn to take notice of your growing professional network. At this stage, learn what belongs in your Career Portfolio, why it is valuable to have one, and start setting it up. Later, as you learn more about careers that interest you, you will begin to tailor your Career Portfolio and seek out opportunities that are handpicked for your career interests.

Step 1. Collect and Organize Materials. Review the list of contents in the Career Portfolio checklist found in the appendix of this text or in CourseMate, then gather any materials you already have, even if they are outdated, old, or directed for another career area. If you choose to upload them, put them in the appropriate sections and name them so that you know they are not current.

Step 2. Store and Save Critical Documents. Plan to store your materials in multiple formats; consider saving materials on an external drive, in the cloud, on your hard drive, and possibly on paper. Select a safe and watertight place to store USB drives and any paper documents, such as letters of recommendation, transcripts, certificates of recognition, and industry-specific materials. Scan or digitally photograph important documents that you have on paper, such as artwork or exhibits.

Step 3. Prepare to Create Job Search Tools. Throughout the textbook and online in CourseMate, there are samples of job search tools, such as résumés, cover letters, e-mails, and other correspondence that you will add to your Career Portfolio. Familiarize yourself with the contents of the Career Portfolio, and consider which materials will be most useful for you at this time in your career.

» Campus and Community Resources

Your career education would not be complete without the resources at your school and in your community. For current students, recent graduates, and anyone with access to their alma mater, colleges and universities are a great first stop for career

The library can be an excellent resource for local or campus career information.

planning. In addition, some campus resources and many community resources are available to the general public.

If you are unable to find what you want using campus and community websites, do not hesitate to confirm critical details such as program times by phone or e-mail. Also consider stopping by the offices, departments, or centers listed. Many have information that you can review when you are there, and this can also be a chance to connect with the people involved in career-building activities on campus or through local resources.

A Career Development Calendar can be found in the appendix of this text or in CourseMate. This is a place to list all important dates and deadlines, such as dates for career fairs, employer visits, and a timeline for recruiting. Highlight important dates on your personal calendar, too.

Below you will find a list of campus and community resources. With a little planning, you can meet important deadlines and locate support and assistance when you need it.

≫ EXHIBIT 1.1 ● Campus and Community Resources

Campus Resources

Just about every resource on campus can help your career development. Here are examples of campus resources that can help you in your career planning. In some cases, these services can be accessed through another department at your college or a community resource, such as the public library.

Career Center	Most career centers offer a wide range of services for students, and often for alumni as well. These may include: ● career counseling ● résumé-writing assistance ● workshops ● mentor programs ● networking events ● campus recruiting ● career fairs ● job and internship listings ● interview preparation ● career resource library
Internship or Co-op Center	Your campus may have an Internship or Co-op Center that is separate from career services. Use this Center to learn: ● requirements ● policies ● internship listings ● timelines
Academic Departments and Academic Advising	Your advisor or faculty may assist with such topics as: ● course selection ● career paths ● networking, particularly with alumni and industry contacts ● requirements for graduation ● internships
Dean's Office	The dean's office may handle academic advising for new and transfer students, and they may also offer: ● professional school advising ● graduate school advising
Alumni Office	Alumni Affairs may connect students with alumni, as well as offer: ● mentoring programs ● networking events
Computer Lab	Although most students have their own computers, most schools offer computer labs where you can go to use a computer, access the Internet, print documents, and seek computer assistance.
Counseling Center	Career development and its many facets can bring up a lot of feelings. Counseling Centers offer individual and group counseling, support groups, and often also have resources and workshops for topics such as dealing with stress, balancing work and family, and handling discrimination.
Financial Aid	Financial Aid handles student loans and applications for financial aid for future academic plans, and may have information on: ● scholarships ● grants ● fellowships ● work-study opportunities

Campus Resources

International Student Services	If you are an international student, International Student Services can help you understand the logistics of working in the United States, and familiarize you with the application process and deadlines for practical training.
Study Abroad or International Education	By living, working, or volunteering in a foreign country, you will be challenged in new ways, discover strengths, develop global skills, and boost your employability. Use this center to identify: • programs • requirements • school policies & forms • application deadlines
Library	Company information, periodicals, and industry publications, as well as many directories and databases, can now be accessed from your personal computer, but you might not be aware of them. A librarian can be an invaluable resource in your career exploration and industry research.
Registrar	The registrar is the place to go for: • official copies of your transcript • details about course registration • graduation requirements
Student Businesses or Entrepreneurial Centers	Students have successfully launched and managed such businesses as bartending, babysitting, tutoring, and student-oriented publications. Many schools have an office to encourage and provide financial support for student enterprises.
Student Activities and Government	Student activities can focus on leisure or professional interests, and participating activities on campus can add to your résumé.

Community Resources

Many community resources are also available for your career development. These resources are often low-cost or free, open to the public, and offered at locations with which you may already be familiar.

Chamber of Commerce	The Chamber of Commerce is your connection to local organizations and businesses. Here are a few possible ways to connect: • join committees • attend events • network with employers • volunteer
Colleges and Universities	Colleges and universities may offer services to the general public, as well as current students and alumni. Contact these offices for more information about available services: • continuing education • counseling center • career center • graduate department of psychology
Community Centers	Community Centers like the YMCA and JCC provide social opportunities, fitness resources, and educational programs. Here are a few resources they may offer: • committee activities • network with community members • job or networking fairs • skill-building classes • career workshops • career or mental health counseling
Department of Labor One-Stop Career Centers	Throughout the United States, the Department of Labor has established local career centers that offer: • career resources • career counseling • wide range of human resource services • job listings
Public Library	Career-planning books, periodicals and industry publications, access to databases and industry directories, computer classes, Internet access, career exploration and job-search workshops are just a few of the resources offered at many public libraries.
Religious Organizations	Many local churches, temples, and other religious organizations offer tailored career programs to meet the needs of their community. These programs may be open to the general public, too.
Local School District	Many school districts offer continuing-education programs that include career-planning classes or career-enhancing subjects like computer skills or business writing.
Online Career Resources	You can also expand your community to include the many online resources available to assist in your career development. Here are just a few online resources (to find these resources, Google the names as listed): • career assessment tools, such as those from CPP, Inc. • secure online career counseling, through organizations such as ReadyMinds • resources for all of your career development needs; start with a resource like The Riley Guide or QuintCareers • consumer information from a professional association, e.g., the National Career Development Association (NCDA)

Your Flexible Plan

Prepare For Your Career

Drafting a flexible career plan offers you an opportunity to apply the content in every chapter of this text to your personal career development goals. Some chapters focus on self-assessment or gathering information about the world of work. These require a plan of analysis. Other chapters prepare you to take action to reach your goals, such as building relationships, making decisions, creating a résumé, or practicing interview skills. These require a plan of action.

Here are the steps of the plans you will create in each chapter.

PLAN OF ANALYSIS

Step 1: Gather Information
Step 2: Evaluate the Information
Step 3: Make Conclusions

PLAN OF ACTION

Step 1: Set Objectives
Step 2: Identify Tasks
Step 3: Define Action Steps

Your flexible plan will help you analyze information and take relevant, meaningful action steps. The chapters are laid out in a step-by-step approach, modeling the cycle of analysis and action throughout your career.

Your Flexible Plan

Plan of Analysis	Chapter 2: Skills	Assess Your Skills
	Chapter 3: Preferences	Define Your Preferences
	Chapter 4: Values	Discover Your Values
	Chapter 5: Explore	Develop a Career Exploration Strategy
Plan of Action	Chapter 6: Relationships	Invest in Your Relationships
	Chapter 7: Decision Making	Commit to Your Next Step
	Chapter 8: Tools	Create Your Job Search Tools
	Chapter 9: Launch	Initiate a Job or Internship Search
Plan of Action and Plan of Analysis	Chapter 10: Career Management	Manage your Career

Performance Appraisal

New research shows that taking a test after learning new information can do more than measure what you know; it can actually help you learn.

How Tests Help You Learn

Students who took tests after reading new material thought they would recall less in the future, compared with students who used other methods for studying (Karpicke, 2010). Researchers hypothesized that the test-takers lacked confidence in their ability to remember information because they were more aware of information they failed to recall. In other words, the test showed subjects what they did not know, and actually caused their minds to work harder to remember the information. While there are many methods for studying, consider test taking another tool that can help you remember new information.

Now that you've read the chapter, answer the questions below and complete the **Tasks**.

1. To prepare for my future, I should expect the following:
   a. Getting a job is exactly the same thing as preparing for a career.
   b. Career development is going to be boring and difficult, because I will have to learn about careers that don't interest me.
   c. There will be many people who can help me prepare for my career.
   d. I will be able to control all the events that impact my career.

2. Which of the following is true about the impact of diversity in the world of work?
   a. There are fewer women and people of color in leadership roles than there were in the 1950s.
   b. Changes have been made to physical structures to allow for greater accessibility.
   c. There are no laws and procedures regarding discrimination and harassment.
   d. None of the above

3. How many generations are now in the workforce?
   a. 1
   b. 2
   c. 3
   d. 4

4. In the twenty-first century, the power structure has become:
   a. Increasingly vertical, with Millennials unwilling to speak or connect directly with those in positions of authority.
   b. Less accessible, because people in leadership roles do not use new technology.
   c. Increasingly horizontal, as communication has increased.
   d. All of the above

5. Career development is:
   a. An academic discipline grounded in theories and models.
   b. A new field developed in 2009.
   c. A foundation for exploring the connection between people and careers.
   d. a and c
   e. All of the above

6. The following are names of theorists who studied careers:
   a. Frank Parsons, Donald Super, and John Holland
   b. Sigmund Freud, Donald Super, and Erik Erikson
   c. Frank Parsons, Erik Erikson, and Marshall McLuhan
   d. None of the above

7. What is the purpose of the Career Portfolio you will create in this text?
   a. To collect documents and send the entire portfolio to as many employers as possible in a job search
   b. To create a collection of paper documents and avoid the use of technology
   c. To enhance your career development
   d. All of the above

Thought Questions

1. Do you believe that you are responsible for your own career success?

2. How will diversity, technology, and globalization impact the world of work you are entering?

3. What are you looking forward to in the world of work?

Notes:

_____

_____

_____

_____

_____

TASK 1.1:

What would you be famous for?

Imagine you are suddenly famous. What are you famous for? Did you discover something? Build something? Help someone? Are you a politician, a celebrity, a TV anchor, a thought leader? Are you suddenly famous for your outstanding talents or natural abilities? What is on your Facebook page? Updates on travel, romance, scientific information, sports statistics? Where are you featured? Are you profiled on *E!*, the *Today Show*, the *Wall Street* Journal, ESPN, WWD, or somewhere else? What major corporations would offer you sponsorships? What products would want to feature you in their advertisements?

Describe as much as you can about your new, famous self and what made you famous.

_____

_____

_____

_____

_____

_____

TASK 1.2:

The Multigenerational Workforce

Using the information in the chapter, consider what you think it would be like to find yourself in the following situations. As you read each scenario, consider these questions:

1. To which generation do you think this person belongs?

2. What assumptions have they made about you?

3. What are your thoughts and reaction to the scenario?

4. How does your reaction reflect the themes of your generation?

You have been assigned a supervisor who has poor technology skills. She has asked for your help with technology tasks, from managing contacts on her phone and computer, to creating presentations and to setting up Web-based conference calls. She has never asked about your ability to perform these tasks, but seems to assume you are more skilled than she is.

Generation: _____

_____

A colleague works from home two days per week. His reputation is excellent, and you are under the impression he completes his work. Although he is not in the office during those days, you are almost always able to reach him immediately by cell phone or e-mail.

Generation: _____

_____

Your supervisor is significantly older than you, and is very well respected in your field. She requires weekly, in-person meetings and frequently comes to your desk and engages you in discussions that are related to company or industry issues, but seem unrelated to your work tasks. When you attend your first company-wide meeting, you learn that she has been instrumental in helping you secure a promotion, based on her trust in you and your loyalty to her and to the organization.

Generation: _____

_____

What do your assumptions tell you about your expectations for working with members of different generations?

Generation: _____

_____

How much do you think generational similarities influence people's behavior?

_____

_____

TASK 1.3:
Life Stages and Life Roles

As you learned in the chapter, Super (1990) identified five stages of career development.

- *Growth* is the time in which many of your attitudes, interests, and skills are developed.
- *Exploration* is the stage when career choices are narrowed but not finalized.
- *Establishment* is the stage in which your experiences help you clarify your interests and career choices.
- *Maintenance* involves the continual adjustment process that involves improving one's working position and situation.
- *Disengagement* involves considerations about retirement, reduced work output, and eventual retirement.

What life stage are you currently in?

_____

_____

How does this impact your career development? For instance, if you are in the Exploration stage, are you narrowing your choices for your career direction?

_____

_____

Super suggested that these life stages are interconnected with nine major life roles, including (1) Child, (2) Student, (3) Leisurite, (4) Citizen, (5) Worker, (6) Spouse (or partner), (7) Homemaker, (8) Parent, and (9) Pensioner (or retiree) (1980). List all of your life roles at the present time.

_____

_____

As you learned in the chapter, life roles also impact career development. For example, are you a student preparing skills for the workforce, and perhaps also a child, parent, or partner? Describe how your career development is impacted by your life roles.

_____

_____

TASK 1.4:
Support Network

Your support network is a great resource in your career development. These are the people and organizations that can provide you with help in a variety of ways. In addition to providing support throughout your career development, they might be able to write references, suggest career fields, ask practice interview questions, or listen when you feel frustrated, anxious, or down.

These are just a few of the resources and people you might include in your support network:

Friends	Classmates	Family	Family friends
Coaches	Employers	Professors	Former teachers
Career center	Community centers	Religious organizations	

Who would have the best things to say about you?

_____

_____

With whom would you want to talk about a new accomplishment?

_____

_____

Who would listen if you felt down, frustrated, anxious, or overwhelmed?

_____

_____

Who might have career information?

_____

_____

TASK 1.5:
Resources

Identifying campus and community resources can help you become aware of deadlines, learn about new or interesting programs, and expand your network. From the list of resources in **Exhibit 1.1**, choose one resource that you will learn more about. Visit this person or organization's website, call, or even stop in.

What resource did you choose?

_____

_____

Where is it located, and what is its website or e-mail address?

_____

_____

Who works there?

_____

_____

What services do they offer?

_____

_____

What else did you learn?

_____

_____

Link to CourseMate

On CourseMate, you can find documents to help you update your Career Portfolio as well as additional resources and activities. Here is some of the information you can find online for **Chapter 1: Prepare.**

CAREER PORTFOLIO
Career Portfolio Checklist
Career Development Calendar
Your Flexible Plan

RESOURCES
Entrance Interview
Career Profile: Thomas Cain
Career Profile: Carlos Rivas

Skills

> Ability will never catch up with the demand for it.
>
> *—Confucius*

What's Inside

What Have You Done?

Skills for Career Success

Assess Your Skills

Evidence of Skills

Prepare to . . .

- Reflect on your experiences and activities
- Learn about important skills for your career
- Assess the skills you are motivated to use in your career
- Identify and build relevant skills

Identifying your skills will help you prepare for the world of work. You will discover the skills you are motivated to use and become more aware of the skills employers are seeking. This can help you select activities, course projects, internships, and work experiences and help you recognize any gaps in the skills you need for the careers that interest you.

» What Have You Done?

Consider your day, and what you have done, as well as yesterday or the day before that. You might have completed coursework, exercised, attended classes, gone to work, socialized, cooked dinner, or spent time reading. In some cases you may have used specific knowledge, as in how to bake cookies from scratch, or highly transferable skills, such as being a good listener or problem solver for friends. If you think about what you do with your time, you can begin to identify the skills you are motivated to use throughout your days, as well as those you would like to spend more time building.

Consider what you have done and the skills you have developed. As you review this list below, add your experiences to **Task 2.1:** What have you done?

Past employment. Any paid work experience, part-time or full-time, short-term or long-term, temporary or permanent, constitutes employment. In your work experiences you can learn many skills, as well as learn to interact with people and better understand professionalism.

Experiential learning. Experiential learning is an opportunity to learn outside the classroom in a work or volunteer setting. Internships, externships, cooperative education, or service learning are all examples. In these experiences, you learn the ropes through mentoring and close supervision. Skills include learning how to take direction and initiative, work in a team, and perform tasks.

Courses and projects. While your degree, certification, or other completed educational credentials are often the most important aspects of your education, any academic work you do has value. Your coursework can help you learn about subjects that interest you, and also help you develop writing, math, science, communication, and reading skills. Team projects can develop leadership, teamwork, and presentation skills.

Extracurricular activities. Extracurricular activities are the experiences in which you participate outside of work and academics. These can include organized activities such as student clubs, professional associations, sororities and fraternities, community service organizations, sports teams, and more. By taking on leadership roles in these settings, you learn about group work, leadership, management, motivating others, communication, and listening skills.

Volunteer experiences. Volunteer work or community service can add another layer to your career preparation. In these experiences, you contribute

© Kumar Sriskandan/Alamy

Working directly with customers develops professionalism, problem solving, and interpersonal skills.

your time, talents, and labor to a cause you value. By participating in food and clothing drives, contributing to fundraising events, helping out directly with people in need, becoming involved in political activities and consciousness-raising efforts you can develop leadership, teamwork, management, administrative, and organizational skills while building meaningful connections.

Hobbies and leisure activities. There are also activities that might occupy your time but are not formalized through activities or other experiences. Reading, journaling, drawing, running, traveling, playing with a pet, shopping, building things, planning birthday parties, talking on the phone, and gardening are all examples of leisure activities.

Achievements. These can include personal or public accomplishments, such as a task you completed, a fear or illness you now manage or overcame, or a goal you reached. We all have achievements that make us proud, and these personal milestones are significant. These can also include achievements that involved awards, honors, or some kind of recognition.

All of these activities require skills that can be used in the workplace. As you think about what you have done, consider which skills you enjoyed using, and where you built these assets.

≫ CAREER JOURNAL ● Motivated Skills

Use the space below to write about your thoughts and feelings.

Describe an experience in which you used or developed a skill that was so enjoyable that you would like to continue developing it. What was the experience? What did you do?

What skill(s) did you use?

What made this skill enjoyable for you to use? Did any aspects of this skill feel like it came naturally for you? Did any aspects pose a challenge for you?

Describe three ways you can build this skill. For instance, is there a course, project, or activity that would help you learn more? Or is there a leadership role or other responsibility you can assume that would help you develop this skill?

1. _____

2. _____

3. _____

Journal Feedback . . . The tasks of performing certain skills are likely to be more engaging and interesting to you. These are the skills you are motivated to use. Many skills are transferable; they can be used in a wide variety of career fields. Identifying the skills that you want to use can help you seek out ways to develop these skills and build evidence of your performance for your self-marketing down the road.

» Skills for Career Success

There are many types of skills that are valued within the world of work. Careers do not encompass only one skill or even one skill area. Employers want to hire employees who add value, can combine skill areas in unexpected ways, and are eager to build new skills. The need for professional and transferable skills is in high demand in all industries, including those where specific career-related skills are also mandatory.

Types of Skills

Transferable skills. Transferable skills are assets that can be used in a variety of career fields and are portable between various jobs and industries. These include communication, teamwork, creativity, research, organizational, technological, listening, observing, decision making, and many other skills. You can develop transferable skills in everything you do, such as coursework, activities, internships, jobs, hobbies, and volunteer activities.

Self-management and professional skills. Self-management and professional skills are used in every career, and can be adapted to meet the needs of your industry. Professionalism in the workplace involves a set of skills that demonstrate that you are ready, willing, and eager to work. Employers want to know that you can manage your time, projects, and relationships in ways that enhance your job performance. These are transferable to all fields, and can help you regardless of the setting in which you work.

Career-related or technical skills. Career-related skills involve knowledge that may not be easily transferable but is useful for specific careers. These skills often involve industry-specific dialogue and terminology that demonstrates experience and familiarity. This may involve technical expertise in one or more areas, such as a fashion designer's ability to do trend research, use Illustrator, create a flat sketch, and

Your ability to organize your commitments and deadlines is a valuable skill.

source fabrics. Skills in other industries could involve understanding the elements of a legal brief or how to design a landscape for optimal sun exposure. In addition, while basic math knowledge is helpful for all occupations, certain skills are critical for careers in science, technology, engineering, and math (STEM) fields.

The 3 Rs and the 4 Cs

Two types of transferable skills are amongst the most valuable to employers, and their abbreviated titles make them easy to remember. These are the 3 Rs, reading, writing, and arithmetic, and the 4 Cs, critical thinking and problem solving, communication, collaboration and team building, and creativity and innovation. The 4 Cs and descriptions of these skills are listed in **Exhibit 2.1**, The 4 Cs. The *Partnership for 21st Century Skills* identified the 4 Cs because they are relevant to many activities, tasks, and environments (*The Partnership for 21st Century Skills*, 2009).

Employers have also recognized the need for these additional skills in the workplace. More than 75 percent of managers and executives surveyed in the American Management Association's (AMA) 2010 Critical Skills Survey believed in the value of the 4 Cs for the future world of work (American Management Association, 2010). In the AMA survey, respondents attributed the need for these skills to four factors:

1. The pace of change in the world;
2. Global competitiveness;
3. The nature of how work is accomplished today; and
4. The way organizations are structured.

As the world changes and becomes more interconnected, more skills will be necessary for workplace success. The 3 Rs and the 4 Cs are highly transferable skills that prepare you for a wide range of employment options, and can be developed in many settings.

>> **EXHIBIT 2.1** ● **The 4 Cs**

New skills for the workplace include the 4 Cs, listed below.

4 Cs	Description
CRITICAL THINKING AND PROBLEM SOLVING	the ability to reason, make decisions, solve problems, and take action as appropriate
COMMUNICATION	the ability to synthesize and transmit your ideas both in written and oral formats
COLLABORATION AND TEAM BUILDING	the ability to work effectively with others, including those from diverse groups and with opposing points of view
CREATIVITY AND INNOVATION	the ability to develop and act on creative ideas

Source: The Partnership for 21st Century Skills, 2009.

How Important Are Transferable Skills?

Wherever you are interested in developing a career, whether it is in an office, a factory, a laboratory, a hospital, or any other setting, it is important to possess broad and specific skills in a wide variety of areas. For instance, in 2006, the Accreditation Board for Engineering and Technology (ABET), an organization that offers accreditation for programs in the sciences, adapted its criteria for student outcomes to include science skills as well as transferable skills such as team skills, communication skills, and a commitment to lifelong learning (Shuman Besterfield-Sacre and McGourty, 2005).

The Job Outlook 2012 survey from the National Association of Colleges and Employers (NACE, 2011) ranked the most sought-after skills by employers. **Exhibit 2.2,** Top Skills Valued by Employers, shows the top five sought-after skills and just a few of the activities that could help you build these assets. All five are transferable skills, and can be attained in many activities and settings, from social clubs, sports, and work environments, or in a leadership role, such as treasurer of your sorority or glee club.

Volunteer work is not only personally rewarding, it also builds leadership, teamwork, and other transferable skills.

Doug Pensinger/Getty Images Sport/Getty Images

Name: Salman Bandukda
Associates Degree: AAS in Fashion Merchandising and Management (*earned 11 years after his bachelor's degree*)
Bachelors Degree: BBA in Marketing and Entrepreneurship
Current Position: Sourcing and Product Development Associate
Employer: Mr. Noah / Feathers

Courtesy of Salman Bandukda

From Salman's Professor

Name: Catherine Geib
Title: Assistant Professor, Fashion Institute of Technology, State University of New York

Courtesy of Catherine Geib

Can you describe the challenges you faced that inspired you to build your skills?

I'm from Pakistan, and I came to the United States and completed a bachelor's degree in Marketing and Entrepreneurship, then I went back to Pakistan and worked in my family's textile and garment manufacturing business. I worked there for 9 years. I would come to NY once or twice a year to meet with buyers. I wanted to start a branch office in NY, and I really wanted to move here, but the economy made it difficult. I had to decide whether to stay in Pakistan, working with my family, or to come to NY, and try to find my own job. I decided to come to NY. I started applying to jobs from WWD, attending job fairs, applying to all the big companies, but I was getting nowhere. I was disheartened. Several people suggested I go to a fashion school. They said that I would build confidence, meet people, and get to know the way the industry works in the United States. I decided to focus on learning another side of the business, which was merchandising.

Tell us about your preparation to enter the job market.

I was 30 years old, and I went to FIT to learn as much as I could, and get experience. My technical skills were excellent, but I didn't know the industry, and I didn't know anyone here who could be a reference for my skills. Besides my classes, I got very involved. I joined the FMM [Fashion Merchandising and Management] Society and the South Asian Cultural Exchange Society – I became the President of that student group. I also did two internships, one at Nautica and another at Calvin Klein. I volunteered at the fashion shows. I worked on more than 10 shows. Diane Von Furstenberg, Zac Posen. I did all the menial tasks. I set up chairs, handed out fliers, and helped backstage to make sure the garments were all lined up. I met a lot of people—people who were setting up tents, makeup artists, models, and backstage production. I exchanged business cards, which I printed for myself, and I followed up with everyone. Being surrounded by the industry professionals helped me understand the industry much better. I wrote thank you notes the same day or the next day, and asked people to connect on LinkedIn. Ultimately, I think I got my job based on my technical skills from my work in Pakistan, my merchandising skills, and my internships and education in the United States. Everything was helpful.

Tell us about Salman's experience in your course.

I remember him well. He came from a production background and was looking to expand his knowledge of the fashion retail business. Salman came to my class wanting to learn the manufacturer's point of view in relationship to buying and merchandising. He was very curious. He was always asking questions, and challenging what I taught in the classroom. That is always my best student, someone who really wants to learn and is interested in taking book knowledge and applying it to industry. I was a senior buyer at Macy's before I joined The Fashion Institute, and I encourage students to think about how they can build on classroom skills with industry experience. Often the first step to get into an industry is by networking with professors who have the contacts and the knowledge of the business. That's how I developed my relationship with Salman. He took a lot of initiative to network with me. It gave him the confidence to speak with executives I knew in a swimwear company, who then hired him as an intern to work in their NY showroom.

What skills did Salman use that helped him transition into the workplace?

His computer skills of course! As an adult, he was already working, and he had experience. In his internship, because of his fantastic computer skills, he helped create retail templates in Excel to help track the business. Through this analysis he gained a lot of insight into how the swim vendors worked with their retail swimwear partners. He also learned how to "show a line," track selling, and analyze data. In his courses and internships, he learned the language of the fashion industry here in the United States, and he learned the merchandising side of the business.

What are Salman's skills?

_____

_____

_____

How did Salman's efforts to prioritize the skills he was motivated to use help him make career decisions?

_____

_____

_____

For additional questions, visit CourseMate. 🖥

The Skills Gap

A skills gap occurs when employers feel that candidates lack the skills necessary to perform a job. These can refer to a lack of advanced skills required for specific careers, or a dearth of transferable skills that could have been gained in a wide range of activities and experiences, as illustrated in **Exhibit 2.2**. Despite high unemployment rates, many employers have unfilled positions and cite a skills gap as the reason.

For instance, in 2011, the Manufacturing Institute reported that manufacturing employers were unable to fill 5 percent of open positions due to the skills gap, which amounts to 600,000 unfilled jobs. In this industry, factors cited for the problem include a changing landscape that requires candidates to possess new, difficult skills in order to meet demands (Morrison, Maciejewski, Giffi, DeRocco, McNelly, and Carrick, 2011). Later in this chapter you will explore how to use your Career Portfolio to maintain evidence for your skills and recognize skills you lack and want to build.

≫ EXHIBIT 2.2 ● Top Skills Valued by Employers

The five skills in the left column are the most sought after by employers, according to the Job Outlook 2012 survey from the National Association of Colleges and Employers (National Association of Colleges and Employers, 2011). The right column lists some of the activities that lead to these skills. As illustrated here, most activities build a multitude of transferable skills for your career.

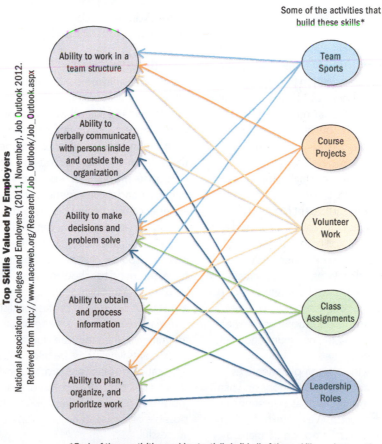

Each of these activities could potentially build all of these skills, and many others. These are only suggestions for common skills that are developed in these activities.

© Cengage Learning 2014

Connecting with others who have similar experiences to your own can help you recognize valuable workplace skills, locate helpful resources, and find support networks. For example, you may discover assets from skills you would normally take for granted, since they are common for those with whom you regularly interact. Finding role models and mentors who share your experience and background, and have accomplished similar goals, can help you learn what helped other people enter into a new career direction, and then assess your strengths to see what you have in common.

Career Change

If you are considering a career change, you bring a wealth of skills, but they may not seem relevant to your current goals. Your prior work history arms you with many transferable skills, including professionalism skills, self-management skills, and workplace skills, amongst others. In addition, if you have read about your new field, taken courses to prepare for your career change, or received any further training, you will be able to emphasize your commitment to lifelong learning. First, assess your transferable skills, then consider whether you would be willing to add value using strengths from your past career. After you learn the skills that are valued in your target work environments, you can assess those skills you need to build further.

Veterans

Every year, approximately 160,000 active duty U.S. military service members and approximately 110,000 members of the Reserve and National Guard service transition to civilian jobs (U.S. Department of Labor, November 3, 2011). While you may be open-minded about your occupational interests or job options, your level of maturity and decision-making experience in the military may increase your desire to make intentional, goal-oriented decisions regarding your education or career.

The skills built during military service are highly transferable and valuable in the workforce. The U.S. Department of Labor's Transition Assistance Program (TAP) Participant Manual (U.S. Department of Labor, n.d.) identifies numerous skills gained during military service. These include an ability to learn, work as a team player, work in a diverse setting, work under pressure and within deadlines, give and follow directions, and take initiative. In addition, the TAP manual lists some of the challenges that can be encountered by veterans, such as lacking educational credentials, facing stereotypes, having unrealistic expectations, or using acronyms and military jargon and lacking the communication skills necessary for civilian employment.

Many veterans may downplay their accomplishments, especially if they were achieved when in crisis situations or when following orders. However, such military skills as operating tanks and weapons and digging ditches occur in a context of leadership and teamwork. The Real Warriors Campaign translates a military experience with those tasks into these transferable assets: "Supervised, trained, and evaluated 40 personnel, supporting over 2,000 troops in four countries, with an inventory list of 1,500 line items, and material assets valued at $65M" (Translating Military Experience to Civilian Employment, November 9, 2010).

Identify the skills you want to use, and then, as you explore job requirements in **SECTION II: Explore Your Options,** look at your military experience for relevant assets and the appropriate way to describe your experience for the civilian job search.

Returning to Work

Returning-to-work parents or others who have been out of the workforce may feel their career and job search skills are out-of-date, and may also feel behind in technology. Although you may not have had consistent, paid employment during this time, life experiences can contribute to your marketability. You may have built new skills through volunteer work, community activism, or part-time employment. These newly developed talents may involve motivating others, organizing people or events, holding leadership positions, or raising funds. Assess your work and volunteer history, your recent experiences, and any training or career preparation. Then, expect that you will need to test your expectations with current industry research and insider information through networking. After you understand the job market, you will be able to accurately assess the skills you have and the skills you want to develop.

Ex-Offenders

Ex-offenders may be concerned that it will be hard to provide evidence of skills or strong references to employers because of such factors as a limited work history, gaps in employment, or a work history that was not through legal employment. Interests, hobbies, and natural talents can all be sources for identifying the skills you want to use. You may have the opportunity to participate in volunteer work and activities while you prepare to transition, and these experiences can help you gain marketable experience using your skills, help you to build new skills, and develop relationships that can lead to networking contacts and references. In addition, you may be eligible for various social-service resources that offer support for entering into the workforce, returning to school, or completing your GED.

Following through on your educational plans or volunteer activities shows skills of professionalism that are valued by employers. These include arriving on time, completing projects and assignments when they are due, and asking questions to clarify assignments when they are unclear. Learning how to address application questions regarding convictions during interviews is also a skill that will help you prepare. Understanding the job search process can help you address your concerns about possible obstacles, as well as prepare you with the tools to be successful.

» Assess Your Skills

To assess your skills, consider what you have done and what you have learned. At this time, focus on assessing all of your skills. Later, you will have the opportunity to identify the skills you want to use in your career by reviewing **Exhibit 2.3**, Motivated Skills, and completing **Task 2.5**, Motivated Skills.

Academic and Work Experiences

Transferable and career-related skills are developed in every experience at school or work. If you are not certain which skills you have attained in college, review the description of your major, courses, or other subject areas to identify skills you have and those you want to build. Your college's course catalogue can provide some of this information. In addition, reading over job descriptions that advertise positions, internships, or leadership roles you have held can help you identify skills you used in your past experiences.

Team and Leadership Roles

The roles you play in your projects and activities demonstrate your skills and provide evidence of your strengths. Interpersonal skills are developed through such activities as team sports, group projects, and committee work. Financial skills can be nurtured by serving as treasurer of a student group, planning a budget for your personal financial decisions, or collecting donations for a fundraising effort. Communication skills can be honed by presenting in front of a group or writing a speech. Some of the skills you use in your activities may be similar to those you are building in classes or work experiences, or they may reflect other talents.

Communication skills are developed in many settings.

Your Unique Combination of Skills

The skills you enjoy using most may not clearly relate to each other, but assessing your range of skills can help you identify preferences, values, and areas for career exploration. In addition, in our global society, there are many opportunities for specific knowledge to be used across industries. To give you insight into the way unrelated skills can add value to work environments, here are two examples.

Outdoor skills from extensive hiking, camping, and team sports and a passion for business and economics. The skill to lead a hike or motivate your soccer team may seem unrelated to an interest in business, but these skills and interests can be connected in unexpected ways. For instance, an ability to connect with business executives in an outdoor setting could help you market yourself for a position at an organization like Outward Bound, a not-for-profit organization whose instructors lead outdoor adventures that help corporate and student groups build leadership and team skills.

Lab skills and an interest in event planning. Knowledge of laboratory equipment is critical as a biologist, but may seem unrelated to event planning. However, if the event planner works for a natural history museum, a better understanding of scientific work is an asset. This unusual combination of assets could also be relevant for event planning, marketing, or public relations positions at pharmaceutical companies, research institutions, and schools or universities.

Assessing all of your skills, especially those you enjoy using, can help set the stage for opportunities that bring you the most satisfaction while also developing a niche and brand for yourself in the workplace. This can help you become the "go-to" person for your talents, and can add value to your contribution in unexpected ways.

Your Personal Motivation

Consider the skills you are not only motivated to use, but motivated to build. The skills you enjoy using most may come from a combination of leisure activities, life experience, and formal training. A high level of motivation will propel you to take the necessary steps to build and maintain skills over time, and can be more important to your long-term success than developed skills that could be outdated in the future. Identify the skills you are motivated to use.

≫EXHIBIT 2.3 ● Motivated Skills

Below you will find a list of skills. Review the list and consider which skills you are motivated to use you in your career. You will explore these further in **Task 2.5**, Motivated Skills. Next, complete the Knowdell™ Motivated Skills Card Sort in CourseMate to identify your values, and complete the Motivated Skills Matrix™ for your Career Portfolio. ▣

Motivated Skills	Definition
COMPUTER LITERATE	Develop, organize and complete tasks and projects using software programs such as Microsoft Word, Excel, and PowerPoint.
PLAN, ORGANIZE	Define goals and objectives, schedule and develop projects or programs.

(Continues)

Motivated Skills	Definition
OBSERVE	Study, scrutinize, examine data, people, or things scientifically.
MAINTAIN RECORDS	Keep accurate and up-to-date records, log, record, itemize, collate, tabulate data.
TEACH, TRAIN	Inform, explain, give instruction to students, employees, or customers.
INTERVIEW FOR INFORMATION	Draw out subjects through incisive questioning.
CUSTOMER SERVICE	Effectively solve problems and challenges that satisfy customers.
ADAPT TO CHANGE	Easily and quickly respond to changing assignments, work settings and priorities.
WORK WITH NUMBERS	Easily calculate, compute, organize, understand and solve numerical and quantitative problems.
CONCEPTUALIZE	Conceive and internally develop concepts and ideas.
MEDIATE	Manage conflict, reconcile differences.
CLASSIFY	Group categorize, systematize data, people, or things.
MAKE ARRANGEMENTS	Coordinate events, handle logistics.
BUDGET	Economize, save, stretch money or other sources.
ENTERTAIN/ PERFORM	Amuse, sing, dance, art, play music for, give a demonstration to, speak to an audience.
READ FOR INFORMATION	Research written resources efficiently and exhaustively.
INITIATE CHANGE	Exert influence on changing the status quo, exercise leadership in bringing about new directions.
DEAL WITH AMBIGUITY	Be comfortable and effective with issues that lack clarity, structure, or certainty.
DELEGATE	Achieve effective results by assigning tasks to others.
MONITOR	Keep track of the movement of data, people, or things.
PERCEIVE INTUITIVELY	Sense, show insight and foresight.
PROOFREAD, EDIT	Check writings for proper usage and stylistic flair, make improvements.
MAKE DECISIONS	Make major, complex, or frequent decisions.
SELL	Promote a person, company, goods or services, convince of merits, raise money.
NEGOTIATE	Bargain for rights or advantages.
DESIGN	Structure new or innovative practices, programs, products or environments.
MANAGE TIME	Ability to prioritize, structure and schedule tasks to maximize effort and meet deadlines.
COUNSEL	Facilitate insight and personal growth, guide, advise, coach students, employees, or clients.
DEAL WITH FEELINGS	Draw out, listen, accept, empathize, express sensitivity, defuse anger, calm, inject humor, appreciate.
EXPEDITE	Speed up production or services, trouble-shoot problems, streamline procedures.
IMPROVISE	To effectively think, speak and act without preparation.
MOTIVATE	Recruit involvement, mobilize energy, stimulate peak performance.
USE MECHANICAL ABILITIES	Assemble, tune, repair or operate engines or other machinery.
IMPLEMENT	Provide detailed follow-through of policies and plans.
PORTRAY IMAGES	Sketch, draw, illustrate, paint, photograph.
ACT AS LIASION	Represent, serve as a link between individuals or groups.
ANALYZE	Break down and figure out problems logically.
TEAM WORK	Easily and effectively work with others to obtain results.
SUPERVISE	Oversee, direct the work of others.
TEST	Measure proficiency, quality, or validity, check and double-check.
VISUALIZE	Imagine possibilities, see in mind's eye.
STRATEGIZE	Effectively plan and develop long-range strategies that successfully accomplish objectives.
INNOVATE/ INVENT	Create unique ideas or combine existing ideas to obtain a new or unique result.
GENERATE IDEAS	Reflect upon, conceive of, dream up, brainstorm ideas.
WRITE	Compose reports, letters, articles, ads, stories, or educational materials.
EVALUATE	Assess, review, critique feasibility or quality.
SYNTHESIZE	Integrate ideas and information, combine diverse elements into a coherent whole.

(Continues)

>> **EXHIBIT 2.3** ● **Motivated Skills** *Continued*

Motivated Skills	Definition
ESTIMATE	Appraise value or cost.
MENTOR	Educate, guide, coach, or counsel a less accomplished or junior colleague.
MUTI-TASK	To effectively manage a variety of tasks and projects simultaneously.
RESEARCH ON-LINE	Able to use search engines and the World Wide Web to gather and organize information and data.

Source: Knowdell™ Motivated Card Sort, 2009. © Richard L. Knowdell. Reprinted with permission. President Career Research and Testing, Inc. Post Office Box 611930, San Jose, CA 95161-1930, Tel: 408-272-3085/Fax: 408-259-8438, rknowdell@mac.com/www.careernetwork.org

>> **TECH SAVVY** ● **Digital Literacy**

 Digital literacy is a critical twenty-first century skill that reflects your ability to manage and utilize the expansive amount of information, media, and technology. The *Partnership for 21st Century Skills* identified many critical skills for the future, including the 4 Cs, which are described in **Exhibit 2.1**, The 4 Cs and these skills to improve digital literacy (*The Partnership for 21st Century Skills,* December 2009):

Access and evaluate information involves accessing information in a timely manner, while critically and competently evaluating content.

Use and manage information involves using information creatively for the task at hand and understanding the legal and ethical issues of using the information.

Apply technology effectively refers to the ability to use technology, including current products, to create, research, organize, evaluate, and communicate information.

Digital Citizenship

By 2011, the Pew Research Foundation found that 78 percent of all adults (Pew Internet, May 2011) and 95 percent of teens (Lenhert et al., 2011) were online. However, membership in the online community does not reflect consistent digital literacy. Today's college students and young adults have grown up with the Internet, and may even be expected to enter the workforce with online skills that surpass their older work peers. Marc Prensky (2001) explored the differences between Millennials and the generations who have had to learn technology, and coined the term "digital natives" to describe the knowledge inherent in growing up with technology, in contrast to the rest of the population, whom he described as "digital immigrants." Although digital natives may bring an instinct and comfort level regarding technology, both digital natives and digital immigrants can lack knowledge of computer software as well as various online activities.

The Impact of Poor Digital Literacy

Knowing where to locate useful information and how to evaluate it is an important transferable skill for life and work. However, in research from the Pew Internet and American Life Project (2011), college students were found to have varied familiarity with the way that online resources operated, and what made information credible. For instance, many students did not know when a link on a search engine was sponsored, or that a sponsored link was an advertisement. In addition, many students were not sure how to evaluate the credibility of information found on Wikipedia; some assumed that the site was reviewed and did not know that Wikipedia is a user-generated site in which entries must be evaluated individually by the end user.

Improving Technology Skills

Build basic skills. For those who lack basic technological skills, such as the ability to use word-processing software, send e-mails with attachments, conduct online banking, or search for information, there is support. Libraries can be a great source for free access to the Internet, with trained librarians to assist. In addition, the United States government has set up a website, www.DigitalLiteracy.gov, that can help users locate resources for career topics, Web design, and technology topics that are helpful in a digital age.

Expand your tools. For those who have mastered basic online skills, or have always used the Internet with ease throughout the day, it may seem more challenging to improve your ability. Focus on locating accurate information faster by using a wider variety of search methods, evaluating the credibility of the resources you find, and learning ethical and legal uses for information. In addition, if you locate an article that offers you statistics or data, see if any key terms are highlighted. By clicking these links you can often locate primary sources or definitions of important terms. For example, the *New York Times* offers links to other resources embedded in key words in the body of its articles.

Research your resources. You can also read more about the sites you use, such as how the information is gathered, or how research was conducted. Many sites have "About Us" pages that offer detailed information about the organization. This is helpful for large organizations as well as personal websites. For instance, there are many blogs that focus on topics that may be of interest. Learning more about bloggers' qualifications and experience can help you understand the context of their recommendations or opinions, and can help you decide whether to connect with them through social media, such as Twitter or Facebook.

Add advanced skills. There are also many advanced skills to expand your digital literacy. Improve results from online search engines by using Boolean operators, which simply involves typing the terms AND, OR, or NOT between search terms in any search engine to narrow your results. Become more knowledgeable about online resources, such as government sites, Wikipedia, and Google Scholar, or use specialized resources through your library such as ERIC, Lexis-Nexis, and ABI-Inform. These sites can help you find business articles, legal cases, and academic research.

Improving your digital literacy can help your career development in many ways. It can aid in your career exploration by making it easier to learn about jobs, industries, and environments that interest you. It can also help you evaluate the information you gather.

»» CAREER PROFILE ● Case Study

Mike Pollan: Building Skills

Mike recently completed an evening and weekend continuing-education program at a university to prepare for an accredited certification exam as a personal trainer. He took the exam and passed, but is now facing a new set of questions about next steps.

Returning to school was a challenge for Mike, who dropped out of high school and worked in numerous short-term jobs. He worked as a valet, a receptionist at a medical office, a busboy, and a salesperson in a retail store, during which time he completed his GED, with hopes for a promotion that never happened. His experiences helped him build skills in sales, customer service, and working in a team. After three years of what he felt were unrelated jobs for which he had no real interest, he went to his public library for a career workshop that was advertised on the board at his gym.

At the workshop, he realized that working out and playing sports were the few constants in his life that he really enjoyed. Based on suggestions in the workshop, he researched careers that involved physical fitness. He identified personal training as a career that would allow him to spend more time working out, and build on skills he had, including how to exercise safely, build muscle and endurance, and motivate people.

Mike was overwhelmed at the start of his program, as he learned about physiology, anatomy, and other scientific areas. However, the focus on exercise and the human body interested him, and his confidence increased. After learning about trends in the workforce and talking with personal trainers and other professionals in health and fitness careers, Mike identified an interest in working with aging adults, especially former athletes looking to maintain fitness levels following injuries, surgeries, or rehabilitation. He is now considering the range of places he could work and their job requirements. He is also exploring where he can gain the best skill-building experience for his credentials, and whether he wants to pursue an associate's degree in the future.

Describe the skills that Mike is motivated to use.
What transferable skills does Mike bring to his new career from his prior experiences?
How has assessing his skills led Mike to reevaluate his career preparation and planning?

To learn more about Mike's career development, visit CourseMate 🖥. View his networking talking points in **Chapter 8: Tools**.

»» WORK WITH AWARENESS ● Overcoming Failure

In school, work, and many other life scenarios, there are times when you may feel challenged by the difficulties you face, or when your goals take longer to achieve than you expected. For some people, this can feel like failure, and that can make it hard to persevere.

Psychologist Carol Dweck started her career eager to learn how people coped with failures (2006). To understand this, she observed children aiming to solve a series of puzzles, starting with simple puzzles and eventually difficult ones. In her book, *Mindset*, she describes how she expected to learn how the

(Continues)

children dealt with failure. Instead, some children expressed excitement and interest in the challenging puzzles. In a huge leap, she understood something unexpected about these children based on their reactions. They did not think they were failing; they thought they were learning.

According to Dweck, there are two mindsets, or ways of thinking: a "growth mindset" and a "fixed mindset" (2006). People with a growth mindset believe they can develop their personal qualities through effort and work. Those with a growth mindset do not aim to validate their skills, because they are more likely to see them as a starting point for something more. Those with a fixed mindset believe that a person's qualities, such as intelligence, personality, and moral character, cannot grow and develop. People with the fixed mindset aim to prove their worth by showing how their skills are valuable, since they see no room for improvement.

Although these mindsets are part of the way people naturally approach life experiences, she suggests that anyone can learn how to develop a growth mindset. This skill can help you reframe even the most difficult scenarios as opportunities for growth, avoid feeling like a failure, learn from experiences when you are evaluated, and avoid the feeling of being judged or failing.

To understand how a mindset can impact your learning experiences, use this guided scenario to imagine yourself in each of the mindsets.

… imagine you've decided to learn a new language and you've signed up for a class. A few sessions into the course, the instructor calls you up to the front of the room and starts throwing questions at you one after another.

Put yourself in a fixed mindset. Your ability is on the line. Can you feel everyone's eyes on you? Can you see the instructor's face evaluating you? Feel the tension, feel your ego bristle and waver. What else are you thinking and feeling?

Now, put yourself in a growth mindset. You're a novice—that's why you're here. You're here to learn. The teacher is a resource for learning. Feel the tension leave you. Feel your mind open up. (Dweck, 2006, p.14)

Preparing yourself to learn is a critical skill for career success. As a student, you are evaluated on new subjects and facts, and as an intern or new hire, you will be required to learn new approaches, techniques, tasks, and workplace behaviors. For those with a fixed mindset, these experiences can present many opportunities to feel like a failure, and to feel confronted by your inadequacies. For those with a growth mindset, these experiences can be seen as a chance to build skills and develop new strengths.

>> Evidence of Skills

As you prepare for your career, you will continually assess the skills that are most relevant, how you can build them, and the steps required to gain evidence of your assets. The Career Portfolio you will create throughout this course can be used to track your skill development and the fit between your strengths and the needs of employers. Identifying areas for improvement based on your interests, personality preferences, values, and your exploration of the world of work will help you notice your own skills gaps—the areas where your assets do not meet the needs of your target occupations. This approach will help you conduct a thorough and informed assessment of your skills, and a plan for building evidence of skills that can help you market yourself in the future.

Recognizing Needed Skills

You may not know all the skills that will help you create your own career success, especially if you are open-minded about your career options. However, you can assess the skills you have, those valued by employers in areas you are considering, and the ones you want to build. This will help you recognize gaps in your skills to determine areas you want to develop. If your skills don't match employers' needs, your job search will be much more difficult. A successful job search is the result of a clear and powerful message; developing evidence of relevant skills through coursework, work experiences, and leadership roles will help you achieve this.

Choosing Skill-Building Experiences

All experiences build skills, but some can help you develop specific, targeted skills that will more closely match the gaps between your assets and employers' needs. If you want to explore art education in the future, but need to earn money now and cannot find part-time paid work teaching art, you may feel frustrated by the limited options to expand your relevant skills. However, with some creativity, you can often turn a regular job into a career-building experience. You will learn more about the job search in **Chapter 9: Launch**, but here is an example to see how you can build evidence of relevant skills for your portfolio.

Suppose you are interested in a career as an art teacher, and are looking for a part-time job. Typically, a part-time job as a cashier will help you build customer-service skills, communication skills, and earn money. These are valuable, and can be transferable to many industries, but do not closely match the most relevant skills for art education. By choosing your location strategically, you may find a part-time job in an art supply store that will allow you to work with artists, art teachers, and art supplies. If the store is flexible and able to allow for a new program, you might be able to add more skills with an innovative project, such as 15-minute art mini-classes to introduce new products once per week. If a new program initiative is not possible, but you focus your energy on learning the products and helping customers buy the most appropriate supplies for their needs, you would demonstrate similar skills, including a knowledge of art supplies, familiarity with the needs of artists and art educators, and ability to communicate about art materials. There are many ways to shape your experiences to build skills.

Masterfile (Royalty-Free Div.)

Reviewing your assets with a mentor can help you identify skills you need and how they can be developed.

Developing References for Your Career

Evidence of your skills is also demonstrated through the strength of your references. Developing relationships with people who can speak about your performance and ability is another important component of your career development. In your career, employers will contact your references to gain insight into your professionalism, self-management skills, technical ability, and more. Learning to work well with supervisors, advisors, and others who are involved in your experiences can help you gain their trust, their support, and their advice. This can help you know what steps they value, learn from their guidance, and prove your worth. A strong effort on your part can provide a foundation for meaningful relationships.

If you recognize a skills gap between your assets and employers' needs, you can build needed skills before a job search or career change. There are many benefits to having this knowledge; it will prepare you to select advantageous opportunities, seek out support and feedback, and help you prepare for career transitions. Since your Career Portfolio is developed to help you track evidence of your skills and knowledge of the world of work, it can help you assess any gaps, allowing you to target the best environments and activities to build evidence of relevant skills.

Your Flexible Plan

Assess Your Skills

PLAN OF ANALYSIS

Step 1: Gather Information

For these questions, reflect on skills you identified using results from the Knowdell Motivated Skills Card Sort, which can be found in CourseMate 🖥 or refer to **Exhibit 2.3**, Motivated Skills.

What skills are you motivated to use in your career?

_____

_____

Which of these skills do you already have?

_____

_____

Which of these skills do you want to build?

_____

_____

Step 2: Evaluate the Information

What is necessary to maintain the skills you have and are motivated to use?

_____

_____

How can you build skills you want to use but need to develop further? What activities or experiences will help you build these skills? Refer to the section "What Have You Done?" in this chapter for skill-building environments.

_____

_____

Describe your level of motivation to take the steps required to maintain and build these skills.

_____

_____

Step 3: Make Conclusions

Following your analysis, create a list of the top five skills that you want to focus on using and building in your career.

1. _____   2. _____   3. _____

4. _____   5. _____

Performance Appraisal

Now that you have read the chapter, answer the questions below and complete the **Tasks**.

1. Where can you develop skills?
   a. Work experiences
   b. Social activities
   c. Community service
   d. All of the above

2. Which of the following is not one of the 4 Cs?
   a. Creativity and innovation
   b. Communication
   c. Commiserating
   d. Critical thinking and problem solving
   e. Collaboration and team building

3. Which of the following is true about transferable skills?
   a. You can develop them only in work experiences.
   b. Employers do not care about them, because they are not technical assets.
   c. You can use transferable skills in any career you develop.
   d. All of the above

4. What is a skills gap?
   a. When you have skills that you did not learn in school
   b. When employees or applicants lack the skills that are sought by employers
   c. When you have skills you perform well but do not want to use
   d. b and c

5. Good ways to assess your skills include
   a. Reading about your courses or major
   b. Reflecting on your experiences and tasks
   c. Thinking about the roles you play in your activities
   d. All of the above

6. Which of the following is true about digital literacy?
   a. Digital literacy is an ability to effectively access, understand, and apply technology.
   b. All digital natives have high levels of digital literacy.
   c. Digital immigrants cannot improve their digital literacy.
   d. Digital literacy is not important unless your job is in a high-tech field.

7. Which of the following is true about a growth mindset?
   a. It is something you cannot develop.
   b. It can help you feel less self-conscious about your shortcomings.
   c. It prevents you from being evaluated by others.
   d. It is none of the above.

Performance Appraisal Answer Key

1. d
2. c
3. c
4. b
5. d
6. a
7. b

Thought Questions

1. Can you identify your skills?

2. Have you identified skills that you want to use in your career?

3. Have you identified any skills that you want to use in your career but do not possess?

Notes:

_____

_____

_____

_____

_____

_____

TASK 2.1:

What Have You Done?

In this exercise, list your experiences. Refer to the section in the chapter entitled "What Have You Done?" for descriptions of the categories. You can also find this exercise in CourseMate. Use it to update your Career Portfolio, and it will be a tool for your résumé development in **Chapter 8: Tools**. 🖥

Past Employment	Degrees, Certificates, and Professional Credentials	Extracurricular Activities
Example:	*Example:*	*Example:*
1. *Camp counselor (summers 2012 & 2011), Roberts Country Day*	1. *HS Diploma (2010)*	1. *College Republicans (2011– Present)*
2. *Lifeguard, Greenboro Community Pool, October 2010– Present*		
1.		
2.		
3.		

Experiential Learning	Courses & Projects	Hobbies and Leisure Activities
Example:	*Example:*	
1. *Investment Banking Internship, Merrill Lynch, summer (2011– Present)*	*Econ courses—all prereqs American Economic Policy International Finance—with team project*	

Volunteer Experiences	Achievements (School or Professional)	Achievements (Personal)

TASK 2.2:
Evidence of Skills

Reviewing your experiences above, identify 10 skills you have developed and note where you built these skills. Refer to the list of skills in **Exhibit 2.3**, Motivated Skills, or list any other skills that are relevant to your experiences. Consider including specific skills that reflect your interests, such as "talented knitter," "great with animals," or "competitive figure skater."

In addition to highlighting valuable skills that may be relevant to employers, the skills you worked hard to develop can provide insight to your interests and values, which you will explore in **Chapter 3: Preferences** and **Chapter 4: Values**.

Skill Developed   Where I Developed This Skill

_____   _____

_____   _____

_____   _____

_____   _____

_____   _____

_____   _____

_____   _____

_____   _____

_____   _____

_____   _____

TASK 2.3:
Expand Your Digital Literacy

What can you do online? Consider the following activities, and use your online skills to complete one or more of these tasks. Consult with a librarian or visit your computer lab for assistance, if you think it would be helpful.

Locate a person online who has been helpful to you in your career development, and connect online, by phone, or in person to say thank you. Create a new social media page for yourself. Look up information on any "how to" question that interests you. Edit an entry on Wikipedia.

After you are finished, describe what you have done.

_____

_____

_____

_____

_____

TASK 2.4:

Transferable Skills and Your Major

Describe the skills you developed in your major. Refer to course syllabi, your course catalogue, or professors' Web pages for reference, if you cannot recall the goals of the course. List the skill you developed and the course or project in which you developed this skill.

Skill Developed   Course or Project Where I Developed This Skill

_____   _____

_____   _____

_____   _____

_____   _____

_____   _____

_____   _____

_____   _____

TASK 2.5:

Build Your Motivated Skills

Now that you have identified the skills you are motivated to use, what will it take for you to build and maintain these skills?

Choose one skill you want to build. What is it?

_____

Now choose one activity that will help you build that skill.

_____

How will this activity enhance your skills? For instance, what do you expect to learn, how will you demonstrate your knowledge, and what evidence and references will you gain for your skills?

_____

_____

Link to CourseMate

On CourseMate, you can find documents to help you update your Career Portfolio as well as additional resources and activities. Here is some of the information you can find online for **Chapter 2: Skills**.

CAREER PORTFOLIO

Your Flexible Plan
What Have You Done?
Motivated Skills Matrix™ Worksheet

RESOURCES

Career Profile: Salman Bandukda
Knowdell™ Motivated Skills Card Sort

© Sigrid Olsson/PhotoAlto/Corbis

Preferences

> I was always making things. Even though art was what I did every day, it didn't even occur to me that I would be an artist. —*Maya Lin*

What's Inside

You Know What You Like

Patterns of Interest: The Holland Codes

Explore Your Preferences: Psychological Type

Applying Type in Everyday Life

Prepare to . . .

- Understand how your preferences connect with career fields

- Identify your patterns of interest according to Holland's RIASEC theory

- Assess your psychological type using the MBTI® instrument*

- Understand how psychological type impacts many experiences

*Your textbook may have been packaged with the MBTI® instrument or you can access this tool through a counselor, school/community career center, or online at www.mbticomplete.com.

Understanding the relationship between careers and preferences can help you identify patterns of interest and explore how these relate to career fields. This can help you choose a career or major, and evaluate your prior choices, as you learn about occupations that are common for people who share your interests. Learning about your natural preferences can also help you consider what you would need in a career for you to be satisfied.

» You Know What You Like

You know what you like, but it may not have led you directly into an obvious career choice. "Find your passion," "follow your dreams," and "make your work feel like play," are all phrases that suggest your interests will lead to a career choice. However, for many people, it is not as easy as turning a love for sports into a career as a professional athlete, or even related fields like personal training or sports marketing. To connect your combination of interests with career fields, you will need to consider important factors, such as your skills, experience, abilities, and motivation.

Connecting personal preferences with careers. There are numerous theories and approaches that look at preferences to help individuals identify career fields that might be of interest. Furthermore, many tools exist to provide additional information that can be used for career assessment. In this chapter you will learn about John Holland's RIASEC theory, which identifies patterns of interest and is the foundation for numerous career assessments. This theory relates patterns of interest to six personality types and corresponding occupational types. Another approach you will learn involves the Myers-Briggs Type Indicator® instrument, a tool developed by Katharine Briggs and Isabel Briggs Myers that builds on psychiatrist Carl Jung's theory about personality. These theories and related instruments will give you the opportunity to learn which career fields are commonly chosen by people who share your preferences.

Identifying careers to explore. The key to using preferences as a source for identifying career possibilities is to look at the activities you choose and the range of career possibilities to which they relate. For instance, whatever your major, suppose you are most interested in socializing, planning social events, texting, and updating your Facebook page. You might like persuading or motivating others, be energized by being around people, or you could be a technology buff. These suggest a variety of careers to explore, each built on a unique combination of preferences.

Your preferences are reflected in all of your choices, from television shows you like to compromises that you are willing to make.

Here are examples of careers that build on certain preferences:

- Public Relations—for the individual who likes promoting social events
- Online Marketing—for the technology buff who likes to sell
- Fashion Merchandising—for the fashion enthusiast who is interested in shopping
- Not-for-Profit Administration—for the community leader and organizer
- Social Work—for the person who enjoys helping and listening to others
- Journalism—for someone who enjoys reporting and storytelling

Learning more about careers that connect to your current interests will provide you with possible directions for career exploration, while allowing you to remain flexible and open-minded as you become exposed to more information about the world of work.

≫ CAREER JOURNAL ● What Do You Like?

Use the space below to write about your thoughts and feelings.

First, list as many of your interests as you can. They can relate to work, school, or your free time. It does not matter if you have experience or whether you feel you have talent or skills in these areas. For example, to appreciate art, you do not need to be an artist.

Choose five interests from the list above that you think you might enjoy learning more about. Describe what attracts you to each interest area and what you like about it.

1. _____
2. _____
3. _____
4. _____
5. _____

Journal Feedback . . . There are many ways to determine areas of interest in the world of work, but reflecting on those that come to mind readily and easily can help you assess some of the areas that energize you most. Assessing your preferences can help you identify themes and learning opportunities that you want to pursue.

Name: Cara S.
College Degree: BA in Anthropology
Current Positions: Volunteer Research Assistant, Winthrop University Hospital EMS, Fire Department Standardized Patient, North-Shore LIJ Health System

Courtesy of Cara S.

Can you describe your career interests?

My current interests are science and innovation. I have always liked science, but I found it challenging. It was a reflex to say I would do premed. It was hard. I ended up deciding to change majors and drop premed. I majored in Anthropology, which was so interesting to me. Towards the end of school, I realized that I still was interested in medical school, and I did my premedical requirements after college. Now, I have three jobs and I'm applying to medical schools.*

Your Holland RIASEC code is Investigative, Realistic, and Social (IRS). How are these interests related to your career activities?

*Investigative—I certainly like exploring and learning why things are the way they are. I also want to do the necessary research to understand the possibilities of developing areas of medicine. I'm excited about the possibility of change within the scientific field. Realistic—I work in a lab, which involves hands-on work, and that's also Investigative. I also work in EMS so that is very hands-on, and I'm training to become an EMT. I do that as a member of the volunteer fire department.
Social—I feel we have a responsibility to understand people around us, and that is one reason I liked majoring in anthropology. My medical interests also are involved with helping people.*

Your MBTI® Type is ENTJ. How do these preferences impact your career?

I am definitely Extroverted. I work as a Standardized Patient. It's my favorite job, and the only paid one. It's like acting. The purpose is to help train medical students and improve communication. It's really fun. When I was reading my type, it says I like to be in charge. I can't take on a leadership role at work, but I seek out the opportunity to plan social events and bring people together, like a dinner with friends who don't know each other well, but who I think will like to meet. I also am very logical in my decision making [as in the Thinking preference], and I'm very organized, like the Judging [preference]. But if I know I have a certain amount of time with my friends, I can be open-minded about what we'll do. I don't need everything planned.

*Since the interview was completed, Cara S. was admitted to medical school and will be attending.

From Cara's Supervisor

Name: Eitan Akirav PhD.,
Title: Research Scientist and Assistant Professor of Research Medicine, Winthrop University Hospital and Stony Brook Medical School

Courtesy of Dr. Eitan Akirav

How do Cara's interests help her in her work?

From a clinical point of view, she has an interest in the well-being of humans, and she is interested in using scientific tools. We conduct mouse-based research to study type 1 and type 2 diabetes. Cara has an interest in disease-based research. Her main interest is to become exposed to the bench side of medicine—we call it "bench to bedside" because there is the research, and then translating the research to directly benefit patients. She could be a natural for translational research, because she is interested in patient welfare and research.

What aspects of Cara's personality help her make a strong contribution?

She's very inquisitive. Most of the science done is hypothesis based, and the orientation to gather information is a significant element of that. Being able to find the needle in a haystack is a required trait of a scientist. Cara has the ability to look at the data, analyze it, and redirect her effort. She's very well disciplined in terms of following the necessary scientific procedures to get meaningful data. She's also very meticulous. She does everything here as a volunteer. I see her in the lab, and she's definitely committed to the project.

What aspects of Cara's interests and personality will help her succeed in the career areas that interest her most?

_____

_____

_____

How are these consistent with Cara's RIASEC code and MBTI® type?

_____

_____

_____

For additional questions, visit CourseMate. 🖥

›› Patterns of Interest: The Holland Codes

John Holland, one of the most well-known career theorists, believed that understanding the role of interests can help people explore activities, occupations, workplace environments, skills, values, and personality (1997). Holland examined the relationship between people and occupational environments, and he developed a theory of personality and work environments that has held up to extensive research scrutiny.

Personality Development

According to Holland, personality development stems from early interests. When you are young, you engage in certain activities while avoiding others (1997). Holland believed that at a young age, activities are influenced by heredity and interests. In time, your preferences develop into interests that make you feel proud, happy, or excited, while also eliciting support, recognition, or approval from parents and peers. As your interests evolve, you choose activities that reflect your interests. This results in the development of related skills, which become your set of competencies. In turn, your competencies impact personality development, including values, traits, and self-concept.

Personality Patterns

Using his theory of personality development as a framework, Holland identified six personality types to describe individuals: Realistic, Investigative, Artistic, Social, Enterprising, and Conventional (RIASEC) (1997). According to Holland, "the more closely a person represents a particular type, the more likely he or she will exhibit the personal traits or behaviors associated with that type" (1997, p.1). A personality is represented by one or more types resulting in a personality pattern. This is referred to as a "Holland Code" or "RIASEC Code," using the first letter of each personality type that most closely matches the pattern of interest. For detailed information on each of Holland's six personality types and to assess your own personality pattern, see **Exhibit 3.1**, A Brief Description of the Holland Personality Typology. Holland acknowledged that more complex theories of personality could explain these factors or others more fully, but he relied on this simple model for his theory. Explore how your interests have developed through **Task 3.1**, Childhood Interests.

Personality Typology

To visually describe his theory, Holland created a model in which the six personality types are positioned around a hexagon in a specific order (RIASEC), reflecting their relationships. The hexagon is illustrated in **Exhibit 3.2**, Holland's Hexagonal Model.

Realistic types enjoy hands-on work such as creating visual displays or exhibits.

≫EXHIBIT 3.1 ● A Brief Description of the Holland Personality Typology

Review the descriptions of each personality type and identify the first, second, and third types that best reflect your patterns of interest. If you have taken a career assessment using the RIASEC codes, read the types that match your results.

A brief description of the Holland personality typology

Attribute	Realistic	Investigative	Artistic	Social	Enterprising	Conventional
Preferences for activities and occupations	Manipulation of machines, tools, and things	Exploration, understanding, and prediction or control of natural and social phenomena	Literary, musical, or artistic activities	Helping, teaching, treating, counseling, or serving others through personal interaction	Persuading, manipulating, or directing others	Establishing or maintaining orderly routines; application of standards
Values	Material rewards for tangible accomplishments	Development or acquisition of knowledge	Creative expression of ideas, emotions, or sentiments	Fostering the welfare of others; social service	Material accomplishment and social status	Material or financial accomplishment and power in social, business, or political arenas
Sees self as	Practical, conservative, and having manual and mechanical skills—lacking social skills	Analytical, intelligent, skeptical, and having academic talent—lacking interpersonal skills	Open to experience, innovative, intellectual—lacking clerical or office skills	Empathic, patient, and having interpersonal skills—lacking mechanical ability	Having more sales and persuasive ability—lacking scientific ability	Having better technical skills in business or production—lacking artistic competencies
Others see as	Normal, frank	Asocial, intellectual	Unconventional, disorderly, creative	Nurturing, agreeable, extroverted	Energetic, gregarious	Careful, conforming
Avoids	Interaction with people	Persuasion or sales activities	Routines and conformity to established rules	Mechanical and technical activity	Scientific, intellectual, or abstruse topics	Ambiguous or unstructured undertakings

Source: Adapted and reproduced by special permission of the Publisher, Psychological Assessment Resources, Inc., 16204 North Florida Avenue, Lutz, Florida 33549, from the Dictionary of Holland Occupational Codes, 3rd Edition. by Gary D. Gottfredson, Ph.D. and John L. Holland, Ph.D., Copyright © 1982, 1989, 1996. Further reproduction is prohibited without permission from PAR, Inc.

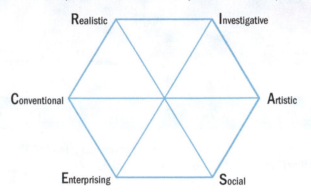

>> EXHIBIT 3.2 ● Holland's Hexagonal Model

The hexagon is a visual representation of Holland's RIASEC Theory (Holland, 1997, p. 35).

Source: Reproduced by special permission of the Publisher, Psychological Assessment Resources, Inc., 16204 North Florida Avenue, Lutz, Florida 33549, from Making vocational choices: A theory of vocational personalities and work environments, 3rd ed. by John L. Holland, Ph.D., Copyright © 1997. Further reproduction is prohibited without permission from PAR, Inc.

Work Environments

Holland recognized that the same patterns and themes that exist in people's personalities are also present within occupations, since people enjoy working with others like themselves (1997). He developed a classification of work environments that reflect the patterns of the people who worked in them. To learn more about how occupations reflect the RIASEC theory, review the dimensions in **Exhibit 3.3**, A Brief Description of the Holland Environmental Typology. To explore a list of majors organized using the six RIASEC types, see **Exhibit 3.4**, Typical College Majors by Holland Code. Keep in mind that occupations, like individuals, often reflect more than one type.

People in Work Environments

The connection between people and work environments is described as person-environment fit. Holland's theory suggests that people with similar interests enjoy working together, and you will find people with a personality pattern similar to yours in occupations that combine your personality types. Explore the relationship

iStockphoto.com/jean schweitzer

Artistic types enjoy creative activities such as performing or appreciating the arts.

between your personality patterns and work environments in **Task 3.2**, Personality and Environment.

Congruence, consistency, and differentiation are some of the concepts used to explain the connections between personality types and occupations. For a visual representation of these concepts, refer to the model in **Exhibit 3.2**, Holland's Hexagonal Model.

Congruence: This describes how closely a person's type matches the occupation types. For instance, the most congruent occupations for Artistic types are Artistic occupations, and the most incongruent occupations for Artistic types are Conventional occupations, which are opposite each other on the hexagon.

Consistency: A personality pattern of types that are close together on the hexagon is consistent, as these types have more in common than personality patterns that consist of types that are farther apart or opposite on the hexagon. Like personality patterns, occupations also often combine types, and those that combine closely related types are more consistent. For instance, a personality pattern or occupation that includes Investigative, Artistic, and Social types is consistent. If you have an inconsistent pattern of interests, you might find it more difficult to choose a career that meets your range of interests.

Differentiation: This is the extent to which a person is similar to a single type and not others. Someone whose patterns of interest most closely match one type is differentiated, and this can make it easier to predict careers that match that persons pattern of interests. An undifferentiated personality pattern is similar to a greater number of types. Someone who has a personality pattern that is similar to more than three types is undifferentiated, and it may be harder to predict careers that match his or her interests.

Applications of Holland's RIASEC Theory

Holland's theory serves as the foundation for many resources of occupational information, including the Dictionary of Holland Occupational Types (Gottfredson and Holland, 1996), and career assessments, such as the Self-Directed Search (SDS) (Holland, 1994) and the Strong Interest Inventory® tool (see CPP at cpp.com). As you learn about the RIASEC themes and occupations that relate to your interests, your self-awareness can help you learn about a greater number of career fields than you might have considered in the past. One approach involves using interest assessments to stimulate learning and identify areas for exploration rather than to identify matching career fields (Krumboltz, 2009). Interest assessments can be used as a starting point for a discussion and exploration about careers, or to examine choices you have already made.

≫EXHIBIT 3.3 ● A Brief Description of the Holland Environmental Typology

A brief description of the Holland environmental typology

Attribute	Realistic	Investigative	Artistic	Social	Enterprising	Conventional
Requires	Manual and mechanical competencies, interaction with machines, tools, and objects	Analytical, technical, scientific, and verbal competencies	Innovation or creative ability, emotionally expressive with others	Interpersonal competencies, skill in mentoring, treating, healing or teaching others	Skills in persuasion and manipulation of others	Clerical skills, skills in meeting precise standards for performance
Demands and rewards the display of	Conforming behavior, practical accomplishment	Skepticism and persistence in problem solving, documentation of new knowledge, understanding, or solution of problems	Imagination in literary, artistic, or musical accomplishment	Empathy, humanitarianism, sociability, friendliness	Initiative in the pursuit of financial or material accomplishment; dominance; self-confidence	Organizational ability, conformity, dependability
Values or personal styles allowed expression	Practical, productive, and concrete values; robust, risky, adventurous styles	Acquisition of knowledge through scholarship or investigation	Unconventional ideas or manners, aesthetic values	Concern for the welfare of others	Acquisitive or power-oriented styles, responsibility	Conventional outlook and concern for orderliness and routines
Occupations or other environments involve	Concrete, practical activity; use of machines, tools, materials	Analytical or intellectual activity aimed at trouble-shooting or creation and use of knowledge	Creative work in music, writing, performance, sculpture, or unstructured intellectual endeavors	Working with others in a helpful or facilitating way	Selling, leading, manipulating others, to attain personal or organizational goals	Working with things, numbers, or machines to meet predictable organizational demands or specified standards
Sample occupations	Carpenter, truck operator	Psychologist, microbiologist	Musician, interior designer	Counselor, clergy member	Lawyer, retail store manager	Production editor, bookkeeper

Source: Adapted and reproduced by special permission of the Publisher, Psychological Assessment Resources, Inc., 16204 North Florida Avenue, Lutz, Florida 33549, from the Dictionary of Holland Occupational Codes, 3rd Edition. by Gary D. Gottfredson, Ph.D. and John L. Holland, Ph.D., Copyright © 1982, 1989, 1996. Further reproduction is prohibited without permission from PAR, Inc.

Realistic (R) PRACTICAL DOERS Realistic students prefer to take an active hands-on approach involving construction, mechanical, or outdoor activities.

Agriculture
Animal Science
Automotive Services
Civil Engineering
Computer Technology
Drafting
Earth Science
Electronics
Facilities Management
Fire Science
Fish and Wildlife Management
Forestry
Heating, Air Conditioning, and Refrigeration

Horticulture
Industrial Arts Education
Landscape Architecture
Law Enforcement
Mechanical Engineering
Medical Technology
Military Science
Natural Resources
Physical Fitness and Training
Plumbing
Transportation
Welding

Investigative (I) SCIENTIFIC PROBLEM SOLVERS Investigative students prefer to take an analytical approach involving research, experimentation, or diagnosis.

Anthropology
Astronomy
Biochemistry
Biological Sciences
Botany
Chemistry
Computer Information Systems
Computer Science
Criminal Justice
Economics
Emergency Health Services
Food Science

Geography
Geology
Mathematics
Optometry
Physical Therapy
Physics
Pre-Dentistry
Pre-Medicine
Psychology
Science Education
Sociology
Veterinary Science

Artistic (A) CREATIVE COMMUNICATORS Artistic students prefer to take a self-expressive or creative approach involving art/design, music, or writing.

Advertising
Architecture
Art Education
Art History
Broadcasting
Cinematography
Classics
Comparative Literature
Creative Writing
Dance
Design
English

Fashion Merchandising
Fine Arts
Foreign Languages
Humanities
Journalism
Linguistics
Mass Communication
Medical Illustration
Music Education
Philosophy
Photography
Theater Arts

Social (S) EMPATHIC HELPERS Social students prefer to take a helping or altruistic approach involving teaching, developing, or caring for others.

Child Development
Counseling
Criminology

Dietetics/Nutrition
Elementary Education
ESL Teaching

(Continues)

>> **EXHIBIT 3.4** ● **Typical College Majors by Holland Code** *Continued*

Ethnic Studies	Public Health
Family Studies	Recreation
Health Education	Religious Studies
Hearing and Speech	Secondary Education
Home Economics	Social Work
Human Services	Special Education
Nursing	Substance Abuse Counseling
Occupational Therapy	Urban Studies
Physical Education	Women's Studies

Enterprising (E) ACTIVE PERSUADERS Enterprising students prefer to influence or lead others through selling the merits of ideas or products.

Business Administration	Management
Business Education	Marketing
Consumer Economics	Personnel and Labor Relations
Finance	Political Science
Government	Pre-Law
History	Public Administration
Hospitality	Public Relations
Hotel Management	Real Estate
Human Resources	Restaurant Management
Insurance	Retail Merchandising
International Relations	Travel and Tourism

Conventional (C) CAREFUL ORGANIZERS Conventional students prefer to take an orderly approach to organizing and managing finances, procedures, or data.

Accounting	Industrial Education
Actuarial Science	Information Technology
Banking and Finance	Mathematics Education
Bookkeeping	Management Information Systems
Business Education	Medical Administration
Computer Programming	Medical Transcription
Computer Systems Operations	Office Systems
Court Reporting	Paralegal Studies
Data Management	Purchasing/Materials Management
Dental Hygiene	Secretarial Procedures
Financial Planning	Small Business Operations
Food Service Management	Statistics
Hotel, Restaurant, and Institutional Management	

Source: Modified and reproduced by special permission of the Publisher, CPP, Inc., Mountain View, CA 94043 from the STRONG INTEREST INVENTORY® PROFILE WITH COLLEGE PROFILE by Jeffrey P. Prince. Copyright 2004, 2012 by CPP, Inc. All rights reserved. Further reproduction is prohibited without the Publisher's written consent. Strong Interest Inventory is a trademark or a registered trademark of CPP, Inc.

>> **EMBRACING DIFFERENCES** ● **Stereotype Threat**

 Stereotypes can limit us, establish incorrect expectations or assumptions about our capabilities at work or in other settings, and make us feel bad about ourselves. In the 1990s, Claude Steele, then a professor at Stanford University, became interested in understanding the high dropout rates of African Americans. He was struck by the fact that these students had similar SAT scores to white students when entering college, and he wondered if race could be a factor in the high rate of attrition. In an illuminating study, he and Joshua Aronson showed that when a person is aware of a negative stereotype about a group to which he or she belongs, even if the individual doesn't believe that stereotype, it can still impact performance.

They described this as *stereotype threat*, the "threat of possibly being judged and treated stereotypically, or of possibly self-fulfilling such a stereotype" (Steele and Aronson, 1995, p. 798).

In this study, undergraduate students were given a portion of the Graduate Record Examination (GRE) and told it was a measure of intellectual ability. Black students scored lower in comparison with white students, but when the stereotype threat was removed, the gap was eliminated (Steele and Aronson, 1995). In another study, white men were shown to do worse on tests of athletic ability than black men because of stereotype threat (Stone, Lynch, Sjomeling, and Darley, 1999). By 2011, more than 300 research studies published in peer-reviewed journals showed that stereotype threat negatively impacts performance (Block Koch Liberman Merriweather & Roberson, 2011).

Stereotypes in American Society

You are probably aware of stereotypes that describe groups to which you belong. Your awareness of stereotypes does not suggest that you believe the stereotypes are true; however, your awareness of stereotypes that exist for your reference groups can make you vulnerable to stereotype threat. Here is a list of some of the stereotypes in American society that researchers have explored.

- *Women are not good at math.*
- *Asian Americans excel in math.*
- *African Americans are intellectually inferior.*
- *White men are not good athletes.*

As you reflect on these and other stereotypes, think about whether you have ever been concerned that you would be judged based on stereotypes.

Stereotype Threat in the Workplace

There are many workplace stereotypes, suggesting, for instance, that women are not ambitious, Asian Americans are introverted, men are better suited for science careers than women, or that people like you are not welcome in an organization. Here are three ways people have been found to respond to stereotype threat in the workplace (Block, Koch, Liberman, Merriweather, and Roberson, 2011).

Fending off the stereotype. This is accomplished by increasing one's effort to improve or demonstrate performance after experiencing stereotype threat. This can put extra pressure on individuals.

Discouraged by the stereotype. After realizing that even increased productivity and performance efforts will not change the perception others have of their group membership, individuals can experience aggression and depression.

Resilient to the stereotype. When someone experiences stereotype threat, this approach involves acknowledging that the stereotype threat occurred, recovering from the experience, and engaging in further development. In this scenario, the individual works toward changing the workplace to reduce the threat, rather than trying to change him or herself.

Those who respond to stereotype threat with *resilience to the stereotype* accept that stereotype threat exists and will impact others' judgments; however, they see the problem as external, rather than a reflection of their own identity (Block, Koch, Liberman, Merriweather, and Roberson, 2011). This has the best possible outcomes, because it does not make you feel that you are the problem. To improve your own resilience to the stereotype, work toward increasing the number and presence of members of your reference group, raise awareness of relevant differences, and make efforts to improve the treatment of your group, which can be achieved by helping others in activities such as mentoring.

» Explore Your Preferences: Psychological Type

Another popular means for exploring the relationship between preferences and careers is the Myers-Briggs Type Indicator® instrument, which was developed using the theory of a Swiss psychiatrist, Carl Jung. Jung, a contemporary of Sigmund Freud, was interested in the study of mentally healthy people, their patterns of behavior, and their quest toward self-fulfillment. To this end, he developed a theoretical model of psychological type outlining basic mental processes and orientation of energy (Myers, Kirby, and Myers, 1998). Building on Jung's theory, a mother-daughter team, Katharine Cook Briggs and Isabel Briggs Myers, developed an instrument to identify and clarify preferences. The tool they created is the Myers-Briggs Type Indicator® instrument, which is also referred to as the MBTI® instrument.

The MBTI® instrument uses a series of forced-choice questions that identify preferences in four dimensions: how we get energized, how we gather information, how we make decisions on information, and how we then act on that information (Myers, Kirby, and Myers, 1998). These preferences create 16 possible combinations or types of recognizable behaviors. This is not to say that individuals are not unique. Rather, type is a framework that can help you understand your personality and how you collect and process information. Contributing to type is each individual's experiences, background, culture, and family history. Preferences can offer insight into many areas that are related to the world of work. Your increased awareness of type can be helpful as you choose a career, enter into professional relationships, work in teams, take on leadership roles, interact with peers or supervisors, and develop your learning and communication styles.

To illustrate how your preferences operate, complete the following activity.

First, sign your name on the line below as you normally do.

_____

Now, sign your name again on the line below, but this time use your other hand.

_____

You probably found that writing your name on the first line was easy and did not require much thought or energy. When you wrote your name the second time using your nondominant hand, you probably experienced some difficulty. It may have felt uncomfortable, took longer, and required more of your attention. However, you *can* write your name with your opposite hand and, if it were required, you could improve your skill.

Both introverts and extroverts may enjoy interacting with people, but introverts gain energy by spending time alone.

The dimensions explored in the MBTI® instrument reflect four dichotomous scales. On each side of the scale is a preference, as illustrated in **Exhibit 3.5**, The MBTI® Preferences Overview. A preference for one dimension does not preclude you from using your other preference; in fact, everyone uses all eight preferences (Myers, Kirby, and Myers, 1998). Your type reflects the preference that is most comfortable and natural for you.

The scales of the MBTI® instrument reflect a continuum with a preference for one side over the other, much like a preference for writing with your dominant hand. Identifying your preferences in each of the scales will result in a four-letter type.

Use **Exhibit 3.6**, Understanding MBTI® Preferences, to assess your preferences on each of the four scales. Then, consider the most popular careers for your four-letter type, using **Exhibit 3.7**, Popular Occupations for MBTI® Types, as well as the most common majors in **Exhibit 3.8**, Common Majors for MBTI® Types. As with the Holland Codes and their corresponding Personality and Occupational Types, the MBTI® instrument can be used to expand your ideas about the careers you might explore and how you can use all of your preferences in ways that will serve you in your career and your life (Krumboltz, 2009).

≫ EXHIBIT 3.5 ● The MBTI® Preferences Overview

Where you focus your attention	**E Extraversion** Draw energy from the outer world of people and activities	**I Introversion** Draw energy from and pay attention to the inner world
The way you take in information	**S Sensing** Like information that is real and factual	**N iNtuition** Like to see patterns and connections, the big picture
The way you make decisions	**T Thinking** Use logical analysis in decision making	**F Feeling** Use their personal values in decision making
How you deal with the outer world	**J Judging** Like a structured and planned life	**P Perceiving** Like a flexible, adaptable life

Source: Modified and reproduced by special permission of the Publisher, CPP, Inc., Mountain View, CA 94043 from the INTRODUCTION TO TYPE® booklet by Isabel Briggs Myers. copyright 1998 by CPP, Inc. All rights reserved. Further reproduction is prohibited without the Publisher's written consent. Introduction to Type, MBTI, Myers-Briggs, and Myers-Briggs Type Indicator are trademarks or registered trademarks of the MBTI Trust, Inc., in the United States and other countries.

≫ EXHIBIT 3.6 ● Understanding MBTI® Preferences

Review the four dichotomies of the MBTI® instrument preferences and check the corresponding boxes of the characteristics that feel most comfortable to you. If you have taken the MBTI® instrument, consider how closely your self-assessed characteristics match your results. **Please note that your self-assessment is not a substitute for the actual instrument and verification.**

Where do you prefer to focus your attention? Where do you get energy? The E–I Dichotomy

EXTRAVERSION

People who prefer Extraversion like to focus on the outer world of people and activity. They direct their energy and attention outward and receive energy from interacting with people and from taking action.

Characteristics associated with people who prefer Extraversion:

- Like a variety of activities with lots of action
- Prefer to work with other people
- Develop ideas by brainstorming and discussing with others
- Learn new tasks by talking and doing
- Enjoy being out and about, away from the office

INTROVERSION

People who prefer Introversion like to focus on their own inner world of ideas and experiences. They direct their energy and attention inward and receive energy from reflecting on their thoughts, memories, and feelings.

Characteristics associated with people who prefer Introversion:

- Like solitude and time for concentration
- Prefer to work alone
- Develop ideas by contemplation and reflection
- Learn new tasks by reading and reflecting
- Like to work in one place

(Continues)

>> **EXHIBIT 3.6** ● **Understanding MBTI® Preferences** *Continued*

How do you prefer to take in information? The S-N Dichotomy

SENSING

People who prefer Sensing like to take in information that is real and tangible—what is actually happening. They are observant about the specifics of what is going on around them and are especially attuned to practical realities.

Characteristics associated with people who prefer Sensing:

- Use past experience to solve problems
- Notice things that need to be done now
- Do things that are practical
- Pay careful attention to details
- Prefer to improve what is
- Like to work steadily, proceeding step by step

INTUITION

People who prefer intuition like to take in information by seeing the big picture, focusing on the relationships and connections between facts. They want to grasp patterns and are especially attuned to seeing new possibilities.

Characteristics associated with people who prefer Intuition:

- Use ingenuity to solve problems
- Envision future priorities
- Do things that are innovative
- Look for new problems to be solved
- Prefer to change things
- Like to work with bursts of energy

How do you make decisions? The T-F Dichotomy

THINKING

People who prefer to use Thinking in decision making like to look at the logical consequences of a choice or action. They want to mentally remove themselves from the situation to examine the pros and cons objectively. They are energized by critiquing and analyzing to identify what's wrong with something so they can solve the problem. Their goal is to find a standard or principle that will apply in all similar situations.

Characteristics associated with people who prefer Thinking:

- Do work that involves logical order
- Use logical analysis to make decisions
- Consider the principles in a situation
- Pay attention to what needs to be done
- Feel rewarded when the job is done well

FEELING

People who prefer to use Feeling in decision making like to consider what is important to them and to others involved. They mentally place themselves into the situation to identify with everyone so they can make decisions based on their values about honoring people. They are energized by appreciating and supporting others and look for qualities to praise. Their goal is to create harmony and treat each person as a unique individual.

Characteristics associated with people who prefer Feeling:

- Do work that involves service to people
- Use personal values to make decisions
- Consider the underlying values in a situation
- Pay attention to the people side of work
- Feel rewarded when people's needs are met

How do you deal with the outer world? The J-P Dichotomy

JUDGING

People who prefer to use their Judging process in the outer world like to live in a planned, orderly way, seeking to regulate and manage their lives. They want to make decisions, come to closure, and move on. Their lives tend to be structured and organized, and they like to have things settled. Sticking to a plan and schedule is very important to them, and they are energized by getting things done.

Characteristics associated with people who prefer Judging:

- Feel comfortable with system and order
- Need to know all about a project to get started
- Produce best with structure and schedules
- Focus on completion
- Need measurable outcomes

PERCEIVING

People who prefer to use their Perceiving process in the outer world like to live in a flexible, spontaneous way, seeking to experience and understand life, rather than control it. Detailed plans and final decisions feel confining to them; they prefer to stay open to new information and last-minute options. They are energized by their resourcefulness in adapting to the demands of the moment.

Characteristics associated with people who prefer Perceiving:

- Feel comfortable adapting to change
- Need only the essentials of a project to get started
- Adapt well to changing situations
- Focus on process
- See outcomes as opportunities for change

The MBTI® instrument type that most closely reflects my preferences is:

_____ISFP_____

Please write the first letter of each of the four preferences that most closely match your preferences on the line above.

≫ EXHIBIT 3.7 ● Popular Occupations For MBTI® Types

ISTJ
- Civil engineer
- Health & safety engineer
- Industrial production manager
- Infantry member
- Nuclear engineer
- Parole probation officer
- Power plant operator

ISFJ
- Administrative assistant
- Bank teller
- Dietician/nutritionist
- Lodging manager
- Physical therapist
- Proofreader
- Registered nurse

INFJ
- Dental hygienist
- Environmental scientist
- General family physician
- Librarian/information services
- Middle school teacher
- Occupational therapist
- Writer

INTJ
- Actuary
- Computer hardware engineer
- Economist
- Food scientist
- Multimedia artist/animator
- Natural sciences manager
- Top executive, military specific

ISTP
- Command & control center specialist
- Computer operator
- Electronics repairer
- Farmer/rancher
- Machinist
- Plant scientist
- Team assembler

ISFP
- Air crew member
- Bookkeeper
- Chemical technician
- Coach
- Data communications analyst
- Driver
- Surveyor

INFP
- Artist/visual artist
- Commercial art director
- Desktop publisher
- Home health aide
- Psychiatrist
- Reporter
- Vocation rehabilitation counselor

INTP
- Biomedical engineer
- Chemist
- Editor
- Graphic designer
- Network systems administrator
- Political scientist
- Top executive, legal

ESTP
- Carpenter
- Fisher
- Inspector/tester/grader
- Materials engineer
- Military officer
- Pilot/copilot
- Tax examiner/revenue agent

ESFP
- Cook
- Licensed practical nurse
- Receptionist
- Recreation worker
- Salesperson
- Teacher's aide
- Veterinary technician

ENFP
- Actor/performing artist/dancer
- Clergy
- Craft artist
- Fitness trainer
- Forester
- Mental health counselor
- Travel agent/services

ENTP
- Architectural drafter
- Cost estimator
- Electrical/electronics technician
- Geologist/geophysicist
- Industrial engineer
- Public relations manager
- Top executive, sales

ESTJ
- Civil engineering technician
- Financial counselor
- Industrial engineer
- Infantry member
- Judge
- Management Consultant
- Sales manager

ESFJ
- Child care worker
- Director of religious activities
- Medical secretary
- Pharmacy aide
- Public health educator
- Surgeon
- Technical writer

ENFJ
- Career counselor
- Elementary school teacher
- Industrial/organizational psychologist
- Interior designer
- Photographer
- Public relations specialist
- Veterinary assistant

ENTJ
- Anesthesiologist
- Commercial art director
- Internist
- Management consultant
- Survey researcher
- Top executive, business & financial operations
- Urban/regional planner

Source: Modified and reproduced by special permission of the Publisher, CPP, Inc., Mountain View, CA 94043 from the MBTI® CAREER REPORT by Allen L. Hammer. Copyright 1992, 1998, 2004 by Peter B. Myers and Katharine D. Myers. All rights reserved. Further reproduction is prohibited without the publisher's written consent. MBTI, Myers-Briggs, and Myers-Briggs Type Indicator are trademarks or registered trademarks of the MBTI Trust, Inc., in the United States and other countries.

EXHIBIT 3.8 ● **Common Majors for MBTI® Types**

ISTJ
- Accounting
- Aviation technology
- Chemistry
- Drafting & technical drawing
- History
- Mathematics

- Statistics

ISFJ
- Accounting
- Child Care
- Cosmetology
- Health & medical sciences
- Mathematics
- Sociology

- Student counseling & personnel services

INFJ
- Anthropology
- Foreign languages
- Library sciences
- Literature
- Performance & fine arts
- Rehabilitation counseling & services
- Women's studies

INTJ
- Geography
- Library sciences
- Literature
- Philosophy
- Physics

- Urban & regional planning

ISTP
- Automotive technology
- Aviation technology
- Computer & information sciences
- Computer technology

- Construction

- Electronics technology
- Welding

ISFP
- Child care
- Computer technology
- Cosmetology

- Culinary arts

- Law enforcement & protective services
- Medical technology
- Social work

INFP
- Applied art & design
- Archaeology
- Architecture

- Earth, atmospheric, & marine sciences
- Library sciences

- Literature
- Performance & fine arts

INTP
- Applied art & design

Computer & information sciences

Geography

Literature

Philosophy

Physics

Urban & regional planning

ESTP
- Agriculture
- Aviation technology
- Construction
- Finance
- Fire science

- Law enforcement & protective services
- Military studies

ESFP
- Child care
- Cosmetology
- Culinary arts
- Fire science
- Law enforcement & protective services
- Medical technology

- Social work

ENFP
- Advertising
- Biological science
- Broadcasting & film
- Fashion design & textiles
- Journalism

- Psychology

- Statistics

ENTP
- Broadcasting & film
- Cultural & foreign studies
- Engineering
- International business
- Philosophy

- Physics

- Urban & regional planning

ESTJ
- Accounting
- Economics
- Engineering
- Finance
- Management

- Political science

- Pre-law

ESFJ
- Education
- Health & medical sciences
- Marketing
- Mass communication
- Rehabilitation counseling & sciences

- Student counseling & personnel services
- Telecommunications technology

ENFJ
- Advertising
- Anthropology
- Journalism
- Performance & fine arts
- Religion & theology

- Student counseling & personnel services
- Women's studies

ENTJ
- Finance
- International business
- Management
- Philosophy
- Political science

- Pre-law

- Urban & regional planning

Jasmine Nouri: Type In Action

Jasmine is studying business at a four-year university in upstate New York. She is a good student, and has always been hard working and motivated, enjoying math, science, and English classes.

As a high school student, she thought she would pursue a career in law, but she is now enthusiastic about the intersection between business and legal issues, following stocks, and reading business and finance magazines and websites. She is friendly and sociable, but wonders whether she will be successful in the competitive fields she is considering.

Her family, while supportive of her aspirations, is not able to provide crucial connections and networking opportunities in these fields. By networking with a former high school teacher, she was able to connect with a commodities broker who hired her to work in the legal department of his firm over two summers.

In the first semester of her junior year, Jasmine participated in the internship recruiting program at her college, hoping to land a competitive, paid, summer internship in finance. As she began the recruitment process, she signed up for a minicourse in her career center. As part of the course, Jasmine took the Strong Interest Inventory® tool and Myers-Briggs Type Indicator® instrument. She learned that her results on the Strong Interest Inventory® tool were Investigative, Enterprising, and Realistic (IER) and

that her MBTI® type was ESTJ. She believed her results to be fairly accurate. She thought the Strong Interest Inventory® tool reflected her interests in research, statistics, and business. She also felt her MBTI® score was accurate, because she values tradition, is willing to work long and hard to complete tasks, is practical, and likes to analyze situations. However, she was surprised to see the focus on engineering careers, and was reminded of her early school interests, such as math and science courses.

Jasmine reviewed her assessment results and felt she could enjoy many of the careers that matched her interests. Her professor assured her that an internship would allow her to explore further, rather than narrow her choices, but she felt doubtful, as she wanted to use her college experience for practical, career preparation.

How can Jasmine learn more about how her preferences will be an asset in the careers she is considering?

Should Jasmine make any changes in her plans based on her assessments? Why or why not? Using Jasmine's MBTI® type, consider how her preferences might shed light on her career development concerns.

To learn more about Jasmine's career development, visit Course-Mate. View her résumé in **Chapter 8: Tools**.

Our preferences guide online behavior such as what information we seek, games we play, sites where we shop, and more. On Facebook and other sites, we share interests and connect with others. But employers are paying attention to online behavior, and it is having an impact on hiring, employee relationships, and career success. Furthermore, the laws and policies that govern online behavior and the workplace are being written and rewritten to reflect rapidly changing technology. Here are several examples of situations and consequences involving real-world online behavior.

- In Seattle, Washington, a star athlete at a public high school tweeted about an academic privilege that led to an investigation revealing inconsistencies and falsified academic records of athletes at his school. The school's athletic director was subsequently fired (Smith, 2011).
- A Connecticut ambulance company employee was fired for posting derogatory comments on her Facebook page about her employer, but the National Labor Relations Board sued the company, claiming the firing was illegal. Two years later, in 2011, the case was settled out of court, with the company

agreeing to broaden its policy concerning online behavior to allow employees to discuss their work (Pepitone, 2011).
- At Anglo Irish Bank's North American branch, an intern was exposed for lying about needing time off for a family emergency when a Facebook picture showed him at party holding a beer (Popkin, 2008). In a twist, the intern's supervisor viewed the photo, sent a follow-up e-mail to him with the photo attached, and copied the entire company. The e-mails went viral and the story was covered in the media, further impacting the intern's reputation.

Manage Your Online Behavior

Expressing your interests through your likes and comments online, allowing pictures of yourself to appear on others' pages, and sharing opinions and ideas through your online activity is part of life. However, this requires you to be more aware of your behavior online and in the real world, and how it can impact your employment, your relationships with others, and your professional reputation.

(Continues)

For advice on managing your online reputation, consider these suggestions from Matt Ivestor, the founder of the former college gossip website, JuicyCampus.com. He intended for the site to be fun, but took it down after it became a source for mean and damaging posts including rumors of sexual promiscuity, accusations of racism, and violent threats (Ivestor, M., 2011). Ivestor suggests starting with these tips:

- **Be proactive.** Claim your own name on various websites and monitor the content reflected about you online by googling yourself and removing digital dirt, which is discussed further in "Tech Savvy: Google Yourself" in **Chapter 4: Values.**

- **Think about the content you create.** The words and images you post, the sites where you post comments, and the discussions you participate in all reflect your reputation. Be aware of the messages you are sending.

- **Defend your reputation.** If something is written about you that is hurtful, potentially damaging, or misleading, step up. Ask your friends not to post pictures of you that you don't want online, be aware of the activities in which you participate and how they could be posted, and participate in real-world and online groups and activities that reflect your reputation, because both usually have online trails.

- **Treat others with decency and respect.** Your online participation should reflect the reputation you are trying to build. Of course, avoid meanness and rude behavior, but also be aware of nuances in written communication. Present your knowledge, insight, and interests, but do all of this with respect for others and their ideas. Online communication does not leave room for the cues we give as we speak, so make sure your posts will not be misconstrued.

The best approach to online behavior may be to use social cues from the real world, while acknowledging the permanence of your online activity. To ensure that your online behavior matches the reputation you want to build, you can also consider how your preferences guide your behavior, and aim to maximize activities that you feel reflect your best assets.

>> **WORK WITH AWARENESS** ● **Proactive Behavior**

In a global economy, where work and rewards are often performance-driven or project-based, and workgroups are the growing norm, proactive behavior exhibits another dimension of professionalism, and is increasingly important. What does it mean to be proactive? It involves taking personal initiative to improve a situation or create new opportunities, and can also involve challenging the way things are being done (Crant, 2000). People who are proactive seek out information and opportunities for growth. They look for ways to build and use their skills. They pursue assignments that help them grow. They recognize how they can be an asset to others and look for ways to contribute.

The Benefits of Proactive Behavior

Proactive behavior is a quality that is sought by employers because it helps them on an organizational level. For instance, by hiring people who take initiative, employers gain employees who will generate ideas and help them evolve. And, as an added bonus, proactive behavior has been shown to benefit you as an employee as well. Here are some of the ways you can benefit in your career and career preparation by engaging in proactive behavior.

Participate in activities. To make a contribution, you must first choose to participate. That requires you to join clubs or committees, take on leadership roles, and manage your time and commitments. Proactive people believe their jobs and responsibilities are bigger than they are actually defined, and they work to expand their duties to include tasks that are not expected of them (Parker, 1998). This has been shown to increase innovation, which is highly valued by employers.

Do extra work. To improve your performance, take active steps to do work that is outside of your responsibilities, and also helps you build skills and generate results for your team. In a study of sales people, those who were more proactive performed better, because they added extra tasks—in their case, they took time to actively solicit new clients (Crant, 1995). If you are in a team project, you could offer to organize the data or research articles that will help your group prepare for a presentation. By collecting and reviewing data, you will sharpen your knowledge of the subject and increase your contribution to the project.

Help others. If you have a talent or skill that can add value, offer to use it. Show your colleagues, peers, or club members that you can do your work and that you will help them with their projects. This will improve their likelihood to want you on their team, and they will grow to see you as a resource for support. This can lead to increased opportunities. People with proactive personalities have been shown to have better career outcomes, including a higher salary and a greater number of promotions (Seibert Crant & Kraimer, 1999). Studies have also shown that proactive people have better relationships with those who supervise their work (Li, Liang, and Crant, 2010). To improve your relationships and increase your rewards, become indispensible by offering to assist whenever you can.

Decide when to be proactive.

Proactive behavior is useful in all occupations and industries, as well as in entrepreneurial ventures, entry-level positions, and seasoned management roles. However, part of developing this aspect of your personality is learning when to take action, and when to let others take the initiative first. Listening and evaluating your environment are important skills that can help you decide when to engage in proactive behavior.

Listen for specific needs.

When you are engaged in a project, listen to others and learn about their needs. Look for opportunities to contribute with specific tasks or added responsibilities, and then consider how these will help you contribute to projects, add skills, build your reputation, and improve your experience.

Evaluate your environment.

Determine what you want to offer, and its value. For instance, offering to perform a task that you have not yet mastered may be helpful in a learning environment, such as a course project, especially if you state your inexperience, but may be damaging in a work setting, where you are contributing to real-world projects. In an entry-level position, consider offering to perform tasks that you know you can do well, such as helping to carry materials to a presentation or packing items for a shipment. If you have an untapped advanced skill, offer to use that, too.

Becoming more proactive can help you feel better about your contribution, become more satisfied with your experiences, and become more committed to your groups, teams, classes, or organization. To improve your experience, take steps to make changes in your role, your responsibilities, your methods of communication, or even look at how you can affect the organization. Your efforts will increase your engagement, and can help you feel that you are making a difference.

» Applying Type in Everyday Life

Understanding more about your psychological type can help you determine how you will feel most comfortable taking initiative, learning, and connecting with others. For instance, your approach to learning can impact where and how you prefer to

» EXHIBIT 3.9 ● Learning Styles Associated with the MBTI® Functions

People Who Prefer:	ST	SF	NF	NT
Interested in:	Facts about real things—useful, practical information about everyday activities	Useful, practical information about people, and a friendly environment	New ideas about how to understand people, symbolic and metaphorical activities	Theories and global explanations about why the world works the way it does
Learn best by:	Doing, hands-on activities	Doing, hands-on activities with others	Imagining, creating with others, writing	Categorizing, analyzing, applying logic
Need:	Precise, step-by-step instructions; logical, practical reasons for doing something	Precise, step-by-step instructions; frequent, friendly interaction and approval	General direction, with freedom to do it their own creative way; frequent positive feedback	To be given a big problem to solve, an intellectual challenge, and then to be allowed to work it out
Want from teacher:	To be treated fairly	Sympathy, support, individual recognition	Warmth, enthusiasm, humor, individual recognition	To be treated with respect, to respect the teacher's competence

Source: Modified and reproduced by special permission of the Publisher, CPP, Inc., Mountain View, CA 94043 from the INTRODUCTION TO TYPE® booklet by Isabel Briggs Myers. copyright 1998 by CPP, Inc. All rights reserved. Further reproduction is prohibited without the Publisher's written consent. Introduction to Type MBTI, Myers-Briggs, and Myers-Briggs Type Indicator are trademarks or registered trademarks of the MBTI Trust, Inc., in the United States and other countries.

Your learning style can influence how you approach tasks, such as whether you prefer to use instructions or figure things out on your own.

build your skills. This can help you take proactive steps to improve your learning and increase your contributions, in ways that are a good fit for your natural preferences.

In school, as an intern or volunteer, or at work, you will have instructors, supervisors, and mentors who prefer to teach and mentor according to their own preferences, and may expect you to learn in the same ways they do. This can lead to frustration on their part, and yours. To apply your MBTI® type to improve your learning, first, locate your preferences in the chart in **Exhibit 3.9**, Learning Styles Associated with the MBTI® Functions, and consider how similar your natural preferences are to those described for your type.

Next, explore how you can improve your ability to learn in various situations, as well as adapt to a variety of teaching styles. For instance, Sensing and Intuitive types may have the biggest difference in learning styles (Briggs Myers, I. Briggs Kirby, L. K. & Myers, K. D., 1998). Sensing types can experience frustration with Intuitive types' orientation toward expressing metaphors and making inferences about the future, and Intuitive types may find it tedious to teach or learn from Sensing types, who prefer carefully plotted, step-by-step instructions. To overcome such challenges, look for ways to ask questions that help you understand others' instructions through your own lens. If you are a Sensing type, ask for clear instructions, and, if you are an Intuitive type, ask about relationships between ideas or potential outcomes.

Understanding psychological type and its many applications in learning and other scenarios can help you expand your self-awareness. Furthermore, as you age, you may notice that you are more inclined to develop and enjoy using your least preferred dimensions. This development and shift over time is a natural process, and can lead to an interest in new career areas, different leadership roles, and other projects in work and leisure activities.

Your Flexible Plan
Define Your Preferences

PLAN OF ANALYSIS
Step 1: Gather Information

What is your RIASEC code? List your self-assessed type or the results of an assessment, such as the Strong Interest Inventory® tool or the Self-Directed Search (SDS).

Three Letter Code: ___R___ ___S___ ___E___

___Social___ ___Enterprising___

What are your preferences according to the dichotomies assessed in the Myers-Briggs Type Indicator®

Four Letter Type: ___I___ ___S___ ___F___ ___P___

_____ _____

List the careers you wish to explore that are consistent with the types in your RIASEC code, your MBTI® type, or both.

_____

_____

Step 2: Evaluate the Information

What did your RIASEC code tell you about your preferences?

_____

_____

What did your MBTI® type tell you about your preferences?

_____

_____

What further information would be helpful to learn about the careers that reflect your patterns of interests and personality characteristics? (These questions will inform your career exploration in **Chapter 5: Explore**.)

_____

_____

Step 3: Make Conclusions

Following your analysis, create a list of your top five preferences that you want to focus on using in your career (such as characteristics of your RIASEC code or MBTI® type).

1. _____ 2. _____ 3. _____

4. _____ 5. _____

Following your analysis, create a list of the top five career areas or jobs that you want to explore further based on your assessment of your preferences.

1. _____ 2. _____ 3. _____

4. _____ 5. _____

Performance Appraisal

Now that you have read the chapter, answer the questions below and complete the Tasks.

1. Your preferences:
   a. Can be assessed using theoretical models and various assessment tools.
   b. Can help you identify the occupations chosen by people with similar interests.
   c. May not seem connected to an obvious career choice.
   d. All of the above.

2. The following is true about John Holland's theory.
   a. There are five personality types.
   b. There are six work environment types.
   c. The theory suggests that the only occupations that are good choices involve an exact match between an individual's personality pattern and occupations with the same pattern.
   d. None of the above.

3. According to Holland's RIASEC theory and Hexagonal Model:
   a. The personality pattern CSI has high consistency.
   b. A person whose personality pattern is IAS and is interested in such majors as international marketing, hotel management, and human resources has high congruency.
   c. It would be easy to predict the best person-environment fit for someone whose personality pattern is ARI.
   d. a and c.

4. The following is true about stereotype threat:
   a. Stereotype threat can occur when someone is aware of stereotypes that exist about their reference group.
   b. Stereotype threat can occur only if a person believes in the stereotypes about their group.
   c. Stereotype threat is limited to school settings.
   d. All of the above.

5. The Myers-Briggs Type Indicator® (MBTI®) is:
   a. An instrument that is based on Freud's theory of psychoanalysis.
   b. Used to help individuals understand their preferences in four dimensions.
   c. An instrument that will assess your RIASEC code.
   d. b and c.

6. The following is true about the MBTI® instrument:
   a. Extroverts like to brainstorm and think out loud, while Introverts prefer to develop ideas by reflecting.
   b. The MBTI® instrument can help you identify career fields that might be of interest.
   c. People with a preference for Judging do not necessarily judge other people; instead, this describes their preference for judging the world in order to live a planned, orderly life.
   d. a and b.
   e. All of the above.

7. The following is true about online behavior:
   a. Short e-mails are always better, even if your message can be misconstrued.
   b. You can post whatever you want as long as you set up your privacy settings because no one other than your friends will ever be able to see it.
   c. It is to your advantage to be thoughtful and intentional about what you do online and off, realizing that any behavior could appear online.
   d. b and c.

Performance Appraisal Answer Key

Thought Questions

1. Can you identify your preferences?

2. Have you identified preferences that will be important for you to consider in your career?

3. Have you identified any preferences that seem to be unrelated to your career interests but are important for you to integrate into your life?

Notes:

_____

_____

_____

_____

_____

_____

TASK 3.1:
Childhood Interests

In this exercise, you will reflect on your childhood interests, relate them to the Holland environmental typology, and then consider if any of these patterns still hold your interests today.

List any activities you greatly enjoyed when you were a child.

_____

_____

_____

Describe the support or encouragement, as well as any discouragement or disapproval, you received for these activities.

_____

_____

Looking at your list of childhood interests, consider the work environments that might include similar activities (see **Exhibit 3.3**, A Brief Description of the Holland Environmental Typology). List any work environments that reflect the patterns of your childhood activities.

_____   _____

_____

Do these work environment types relate to your current career interests? Why or why not?

_____

_____

_____

TASK 3.2:

Personality and Environment

Using **Exhibit 3.1**, A Brief Description of the Holland Personality Typology, you assessed your personality type. Then, using **Exhibit 3.3**, A Brief Description of the Holland Environmental Typology, you considered the types of work environments you might enjoy. In this exercise, compare what you have learned about yourself and occupations, according to Holland's RIASEC theory.

Which work environments interest you most? Why?

_____

_____

Now, look at the work environments that include the types that are in your personality pattern. The extent to which occupations match your personality is described as congruence. Describe your thoughts and reactions to these work environments. Are these the work environments that interest you most?

_____

_____

In which work environments do you feel you could be most successful? Why?

_____

_____

TASK 3.3:

Exploring Psychological Type

Depending on the strength of your preferences, your MBTI® type may reveal a very strong picture of your personality or you may feel that it reflects your personality sometimes, but not at other times. Describe your reaction to your MBTI® type.

Overall, how closely does your MBTI® type match your personality?

_____

_____

Circle your preference in each of the four dichotomous scales and then describe how this is reflected in your personality.

E vs. I _____

S vs. N _____

T vs. F _____

J vs. P _____

TASK 3.4:
Psychological Type and Careers

Your MBTI® type can be used to identify career fields that might be of interest to you. Use **Exhibit 3.7**, Popular Occupations for MBTI® Types, to explore occupations, and then consider what you have learned about type to help you expand your range of career possibilities.

Which types are commonly employed in the occupations that interest you most?

_____

_____

Now, look at the occupations that are popular for your MBTI® type. Describe your thoughts and reactions to these occupations. Are these the occupations that interest you most?

_____

In which occupations do you feel you could be most successful? Why?

_____

_____

How closely does your MBTI® type match your personality?

_____

_____

TASK 3.5:
Career Fields to Consider

Reviewing your responses in **Task 3.2** and **Task 3.4**, consider the occupations and work environments that are of interest to you. Now, review the information about college majors in **Exhibit 3.4**, Typical College Majors by Holland Code, and **Exhibit 3.8**, Common Majors for MBTI® Types.

Are there particular work environments, occupations, or college majors that interest you and also reflect both your RIASEC code and your MBTI® type? What are they?

_____

_____

Do these interest you? Why or why not?

_____

_____

Why do you think people who have the same preferences as yours are often interested in these career areas? Do any of your preferences seem to be present in these career areas?

_____

_____

Link to CourseMate 🖥

On CourseMate, you can find documents to help you update your Career Portfolio as well as additional resources and activities. Here is some of the information you can find online for **Chapter 3: Preferences**.

CAREER PORTFOLIO

Your Flexible Plan
Holland RIASEC Code / Personal Summary
MBTI® Type / Personal Summary

RESOURCES

Career Profile: Cara S.

Values

iStockphoto.com/Steve Debenport

> The more boundless your vision, the more real you are.
> —*Deepak Chopra*

Learning about your values can help you identify what motivates you, what is important to you, and what you want in a career for it to meet your personal goals. Assessing your values allows you to make comparisons with values in the workplace while building and evaluating your evolving professional reputation.

What's Inside

That Motivates Me

Values and Your Career

Building Your Reputation

A Life Worth Living

Prepare to . . .

- Understand how values are defined
- Learn how values impact aspects of career development
- Define the type of reputation you want to build for your professional identity
- Explore approaches to creating personal fulfillment

» That Motivates Me

Values describe what is important to you and what motivates you in all aspects of your life. They are subjective and deeply personal, reflecting your beliefs about what is right for you, others, and society at large. Your values are shaped by many factors, including your experiences, family, culture, gender, ethnicity, friendships, education, and environment. Numerous theories have addressed what motivates us, and how personal values impact motivation.

Consider the last time you were highly motivated. Were you aiming to complete a school task, do a favor for a friend, or make something happen in your life? Were you trying to meet your needs, such as earning money to pay your bills? Were you looking for ways to please someone, or strengthen a relationship? In the workplace, employers are looking for workers who are motivated to work hard, stay focused, and act professionally. Your enthusiasm to perform at your peak depends on whether your work meets your needs and how closely the tasks and environment connect with your values.

A Hierarchy of Needs

In 1943, Abraham Maslow identified a hierarchy of five needs to describe how individuals are motivated. According to his theory, only as lower-order needs are satisfied, will people pursue higher-order needs. The hierarchy of needs include (1) physiological needs, such as having food and drink, (2) safety needs, which include being safe and free from harm, (3) belonging, including connecting with others and building relationships, (4) self-esteem, including feeling valuable and worthwhile, and (5) self-actualization, in which people gain self-awareness and strive to contribute to society, the arts, philosophy, or some cause other than themselves. His theory is represented in **Exhibit 4.1**, Maslow's Hierarchy of Needs.

There are many experiences that can influence your values, including time with your family.

Monkey Business Images/Shutterstock.com

Employees cannot perform well without meeting lower-order needs, such as having restroom breaks or a safe workplace. However, independent contractors, freelancers, and part-time employees make their own hours and cover their own health expenses, and may decide to work without breaks to meet deadlines for a project, or avoid seeing a doctor due to out-of-pocket costs. On the other hand, benefits provided to full-time employees often include health care as well as vacation and sick days. To ensure that safety and health needs are met in the workplace, organizations such as the Occupational Health and Safety Administration (OSHA) provide legal guidelines for employers as well as support for employees. When you consider your employment options, explore how you will ensure that your lower-order needs are met.

Higher-order needs, including belonging, self-esteem, and self-actualization, can be met through such activities as: office parties and sports leagues, which increase opportunities for connectedness; recognition programs, which build self-esteem; and job mobility, which can involve identifying employees for positions that closely match their interests and talents. To explore how your needs could be fulfilled through work, imagine the type of rewards and motivation that would help you perform at your peak.

Intrinsic Versus Extrinsic Motivation

In addition to meeting our needs, we are all motivated by intrinsic and extrinsic rewards. Intrinsic rewards can include self-acceptance, connectedness, community feeling, and physical health. Extrinsic rewards include earning money, pleasing others, being attractive, or becoming popular or famous.

Many people are motivated to work for extrinsic rewards, such as earning money, rather than intrinsic rewards, such as self-fulfillment. In fact, research has shown that when people are presented with an extrinsic motivator, such as being offered a cash incentive, it can actually decrease their intrinsic motivation (Deci, Koestner, and Ryan, 2001). This can make it even harder to enjoy learning for learning's sake or to stay motivated to solve challenging problems, because people begin to work only for the extrinsic motivator—essentially, the prize. Exploring the connection between motivation, positive emotions, health, and well-being, research found that people who are motivated by intrinsic rewards report that they feel better than those who are motivated by external rewards regardless of whether they attain their goals (Kasser and Ryan, 1996). As you consider your values and what motivates you, consider how you stay motivated in the short-term and the long-term, and how you feel as you strive to reach your goals.

Values as Motivators

Finding work that motivates you when there are no immediate rewards can help you improve your performance by keeping you interested, engaged, and focused. Doing your best work also increases your value to an organization, making it easier for you to negotiate for higher pay, better job assignments, and greater responsibilities. Therefore, aiming for a career that offers intrinsic rewards can also increase your likelihood of attaining extrinsic rewards in the long run.

To identify the values that are most important to you, look at the choices you have made, including courses you selected, activities in which you participated, and friendships that have meaning for you. Answering "why" you enjoy certain activities or "why" you make your choices will highlight your values and how they motivate you in your actions.

Yuri Arcurs/Shutterstock.com

Your motivation to work hard and succeed is often higher when your tasks are fulfilling.

>> **EXHIBIT 4.1** ● **Maslow's Hierarchy of Needs**

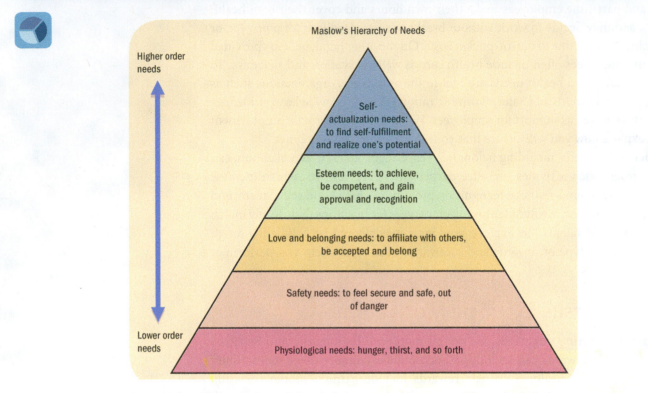

Source: Maslow, Abraham H., Frager, Robert D., Fadiman, James, Motivation and Personality, 3rd edition. Copyright © 1987. Reprinted and Electronically reproduced by permission of Pearson Education, Inc., Upper Saddle River, New Jersey.

>> **CAREER JOURNAL** ● **What is Important to You?**

Use the space below to write about your thoughts and feelings.

Consider a course, job, club, leadership role, hobby, important friendship, or something else that has meaning for you. Why is it important to you?

What motivates you to engage in the activity you selected, nurture the friendship you described, or perform the job you listed? Does it make you feel good, pay you money, or enhance your learning? Do you find it exciting, engaging, or challenging?

Consider what you learned about intrinsic and extrinsic motivation. Now, look at your answers above, and consider whether they reflect intrinsic or extrinsic motivation. List your motivators according to their importance to you.

Extrinsic Motivation (such as receiving recognition, aiming for popularity, earning money, or improving physical appearance)

1. _____
2. _____
3. _____

Intrinsic Motivation (such as building connections with others, achieving intellectual or spiritual growth, improving physical health, or feeling self-fulfilled)

1. _____
2. _____
3. _____

Journal Feedback . . . The choices you make about how you spend your time reflect what is important to you. We are all trying to maximize our human experience, and our values help us choose how we feel we can accomplish this. Assessing whether you are largely motivated by intrinsic or extrinsic rewards can add another dimension to your understanding of your values.

›› CAREER PROFILE ● Monica Baldwin, Federal Law Enforcement

Name: Monica Baldwin
College Degree: BA in Communications
Graduate Degree: MS in Education, Administration, and Supervision (*achieved more than 10 years after college*)
Current Position: Special Agent Recruiter
Employer: Government

Courtesy of Monica Baldwin

From Monica's Supervisor
Name: William DeSa, Jr.
Title: Supervisory Special Agent
Employer: Government

Can you describe Monica's contribution to your team?
Character, competence, collaboration, and courage are cornerstones in the FBI. Monica has outstanding character and is always professional in her role as recruiter for our

Courtesy of William DeSa, Jr.

(Continues)

I understand you made a career change. Can you tell us about that experience?

After completing college, I started working in advertising and marketing. My first job involved association management where I organized and hired talent for large trade and auto shows. Six months later, I was hired as an advertising coordinator for a bank where I handled advertising campaigns and branch openings. Several years later, I moved to a midsized advertising agency as Media Director. I was only a few years out of school, and I was a supervisor responsible for budgets of several million dollars and managing a small staff. Two years later, a larger agency bought us out, and I was laid off because they already had someone in my position. I ended up working three jobs. I was a receptionist and managed a telemarketing program in an insurance agency, worked nights as a cashier in a drug store, and did freelance media buying for small agencies. It was very humbling, but I was raised to work hard and never give up. During that time, I applied to the FBI, took and passed a written test and a structured interview, and began the background check and clearance process.

Tell us about your transition to the FBI and your career as an agent.

I've been an agent with the FBI for almost 25 years. After completing the rigorous training program, I was assigned to Newark where I worked a variety of investigative areas from violent crime to white-collar crime. During that time, I realized I wanted to teach and completed my master's degree as a part-time student. I've always established a 5-year and a 10-year plan for myself. After obtaining my master's degree and completing 10 years in the field, I applied for and received a promotion to a supervisory position at the FBI Academy in Quantico, Virginia, where I designed and delivered classroom and computer-based training programs. Later, I returned to the field as a supervisor, and managed the administrative squad including internal, firearms, and police training. Next, I supervised the cyber-crime squad, dealing with computer intrusion, child pornography, Internet fraud, and intellectual property rights. Now, as the special agent recruiter, I am reinvigorated through my interaction with college students and young people who will be the future of the FBI.

How did your values impact your career?

My values include honesty, hard work, strong family ties, and remaining true to myself. I followed my passion, which for me was advertising and marketing. But, after the layoff, I had to re-evaluate my career. I considered the volatility of the advertising field versus the stability and new challenges a government job offered. In this career, you realize you're working for the greater good, not just for the bottom line from a financial standpoint. Here, the bottom line is saving lives. I've also blended my education and prior work experience into my present career. For example, I've been a public affairs coordinator for the FBI and now I'm recruiting, which is a form of marketing. I'm always thinking about how I will reinvent myself. As I approach retirement eligibility from the FBI, I'm developing my next 5- and 10-year plans.

agency. Continually meeting or exceeding expectations placed upon her demonstrates her on-the-job competence. Although Monica is senior to me in years of service to the FBI, I am her supervisor. I am able to collaborate with Monica and learn from Monica's feedback to my ideas. The vision for the squad is my responsibility and I appreciate having Monica's advice and occasional criticism regarding my ideas. Monica displays courage by not being afraid to say "We're doing it wrong," or speaking up regarding an idea or business practice, even though her view may be the minority view.

How do Monica's values come through in her work?

Monica is one of the more senior agents, not only on my squad, but also in our entire field division. She demonstrates characteristics all supervisors hope to see in an agent. A remarkable characteristic continually demonstrated by Monica is her enthusiasm for her work. Not many agents with her years of service retain the enthusiasm she exhibits on a daily basis. Her tenure with our agency has given her a broad base of experiences upon which she can draw while recruiting individuals to become new agents. The FBI motto is "Fidelity, Bravery and Integrity http://www.fbi.gov/about-us/history/seal-motto." Perhaps the most important aspect of our motto is the "I" for integrity. We, as an agency, cannot be successful if the American public does not trust us. Senior agents, like Monica, have often had their integrity and ethics challenged. Monica maintains a high level of integrity and displays this through her work.

What are Monica's values?

_____

_____

_____

How have Monica's values influenced her choices and helped her build her career?

_____

_____

_____

For additional questions, visit CourseMate. 💻

» Values and Your Career

Values can shape the workplace and guide your career decision making throughout your lifespan. Consider the ways your values might connect with different aspects of your work experiences, and then review the list of career values in **Exhibit 4.2**, Career Values, to explore which are most important to you. **Task 4.2**, Assess Your Career Values, will give you an opportunity to explore the values that are most important to you in your career.

Tasks

To succeed at work, you must have the skills to perform your job responsibilities. If the tasks interest you and are aligned with your values, your motivation will increase and, ultimately, so will your performance. On the other hand, if you enjoy your job tasks but your values are inconsistent, you might become frustrated and lose motivation. For example, if you value working alone, frequent interruptions by colleagues could make your work less enjoyable.

If you are energized by a demanding work environment, you may also find yourself willing to work long hours.

Environment

Work environments can vary greatly, and values are also reflected in an organization's image, branding, policies, programs, goals, and culture, such as dress codes, formality, work schedules, work activities, and employee interactions. In addition, many organizations reflect their culture through the impact they have on society at large. For example, companies may offer financial support or sponsorship of social causes or make conscious choices about the way their products or services impact the world, such as choosing not to test products on animals. Values may also be reflected in employees' beliefs about gender, race, culture, and other attitudes and expectations about others. For instance, some people automatically assume that a woman would not want a demanding career track and a man is more likely to hold a senior-level position. These perspectives reflect gender biases that nevertheless exist in the workplace. Exploring how your personal values compare to organizational and industry values can help you consider how and where you will locate mentors and support within an organization or industry.

Relationships

Your values also impact your relationships with others in the workplace. Values are revealed through a sense of humor, what people do in their free time, and choices people make. Being aligned with your coworkers' values can make it easier to build relationships. Values can also guide you toward the types of relationships you seek, such as looking for high achievers to serve as role models, or creative types working in teams if you value collaboration and innovation.

Work-Life Balance

In **Chapter 1: Prepare**, you learned about life roles and life stages. Right now, you may experience such life roles as student and worker; you may also identify yourself as someone's child, especially if you are financially dependent on your parents or if you are exploring a career reentry or career change as you care for sick or elderly parents; or you may be a parent yourself. In addition to work, you may want time for sports activities, socializing, dating, family, or personal time. Individuals who are energized by a tremendous opportunity for financial reward might be attracted to high-stakes positions with 70+ hour schedules. Others might prefer to sacrifice potential earnings and prestige for more personal time. Considering what is important to you now and in the future can reveal your values concerning work-life balance.

Personal Values in the Workplace

Understanding the value you can add to the workplace is another way to ensure that you are pursuing careers and job tasks where your assets are appreciated. Considering the personal characteristics and traits that you possess is one way to identify your attributes. Here are a number of positive attributes that can describe how you interact with others, perform tasks, or engage in your work.

friendly	smart	innovative	happy
compassionate	knowledgeable	insightful	fun
good listener	hard worker	creative	eager
strong communicator	persistent	athletic	motivated

Consider how you would describe yourself, how others might describe you, and which attributes connect with the professional reputation you would like to build. To turn your asset into an affirmation, add it to the phrase, "I am _____."

"I am persistent." "I am a hard worker." "I am motivated."

When you think of the assets you want to demonstrate in the workplace, consider how your affirmations fit the tasks you see yourself performing. Use **Task 4.1**, Choose Your Affirmations, to list your personal values and develop your own affirmations. Explore how your personal values compare with the career values you would like in your work experience.

≫EXHIBIT 4.2 ● **Career Values**

This is a list of career values. Review the list and consider the values you want in your career. You will explore these further in **Task 4.2**, Assess Your Career Values.

Next, complete the Knowdell™ Career Values Card Sort in CourseMate to identify your values, and complete the Summary Sheet of Prioritized Values for your Career Portfolio.

Career Values	Definition
INDEPENDENCE	Be able to determine the nature of my work without significant direction of others. Not have to follow instructions or to conform to regulations.
CHALLENGING PROBLEMS	Engage continually with complex questions and demanding tasks, trouble-shooting and problem-solving as a core part of my job.
EXERCISE COMPETENCE	Demonstrate a high degree of proficiency in job skills and knowledge; show above average effectiveness.
JOB TRANQUILTY	Avoid pressure and "the rat race" in my job role and work setting.
CREATIVE EXPRESSION	Be able to express in writing and in person my ideas concerning my job and how I might improve it; have opportunities for experimentation and innovation.
WORK UNDER PRESSURE	Work in time-pressured circumstances, where there is little or no margin for error, or with demanding personal relationships.

Career Values	Definition
PHYSICAL CHALLENGE	Have a job that requires bodily strength, speed, dexterity or agility.
PRECISION WORK	Deal with tasks that have exact specifications, that require careful, accurate attention to detail.
KNOWLEDGE	Engage myself in pursuit of knowledge, truth and understanding.
AESTHETICS	Be involved in studying or appreciating the beauty of things or ideas.
STATUS	Impress or gain the respect of friends, family and community by the nature and/or level of responsibility of my work.
INTELLECTUAL STATUS	Be regarded as very well-informed and a strong theorist, as one acknowledged "expert" in a given field.
FAST PACE	Work in circumstances where there is a high pace of activity and work is done rapidly.
EXCITEMENT	Experience a high degree of stimulation or frequent novelty and drama on the job.
SECURITY	Be assured of keeping my job and a reasonable financial reward.
CHANGE AND VARIETY	Have work responsibilities frequently changed in content or setting.
ADVANCEMENT	Be able to get ahead rapidly, gaining opportunities for growth and seniority from work well-done.
WORK ON THE FRONTIERS OF KNOWLEDGE	Work in research and development, generating information and new ideas in the academic, scientific, or business communities.
WORK ALONE	Do projects by myself, without any amount of contact or input from others.
INFLUENCE PEOPLE	Be in a position to change attitudes or opinions of others.
HELP OTHERS	Be involved in helping people directly, either individually or in small groups.
STABILITY	Have a work routine and job duties that are largely predictable and not likely to change over a long period of time.
FRIENDSHIPS	Develop close personal relationships with people as a result of work activity.
MAKE DECISIONS	Have the power to decide courses of action, policies, etc., a judgment job.
POWER AND AUTHORITY	Control the work activities or destinies of others.
HELP SOCIETY	Do something to contribute to the betterment of the world.
PUBLIC CONTACT	Have a lot of day-to-day contact with people.
AFFILIATION	Be recognized as a member of a particular organization.
COMPETITION	Engage in activities which pit my abilities against others.
CREATIVITY (GENERAL)	Create new ideas, programs, organized structures or anything else not following a format developed by others.
COMMUNITY	Live in a town or city where I can meet my neighbors and become active in local politics or service projects.
TIME FREEDOM	Have responsibilities at which I can work according to my time schedule; no specific working hours required.
RECOGNITION	Get positive feedback and public credit for work well done.
MORAL FULFILLMENT	Feel that my work is contributing to ideals I feel are very important.
LOCATION	Find a place to live (town or geographic area) conducive to my lifestyle, a desirable home base for my leisure, learning and work life.
ARTISTIC CREATIVITY	Engage in creative work in any of several art forms.
WORK WITH OTHERS	Have close working relations with a group and work as a team to common goals.
HIGH EARNINGS ANTICIPATED	Be able to purchase essentials and the luxuries of life that I wish.
PROFIT, GAIN	Have a strong likelihood of accumulating large amounts of money or other material gain through ownership, profit-sharing, commissions, merit increases, etc.
SUPERVISION	Have a job in which I am directly responsible for work done by others.
ADVENTURE	Have job duties which involve frequent risk-taking.
FAMILY	Insure that the type of work I do and the hours I work fit with my family responsibilities.
SPRITIUALITY	Work in a setting that is supportive of my spiritual beliefs.
WORK-LIFE BALANCE	Have a job that allows me adequate time for my family, hobbies and social activities.
ENVIRONMENT	Work on tasks that have a positive effect on the natural environment.
HONESTY AND INTEGRITY	Work in a setting where honesty and integrity are assets.
FUN AND HUMOR	Work in a setting where it is possible (and appropriate) to joke and have fun.
STRUCTURE AND PREDICTABILITY	Do work with a high level of structure and predictability.

(Continues)

>> **EXHIBIT 4.2** ● **Career Values** *Continued*

Career Values	Definition
STEEP LEARNING CURVE	Be presented with new, unique or difficult tasks to be quickly mastered.
PERSONAL SAFETY	Have a high probability of being safe and healthy at work.
GROUP AND TEAM	Work with a group to obtain team (rather than individual) results.
TRADITION	Be involved in work that is consistent with the social traditions in which I was brought up.
PRACTICALITY	Be involved in work that yields a practical or useful result.
DIVERSITY	Work in a setting that includes individuals of diverse religious, racial or social backgrounds.

Source: Knowdell, Career Values Card Sort, Career Research and Testing, Inc. Copyright © Richard L. Knowdell. Reprinted with permission. President Career Research and Testing, Inc. Post Office Box 611930, San Jose, CA 95161-1930, Tel: 408-272-3085/Fax: 408-259-8438, rknowdell@mac.com/www .careernetwork.org

>> **WORK WITH AWARENESS** ● **Corporate Social Responsibility**

In 1953, Howard Bowen, an economist, wrote a book about the obligation of individuals in business to make decisions that support the desirable values and ethics of society. Although it has taken many years to become the popular and growing trend it is today, corporate social responsibility (CSR) describes the business world's activities that benefit society, not just shareholders or their bottom line.

CSR enables organizations to connect their corporate identity with social values, while attracting like-minded customers and employees. In fact, one report indicated that 86 percent of new college hires will consider leaving an employer if the corporate social responsibility values are no longer consistent with their own (Meister and Willyerd, 2010). In 2011, a survey of 300 companies from 20 industries found that 72 percent of companies had formal CSR programs, 60 percent had budgets dedicated for CSR programs, 62 percent had a designated position for CSR in leadership, and 66 percent of CEOs led a CSR-related program in the past year (Crespin, 2011). As you consider your values in the workplace, explore how they could also be reflected in a business environment through corporate initiatives. Here are several examples of programs and efforts that reflect corporate social responsibility.

Volunteer opportunities. Through outreach efforts, employers offer interesting volunteer opportunities for employees that help them connect with neighboring or distant communities: to support educational programs; upgrade schools, libraries, and parks; and raise funds through such efforts as walk-a-thons. In many cases, the business pays for supplies or will make a donation to the benefiting charities, or may allow workers to perform such activities during paid work hours. Such activities also offer employees the opportunity to network with those outside their core group and develop additional skills while doing good. Merrill Lynch employees serve as guest speakers and content experts to middle and high school students in a program supported by the U.S. Department of State, (UNA-USA., n.d.).

Through Target's school library program, employees help upgrade libraries in partnership with The Heart of America Foundation (Target Volunteers, n.d.).

Charitable giving. Many businesses offer matching donation options for employees contributing to their favorite causes or make a contribution to a cause they have chosen when customers make a purchase. Since its inception, TOMS Shoes has donated a pair of shoes to a child in need for every pair of shoes purchased, and has now extended their giving to support health, education, hygiene, and community development programs (Toms, n.d.).

Sustainability. By decreasing their carbon footprint, implementing recycling or upcycling programs, reducing waste, and using eco-friendly materials, companies are making sustainability part of their corporate policies. In addition, some companies are developing cradle-to-cradle programs in which their products are developed to be safe for humans and the environment for current and future lifecycles. Flor develops carpet that considers the environmental impact of every aspect of its product lifecycle, including design, manufacturing, use, delivery, and reclaiming. For example, Flor starts with recycled content and is fully recyclable (Flor, n.d.).

Human rights. While many companies do not own the overseas manufacturing plants where their goods are produced, addressing human rights issues ensures that employees are not children, are treated well, and are paid fairly. This can involve preventative methods as well as the existence of management programs that can help businesses respond to violations. For instance, in 2010, a report alleged that one of General Electric's (GE) suppliers violated Chinese law. GE responded with a team of investigators through their "eyes wide open" program and has worked closely with the supplier to make changes that meet requirements (GE Citizenship n.d.).

» Building Your Reputation

Your values reflect who you are, and are revealed to others through your actions, lifestyle, and appearance. Combined, these shape your reputation. Everyone has a reputation, and for most people, it is not two dimensional, as in good or bad, friendly or mean, smart or unintelligent.

Your reputation is often nuanced, and can vary with different groups of people. For example, in your courses, you may be known as studious and responsible, and your friends may think of you as a good listener and kind-hearted. Your professors may not know of your ability to listen, aside from knowing that you pay attention in class. However, if you are assigned a team project, you might act as a synthesizer, listening and empathizing as everyone in the group contributes ideas, and work towards helping members choose a topic and method for sharing the work that allows everyone to contribute their best assets. This would reflect your capacity for listening. The more experiences you have, the greater the opportunity for your reputation to develop.

Your Reputation and Your Career

Being aware of your reputation is important for your career development. The choices you make shape the impressions of those who will act as advocates for you, such as the professors and supervisors who write references for your job or school applications, as well as your friends, mentors, faculty, work colleagues, and family, who all make decisions based on your reputation. This influences the type of information they share with you, whom they want to introduce to you, and what they think you are motivated to achieve. Your reputation is the foundation for your personal brand, which you will explore further in **Chapter 8: Tools** as you prepare your marketing materials and develop a consistent image that reflects your greatest, genuine assets. You can control your reputation, but this involves taking an honest assessment of how you connect with others in your relationships, and how your choices influence people's perception of you.

© Beau Lark/Corbis

You will build your reputation through actions that reflect your values, such as working hard and showing appreciation for the assistance you receive.

The Message You Send

To build a reputation that reflects the characteristics and qualities that are important to you, pay attention to the message you send through your relationships, activities, lifestyle, and appearance. Consider what impression you would like others to have, and how your choices help reinforce or detract from that message.

Your relationships. Your relationships with friends, family, peers, faculty, and professional contacts demonstrate your reputation. Are you reliable, loyal, fun, sensitive, or are there other words your connections would use to describe you? How you behave towards others and how they view you is a key component of your reputation.

Your activities. When you put together your résumé or apply for an internship, you will look at your school activities, courses, hobbies, and prior work experiences. These activities show how you spend your time. Consider which of your values are reflected in each of these different types of personal or professional activities. You may want to refer to the **Task 2.1**, What Have You Done?, for the list you created of your experiences.

Your lifestyle. Do you spend your time in the library, the gym, or the art studio? Where would your friends or family expect to find you at various times throughout the week? Do people think of you as family-oriented, social, or studious? Explore which of your values are reflected through your lifestyle to see how consistent your values are in different areas of your life.

Your appearance. Your style of dress, haircut, makeup, jewelry, or body art offers people insight into the image you want to project. Reflecting on the choices you make about your appearance will help you consider the impression you are making outwardly. For instance, your appearance might reflect your creativity, your conservative attitude, or your value of eco-friendly materials.

To make connections between your personal values and the values that you want in your career, assess your current choices and your relationships, and explore how these can impact the professional reputation you want to build.

⟫TECH SAVVY ● Google Yourself

In the digital age, your offline activities, such as your participation in social events, work and school achievements, and volunteerism often have an online digital footprint, in the form of documents and records that are easily searchable via search engines. In addition, your online activities show an online persona that may differ from the reputation you are aiming to build. Your values show up through all of your experiences, and sometimes activities that play a small role in your real life can play a very large role in your online presence.

Your Online Persona

To see what information is online about you, write your name into a search engine, such as Google.com or Dogpile.com, which provides results from many search engines. Try several different versions of your name as well as more than one search engine. Include your first and last name, your name with your middle name or middle initial, your first and last name in quotes, your maiden name, or any nickname you use. Review all the pages of results to see where your name shows up, and if it is you. If you find content about another person with your name, you can add content and increase your own online presence. Now you are aware of your online persona, and you can evaluate how consistent it is with your reputation in the real world.

There are many ways to create or tweak your online persona so that it accurately reflects your best assets. As you review the information you find online, note websites where you are represented positively or negatively. Bookmark or print pages of your online presence to have records of accomplishments, or evidence of negative representations that you would like to wash over or remove. Consider the values you want to show and the activities and accomplishments that support this message. Next, develop a strategy to improve your online reputation by adding positive content, such as a professional profile on Google+ or LinkedIn, and removing digital dirt.

Digital Dirt

Negative online information has been referred to as "digital dirt," and can include personal information, controversial associations or activities, embarrassing photos, disparaging information including gossip or rumors shared in public forums, public records such as lawsuits or criminal records, inconsistent information about degrees or credentials, or other reputation-damaging information. In this area, the Internet has also led to a new area of professional services, those who improve your digital image, as well as those who scrutinize online information to assist people in finding online information. At best, digital dirt can distract an employer from seeing online information that reflects your best assets; at worst, it can cost you a job or professional relationship.

If you have found digital dirt that you would like to clean up, Sautter and Crompton (2008, see pp. 30–31) recommend the following three tips:

- **Wash over it.** They suggest creating new content so that digital dirt moves down to another page, and is harder to find. Creating a LinkedIn profile, blog, personal website or online portfolio can help you develop and control the online presentation of your accomplishments.

- **Wash it out.** If you know the person or organization that created the content, you may be able to have them remove it. Contact the source of the information, and explain the exact content you want removed. If you do not know the creator of the content, Sautter and Crompton maintain that this can be difficult.

- **Wait it out.** If you are involved in professional activities and building your career, you may find that your newer activities naturally overshadow past online activities. If your favorable activities are not listed online frequently, this may not be as effective.

≫ EMBRACING DIFFERENCES ● Cultural Values

We live in a global economy, in which cross-cultural interaction is common. For every cultural group, there are a set of values that reflect cultural experiences, and a way of looking at the world. By understanding how cultural values impact your point of view, and may impact others' perceptions and behaviors, you can be more effective and understanding when dealing with people of different cultural backgrounds or from different countries.

American Cultural Values

If you are first generation American, or not American, you may be more aware of the differences between American cultural values and your culture. For Americans who have traveled abroad, there is also often an increase in cultural awareness. You might be aware of foods that are common in other countries, or cultural differences in dealing with time and punctuality. In social activities, Americans often expect guests to arrive at the exact time of an invitation, whereas Latin Americans expect guests to arrive later than the recommended time. These are just a few examples of how culture differences may reflect values.

Understanding Cultural Differences

For those who have a strong understanding of cultural differences, miscommunication is more easily avoided or worked through. To understand the relationship between cultural values and many aspects of life, Stewart and Bennett (1991) look at different dimensions that impact how cultures differ.

Perception and thinking. Perception and thinking involve how people from different cultures think when they see the

same thing. Some cultures prefer to make comparisons and look at distant situations as related, while others are oriented towards comparing data and clearly connected concepts.

Communication. Another example of differences can involve language and nonverbal behavior. In Italian culture, large nonverbal gestures may help tell a story that is still predominately shared through verbal language, while in Japan, specific nonverbal language may be very significant in certain interactions, particularly in settings where respect or status is relevant. In contrast, Americans are largely oriented toward verbal communication, relying less on nonverbal gestures.

Social relations. In many cultures, class and social position is rigid, and there is not the assumption of equality that exists amongst Americans. In Europe, heritage, inheritance, and dialect all contribute to these views. On the other hand, Stewart and Bennett tell us that most Americans would describe themselves as middle class, and also believe that individuals can move between social class groups. This informality is often reflected in communication between class groups, as well as generations, even in the workplace.

Of course, there are many other ways that cultures differ. By thinking, communicating, and interacting in different ways, cultural values can represent significantly different approaches to the world which can impact career exploration, decision making, and on-the-job success.

Alex Moreno: Values in Conflict

The youngest of four children, Alex Moreno grew up in an urban Hispanic community in southern Florida. Throughout his childhood, his parents both worked in physically demanding jobs and attended church every Sunday. At home, they spoke Spanish, and pushed their children to have careers and independence. When he was accepted into the University of Florida with an academic scholarship, his family hosted a large celebration where both of his parents expressed great pride in his accomplishments and hope for his future.

His older brother and sisters had already developed careers with competitive salaries as a bank teller, police officer, and government employee. Nevertheless, Alex felt extra pressure to achieve because of his scholarship and his parents' expectations. He was hoping to develop a medical career, inspired by his Uncle Eduardo, a practicing physician in a small community near Miami. Becoming a doctor and having a professional income would help his family, and he believed he could handle the academic rigor of medical school.

As an undergraduate, Alex worked as a research assistant for a faculty member and learned that he enjoyed the research side of medicine. When he discussed his new plan to pursue a medical research career with his family, he sensed his parents were confused and frustrated with his plan to attend medical school or a doctorate program or both, but not to become a practicing family doctor or a surgeon. Alex could not promise them that he would be guaranteed employment as a researcher, where he would work, or what he would earn, and he could not make a decision without the approval of his family. He felt conflicted and not sure how to proceed.

Alex contacted his Uncle Eduardo who counseled him to postpone medical school and find an interim job that would help him explore his interests while gaining experience.

He learned that research assistant positions would expose him to the research that interested him most, while helping him prepare for medical school. Despite his excitement about the nature of the work he was exploring, he was concerned that he would be seen as a failure by his family, because he would still need more education and his early job targets were relatively low paying and low status.

What values are important to Alex, his parents, and his culture?
What values must Alex resolve in order to move forward in his career?
What could Alex do to begin to resolve his values-based conflict?

To learn more about Alex's career development, visit CourseMate ⬛ . View his résumé and job-search materials in **Chapter 8: Tools**.

>> A Life Worth Living

The ancient philosopher, Socrates, explored the nature of a life worth living in Plato's *Republic* (Cornford, 1945). For Plato, the examined life held meaning. Another value that people often associate with a life worth living is happiness. For others, relationships and community signify meaning in life, as can lasting contributions to science or the arts. Religion, philosophy, sociology, political theory, and other disciplines have looked at these central questions to human existence. Very recently, the field of positive psychology has emerged to explore happiness and other values, such as courage, generosity, creativity, joy, and gratitude to learn more about how personal fulfillment is attained, and how people can improve their ability to feel good, enjoy life, and create a life worth living (Csikszentmihalyi and Nakamura, 2011). There are many contributions in this new field that have far-reaching implications for career development. Here are two of the ideas that have been studied.

Optimizing Your Experiences

Have you ever been so engaged in a task that you became unaware of the time, and was it not until after you were done, and reflecting on the experience, that you even considered whether you enjoyed yourself? Mihaly Csikszentmihalyi, who named this experience "flow," found that to increase the likelihood of such optimal human experiences, we must (1) set and strive for challenging goals, (2) become immersed in chosen activities, (3) pay attention to what is happening, and (4) learn to enjoy immediate experiences (2008). This reflects such career values as being engaged in your work tasks, being challenged, and mastering skills. This theory suggests that everyone has the capacity to experience—and benefit from—flow.

Aiming to Flourish

In work, as in life, your values might be very broad, such as a desire to flourish. According to Martin Seligman, we can all improve our well-being, and he outlined five specific elements that contribute to well-being and allow us to flourish in all areas of life (2011). These include (1) positive emotion, which reflects your mood, happiness, and life satisfaction, (2) engagement, such as when time stops for you, (3) positive relationships, in which you connect with and help others, (4) meaning, as in meaningful experiences, and (5) accomplishment, whether for something personally rewarding or that contributes to society.

Seligman also developed a list of signature character strengths, and a free online resource at http://www.authentichappiness.com that allows individuals to identify strengths they have and others to develop. These strengths reflect beliefs and values, such as wisdom, knowledge, love, originality, justice, fairness, leadership, self-control, beauty, gratitude, hope, and sense of purpose (Seligman, 2011). Explore how your signature strengths are reflected in your career interests to ensure that your career will support your life goals.

RubberBall Productions/Jupiterimages

When you are deeply engaged in your work, you may not notice that time has passed. This optimal human experience is called "flow."

Your Flexible Plan

Discover Your Values

PLAN OF ANALYSIS

Step 1: Gather Information

For these questions, reflect on personal and career values you identified in the chapter or in CourseMate, using results from the Knowdell™ Career Values Card Sort.

What values did you identify that are important to you for your work and your career?

_____

_____

How are your values reflected in your reputation?

_____

_____

What values are important to you, but not well-represented by your current career-related choices?

_____

_____

Step 2: Evaluate the Information

What must you do to ensure that your values are consistent with your career goals? For instance, if your goal is to earn a high salary, you might want to explore careers where earnings are higher. If creativity is important to you, you will need to identify career fields where you are able to be creative, and nurture this skill.

_____

_____

What further information do you need about jobs, career fields, or organizations in order to assess their compatibility with your values? For example, to explore careers with earnings comparable to your goals, you must learn about salaries for various jobs in the careers you are exploring.

_____

_____

What further information would be helpful to learn about careers that reflect your values? (These questions will inform your career exploration in **Chapter 5: Explore**.)

_____

_____

Step 3: Make Conclusions

Following your analysis, list the top five values that you want to focus on in your career.

1._____   2._____   3._____

4._____   5._____

Reflecting on your skills, preferences, and values assessment, consider how these complement each other. List career fields that interest you at this time and encompass all three areas you have assessed.

_____

_____

Performance Appraisal

Now that you have read the chapter, answer the questions below and complete the Tasks.

1. According to Maslow's Hierarchy of Needs (1943), the following is the order of our needs, from lowest-order needs to highest-order needs:
   a. Self-actualization, self-esteem, safety needs, physiological needs, and belonging
   b. Physiological needs, safety needs, belonging, self-esteem, and self-actualization
   c. Self-esteem, self-actualization, physiological needs, belonging, and safety needs
   d. Belonging, safety needs, physiological needs, self-esteem, and self-actualization

2. Examples of intrinsic motivation include:
   a. Enjoying your work tasks.
   b. Developing meaningful professional relationships.
   c. Striving for a promotion.
   d. a and b

3. Which of the following is true about careers and your values?
   a. Work environments do not reflect cultural, organizational, or individual values.
   b. Your personal values will not impact your work experience.
   c. Your values can make it hard to build relationships with colleagues who are not like you.
   d. All of the above

4. Affirmations can:
   a. Reflect your skills, but cannot be used to reflect your personal attributes.
   b. Help you see the value you add to the workplace.
   c. Reflect your personal characteristics and traits.
   d. b and c
   e. None of the above

5. Corporate social responsibility is a way for businesses to:
   a. Do good.
   b. Demonstrate corporate values.
   c. Attract like-minded employees.
   d. All of the above

6. Which of the following is true about your professional reputation?
   a. You cannot change your reputation.
   b. Your reputation can influence your career.
   c. Your personal reputation does not matter for your career.
   d. How you dress is your business, and you will not be judged in the workplace based on your appearance.

7. To create a life that is worth living:
   a. Identify what would make your life meaningful.
   b. Avoid any activities that could be challenging.
   c. Look for opportunities to use and develop your strengths.
   d. a and c

Performance Appraisal Answer Key

1. b
2. d
3. c
4. d
5. d
6. b
7. d

Thought Questions

1. Can you identify your values?

2. Have you identified values that will be important for you to consider in your career?

3. Have you identified any areas where your personal, family, career, or cultural values might conflict with your career interests or career goals?

Notes:

_____

_____

_____

_____

_____

_____

TASK 4.1:
Choose Your Affirmations

We all possess attributes that describe our best qualities. By stating these attributes as affirmations, you confirm your commitment to the actions that support your statement. Affirmations keep you focused on the positive qualities you value, and help you focus on the skills and behaviors you want to develop further.

- *"I am a caring friend"* is an affirmation that could show that you spend time with your friends, listen to them, and help them with personal concerns.
- *"I am good with numbers"* probably means you are a frequent choice for dividing a check amongst a group at the end of a meal, adept at estimating your bill at the supermarket, or able to solve problems easily in your math assignments.
- *"I am ambitious"* suggests you work hard and persevere when the going gets tough.

Choose three affirmations you think reflect your best qualities. To embrace these qualities in your career, consider how you will continue to build them. To see a list of possible attributes, refer to the list in "Values and Your Career" in this chapter. Next to each affirmation, write at least one action you can take to further develop the skill, characteristic, or trait.

1. *I am ...*

_____

To develop this quality, I will ...

_____

2. *I am ...*

_____

To develop this quality, I will ...

_____

3. *I am ...*

_____

To develop this quality, I will ...

_____

TASK 4.2:

Assess Your Career Values

Review **Exhibit 4.2**, Career Values. In CourseMate, complete the Knowdell™ Career Values Card Sort to sort the career values by how important they are to you in your career (ALWAYS VALUED, OFTEN VALUED, SOMETIMES VALUED, SELDOM VALUED, and NEVER VALUED). After you complete the Knowdell™ Career Values Card Sort, you will be prompted to complete the Summary Sheet of Prioritized Values and the Career Options Worksheet for your Career Portfolio.

List up to 10 career values you identified as ALWAYS VALUED here.

1. _____   5. _____   8. _____

2. _____   6. _____   9. _____

3. _____   7. _____   10. _____

4. _____

TASK 4.3:

Values, Jobs, and Work Environments

Review **Exhibit 4.2**, Career Values, and choose three to five values you would like to be held by each of the following:

Your coworkers.

_____

Your supervisor.

_____

Your organization.

_____

Your industry.

_____

Would you prefer for these groups to share all of the same values or to represent different values? Why?

_____

_____

_____

TASK 4.4:

Analyze Your Reputation

To understand your reputation, there is no better method than asking the people around you. Choose three people who would know your reputation. Consider including a friend, family member, teacher, classmate, or coworker. Ask for three words that describe your reputation, in their eyes.

Whom Did You Ask?   **Three Descriptive Words**

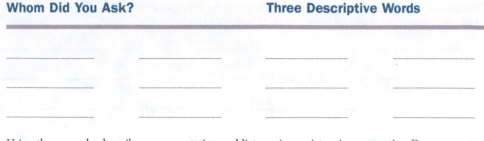

Using these words, describe your reputation and list any inconsistencies you notice. Do you want to improve your reputation in any ways? What affirmations can help you focus on strengths to build?

TASK 4.5:

That's a Life Worth Living

Imagining what would make your life worth living involves contemplating the values that are most important to you. However, it might be hard to identify these. Instead, consider allowing your mind to wander to all the thoughts and ideas that come up when you think about what would make your life worth living. This can be done by creating a cluster map that illustrates your thoughts, by writing down words that relate to a central theme.

In this exercise, you will create a cluster map that illustrates your ideas about a life worth living, starting with this central theme: "My Life." Next, write in words or phrases that reflect your thoughts about the values, ideas, activities, skills, preferences, and anything else that comes to mind. Write the first thoughts that come to your mind, without questioning them. They do not need to be related to each other, and they can reflect your stream of consciousness. Aim to fill in as many words as you can. After you are finished, review your cluster map to see which ideas came to mind and any themes that you notice in this quick, unedited exercise.

Here is an example:

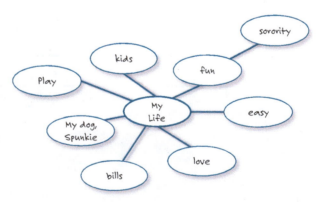

Use the space to create your own cluster map of ideas and inspiration for a life worth living.

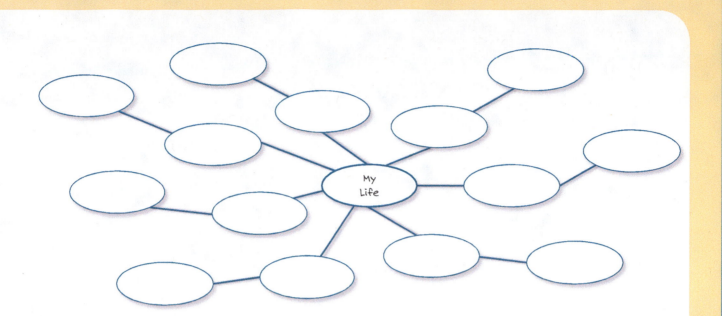

Link to CourseMate

On CourseMate, you can find documents to help you update your Career Portfolio as well as additional resources and activities. Here is some of the information you can find online for **Chapter 4: Values**.

CAREER PORTFOLIO

Your Flexible Plan
Summary Sheet of Prioritized Values
Career Options Worksheet

RESOURCES

Career Profile: Monica Baldwin
Knowdell™ Career Values Card Sort

SECTION II

Explore Your Options

Fabrice Lerouge/Jupiterimages

Explore

I long, as does every human being, to be at home wherever I find myself.   *—Maya Angelou*

What's Inside

Connect to the World of Work

Four Steps to Conduct Career Research

Expand Your Options

Education, Majors, and Careers

Real-World Career Exploration

Prepare to . . .

- Learn about careers that interest you and discover new careers

- Use technology and other resources efficiently in your career exploration

- Consider ways to expand your career exploration into new directions

- Become aware of skills and educational requirements for various career paths

- Discover how internships and experiential learning can help you prepare for your career

Exploration can help you learn about career fields before you start a job, take further steps for your career, or prepare your job application materials. Connecting your skills, preferences, and values to the world of work will help you evaluate organizations, careers, and industries based on your personal goals and dreams.

» Connect to the World of Work

Your skills, preferences, and values influence the types of activities and careers you might like, while the world around you continually shapes and influences how jobs and careers evolve. Connecting what you know about yourself with information about the workplace can help you identify areas to explore.

Periods of Economic Change

As our economy responds to technological, political, and social developments, needs in the workplace change. Throughout the past 150 years, there have been three periods defining our economy, and we may be entering a fourth.

- **Agricultural Age.** The Agriculture Age was dominated by farming in the eighteenth century.
- **Industrial Age.** The Industrial Age was led by manufacturing and factory work during the nineteenth century.
- **Information Age.** In the Information Age of knowledge-workers in the twentieth century, education became critical, as jobs required greater professional and technical services and, ultimately, computer knowledge (Drucker, 1959). Many theorists are now suggesting that knowledge and technical expertise may no longer be enough.
- **Conceptual Age or Age of Innovation.** The case is growing for the beginning of a Conceptual Age (Pink, 2005) or Age of Innovation (Walshok et al., 2011). This may also include the rise of a Creative Class (Florida, 2002). Combining knowledge with creativity is increasingly important in the workplace, as the need for knowledge workers expands into a much wider range of jobs and industries.

In the future, many careers will likely use knowledge and information as a foundation, while efforts to integrate innovation, address global problems, and explore issues of sustainability become a central focus for many new as well as evolving jobs and careers. For example, a contractor who can identify and recommend energy-saving solutions that save money for clients in the long-run can provide more specialized services than a contractor who fails to think creatively. An attorney who expresses empathy and understanding provides an indispensable service that cannot be outsourced as easily as the services of an attorney who prepares form letters, since such letters can now be ordered online and prepared locally or overseas at a low cost and a high speed.

Connecting Careers to Skills, Preferences, and Values

Everyone has a diverse set of skills, preferences, and values, and can use these to build careers for the future. Some of these will come from your work, education, and training. Activities, volunteer work, and hobbies can also help you build unique assets.

Imagine going back many years to the time when the horse and carriage dominated transportation. Two carriage drivers, Sam and John, both loved their work, but when cars became less expensive and more common, each knew it was time for a change.

Advances in technology have continually altered the workplace since the start of the Industrial Revolution.

- **Customer Service and Transportation.** Sam enjoyed providing a service to customers, and was proud to bring people from one place to another with speed and grace in his horse and carriage. He had strong relationships with his customers and others in transportation. When cars were introduced, he was eager to learn how new models functioned and were maintained. With his customer relationships and knowledge of cars, Sam stayed within the field of transportation and found a job as a chauffeur.

- **Raising and Caring for Horses.** Unlike Sam, John was more interested in horses than transportation. Driving a horse-drawn carriage allowed him to care for the animal, enjoy the sound of the horse trotting, and appreciate the animal's strength and grace. He was excited about the growing field of horse racing, and had built strong relationships with those who raised horses, as well as trainers and jockeys. He found work caring for racehorses.

Sam and John both enjoyed their jobs, but for different reasons. When necessity forced them to rethink their next steps, each connected past experiences, skills, preferences, values, and relationships to embark on a new direction. By continuing to learn and explore throughout his career, each was prepared to adapt and reinvent himself successfully.

Change in Our Present Economy

While we are not experiencing a single dramatic shift like Sam and John, we live in a world of constant change, which impacts everyone. While the youngest generation has grown up with the Internet, everyone else, including Generation Xers, Baby Boomers, and older workers, remember work without cell phones, and high school and possibly college, without computers or e-mail. At work, the mingling of four generations results in different expectations about the pressure to develop skills for ever-shifting workplace demands, as well as varying levels of comfort and familiarity with new technology.

Here are some possibilities for how careers may continue to evolve. Many current events are setting the stage for changes such as these.

- **Health Care Will Change.** Health care will <mark>become more efficient</mark> as health care professionals integrate the latest technologies and problem-solving approaches; patient time and personal attention will continue to decrease.
- **Outsourcing Will Increase.** For careers such as law, accounting, and finance, many services will continue to be replaced by technology or performed by people in other parts of the world.
- **Jobs Will Be Eliminated.** Service jobs that require hands-on work will not be outsourced, nor will people-centered service jobs, management positions, and those addressing infrastructure. However, the number of these jobs will shrink due to automation, technology, and product development. These include such areas as landscaping, gardening, construction, and jobs in restaurants, hotels, and retail stores.
- **All Careers Will Evolve.** Technology, globalization, and sustainability will impact all fields, not just high-tech, international, and green careers.

Many of these changes are already taking place. For instance, the use of low-cost software programs like TurboTax have replaced many accounting jobs; firms offer inexpensive graphic design and legal services through overseas employees; and some companies, including Google, have hired chief sustainability officers. Becoming familiar with how careers are evolving can help you prepare for the future.

To see which careers are currently growing, review the occupations in **Exhibit 5.6**, Fastest-Growing Occupations. Notice that many growing areas are in renewable energy, technology, and professional services. Many of these career fields were unheard of even a few years ago.

Innovate, Adapt, and Learn

Change has been a theme impacting all aspects of work, such as production, sales, communication, and consumer activities. <mark>The ability to adapt to change is critical for organizations as well as individuals.</mark> Consider how change has impacted the music industry, and how organizations have responded. In and before the 1970s, listeners bought vinyl records; then, in the 1980s they bought tapes and eventually CDs; and, by the late 1990s, digital music had fully arrived. All of these required different production, manufacturing, and even recording devices.

Despite the introduction of new products and services, and opportunities for new ventures, many companies failed to reinvent themselves, including large retail chains like Tower Records and Sam Goody, which declared bankruptcy. On the other hand, Apple, once known only as a computer company, defined itself broadly and prospered. Apple's digital music retailer, iTunes, is now the top music retailer in the United States (Neumayr and Roth, 2008). While Apple still makes computers, it has also expanded its product lines to include online retailing, including new products such as iPods, iPhones, iPads, and apps. The same approach can be applied to career development. Consider how to broaden your exploration into areas that are currently developing, or look for ways to combine your skills in unexpected ways. As you gather information, your exploration may take you in unexpected directions that call for further research or reflection.

© Newscast/Alamy

Successful organizations look for ways to reinvent themselves through new products or services and value employees who can participate in their growth.

Use the space below to write about your thoughts and feelings.

> Consider a situation in which you made a decision that was important to you. It could be an important financial decision such as buying a car or a life decision such as whether to go to college. Describe the situation.

> In reviewing this important decision, how did you gather information that was helpful to you? Describe your experience of learning critical details before making a decision.

Choosing a career direction, deciding which jobs to pursue, or committing to further training requires you to gather information and evaluate it. Your preferred methods of career exploration will likely be no different than your experience gathering information for other significant decisions.

Some people find that they prefer to gather concrete information based on what they learn from their five senses (sight, hearing, taste, touch, smell), often by comparing data, such as product reviews, writing pro/con lists, or through hands-on learning. Others prefer using their intuition, sometimes referred to as "trusting their instincts," "the sixth sense," or having a "gut feeling" about something. In **Chapter 3: Preferences**, you assessed your preferred approaches for gathering information using the dimensions of the Myers-Briggs Type Indicator® (MBTI®) and you may have also taken the MBTI®.

> Returning to the experience you described above, how did your preferences impact your information gathering? What did you value more: information gained by your five senses *or* information gained by your instincts? Why?

Journal Feedback . . . Important career insights can be gained from many resources, such as talking to others or reading about facts. But for many people, it is common to rely on preferred methods of gathering information. By gaining awareness of your preferred methods for exploration, you can become more aware of the need to include other approaches that might add important information, such as the perspective of individuals in the field or data about industry growth and earnings.

Name: Cody Grant
College Degree: BS in Accounting
Graduate Degree: MS in Accounting, with a concentration in Finance *(Received both degrees in 4 years)*
Current Position: Senior Associate, International Tax
Volunteer Positions: Board Co-Chair, United Neighborhood Houses Junior Board
Board Member, Binghamton University School of Management, Young Alumni Metro Advisory Board
Employer: Ernst & Young, LLP

Courtesy of Cody Grant

How did you explore career fields?

When deciding on a major in college, I remember thinking forward and asking myself, "What do I want my career to be?" More importantly though, I thought long and hard about how my decisions would impact the path I would take leading up to the beginning of my career. From that start, I decided I wanted to work in business. I discovered that the career of a public accountant was really more in line with my professional and personal goals. For starters, it was a little more flexible. I knew I'd be able to spend time as a volunteer and have time for other aspects of my life. From there, I decided that I wanted to work at a large firm where the opportunities are endless. In public accounting, this meant working for one of the "Big 4" accounting firms, but the next step was to decide which firm. By talking to people at each firm and learning about their personal experiences, I learned about the environment and culture at each.

How important are internships in your field and extracurricular activities?

Interning in public accounting allows you to see what you'll be doing day in and day out, learn the culture of the firm, and can potentially lead to a full-time position. However, an unpaid internship, working for a local company in your field of study, or charity work are all ways to make your summer time off useful if internship opportunities are not available. Before starting my full-time career, I interned with Motorola in Supply Chain Finance and with Ernst & Young in the group in which I currently work. It's clear to me that both opportunities helped cultivate different skill sets, and contributed greatly to my opportunities after graduation. In a similar light, participating in extracurricular activities lays the groundwork for future success—it proves you can take on responsibility, prioritize multiple task at once, and provides employers with a sense of your interests. At Binghamton, I was a Resident Assistant, a member of a professional business fraternity and a teaching assistant for both business and non-business courses.

From Cody's Supervisor
Name: Daniel Fletcher
Title: Manager, International Tax Transactions

Courtesy of Daniel Fletcher

How does Cody demonstrate his ability to learn on the job?

Cody is very eager to learn. He's done a great job building his technical tax knowledge, which is the key that lays the foundation for a successful career as a tax professional. In the early years of your career, it's important not to focus too narrowly; Cody does a great job broadening his skill set by working on a variety of projects. This broad base of skills will pay off for him as his career advances.

Cody also does a great job building rapport with his peers and superiors (all the way up to the partner level). He manages his personal brand very well. In this business, having a reputation for integrity and technical competence—both internally and externally with clients—is crucial to your success as a tax professional. Cody has quickly become a "go-to" member of our team. This is, in large part, due to his focus on producing high quality work and developing strong relationships with his coworkers.

How important is industry knowledge and career research for ongoing success in your field?

The only constant in the tax profession seems to be the continuously changing landscape. A person who's successful in this field keeps up with changes in the law, while applying the law to his or her client's facts to obtain the best result possible. And, as far as industry knowledge goes, it's very important to understand each client's business. Without that knowledge, you can't properly apply the tax law or effectively develop solutions for your client and achieve the ultimate goal, which is to become one of your client's trusted advisors.

I think Cody takes the right approach. He keeps himself up-to-date with the latest tax law changes and the trends among our clients. I also think he asks the right questions, meaning, he seeks to understand our clients' businesses, which is not always easy in the financial services world. He's building a solid foundation for success and, one day soon, he'll be passing those skills on by helping develop the next generation of professionals.

How did Cody explore career fields?

_____

_____

_____

What else did you do to prepare for career decisions?
When I wasn't sure how to get from point A to point B regarding any aspect of my career preparation, I reached out to multiple people for a wide range of advice. Always asking questions is a good practice. I could say that making a good group of friends with the same drive and similar goals was one of most helpful things I did. I really believe that throughout your college years it is extremely important to surround yourself with people who have similar goals—people who are motivated and passionate in everything that they do. Ultimately, they will rub off on you and, collectively, your group—your peers, your friends—will have that drive to excel.

What type of career information do you think Cody learned through his experiences?

_____

_____

_____

For additional questions, visit CourseMate. ▣

>> Four steps to Conduct Career Research

Researching an industry, organization, and position before you begin your job search can help you gain valuable information, search for trends and growth areas, learn where insiders look for job listings, and improve your questions and answers throughout networking and job interviews. These four steps can make your career exploration more thorough and time efficient.

There are many resources to help you gather career information.

Diego Cervo/Shutterstock.com

Step 1. Create a list of questions.
Step 2. Identify resources.
Step 3. Group your questions.
Step 4. Start your research.

Step 1: Create a List of Questions

To start your career exploration, create a list of questions you have about careers, industries, organizations, and positions. These questions should be designed to help you gather information. Self-assessment gives insight into your skills, interests, and values, and career exploration links your self-reflection to the world of work (see **Exhibit 5.1**, Career Exploration Questions).

If you are not certain which careers interest you most, or what you need to learn to make important decisions, start with the information you gathered in your self-assessment in **Chapters 2: Skills**, **Chapter 3: Preferences**, and **Chapter 4: Values**. Create questions that connect what you like to do, what you do well, and what you value with the world of work. Include any question you have about jobs, organizations, and industries.

Step 2: Identify Resources

Go through your questions and decide, one-by-one, where answers can be found to your questions. If you do not know, *do not* just skip it or take an educated guess. Information can be found in many places. If you are trying to answer a question, and do not know where to look, start with the online resources in **Exhibit 5.2**,

---

》EXHIBIT 5.1 ● Career Exploration Questions

 Consider what you want to learn. Additional questions can be found on CourseMate, and think of your own, too.

Exploring Careers
What careers use the skills that I want to use most?
What careers are common for people with my preferences?
How can I learn more about the relationship between my values and career fields?
What are common entry-level positions in these fields?
What are the educational and experiential requirements for entry-level positions?

Exploring Industries
What are major recent trends in the industry?
Who are some of the influential employers? What makes them so successful?
Where can I meet networking contacts?
Where are job openings listed for this industry?

How might employers respond to someone changing careers or reentering the workforce?

Exploring Organizations
What is the organizational culture?
What helps people to succeed within this organization?
How diverse is the workforce?
Is corporate responsibility a part of the company's mission?
Does the organization promote work-life balance?

Exploring Positions
What salaries are offered?
What is a typical day like?
What skills will be developed in this position?
In what directions could this position lead within (or outside) the organization?
Are additional educational or other credentials required for promotion?

Online Resources for Career Exploration, professional associations, such as those in **Exhibit 5.3**, Professional Associations, or the campus and community resources listed in **Chapter 1: Prepare.** Here are several suggested resources for locating information on careers that connect with your skills, preferences, and values.

- **Skills.** Consider your skills and the previous experiences you have enjoyed, and learn more about careers that build on these. Resources to identify careers that match your skills include: O*Net, the Occupational Outlook Handbook, job listings, careers related to your major, or past jobs and internships.
- **Preferences.** Explore fields and industries that match your patterns of interest and personality type. Resources to identify careers that match your preferences include: O*Net, the Bureau of Labor Statistics Occupation Finder tool, and recommended careers from assessments you have completed, such as the MBTI® insrument or the Strong Interest Inventory.
- **Values.** To connect your values to careers and work environments, review your self-assessed values, and compare them to corporate responsibility reflected in company and industry websites. You can also network with insiders to learn more about attitudes and activities that reflect industry values.

Step 3: Group Your Questions

Now that you have a list of questions, and have considered where to gather the information to help you find answers, you might notice that you are planning to use the same resource to answer a number of questions. Using the Internet can be an excellent starting point, but when online information from a homepage is incomplete or confusing, go to the "contact us" page available on most websites and consider calling or e-mailing with your questions. Before going to any resource, whether a website or a personal contact, plan all of the questions for which you intend to seek answers.

Here are two examples of grouped questions, but, of course, each resource would help you answer many more questions as well.

Resource		Career Exploration Question
Industry websites	→	What are major recent trends in the industry? What are common entry-level positions in these fields? Who are the largest and most influential employers?
Networking contacts	→	What major recent trends in the industry have impacted your career? What entry-level positions are appropriate for someone with my level of education and experience? What are the best resources for entry level job listings in this industry?

Step 4: Start Your Research

As you start your research online, in a library, at your career center, or in the field, plan to get the information you need without wasting time. As new questions come up, categorize them quickly so you continue to access the best resources first. Ask for contact information from those who are helpful and send a thank you note or e-mail to express your appreciation. Consider connecting on LinkedIn or follow up with an e-mail to build your network.

If you like to learn by talking with people, you might be eager to start reaching out to ask questions that will help you gather information. However, building a foundation through career research and an informed set of questions will help you network far more effectively. With preliminary research about companies and industries, you will have informed questions for your networking meetings. Similarly, meeting people in industry can add depth and breadth to the written information you evaluate.

≫EXHIBIT 5.2 ● Online Resources for Career Exploration

To locate these resources online, enter the website names into a search engine. This is a limited list, many more resources can be found online, and an expanded list is available on CourseMate.

Topic	Types of Online Resources	Website Names (this is a limited list)*
General	Government Resources	Bureau of Labor Statistics Career Information O*Net Online Occupational Outlook Handbook
	A-Z Index of Career Topics	The Riley Guide QuintCareers
	Web-based Videos	Inspired2Work Vault—Job Talk
	Salary information	salary.com wetfeet.com monster.com
	Values & Careers	Graduation Pledge Vault—Job Talk
Industry & Organizations	General Industry Information	Hoovers Wetfeet Vault BLS Career Guides to Industries (CGI)
	Company Profiles	Hoovers Glassdoor
	Company Websites	Employer Sites, "about" page or "annual report"
Positions	Databases of job information	O*Net Occupational Outlook Handbook Inside Jobs
	Job listings on industry specific websites	Hcareers Style Careers Media Bistro Idealist Mashable Star Chefs Creative Heads
Diversity	General	Diversity Jobs Hire Diversity IM Diversity Diversity Employers Magazine Online

>> EXHIBIT 5.3 ● Professional Associations

This is a limited list; many more professional associations can be found online, and an expanded list is available on CourseMate. ⌨ To locate professional associations online, enter the full name of the professional association or the career field and the words "professional association" (e.g., "dental hygienist professional association") into a search engine, such as Google.

Industry	Professional Associations
Accounting/Finance	American Institute of Certified Public Accountants, Association for Financial Professionals, American Accounting Association
Advertising/Public Relations	Advertising Research Foundation, Public Relations Society of America, American Association of Advertising Agencies, Council of Public Relations Firms
Arts	College Art Association, National Endowment for the Arts, American Society of Interior Designers, Society of Illustrators, New York Foundation for the Arts
Biology/Biotechnology	American Institute of Biological Sciences, American Society for Microbiology, Biotechnology Industry Association, Society for Experimental Biology and Medicine
Building and Real Estate Management	National Association of Residential Property Managers, Institute of Real Estate Management, Building Owners and Managers Association International
Business	American Management Association, Small Business Administration, Toastmasters International
Computer	American Society for Information Science and Technology, Association for Information Systems, Society for Information Management, Network Professional Association, Programmers Guild, Software and Information Industry Association
Construction	Construction Management Association of America, Professional Women in Construction, American Society of Construction Professionals and Engineers
Data Processing	Association of Information Technology Professionals, Black Data Processing Associates
Education/K-12	American Association of School Administrators, American Federation of Teachers, National Education Association, Association for Middle Level Education
Engineering	American Society of Civil Engineers, Institute of Electrical and Electronics Engineers, Institute of Industrial Engineers
Fashion	Fashion Group International, American Apparel and Footwear Association, Council of Fashion Designers of America, The Fashion Center
Government	Federal Employee Association, National Active and Retired Federal Employees
Graphic Arts	CG Society of Digital Artists (name), Graphic Artists Guild, American Institute of Graphic Artists, The Society of Publication Designers
Health Care	American Medical Association, American Association of Healthcare Administrative Management, American Health Care Association, American Dental Association, American Hospital Association, American Nurses Association
Legal	American Bar Association, The Association of Legal Assistants, The Association for Legal Professionals, National Lawyers Association
Logistics/Transportation	Advanced Transit Association, American Public Transportation Association, Transport Workers Union, United Transportation Union, United Auto Workers, American Road and Transportation Builders Association
Music	American Federation of Musicians, National Association of Music Merchants, National Music Publishers Association
Retail	National Retail Federation, National Association of Retail Buyers, Retail Merchants Association, The Association of Resale Professionals
Sales/Marketing	American Marketing Association, Sales and Marketing Professionals Association, Association of Marketing and Communications Professionals, National Association of Sales Professionals, United Professional Sales Association
Sports/Recreation	International Sports Professionals Association, North American Society for Sport Management, International Fitness Professionals Association, National Association of Recreation Resource Planners
Transportation	American Association of State and Highway Transportation, International Right of Way Association, American Public Transportation Association, American Transportation Association

© Cengage Learning 2014

Social media has added a new spin on career exploration. Now you can filter the news, search easily for information in your industry, and have current events and employer updates sent to your e-mail or social media accounts. Here are some of the most common social media resources and how they can help you stay up-to-date.

Facebook. On Facebook, anytime you "like" a company or professional organization, updates will show up in your newsfeed. To have industry-specific information come to you, consider "liking" a news source or informational site for your industry. Some suggestions include Mashable for techies, MediaBistro for media-related fields, or Stylesight for fashion trends.

Twitter. Twitter allows you to "follow" companies or people in the fields that interest you. With Twitter, you stay on top of your industry by reading brief entries that are 140 character or less, may include links to helpful articles or blogs, and are connected by an archival system using hashtags (e.g. #education). To find people and organizations for your professional interests, choose "#discover" on the top bar, then "browse categories" on the far left, and type the name of any topic that interests you.

Pinterest. Pinterest is a great resource for learning more about people's interests and sources for inspiration, from products to images. By looking up the Pinterest pages of organizations, people in your industry, and bloggers who comment on your industry, you can search images that impact their ideas. These may also include comments and links to related blogs or websites. Although Pinterest has gained in popularity, you may find more professional activity on Pinterest in visual fields, such as fashion, design, art, and architecture.

LinkedIn. LinkedIn allows you to join groups related to your career interests and follow companies of interest. When you join a group, you will be prompted to decide the frequency with which you want to receive updates and how you wish to be contacted. Searching directly for companies and looking to see if any of your connections work there is a great way to find networking resources for the organizations that interest you.

YouTube. YouTube is a great source for videos posted by companies to share information, promote new ventures and products, and communicate their values. There are also a number of videos on career topics such as interviewing, creating an elevator speech, and networking.

Delicious. On Delicious you can organize bookmarks and see the bookmarks of others. To get started, choose any interest, such as photography, and search others' bookmarks for professional associations, articles, blogs, and more by combining any words you choose with the tag "photography" in the search bar.

Digg. Users vote on Digg for online favorites, including blogs, pages, articles, and resources. Search by keyword to get results that match the term you choose. This can help you find popular resources for the subjects that interest you.

StumbleUpon. Use StumbleUpon to search for sites that match your interests, and find sites recommended by friends or other StumbleUpon users. This can help you eliminate the need to search through pages that are a poor match, helping you reach search results that are recommended.

Specialized social media hubs. Your field of interest may have its own specialized social media hub; for example, deviantART.com or behance.com connect individuals in creative professions. In addition, many alumni associations and professional organizations have introduced social networking for members, allowing a more private exchange of information.

By using social media to narrow your research into areas that interest you, you may learn about new jobs, niche fields, and specialized careers that require multiple talents.

>> Expand Your Options

As you research career fields in a global economy, exploring how to combine your skills, develop a creative mindset, and add value can help you think more broadly about your career options.

Combine Your Skills

Exploring how various careers combine your skills in creative and unexpected ways can help you expand your options. Your coursework, activities, hobbies, volunteer work, and leadership roles have helped you build skills that prepare you for many

In the world of work, your assets and creativity can help you add value in unexpected ways.

settings. For instance, a student who has studied a science field and enjoys writing might find work as a technical writer for a pharmaceutical company. Use **Exhibit 5.4**, Careers and Transferable Skills, to look at how skills from your major combine with student activities to suggest alternative career options.

Increase Your Creative Thinking

If thinking outside the box is a challenge for you, you can use Daniel Pink's "six senses" to identify new areas to explore (2005). This list is designed to help you cultivate creative, right-brain thinking. Consider how these concepts are present in the world of work, and look at how your activities, projects, or coursework have prepared you to contribute in these areas.

1. **Design.** The importance of design can be seen by the relationship between product packaging and product success (also see Gladwell, 2005). Pink recommends thinking beyond functionality and aiming for design that is attractive, fun, or engaging. This can be part of how you create presentations and projects, as well as how you approach developing your professional image.
2. **Story.** When stating your case or making a point, create a story that is compelling, rather than merely telling facts. This can help you connect with people, and help them understand your points. Jobs that involve communication skills offer opportunities for storytelling.
3. **Symphony.** Formerly, analysis and knowledge equaled power, but connecting ideas together is critical when information jobs are easily outsourced or computerized. Pink describes this as putting the pieces together, seeing the big picture, or crossing boundaries. In many work environments, whether dealing with projects or people, this can be helpful.
4. **Empathy.** Understanding others, developing relationships, and caring will be important skills in developing meaningful connections. Consider how empathy can help you perform jobs.

5. **Play.** Making time for personal interests, balance, and humor is fun and engaging, and can help you develop a wider network and skill set. Many careers evolve from hobbies and the talents fostered in those activities.

6. **Meaning.** Find meaning in the world around you. Connect your activities and interests to social causes and experiences that are personally relevant and make a difference. Connecting with organizations that have similar values to your own can help you feel more passionate about your work.

Plan to Add Value

As you explore career fields, look at jobs, organizations, and fields to which your unique combination of skills, preferences, and values can add value. For instance, if you're organized and can combine this with technological know-how, you could add value by reorganizing data storage at your work setting. A project like this doesn't have to be part of your assigned tasks, and could apply anywhere, not just in an office, since every work setting maintains contacts, sends bills, and receives payments. Of course, you must do your actual job first, and do it well, but seeing beyond your immediate tasks is important in today's economy.

Gathering information about how your unique assets add value to the workplace will help you think creatively about careers that might be right for you, and expand your list of careers to explore.

≫ WORK WITH AWARENESS ● Sustainability and Green Careers

A growing segment in the job market is represented by green careers. Green careers involve jobs that preserve and restore the quality of the environment. There may be many reasons for the growing trend for green careers, including such issues as long-term cost savings, an interest in preserving the environment, or a desire for companies to appeal to environmentally conscious consumers. Regardless of the determining factors, green careers are expanding significantly.

In fact, the growth of green careers has far exceeded growth in other areas. Between 1987 and 1997, green careers grew at almost triple the rate of traditional jobs (3.7% vs. 9.1%)

(Coulter, 2011). Furthermore, green careers are not only for scientists and white-collar managers. For instance, 69 percent of all green careers are in manufacturing, compared to 43 percent of all U.S. jobs (Kuang, 2011). In addition, many opportunities are opening for green jobs in a wide range of industries including traditional fields, such as banking, consumer products, marketing, or the law, in ways that are indirectly related to the green movement, environmental issues, or sustainability. An example is a consumer-goods company aiming to reduce the plastic involved in packaging for their products.

Environmental Preservation	Related Job Titles
Care for the earth, natural resources, wildlife	conservationist, environmentalist
Design and implement green infrastructure, IT, distribution channels	logistics specialist, systems specialist
Design and manufacture green products, materials, and processes	designer, inventor, manufacturer
Educate and inspire	teacher, writer
Generate clean, renewable energy	solar sales consultant, wind resource assessment specialist
Help companies and organizations green their business	sustainability consultant, in-house sustainability manager
Motivate and persuade people to take green actions	marketing director, sales manager
Provide green services	event planner, real estate broker

(Continues)

Remodel, retrofit, build green buildings and spaces	contractor, green rater
Secure funding, invest	investor, fundraiser, financial planner
Set policy, regulate, advocate	advocate, policy maker

McClelland, C., Making Sense of the New Green Career Frontier: A Framework of Green Industries. Chapter 5, Career Planning and Adult Development Journal, p. 51. Career Planning and Adult Development Network, 2008. Copyright © Richard L. Knowdell. Reprinted with permission. President Career Planning and Adult Development Network. Post Office Box 611930, San Jose, CA 95161-1930, Tel: 408-272-3085/Fax: 408-259-8438, rknowdell@mac.com/www.careernetwork.org

As you can see from this varied list of occupations, green careers are not limited to science, technology, engineering, and mathematics (STEM) fields, although an understanding of these areas will help you appreciate and communicate concepts that are fundamental to sustainability. Every career field can potentially involve green occupations, and knowledge about sustainability is another asset for your future.

>> Education, Majors, and Careers

Your academic preparation may not relate directly to all the jobs you perform in your lifetime, but it should offer you a basic set of transferable skills and a foundation from which you can draw, whatever type of career you build. Using **Exhibit 5.4**, Careers and Transferable Skills, consider how your education and activities have helped you add skills that are relevant to the workplace, while demonstrating your interests.

Career-Related Majors

Many careers require or can benefit from technical or career-related education and training. Examples of these include dental hygienist, nurse, electrician, computer programmer, accountant, and graphic designer.

If you have chosen a business, technical, art, design, or vocational major, and are looking for ways to expand your career options, consider fields that build on the transferable skills you have already developed, and where you might like to add skills. For instance, a major in nursing will help you develop project management, organizational, math, team, and communication skills. These can be applied to business, not-for-profit management, helping fields, and education. Determining the direction you want to go can help you decide which skills need to be developed further.

Liberal Arts Majors

Studying a liberal arts subject area will provide you with transferable skills as well as the opportunity for specialized training. Most liberal arts majors provide a foundation in such skills as written and verbal communications, critical thinking, research, project management, as well as others. Employers no longer expect your major to signal your career direction; rather, they expect your entire experience to signal your career direction. To increase your career options, build skills, and demonstrate your interests, get involved in campus activities, take on leadership positions in student clubs, or gain experience through part-time work, volunteer roles, and internships.

Echo/Cultura/Jupiterimages

Coursework helps you develop transferable skills, but it is up to you to learn how your assets are relevant in the workplace.

Science, Technology, Engineering, and Mathematics (STEM) Majors

For students in science, technology, engineering, and mathematics (STEM) majors, your education may have emphasized math and technical skills, including laboratory work. In these majors many transferable skills are developed, such as the ability to perform research and present results, work in a team, think analytically and critically, and understand how to manage data. Many careers require these assets, but it is often up to the job applicant to understand and communicate the connections between his or her skills and those sought by employers.

Exploring Education and Opportunity

Although there are many paths to success, statistical data from the Bureau of Labor Statistics illustrates that for the greatest number of people, higher levels of education lead to increased earnings and lower unemployment (see **Exhibit 5.5**, Education, Earnings, and Unemployment). Given the opportunity that college and graduate study offer, researchers who studied Millennials recommend viewing education as an investment, rather than an expense (Settersten and Ray, 2010). Having invested in their future through education, graduates can expect their skills and credentials will set them on a higher track for lifetime earnings, affording greater opportunity as well as financial return in the long run. Despite the short-term difficulty of a competitive entry-level job search in a downturn economy, data on lifetime earnings reflects a clear advantage for those with more education.

Consider how your major can prepare you for many fields. This is a limited list of transferable skills and career options. Many more skills are earned in each major and activity, and these majors prepare you for many more careers than those listed. Visit CourseMate for more information about majors and careers.

» EXHIBIT 5.4 ● Careers and Transferable Skills

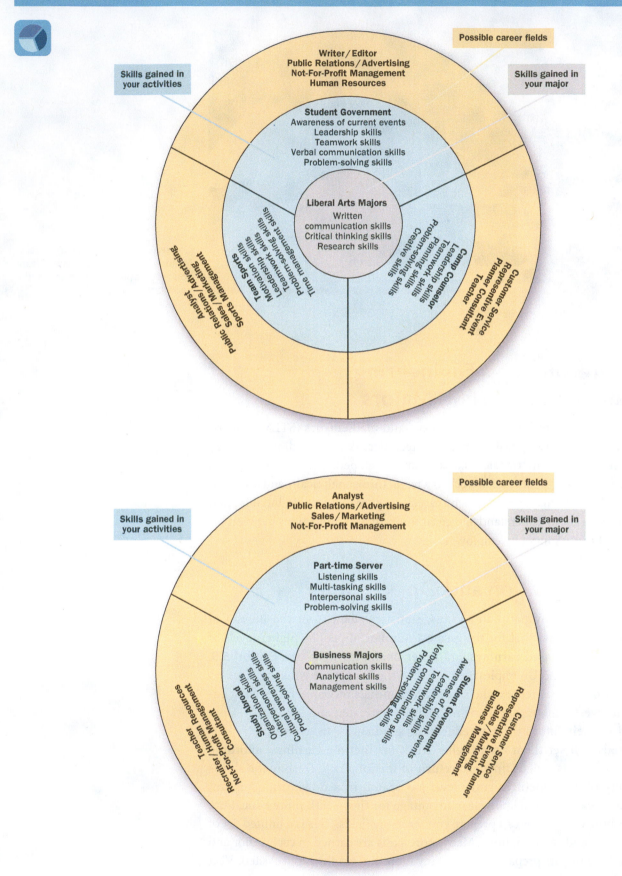

Diagram 1

Possible career fields
Skills gained in your activities
Skills gained in your major

Writer / Editor
Public Relations / Advertising
Not-For-Profit Management
Human Resources

Student Government
Awareness of current events
Leadership skills
Teamwork skills
Verbal communication skills
Problem-solving skills

Liberal Arts Majors
Written communication skills
Critical thinking skills
Research skills

Team Sports
Motivation skills
Leadership skills
Problem-solving skills
Time-management skills

Camp Counselor
Leadership skills
Teamwork skills
Problem-solving skills
Creative skills

Analyst / Advertising
Public Relations/Marketing
Sports Management

Customer Service
Representative
Event Planner
Teacher Consultant

Diagram 2

Possible career fields
Skills gained in your activities
Skills gained in your major

Analyst
Public Relations / Advertising
Sales / Marketing
Not-For-Profit Management

Part-time Server
Listening skills
Multi-tasking skills
Interpersonal skills
Problem-solving skills

Business Majors
Communication skills
Analytical skills
Management skills

Study Abroad
Organizational skills
Interpersonal skills
Cultural awareness
Problem-solving skills

Student Government
Awareness of current events
Leadership skills
Teamwork skills
Verbal communication skills
Problem-solving skills

Teacher Resources
Recruiter / Human Management
Not-For-Profit Consultant

Customer Service
Representative
Creative Event Planner
Business / Marketing
Sales / Marketing
Management

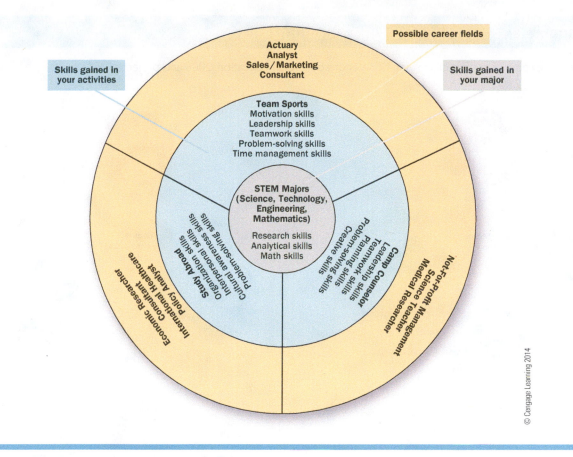

Possible career fields

Skills gained in your activities

Skills gained in your major

Actuary
Analyst
Sales / Marketing
Consultant

Team Sports
Motivation skills
Leadership skills
Teamwork skills
Problem-solving skills
Time management skills

STEM Majors
(Science, Technology,
Engineering,
Mathematics)

Research skills
Analytical skills
Math skills

Organization skills
Interpersonal skills
Cultural awareness skills
problem-solving skills

Study Abroad

Economic Researcher
Consultant
International Healthcare
Policy Analyst

Leadership skills
Teamwork skills
Planning skills
Problem-solving skills
Creative skills

Camp Counselor

Medical Researcher
Science Teacher
Not-For-Profit Management

≫EXHIBIT 5.5 ● Education, Earnings, and Unemployment

Higher education results in higher earnings and lower unemployment rates.

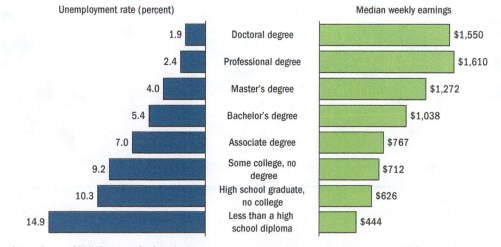

Unemployment rate (percent)		Median weekly earnings
1.9	Doctoral degree	$1,550
2.4	Professional degree	$1,610
4.0	Master's degree	$1,272
5.4	Bachelor's degree	$1,038
7.0	Associate degree	$767
9.2	Some college, no degree	$712
10.3	High school graduate, no college	$626
14.9	Less than a high school diploma	$444

Source: Current Population Survey (CPS). Bureau of Labor Statistics.

>> **EXHIBIT 5.6** • Fastest Growing Occupations

These are some of the fastest growing occupations by level of education, 2008 and projected 2018.

Source: Employment Projections Programs, U.S. Department of Labor, U.S. Bureau of Labor Statistics, viewed on August 22, 2011

In a global economy, learning to interact successfully with others who are different from you is critical.

Although there are some jobs that focus primarily on skills addressing issues of diversity, such as researching issues of poverty or teaching English as a second language (ESL), many more work environments draw on global awareness to add value to other skills sets, such as marketing to broad customer bases, interacting with employees around the world, or showing respect to fellow employees.

Here are a number of ways you might have developed your understanding of diversity.

- Growing up in a diverse neighborhood, where cultural differences are part of everyday life
- Traveling to a part of the world where people celebrate different holidays, eat different foods, or wear their clothes differently than in the United States
- Volunteering in an environment that raised your awareness of relevant issues facing various groups of people

The American workforce is expected to become more diverse. (see **Exhibit 5.7**, Diversity in the Labor Force). In **Chapter 3: Preferences**, you explored how stereotype threat can impact performance, and how being the "only" of any group within a work setting can increase the risks of stereotype threat. Therefore, conduct research to understand how specific organizations address diversity. Consider how diverse your target organizations are, whether their leadership is diverse, and whether mentoring or other internal support programs exist to support diversity. If the organizations you are targeting are not diverse, consider what you can do to reduce the impact of stereotype threat. Be mindful that all groups can experience stereotype threat.

With four generations represented in the workforce, understanding generational differences and succeeding with others of varying ages will also be important. As you research industries and organizations, consider how representative they are of the ages of the population currently in the workforce (**Exhibit 5.7**, Diversity in the Labor Force), and how this is represented in leadership as well as entry-level opportunities.

There are many other differences that are present at work, and your understanding and appreciation of others can help you connect and build relationships, regardless of race, ethnicity, gender, age, disability, or sexual orientation. Efforts to build sensitivity and awareness can help you prepare for increasing diversity in the U.S. workforce and globalization in the years ahead.

>> **EXHIBIT 5.7** ● **Diversity in the Labor Force**

Diversity in the labor force, by race and ethnicity, 2008 and projected 2018 (numbers in millions). By 2018, the population is expected to become more diverse.

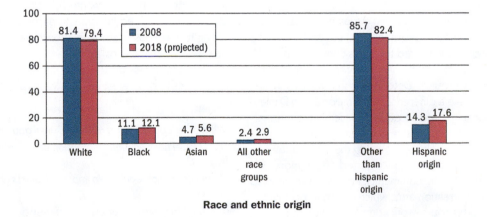

Race and ethnic origin

(Continues)

>> **EXHIBIT 5.7** ● **Diversity in the Labor Force** *Continued*

Diversity in the labor force, by age (numbers in millions). By 2018, the projected number of workers in the primary working age group, from 25–54, is expected to decline, with workers 55 and older increasing significantly.

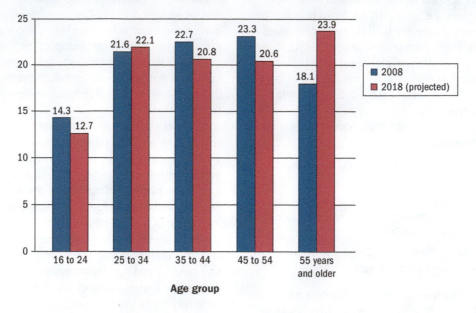

Age group

Source: Occupational Outlook Handbook, 2010–11 Edition, Overview of the 2008–18 Projections, U.S. Department of Labor, U.S. Bureau of Labor Statistics, viewed on August 22, 2011.

>> **CAREER PROFILE** ● **Case Study**

Daniel Chee: Exploring Possible Alternatives

In high school, Daniel Chee had been a "C" student, and preferred spending time with his friends, making things, and camping. He accepted a part-time job in construction after graduation, and enrolled in community college hoping to expand his future options. By the end of the first semester, he had failed one class and received poor grades in the others. He met with an advisor who suggested career counseling.

Daniel's career counselor helped him discover a preference for hands-on work, motivating and leading others, and organizing information or materials. He related this to his construction work, but also told the counselor that he had volunteered often to clean up parks and local playgrounds. Determining that working in nature and helping to make a difference were important to Daniel, his career counselor suggested he explore these interests further.

Inspired by her suggestion, he read about careers in parks and recreation, but had trouble connecting the information to his real life. The career counselor suggested he get more involved on campus or in the community. He joined an effort to protect a forest and recreation area, which was so important to him that he stopped his coursework completely, opting to work in construction and volunteer. Once active as a volunteer, he could see that many paid positions in not-for-profit management

and politics required a degree, and he suddenly felt certain that he should continue his studies. He returned to community college, and declared a major in political science.

He found his classes difficult, and his grades were not as high as he had hoped. He returned to the career counselor and told her that he wanted to complete a BA degree and have a career in community outreach, but since school had been such a challenge already, he did not know if he would be able to complete another degree nor if he wanted to take more loans for his education. She suggested he apply to Bachelor Degree programs, telling him he could defer and attend later. She also suggested he research AmeriCorps, a program that would allow him to work for a year, postpone paying his loans, and gain experience that relates to his interests, all before making a decision.

What other approaches could help Daniel gather information?

Does Daniel have enough information about entry-level jobs? Why or why not?

What information would help improve Daniel's ability to choose a next step?

To learn more about Daniel's career development, visit CourseMate. 🖥 View his résumé and job search materials in **Chapter 8: Tools**.

© Cengage Learning 2014

» Real-World Career Exploration

In 2011, the Bureau of Labor Statistics listed over 800 occupations and 400 industries (Bureau of Labor Statistics, 2011). It would be impossible to even try to learn about all the choices for your future. Nevertheless, with a lifetime of work ahead, and so many options, few people feel ready to fully commit without getting their feet wet first.

That is what happened when Sean Aiken graduated, and his adventure grew into a career about exploring the future and its possibilities. With a degree in business, Aiken was undecided about a career direction. Using entrepreneurial, marketing, critical thinking, problem-solving, and communication skills, he arranged for a job search website to sponsor travel expenses. From February 2007 to March 2008, he worked in various locations throughout the United States and Canada, trying a different job every week for a year, hoping to find his passion in the world of work (Belkin, 2007). Instead of receiving wages, he asked employers to donate all of his earnings to a charity, ONE/Make Poverty History, for which he successfully raised $20,401.60 (About the Project, One Week Job). Aiken's journey included such jobs as pilot, preschool teacher, park ranger, Hollywood producer, aquarium host, advertising executive, and veterinary assistant.

After exploring careers for a year, Aiken didn't narrow his choices by selecting one; instead, he widened them to create an entirely new career. He turned his journey into a career as a public speaker and author, in what Lisa Belkin in *The New York Times* described as, "Sean—the-vocation-seeker" (2007). Aiken did not know his passion at the start of his journey, but, having learned about himself and honed many diverse skills along the way, he was prepared to recognize and take advantage of opportunities in the future in an innovative way. While a career exploration tour may not be on your horizon, experiential learning in the world of work can help you gain insight, improve your skills, and lead you in directions that point to the right choices for you.

Job Hopping Pros and Cons

Like Sean Aiken, many young adults find themselves unsure about their career direction, trying one entry-level job and then another. Changing jobs or career fields frequently, or job hopping, has become so common that today's job hopping has been reframed by researchers as "job shopping" (Settersten and Ray, 2010). For those with strong credentials, job shopping offers the chance to see different companies and office cultures, and may lead to salary increases and added responsibilities with each transition. However, for those who struggle to find their footing in the workplace and lack critical skills or education, job hopping can make it harder to transition to the world of work. Frequent job changes may limit opportunities to develop strong mentor relationships and support networks within industries. In addition, many employers look unfavorably on candidates who have bounced from job to job, assuming they have a lack of interest, motivation, or competence.

There are many opportunities to gain real-world exposure to careers before you start your first career-related job. This can help you make better career decisions and decrease early career job hopping. Many of these opportunities can be found through existing programs at the career center at your college.

Peter Dazeley/Digital Vision/Jupiterimages

Experiences in the workplace help you test career decisions as you build your résumé and widen your professional network.

Learn by Doing

Gaining experience in work settings may help you become more directed for your early jobs, even if you still shop around. For some career fields, internships are expected prerequisites, and it would be difficult to gain those entry-level opportunities without prior experiential learning. Exploration in the world of work can also help you learn about employers' expectations and build your network while gaining experience for your résumé.

Internships, externships, or cooperative programs. An internship, externship, or cooperative program give students the chance to combine classroom experience with hands-on learning gained by working in the field. Internships are the most common form of experiential learning and can be completed during the school year as well as summer breaks. According to the National Association of Colleges and Employers (NACE), for an experience to be an internship and not just a part-time job, whether it is paid or unpaid, it must include learning objectives that will help the student gain transferable skills, supervision with feedback, a clear start and end date, and offer proper resources for learning (Artim, Devlin, and Mackes, 2011).

Job shadowing. Job shadowing involves observing and following a person in a work setting. Attending meetings, observing activities, and experiencing the workplace firsthand are all benefits of job shadowing. Although you will not participate in work-related activities, you have the chance to learn and ask questions.

Mentors. Mentor relationships offer opportunities to connect with people in the field, visit places of work, and receive feedback on your ideas, decision making, and job search tools.

Site visits. Many employers offer the opportunity for students to visit their sites through arrangements with career centers. Site visits often include descriptions of the workplace and job opportunities that may be of interest.

Employer visits on campus. Employer visits involve employers coming to your campus to discuss job or internship openings. Although you won't set foot in the work environment, you will meet employees and hear about their experiences on the job. This insight can help you decide whether a particular workplace is interesting to you and how to present your qualifications.

Part-time work. Part-time work can give you the chance to experience a work environment that interests you, and earn money while you contribute your skills. Part-time work can also expose you to an industry and help you build relationships.

Volunteer work. Volunteering in a workplace of interest will offer you the chance to build skills and relationships. This can be a great choice when employers do not have the funds or time to develop an internship, but are still willing to have someone contribute their skills and knowledge. In return, this offers you the chance to observe, learn, gain industry knowledge, and build relationships.

Temporary work. "Temping" can allow you to earn money by performing tasks you have already mastered, such as administrative tasks, while you observe and experience work environments. Many employers also offer temporary-to-permanent employment, where temping serves as a trial period before hiring for entry-level positions.

Informational interviewing. Networking for information, or informational interviewing, allows you to meet with people in your field to learn more about what they do. Road Trip Nation, for instance, is a long-running PBS series that chronicles the journeys of young people as they set out to find answers to their career-related questions. In one episode, the show features students conducting informational interviews with U.S. Secretary of Education, Arne Duncan; California State Superintendent of Public Instruction, Jack O'Connell; and former NFL coach, Darryl Rogers (August 23, 2011, roadtripnation.org). With insider information, viewers learn what it takes to succeed in various fields directly from those who have already built their own success. Learn more about setting up your own informational interviews in **Chapter 6: Relationships**.

Additional opportunities. There are also programs and opportunities for experiential learning for experienced individuals who cannot commit to semester-long internships or to leave their jobs to temp or volunteer. One such program is Vocation Vacation, in which participants pay to engage in short-term experiential learning opportunities set up for potential career changers.

Benefits of Experiential Learning

Here are several additional benefits of experiential learning.

Test career decisions. Education and training is a huge investment of time and money. Experiential learning can help you learn about the industry and change or refocus your direction if you find the real world is not what you expected.

Gain real-world experience. An experiential learning opportunity can expose you to the culture, values, and environment of a workplace. This can help you determine if you feel comfortable and can build relationships, or if you would like to explore other environments.

Build skills. Experiential learning can help you build skills through work tasks. Your participation in real-world projects will help you decide if you like the work and gives you assets for your résumé and self-marketing.

Develop relationships. Any opportunity to work in your field of interest will help you build your network for feedback and advice, to help you learn about job openings in the field, and gain references for future employment.

For students, experiential learning is an important and necessary aspect of preparing for your career launch, because it provides a foundation for decision making and self-marketing for your future job search.

Your Flexible Plan

Explore Career Fields

PLAN OF ANALYSIS

Step 1: Gather Information

What jobs, careers, and industries did you identify as targets for your career exploration?

_____

_____

What skills, preferences, and values are important for these targets?

_____

_____

Describe major trends and key issues concerning the economic, geographic, and other concerns for your target jobs, careers, and industries.

_____

_____

Who are the industry leaders?

_____

Step 2: Evaluate the Information

How reliable and accurate is the information you gathered? How many sources confirmed your findings?

_____

_____

What further information do you want to obtain about jobs, career fields, industries, or organizations in order to assess their compatibility with your self-assessment?

_____

_____

Step 3: Make Conclusions

In the next chapter, you will begin action steps. The first plan of action will involve building connections. Based on your self-assessment and research, list five targets, such as jobs, careers, industries, and/or organizations, in which you want to meet people and build relationships.

1. _____   2. _____   3. _____

4. _____   5. _____

What would you like to learn more about before choosing a direction or applying for jobs? This might include information about diversity in your field of interest, typical career paths, the need for advanced degrees or further training, types of activities that are common for an entry-level employee, or an overview of a typical day. List three topics for further exploration.

1. _____

2. _____

3. _____

Performance Appraisal

Now that you have read the chapter, answer the questions below and complete the Tasks.

1. To explore career fields for your future, a thorough approach requires you to:
   a. Learn about the skills that prepare you for careers of today.
   b. Learn about emerging career trends and the skills they require.
   c. Try out different paths through internships, job shadowing activities, and coursework that relate to your career interests.
   d. All of the above

2. The following reflects changes in the world of work:
   a. Knowledge-workers who provide analysis without creativity are nevertheless likely to find stable, long-term job security.
   b. There is a greater need for specialized or expert skills combined with a broad variety of transferable skills.
   c. Outsourcing is likely to diminish.
   d. None of the above

3. Which of the following is an example of a good, career-exploration question?
   a. Where can I learn about career fields?
   b. What can I do with my major?
   c. Where can I learn about internships?
   d. All of the above

4. Which of the following is true?
   a. To gather information, you must review every website available.
   b. Information is most useful if it comes directly from someone in the field, not from a book or a website.
   c. The best approach to gathering information is to use multiple approaches, including conducting research, informational interviewing, and experiential learning.
   d. Students cannot gather information about careers because they are still in school and not in the real world.

5. Social media can do the following:
   a. Help you attract career information directly to you.
   b. Organize career information.
   c. Locate resources others find helpful.
   d. All of the above

6. Green careers are which of the following?
   a. A fad
   b. Limited to science, technology, engineering, and math (STEM) fields
   c. Becoming integrated into all fields in a variety of positions
   d. Not for recent graduates

7. Which of the following is true about careers and areas of study?
   a. You should limit your career exploration to fields that are common for your major.
   b. Employers will not consider candidates with unrelated majors.
   c. Learning about the transferable skills required for careers can help you assess areas to develop through your coursework and experiential learning.
   d. None of the above

Performance Appraisal Answer Key

1. d 2. b 3. d 4. c 5. d 6. c 7. c

Thought Questions

1. Do you feel prepared to enter a constantly changing world of work? Why or why not?

2. Have you identified information that is important to you, and have a plan and timeline for gathering information?

3. What skills have you identified that are relevant to your career interests? Describe how they relate to your major, activities, and other experiences.

Notes:

_____

_____

_____

_____

_____

TASK 5.1:

What I Want to Know: Four Steps of Career Exploration

What information would help you make decisions about your career options, and the positions, organizations, and industries that would be most appealing to you? First, list five questions for which you would like to find the answers. Next, list the resources you think would be helpful in locating your answers. Use the resources in **Exhibit 5.1**, Career Exploration Questions, **Exhibit 5.2**, Online Resources for Career Exploration, and **Exhibit 5.3**, Professional Associations, to get started, and then go online to see if your resources are guiding you toward the answers you want.

Step 1: Create a List of Questions	Step 2: Identify Resources
Example: 1. What can I do with an English major?	Careers for English Majors (books/online), networking contacts, Occupational Outlook Handbook (OOH), career center, professors
Example: 2. What entry-level jobs are available in publishing?	Professional associations, OOH, career books for English Majors, career center, job listings
1.	
2.	
3.	
4.	
5.	

Step 3: Group Your Questions

Resource	Which Questions Can Be Answered
Example: Occupational Outlook Handbook	use for question 1 & 2

Step 4: Start Your Research

Choose one of your career exploration questions above, and learn about it using the resources you identified. What did you learn?

_____

_____

TASK 5.2:
Explore Your Creativity

If we are entering a new period in which creativity and innovation will be critical career skills, connecting your skills, preferences, and values in creative ways will be important to your future success.

What careers interest you that could combine your assets in unique ways?

_____

_____

How would you develop your assets to increase your marketability for these fields?

_____

_____

TASK 5.3:
Transferable Skills and the Workplace

Every job or career-related experience you have will expose you to certain information, help you build skills, and lay a foundation for your future.

What skills are important for the fields that interest you? Which skills do you have and/or want to develop?

Career that you are considering	Typical tasks and skills used in this field List the skills you expect to use in the related entry-level position	Transferable Skills List transferable skills you have and/or want to develop for the future
Example: *Interior design*	Drawing, sketching, knowledge of interior design, measure spaces, select fabrics, organize materials, space planning, attention to detail	Drawing, sketching, listening, communication, business, project management, creative, color sense

TASK 5.4:
Careers and My Major

There are careers that are directly related to your major. There are also transferable skills you have gained because of your major. In this exercise, you will explore what you studied, what it prepares you for directly, and how it is transferable.

List your major, and three transferable skills that you have gained from your major.

_____

_____

List three career fields for which you are prepared based on your major, activities, and other experiences.

_____

_____

Using the Occupational Outlook Handbook, look up each of the careers. After reading about the field, list and describe the career field that stands out as most interesting.

_____

_____

_____

TASK 5.5:
Experiential Learning

Learning by doing gives you an opportunity to explore careers in the real world.

List three career fields, jobs, or industries you would like to experience.

_____

_____

What experiential learning methods would you consider to learn more in these areas?

_____

_____

Link to CourseMate

On CourseMate, you can find documents to help you update your Career Portfolio as well as additional resources and activities. Here is some of the information you can find online for **Chapter 5: Explore**.

CAREER PORTFOLIO
Your Flexible Plan

RESOURCES
Career Profile: Cody Grant
Career Exploration Questions
Online Resources for Career Development
Professional Associations

StockLite/Shutterstock.com

Relationships

> The end result of kindness is that it draws people to you.
> —*Anita Roddick*

Relationships are a critical component of your ongoing career development. Throughout your work and life, many of your most interesting and rewarding opportunities develop out of your relationships. Building and nurturing genuine relationships can help you gain support, information, and access throughout your career.

What's Inside

Prepare to . . .

- Understand the connection between relationships and career development

- Find information, gain support, and learn about opportunities

- Develop a strategic approach to building your social network

- Learn how to find out about internships

» Real Relationships

Building relationships in your career can provide you with the foundation for many aspects of career success. Your contacts will help you learn about information, find job openings, and offer suggestions for your career. In addition, mentors and connections can provide support and advice for decision making and career exploration. Networking is also invaluable for your future job search. Many estimates suggest that 75 percent or more of all jobs are found through networking. For this reason, networking has been referred to as the "hidden job market." However, to gain access to the hidden job market, it is critical to build relationships and nurture them throughout your career. To take advantage of the benefits of relationships in your career, aim to expand your social network as early as possible, before you are ready for a job search and, ideally, when you are not looking for anything in return.

A real relationship is rooted in trust, respect, and mutual support. A contrived connection is one that is inauthentic and lacks sincerity. Often, when relationships are discussed in the context of one's career, it is about what you can get. Job seekers are often looking for job listings, contacts for business opportunities, or references. However, all of these benefits are more likely to come from real relationships that evolve over time and through genuine interests, rather than contrived connections developed for short-term personal gain.

In *Energize Your Workplace*, Jane E. Dutton explores how interactions characterized by such feelings as trust and mutual positive regard can improve a workplace, while a low-quality interaction that is marked by distrust can be harmful to the individuals as well as the organization (2003). Building meaningful relationships even before you launch your career will help you develop your career and also prepare you with a valuable asset on the job skill. Consider the strategies below for building real relationships that will benefit you throughout your career.

Speaking with professors can lead to stronger relationships and help you learn about additional resources.

Clerkenwell/the Agency Collection/Jupiterimages

Connect through Your Interests

Following up on a genuine interest in your courses can help you expand your network. Choose your most interesting course, and visit the professor during office hours to learn more about his or her area of study or related career fields. In turn, this could lead to greater knowledge about the industry, introductions to former students who are now in the field, and a stronger relationship with a professor who could serve as a reference for future employment opportunities. If the professor recommends additional readings, read them. If he or she recommends a student group, attend the meeting. Then, follow up with an e-mail to share what you learned and develop a dialogue. Real relationships take time to evolve, but your interests can be a great starting point.

Connect through Your Career Exploration

As your career interests develop, meeting people in the world of work will add a personal element to your research. These can include people working in fields that interest you, such as recent graduates from your school and individuals at various levels, as well as those responsible for hiring decisions. You can also develop connections with those who train others for career fields, such as professors or coaches. Having connections in industries, organizations, and positions that interest you will help you learn insider information, gain perspective from others, and learn about jobs when you are ready.

Connect through Online Social Networks

With online social networks, you may have many more "friends" than in the real world. While connecting with someone you never met does not make that person a part of your inner circle, inviting an industry leader or journalist you admire to connect on LinkedIn will allow you to receive updates and potentially interesting insider information. That could include books the person recommends, thoughts about industry issues, and links to articles or blog entries. In a technologically connected world, there is room for different types of online relationships.

Building relationships in terms of how you can mutually benefit, rather than merely how you can benefit, will help you develop a meaningful career network. You may not feel you always have something valuable to offer to the people in your network, but look for opportunities to share ideas, resources, and information when you can. As you learn more about how social networks develop and what you can do to expand your network, you will be positioned to build many types of real relationships for your career development.

>> CAREER JOURNAL ● A Person I Would Like to Meet

Use the space below to write about your thoughts and feelings.

Are there any people you would like to meet for your career development? Who would you seek out for a conversation or advice? Consider one or more of the following: a business owner, industry leader, politician, celebrity, household name, someone in a position of hiring, a person you admire, or a person who has made a difference in the lives of others.

How might he or she help your career development? Is there certain information you think he or she could share? Resources that he or she might suggest? Insight about career paths or suggestions for training, certification, or education?

(Continues)

What other questions would you like to ask? If he or she could tell you anything, what would you most like to know?

How can you reach that person, or reach someone who might be easier to access that would have similar information or advice to offer? For instance, can you find out if the person's organization recruits on your campus? Is there someone within that organization who might offer similar insight? Is there a similar organization that recruits if that one does not? Are there any alumni who work at that organization, or similar organizations? This line of questions will help you target someone with the ability to help you find answers to some of your questions.

How will you thank this person for his or her insight? How important are the answers they can provide? What does this mean to you, and how will it help you?

Journal Feedback... Your career exploration questions and concerns can come to life when a person with real-world experience addresses them. Hearing firsthand about the successes and difficulties others have experienced, and their advice for you, can give you insight. As you reach out to others, becoming more aware of your appreciation for their assistance can help you express gratitude that is sincere and has meaning.

» Types of Social Network Structures

Your social network consists of all the people you know. Your family, friends, professors, work supervisors, colleagues, and coaches are just some of the people already in your network. If you use online social networking, you might already have 300 friends on Facebook, or 150 connections on LinkedIn, and that's great, too. However, developing a meaningful professional social network requires some knowledge about how relationships can impact your career.

Name: Jesse Savran
College Degree: BFA in Communication Arts
Graduate Degree: MA in Communication Arts with a concentration in Media Management *(achieved while working full-time)*
Current Position: Booking Agent and Manager
Employer: Greg Raposo

Courtesy of Josh Freeman

Describe your work.

For the past seven years, since I was 18, I've been booking concerts for Greg Raposo, who has been active in the music industry for close to two decades. He's a solo artist, but he was a member of Dream Street, a five-member boy band with Jesse McCartney that sold close to a million CD's before breaking up in 2002. I've booked well over a hundred concerts and 7 tours for Greg. I've booked him at venues, colleges, festivals, military bases, and as a headliner at several charity events I produced. I've also been Greg's tour manager for two tours of Costa Rica. In addition to booking and managing Greg, I also work full-time for an agent who handles client management for high profile television talent, where I get a lot of training and experience.

Tell us how you started your career.

I have two older brothers who were both in bands, so I was always around music and local musicians. When I was 16, I started booking shows, first at our local community center, then all over the area. I developed relationships with many of the bands and started creating professionally packaged compilation CDs that sold for a profit. I produced four CDs in high school and college that sold over four thousand copies in total. Through connections I made at the venues, I also took a job as security at one of the clubs. One night, a kid from my high school, Greg Raposo, was performing. I knew who he was and that he was in a boy band, and he knew who I was—that I was involved in the local music scene. We became friends, and we'd brainstorm about our ideas. I didn't become his booking agent and manger right away. That happened later.

Tell us a little about your academic experience.

I had a great time in high school but was never the best student. I definitely wasn't thinking I'd be in six more years of school. But with touring in-between semesters and shows on the weekends, undergrad went really quick. I wanted to graduate on time, and I wanted to do well. I did—and I graduated with honors. I also got the idea that when you took classes you were interested in, it was more fun, and easier, because you wanted to learn the topics. Now at 25, I feel like a professional. Even the idea of going to law school excites me. I don't think of it as more school, just a stepping-stone.

From Jesse's Employer

Name: Greg Raposo
Title: Musician, Solo Artist

Courtesy of David Sanders

How does Jesse demonstrate his ability to make genuine connections with people?

Jesse talks to everyone, and he is a real person. With me, he showed interest, and respected what I did. He wanted to learn. As the artist, I always felt like he was genuinely interested, not trying to take advantage. I trust him and the ideas he brings to the table. He'll call people and talk to them. Here's an example. We covered a song from the band Akcent, based in Romania, and we needed to get permission to put the song on our album. Jesse went online to research who to speak to, and, with the seven-hour time difference in Romania, he coordinated everything in the middle of the night. After a week of talks, he finalized the deal. He's passionate about what he does. He really loves it. He loves being on tour, meeting everyone, and making things happen.

What skills and assets help make Jesse a team player?

Jesse's a very positive person. Even if he's upset, he never wants to give up. He listens to people, he talks to them, and he really cares, so he tries to make things work. Jesse's the kind of person who's always thinking of new things, different ways to promote our band or plan our budget. He's also very detail-oriented. If we want to do a show, I'll run it by him and he'll figure out every last detail on how to make it run as smooth as possible. He has great math skills, and we need that for the budget. He also takes initiative. If I give him an idea, he'll just take it and run.

How did Jesse build relationships that helped him develop his career?

_____

_____

_____

How would you describe Jesse's professional reputation?

_____

_____

_____

For additional questions, visit CourseMate.

Developing connections beyond your inner circle can help you learn about opportunities.

(Photo credit: © John Lund/Blend Images/Corbis)

Understanding Social Networks

As you develop real relationships throughout your career, you may find some connections provide more meaningful career information, support, or resources than others. Understanding types of social networks can help you plan an approach for building your network that widens your circle while helping you nurture your existing relationships.

Strong and weak ties. One theoretical approach separates your strongest relationships from your weakest (Grannovetter, 1973). The people you know well make up your closest circle, or "strong ties." This may include your family, close friends, and others with whom you communicate often. These connections provide personal support, advice, and camaraderie. If they know of job openings or leads, they will tell you right away, because they are in close contact with you. People you know, but not very well, such as a family friend, a professor, or a former employer are your "weak ties." They may have information about job openings or connections with others in your fields of interest, but would never think to tell you, because they may not know about your interests or career needs.

Social resources theory. This theory suggests that the value of your connections is built on the extent to which you build a network that has access to the knowledge, information, and people you want to contact (Lin, Ensel, and Vaughn, 1981). However, adding weak ties with social resources is also important in this approach. For example, you may need to go outside your network of strong ties to meet people with additional social resources. If you meet many connections, but none have the resources you want, you might find yourself frustrated by the time and effort you have spent networking.

Structural holes theory. Another theory addresses patterns of relationships by identifying "structural holes" in social networks (Burt, 1992). Structural holes theory suggests that it is not enough to have weak ties; the ties themselves must not have strong ties to each other. In other words, your connections should belong to a number of different social networks, so that with each new connection, you network into a new group.

Applying the Theory to Your Own Social Network

Theories about social networks can help you build relationships because each approach helps you expand your network in different ways. Here are some strategies for expanding your social network using these theories.

Let your extended network know your needs. Because your weak ties could have information that could help you, but will not necessarily know your needs, you may have to spread the word when you want support, insight, or assistance. E-mail and social media provide easy methods for sharing news about graduation, a job search, or a new internship. Letting others know about your accomplishments and when you want more information can help them connect with you if they can help. Personal e-mails or phone calls can also help you connect.

Nurture relationships outside your inner circle. Many people spend more time nurturing relationships with those in their inner circle than developing a wide circle of weak ties. A next step could include strengthening your connections with the weak and strong ties you already have. If you read an article that seems useful for a weak tie, send it along with a personal note. If the person comes to mind, say hello and ask them how they are doing. If you notice an accomplishment or new activity through a post or update, comment and engage in a conversation.

Add weak ties. There are many ways to add connections you do not know well. Social media is an excellent resource for developing weak ties because it is easy to add connections who are mere acquaintances. By following them or reading their updates and posts, you can learn more about them and respond regularly to build a connection. Another way to build weak ties is to meet people through alumni events or professional association meetings.

Add connections with social resources. To seek out connections with social resources, it is not always necessary to aim solely for high-status or high-level connections. You can include people in your target industries, organizations, and career fields. Mentor programs, student and alumni networking events, and committee work through professional associations offer a structured environment for you to meet and build career-related connections.

Build relationships with structural holes. To build relationships with people who are not connected to each other, first assess your network to see which of your contacts know each other. Build your network with connections from different colleges, different positions and organizations, and even different parts of the country, or the world.

Theories about networking can help you build a results-oriented network without lacking the genuine quality of real relationships. By increasing the number of your connections and types of relationships, you can be assured that when you have a specific question or career development concern, you will have a wider circle that can help you address your needs.

» Expand Your Social Network

Building your social network involves some strategy, a bit of effort, and may take a dose of courage to talk to people you don't know, but the benefits are well worth it. Because an effective network is rooted in genuine relationships and common interests, building your network does not involve gimmicky sales pitches or self-promotion. This straightforward three-step approach can help you build connections and develop them for your career.

Identify Your Connections

Start building your social network by looking at your existing relationships. Consider people you know well, such as your inner circle of friends, your family, and the people closest to you. Then, start to think about people you know, but do not know well, and those you know through specific tasks or interests, such as members of a study group, teammates, or work friends. All of these groups exhibit varying qualities and strengths of relationships. Shifting gears to online relationships, review your lists of friends, contacts, and followers. Given all of your relationships, consider where you have strong ties, weak ties, structural holes in your social networks, and how you can develop relationships with those who have the most social resources. This assessment of the types of networks you have already developed can help you identify areas where your networking can be improved.

Taking the time to follow up and thank others shows your appreciation for their time and assistance.

Malyugin/Shutterstock.com

Reach Out to Others

Building your social network can start out naturally. One approach is to reflect on your career research questions and what you want to know. Next, consider who might have this information. Ask people in your inner circle—your strong ties—and your extended network—your weak ties—if they know anyone who might have that information. Consider reaching out to your friends' friends, family's friends, and your friends' families, as well as advisors, school administrators, professors in your major and in other departments, coaches, and religious leaders. You can also join a mentor programs, access an alumni database, attend alumni events, and speak to people in student groups or professional associations. Asking for an introduction from someone you already know can help break the ice, and create a deeper bond. An introduction can be helpful for online networking, too. After you reach out to others, let them know why you want to connect and thank them when they have helped. (See **Exhibit 6.4**, LinkedIn request, and **Exhibit 6.5**, Networking E-mail Thank You Letter.)

Turn Connections into Relationships

Now that you have made a connection, make it count. Learn more about your connections by reading their online profiles or bios, offer information that you think could interest them, and follow up. Let your career-related connections know when their advice has been useful, such as in an interview or if you pursued a volunteer opportunity that was recommended. Although you may appreciate help that was offered by a networking contact, without a thank you note, e-mail, or other gesture, your contacts may not know how helpful they were. If a contact does not seem to be able to provide the type of assistance that can help you, acknowledge your contact's effort and show respect for his or her time and limitations.

≫ WORK WITH AWARENESS ● Connect Around Causes

Connecting with people in the careers that interest you, in other social networks, and at different stages of their careers may seem like a challenge. These are not your everyday friendships or relationships. The truth is, it can be challenging to develop sincere, meaningful relationships with people you call through an alumni database or meet at a networking event. You may have nothing in common, or, at best, find it difficult to reach common ground. Getting involved in social causes that are truly important to you can be a great way to expand your network and forge authentic connections that lead to real relationships.

Volunteerism Showcases Workplace Skills and Values

When you work hard for something that is important to you, it shows. As a volunteer, your interests and talents are revealed to a wide social circle, because volunteering brings people together from diverse backgrounds to benefit a common cause. Volunteering is also an opportunity to showcase your punctuality, work ethic, dedication, and positive attitude. All of these demonstrate workplace skills. As a volunteer, the people you meet will be more likely to extend an offer to help you, because you have shown that you share similar values and are willing to contribute your time and effort for these causes.

How Volunteer Activities Help Build Connections

As you volunteer, you meet people and get to know each other. You can build trust, friendships, and respect as you prove your value on projects and tasks. Because all volunteers have their own social networks, unconnected to yours, there is a greater likelihood your new connections will know someone who is not already connected to your social groups.

Choose Meaningful Volunteer Activities

To learn more about volunteer opportunities, search online by the cause that interests you or search websites dedicated to volunteering. The closer your activities match your real interests, the easier it will be for you to connect with others involved in the cause.

Here are a few suggestions for locating volunteer opportunities by location:

serve.gov

idealist.org

dosomething.org

volunteermatch.org

Tell Others about Your Social Causes

Once you have picked your causes, share the news. You can like or follow many charitable organizations, and then, when people view your social media profiles, they can learn about the social causes you value. This can help strengthen your bond with connections who share your social concerns, or help you find others with similar values. You can also use LinkedIn's Volunteer Experience and Causes feature to highlight your volunteer activities. A survey of LinkedIn users suggests employers prefer those who contribute through volunteer work (Subbaraman, 2011). Your volunteer activities can get employers' attention for your internship search as well.

Social media is a great tool for relationship building. You can search online for the names, organizations, and positions of many of the people in the networks of your friends, family members, and acquaintances. Having this information available to you can help you identify people with whom you want to network, and it gives the names of those who can provide the introductions.

Learn about your connections. To expand your social network, use LinkedIn, Google+, and Facebook to learn about those in your circle. First, read about your connections. You may not realize what they have been doing recently, how many interesting people they know, where they have worked, or the activities or professional associations to which they belong. You can request introductions to people in their network, or explore information or organizations that seem interesting.

Expand your network. To connect with others, instead of sending random, automatic invites, build new connections through existing connections and personal requests. Write a note to the person you know, and ask her to forward the message to her connection. Prepare messages that are professional and respectful. Increase your chances for success by writing clear, concise, and gracious messages that explain why you are writing. If you don't know the person you are contacting, let him know why you want to "connect" or be "friends" and add the name of your mutual acquaintance. (See **Exhibit 6.4**, LinkedIn Request, for personalizing a request on LinkedIn.)

Social networking etiquette. Lindsey Pollak gives the advice, "If You Wouldn't Do It in Person, Don't Do It on LinkedIn!" in the title of a blog post, where she adds, "Say thank you early and often," "customize every connection request you send," and "don't pester." These simple suggestions reflect traditional networking tips, and are a reminder that online networking should follow the same rules as offline relationship building (Pollak, 2011).

>> Six Steps for Informational Interviewing

To explore careers, you may have some questions that are best answered through research and online resources, while other questions require the perspective of someone in an industry. Informational interviewing is your opportunity to find these answers and generate new questions. In addition, through informational interviews, you can learn what employers are seeking, where jobs are listed, and you may even learn about jobs that have not been listed. Learning about the hidden job market is a valuable resource in your career development and is also explored in **Chapter 9: Launch**, but if you set up informational interviews in the hopes of receiving a job offer, you will most likely be disappointed. These meetings are a chance for you to learn about employers and gather as much information as possible.

You are the interviewer in these meetings, and your goal is to ask questions that help you gather information while making a connection. You will be expected to have questions to ask and to keep track of time during the meeting.

In addition to prepared questions, you should prepare answers to the most common interview questions before your networking meetings, as your contact may seek to gauge your knowledge or interest in the field. Your preparation should also include a basic understanding of the person's position, organization, and industry. Follow

iStockphoto.com/Phillip Jones

Preparing in advance can help you make the most of informational interviews.

these steps to develop a plan for informational interviewing that provides you with the information you want while using time effectively.

Step 1: Review Your Research Questions

If you have already developed a list of career research questions, review the resources where you expect to find the best answers. Assess which questions you would like to look up online or in books, and which are most appropriate for asking the people in your network. Then you will be ready to develop a list of networking questions.

Step 2: Develop Networking Questions

Listing networking questions can help you organize your thoughts, and you will start to see that your questions may fall into categories (see **Exhibit 6.1**, Networking Questions). Consider the questions that will best help you gather the information that is most important to you, and leave time for natural conversation. This will prepare you to plan who will have the best information for the areas in which you want insight.

Step 3: Determine Whom to Contact

Much like your evaluation of online resources for career information, some contacts are better for some questions than others. Not all of your questions will be appropriate for all meetings or for all contacts. Realizing how your questions could differ with someone in an entry-level, mid-level, or senior-level position is also useful. In other words, everyone is a potentially great contact, if you ask questions that are suited for his or her knowledge areas, experience, and time in the industry, field, or position.

Networking Contacts	Possible Information
Entry-Level Contact or Recent Graduate	job search information, entry-level job requirements, transitioning into the field, adjusting to the culture of the industry
Mid-Level Contact or Mid-Career Individual	educational or training required for mobility within the field, professional associations and organizational committees to join, experiences that help new hires shine and demonstrate star potential, various alternatives for career paths over time
Senior-Level Contact, Experienced Individual, or Retiree	trends and shifts in the industry, history of major industry-related events, weaknesses and strengths of key organizations and leaders, forecasting of possible future developments

Step 4: Request Informational Interviews

To request informational interviews, first send an introductory e-mail. Most informational interviews will be with people you don't know, including referrals from friends and family as well as alumni contacts or others in the field. Your e-mail request can include details about you and what you hope to gain from the conversation, as well as how you learned of the contact and any other critical details about your referral. (See **Exhibit 6.3**, Informational Interview Request.) If possible, arrange for the amount of time your interview should take, so that you can plan your schedule accordingly. Generally, a half hour is appropriate.

Step 5: Conduct Informational Interviews

As you start the meeting, you will want to introduce yourself and reiterate what interested you in setting up the meeting. Then, allow for conversation while asking as many of your questions as you would like within the scheduled time. (See the tips in **Exhibit 6.2**, Sample Structure of an Informational Interview.)

Step 6: After the Meeting

At the end of a networking meeting you are expected to send a thank you letter. This can be done via e-mail, in a business-style letter, or using a personal note card. Use your judgment regarding the formality of the meeting as well as the nature of how you met the contact to determine the method to thank them as well as what you might say. (See **Exhibit 6.5**, Networking E-mail Thank You Letter.) Thank you notes should be sent within 24–48 hours.

≫ EXHIBIT 6.1 ● Networking Questions

General Questions
These questions will help you understand more about your networking contact and his or her job or organization.

- What led you to pursue a career in _____?
- What do you like most/least about your job?

- What other positions have you held in this field (or other fields if the person changed careers)?
- What educational background or training do you have? Do you feel that prepared you well for this field?
- What motivates you in your work?
- Why do you like most/least about working for _____ (name or type of organization)?

- What do you like about your colleagues, supervisors, and, in general, your work relationships?
- How would you describe the office culture?
- Is there a lot of opportunity to work in teams? Is there a lot of opportunity to work independently?
- What is a typical day or week like?

Career Path Questions

These questions will help you understand more about your networking-contact's knowledge of how to develop a career in the industry.

- What advice would you give to someone starting a career in _____?
- Is there anything you would do differently if you were to start your career over?
- What education or training do you think would prepare me best for this field?
- What is the typical next step if I were to start in an entry-level position in _____?
- What directions have you seen this career path lead to?
- What degrees, certification, or licensure will help someone move ahead in this career?
- What trends have you noticed?

"What to do next" Questions

These questions will help you understand more about your networking-contact's ideas about how you can continue your exploration process.

- Are there any organizations you would recommend joining?
- I have heard of the _____ association; is this one you would recommend becoming involved with?

- Is there anyone else you would recommend I contact? *If yes, then follow with:* Can I mention your name when I contact her or him?
- Are there any websites or books you would recommend I read to learn more about the field?
- May I follow up with you? What would be the best method to contact you (phone, e-mail, traditional mail)? [Always obtain the information you need to send a thank you note, too.]

Internship or Job Search Questions

Part-time and full-time job seekers or those seeking to build credentials through work opportunities often want to ask a few questions, namely, "Do you have any positions open?" and "Can you recommend me?" While these certainly cover the information you may want, they can have a negative outcome; the direct style can be off-putting to some, informational interviewees may not know all the jobs available, and most networking contacts will not provide a formal recommendation unless they know a candidate well (although they may be willing to have their name mentioned).

Nevertheless, there are questions that are absolutely appropriate. Here are some examples:

- Where are jobs in this field most typically listed (e.g., company websites, professional association websites, journals, other)?
- I would be interested in finding out about positions in your organization; how does your organization typically list open positions? Could I mention your name, and that we met/spoke/other?
- I want you to know that I recently applied for the _____ position listed on your company's website; could I send a follow-up letter mentioning some of the details I learned about the company from our conversation?

>> **EXHIBIT 6.2** ● **Sample Structure of an Informational Interview**

- Thank the contact for meeting with you.
- Mention the amount of time you initially agreed to speak (15 minutes, 1/2 hour, hour, more). For example: "I know you said you would be available for a 15-minute conversation. I will keep track of the time for us, as I know you have a very busy day."
- Give a brief description of why you wanted to set up the meeting (can be similar to your answer for "Tell me about yourself" in interviews).

- Start with a general question that truly interests you.
- Several minutes before the conversation is scheduled to end, wind down the conversation and do not ask additional questions that require detailed answers.
- If the contact wishes to speak longer, request an additional meeting (perhaps at their office or over coffee), rather than extend the existing meeting. Prepare a new set of questions and areas you wish to discuss.

Leticia Beason: Networking for Information

Leticia entered college without a clear focus, and chose a major and activities based on her interests and the classes she enjoyed. She hoped her career direction would become clear later on. This led her to major in sociology, join a sorority, and successfully land a place on the university dance team.

After a semester abroad in the fall of her third year, Leticia returned to school unclear about her career interests. In addition, she was about to hold two very demanding, year-long leadership roles, as captain of the dance team and public relations (PR) representative of her sorority.

Leticia approached her academic advisor to discuss her career concerns. She was encouraged to visit the career center, and participate in an alumni-student mentor program in which she could be paired with a recent graduate in a career areas that interested her. After reading the list of alumni in the program, she chose a mentor working in public relations, since she was holding a related position in her sorority.

At the career center, Leticia was directed to online resources where she could learn about the field. She contacted her mentor and shared her interests and career uncertainty. Because the mentor lived nearby, they planned an in-person meeting. Leticia followed the recommendations in the mentor program handbook, dressing in professional attire and bringing her résumé to the meeting.

What steps did Leticia take to gather information for her career exploration?

What questions could Leticia ask during the meeting with her mentor? How would these questions help Leticia?

To learn more about Leticia's career development, visit CourseMate 💻. View her résumé and job search materials in **Chapter 8: Tools.**

© Cengage Learning 2014

▶▶ EXHIBIT 6.3 ● Informational Interview Request

Here is an example of a request from a student with no experience in the field.

To:	rkdonald@donaldgorhamevents.com
Cc:	
Bcc:	
Subject:	Student Referred by Professor David Wheeler

Dear Mr. Donald,

I am a junior at University of Arizona and am writing at the suggestion Professor David Wheeler. After discussing my interest in exploring a career in event planning, Professor Wheeler recommended I contact you. He spoke very highly of your success as an event planner, and I was hoping you might be available for an informational interview. I have researched the field online and am trying to decide if event planning would be a good fit for me. I hope to learn more about your experiences, as well as the skills and abilities that you think are essential. I would also like to learn more about what I can do now as a college student to prepare myself for this field.

I would greatly appreciate it if I could meet with you for a short informational interview. I will call you next week to set up an appointment. In addition, I can be reached at 702.555.5555 or at this e-mail address. I would like to thank you in advance for your assistance.

Best regards,

Leticia Beason

© Cengage Learning 2014

LinkedIn generates an automatic request to request a connection, shown here. Note that it does not help the recipient understand the context of the request, nor remind the recipient of any details about the sender.

LinkedIn

Leticia Beason requested to add you as a connection on LinkedIn:

I'd like to add you to my professional network on LinkedIn.

-Leticia

[Accept]   <u>View invitation from Leticia Beason</u>

By modifying your request on LinkedIn, as shown here, you can be more specific and personal when you request a connection on LinkedIn. LinkedIn restricts the number of characters allowed per message. Note that although this is short, the note offers enough information to inform the recipient of details about the sender. Use a formal greeting, such as Mr. or Ms., unless you are certain that addressing your contact by a first name is appropriate.

LinkedIn

Leticia Beason requested to add you as a connection on LinkedIn

Dear Ryan,

It was great to speak with you yesterday. I really enjoyed our conversation regarding my interest in a career in event planning, and would like to add you to my network. Thank you.

Best Regards,

Leticia Beason

[Accept]   <u>View invitation from Leticia Beason</u>

It is also possible to send a personalized message on LinkedIn to be introduced to someone you have never met, shown here. Select the category "expertise request," and the subject can be written "informational interview."

Your message to Donna O'Grady: *Include a brief note for Ryan Donald:*

Send Donna a message   ✕

Include others on this message

To: Donna O'Grady

Subject: | Informational interview |

Dear Ms. O'Grady,

We have a mutual connection, Ryan Donald, who is an alumnus from my college, University of Arizona. I am interested in a career in event planning, and hoping to learn more about the field. I was impressed by your profile, and would like to schedule a brief conversation or informational interview.

Best Regards,

Leticia Beason

[Send Message]   or Cancel

Send Ryan a message   ✕

Include others on this message

To: Ryan Donald

Subject: | Informational Interview |

Dear Ryan,

Thank you again for our meeting. I was reviewing your profile, and noticed you have a connection, Donna O'Grady, at Jones Event Productions in Phoenix. I was hoping you would forward her this message exploring the possibility of scheduling a brief conversation or informational interview. Thank you very much.

Best Regards,

Leticia Beason

[Send Message]   or Cancel

>> EXHIBIT 6.5 ● Networking E-Mail Thank You Letter

Everyone in your networking experience should be thanked with personal notes that address the type of assistance provided. Mentors, friends, and family who provide insight, information, contacts, and other types of career support are also worthy of personalized thank you notes. In many cases, e-mail is an appropriate method of communication; occasionally, business letters, handwritten notes, or brief and immediate text or e-mail messages may be most appropriate.

To: davidwheeler@rcc.edu
Cc:
Bcc:
Subject: Thank you

Dear Professor Wheeler,

Thank you so much for encouraging me to contact your former student, Ryan Donald. He invited me to meet with him at the Marriott Hotel, where he is working with their in-house event-planning team. I greatly enjoyed learning more about the process of developing a large-scale corporate event. Ryan introduced me to his colleagues, and answered many of my questions about the industry. In addition, he provided feedback on my resume, and gave me suggestions for highlighting my activities in my cover letters and during interviews. Although Ryan's firm does not have any openings, I learned that the Marriott offers an internship program and I intend to apply.

Again, thank you for your offer to serve as a reference, too. I will stay in touch with details about my ongoing exploration, including which positions I consider and when you might be called as a reference. My conversation with Ryan further confirmed that this is the right direction for me, and I am looking forward to building my experience! I look forward to following up with you soon.

Best regards,

Leticia Beason

>> EMBRACING DIFFERENCES ● Disclosing a Disability

If you have a disability or special needs, you may be wondering when and how to discuss your disability with contacts in your industry or whether you should disclose your disability at all. You may want to learn more about whether a career is a good fit for someone with your needs. Informational interviews can help you explore these questions.

When to Disclose Your Disability

There is no requirement to share information about your disability. However, if you are planning for an informational interview, you may need accommodations or require information that can help you ensure that your meeting will run smoothly, for example, being able to easily access the meeting location. In addition, you may want to disclose information to help your networking contact understand or prepare for some of the networking questions you wish to discuss, especially if your purpose is to explore information about working with a hidden or visible disability. Consider your needs and your goals for the meeting, and then determine the best time and place to disclose your disability, or whether to disclose it at all.

If you are in a job or internship search, your concerns may be different. The Department of Labor's Office of Disability Employment Policy suggests that, if you decide to disclose your disability, consider doing so at one of these stages of a job search (n.d):

1. In a letter of application or cover letter
2. Before an interview
3. At the interview
4. In a third-party phone call or reference
5. Before any drug testing for illegal drugs
6. After you have a job offer
7. During your course of employment
8. Never

How to Disclose Your Disability

To disclose your disability, consider directing the discussion toward your strengths and assets, while giving practical solutions for reasonable accommodations if they are needed. Developing talking points that address your needs, as well as your ability to perform the job well, can provide a foundation for strong, effective communication. Developing a script that you practice in advance can help you prepare. A career counselor, family member, friend, or mentor may be a good person to help.

A positive approach can help you connect with others, build your network, display your enthusiasm, and help you determine that a job or career is not right for you. It is up to you to determine your goals for the discussion, and whether they have been achieved.

What to Disclose

If you decide to disclose information about your disability, the Department of Labor's Office of Disability Employment Policy suggests that the following information may be the most important (n.d):

- General information about your disability
- Why you are disclosing your disability
- How your disability affects your ability to perform key job tasks
- Types of accommodations that have worked for you in the past
- Types of accommodations you anticipate needing in the workplace

These topics are options that can form the foundation for talking points in the script you prepare. This will allow you a goal-oriented discussion that addresses your needs while helping you move forward toward building a connection with the person with whom you are meeting.

» Networking for Internships

Networking for internships is a lot like networking for information, except that you are seeking concrete information about current openings. This type of networking should involve contacting people with whom you have real relationships, as well as building genuine connections with new contacts. Following up with information, appreciative thank you notes, and new information that can help your contacts will lead to more information and new leads.

Locate Opportunities

There are many places to find out about internships, and these include the websites of organizations where you would like to work, job boards, volunteer boards, your

wavebreakmedia ltd/Shutterstock.com

Research company and industry websites before reaching out to your network to explore internships.

career center, and industry-specific websites. It is easy to apply for open positions, but, even in these cases, your résumé will get more attention if you can add the name of a person who is connected to the organization or position.

Create a List of Potential Opportunities

If you cannot find internships, or if you have specific companies in mind that are not listing any opportunities, consider soliciting them. By identifying target organizations, you can create a list of places where you would like to intern, work, or volunteer. Many times, employers would like to add someone to their team, but have not yet developed a position, or would rather not start the involved process of listing a position, especially for volunteer projects, part-time work, or internships. In fact, many organizations take so few interns each year that they never formally list these opportunities. If an organization is of particular interest to you, do not hesitate to add them to your target list, even if no position is listed. In these cases, find a person to whom you can direct your résumé and cover letter, such as a department head or human resources executive. Then, send an e-mail cover letter explaining your skills and experience and describing the type of position you are seeking. Following up with a phone call and e-mail may also be necessary to learn whether an opening is available.

Identify Connections

If you have connections at your target organizations, contact them and discuss the positions that interest you or those you would like to create. In most cases, you will not have connections at these organizations, and you will have to build them. Finding the friends of friends by speaking with people directly and reading about your contacts online are two ways to find people through your network. Speaking with others can help you find insider information, like details about a position or information about the company. This can help you tailor your cover letter and résumé for the specific needs of the organization and make your application stand out.

Your Flexible Plan

Invest in Your Relationships

PLAN OF ACTION

Step 1: Set Broad Objectives

To set objectives, consider your answers to the following questions.

Can you answer this question?	If not, what must you do next?

Whom do you want to meet?

What do you want to discuss?

When—what is your timeline for building connections?

Where do you need to go to meet people and build your network?

Why will this be helpful to you at this time?

How will you reach these people?

Using the Who, What, When, Where, Why, and How questions as a guide, state three broad objectives for building relationships at this stage in your career.
Example: I want to meet people in my field and learn more about how they got started.

1. _____

2. _____

3. _____

Will your objectives for building connections help you make decisions and market yourself for your career? If they will not help you, then you must rework your objectives.

Step 2: Identify Specific Goals

Identify three goals that will help you meet your broad objectives. Aim for goals that you believe you can achieve.
Example: Meet people (broad objective) by talking with alumni (goal).

1. _____

2. _____

3. _____

Step 3: Define Action Steps

Choose one goal and list the steps you will take to achieve it.
Example: (1) Contact the alumni association at my college. (2) Learn how to reach alumni. (3) Choose alumni to contact. (4) Write an e-mail to each person to introduce myself. (5) Prepare networking questions while waiting for responses.

List your action steps.

Goal: _____

1. _____

2. _____

3. _____

4. _____

5. _____

6. _____

Performance Appraisal

Now that you have read the chapter, answer the questions below and complete the Tasks.

1. To build relationships for your career, you must do the following:
   a. Focus only on building relationships with contacts who give you job leads.
   b. Contact people only when you need something.
   c. Make genuine connections with a wide range of people.
   d. b and c.

2. The following information is based on theories about social networks:
   a. Strong ties are more important than weak ties.
   b. It can be helpful to build relationships with people who do not know each other.
   c. You do not need to build relationships with people who have social resources, because students already have these.
   d. None of the above.

3. Which of the following is an example of a good networking contact?
   a. A professor
   b. A graduate of your school
   c. A family friend
   d. All of the above

4. Which of the following is true?
   a. To build meaningful relationships, send a form letter to everyone you know and ask them to forward it to everyone they know.
   b. To build meaningful relationships, think about topics that genuinely interest you, and follow up with people who might know more about these topics.
   c. To build meaningful relationships, send personalized e-mails that explain why you are writing, and follow up with thank you e-mails or letters to everyone who has offered to assist you.
   d. b and c.

5. The following is true about volunteer work:
   a. It can help you meet people with common interests, in different social networks
   b. You cannot expand your network in volunteer positions.
   c. Volunteer work does not help you build your career.
   d. b and c.

6. Online social networks are a way to do the following:
   a. Learn about people who work in organizations and careers that interest you.
   b. Identify active professional associations in your field.
   c. Connect with friends of friends through introductions.
   d. All of the above.

7. Which of the following is true about informational interviewing and networking?
   a. Your connections can help you find out about volunteer work, internships, and job openings that are never formally listed.
   b. Your social connections will not help you unless you are ready for a job search.
   c. You do not need to have answers to basic interview questions for informational interviews, because none of your contacts will ask you questions or seek to learn about your skills, experience, or interests.
   d. If you discuss your career interests with someone in an informal setting and they are especially helpful, such as meeting someone at a social event who gives you the names of additional networking contacts, you do not need to send a thank you note because it was not a formal informational interview.

Performance Appraisal Answer Key

1. c
2. b
3. d
4. d
5. a
6. d
7. a

Thought Questions

1. Do you feel prepared to speak with people in the world of work? Why or why not?

2. Have you developed a list of questions about careers that will help you gather information from people during your career exploration?

3. What can you do to improve your ability to build real relationships and connect with others in careers that interest you?

Notes:

_____

_____

_____

_____

_____

_____

TASK 6.1:
Identify Your Social Network

Who is in your social network, and whom else do they know? List three people . . . who you think might have information for your career. Then, using your knowledge of the friends of your connections, or online resources such as LinkedIn or Facebook, list three more people each of your contacts knows whom you would like to meet.

1. _____   1. _____ (names of three connections of your contact)

   (your contact)   2. _____

                        3. _____

2. _____   1. _____ (names of three connections of your contact)

   (your contact)   2. _____

                        3. _____

3. _____   1. _____ (names of three connections of your contact)

   (your contact)   2. _____

                        3. _____

Describe the information or resources these contacts might offer.

_____

_____

_____

TASK 6.2:
Create a Networking Wish List

Creating a networking wish list is a chance to dream up all the people you would like to speak with in your job search. Networking can involve an in-person meeting, a phone call, a chance encounter, an e-mail exchange, or any type of personal encounter. You already identified the questions you would like to know; now, you will be listing the people you would like to speak with to ask some of these important questions. Perhaps you know someone who knows someone else in the industry where you want to work. Right now, you may not know whom others know, but, when you are in a job search, by networking graciously and appropriately, you will begin to find contacts in many places!

List both the people you know, people with whom you think you could meet through others, and anyone you don't know but with whom you would like to speak. Do not restrict yourself! List friends, family, family friends or friends' families, past employers or colleagues, people you know through social activities, or people you would like to know, but can't imagine you would ever meet! Would you like to contact the CEO of your dream company, someone in your ideal position, a person who has the power to hire you, or maybe someone who would be your boss? The point of this exercise is to create a wish list, and then develop a more concrete, actual list of "real" contacts.

Step 1: List the people you wish you could meet or speak with.

Step 2: List people you know who might have similar information.

Step 3: List people who might know someone else with similar information.

People You Wish You Could Meet	What You Want to Learn from This Person	People *You Know* Who Might Have Similar Information

TASK 6.3:

Develop a Networking E-Mail Letter

Using **Exhibit 6.3**, Informational Interview Request, create your own sample e-mail networking letter. Choose an actual person you wish to reach, and then write a letter that details the type of information you would like. You can request an informational interview, or ask for feedback on your résumé or other materials. This is your opportunity to get the information and assistance that will help you. Add this to your Career Portfolio for future reference.

_____

_____

_____

_____

_____

TASK 6.4:
Identify Your Talking Points

During your networking meetings and informational interviews, your contacts might ask you about your experiences, your career interests, and your relevant skills. Having a few talking points will help you answer these questions and demonstrate that you have prepared for the meetings. Reflect on your self-assessment to address the following key areas that influence your career preparation.
Possible Talking Points:

Career Interests. List up to three areas that you are exploring, and why they are of interest to you.

_____

_____

Experience. List coursework, activities, and other experiences that have helped you build skills for the career areas that interest you most.

_____

_____

Skills. List the most significant skills you have for the career areas that interest you most.

_____

_____

TASK 6.5:
Conduct an Informational Interview

Using contacts through family or friends, your career center, alumni contacts, or anyone in your network, schedule an informational interview. Use the chart below to prepare.

Time and Date of Informational Interview:

Contact Name:

How You Know This Contact:

Organization or Affiliation:

What You Hope to Learn:

Questions You Most Want to Ask:

Link to CourseMate 🖥

On CourseMate, you can find documents to help you update your Career Portfolio as well as additional resources and activities. Here is some of the information you can find online for **Chapter 6: Relationships**.

CAREER PORTFOLIO
Your Flexible Plan
Informational Interview Request
Networking E-mail Thank You Letter

RESOURCES
Career Profile: Jesse Savran

iStockphoto.com/Aldo Murillo

Decision Making

> Life is the sum of all your choices. —*Albert Camus*

What's Inside

What Decisions Are Next?

Improve Your Decision-Making Skills

Create Opportunity from Unexpected Events

Choose a Major, Further Education, or Training

Move from Decisions to Action

Prepare to . . .

- Explore decisions you will make throughout your career

- Consider approaches to decision making and the value of a decision-making model

- Understand how to make decisions in an uncertain world

- Consider key questions to improve your educational choices

- Learn strategies for difficult decision making and move towards action steps

Making career decisions involves reflecting on your self-assessment, prioritizing your concerns, and incorporating them into your understanding of the world of work. Throughout your career there will be big decisions, such as choosing a major or a career direction, as well as small steps, like selecting activities and courses that will help you build skills and credentials. Improving your career decision-making skills will help you in all of these areas.

» What Decisions Are Next?

You make decisions all the time to help you deal with natural parts of your day. From deciding what to have for breakfast, whether or not to go to the gym, and which route to take through campus, you constantly weigh your options and make choices. Throughout your career, you also have many decisions to make. There are some decisions you may have made already, such as choosing to pursue higher education, selecting a school to attend, or engaging in part-time or full-time work.

Your choices helped you confirm your personal preferences and values, build relationships, and identify areas where you want to build skills or gain experience. Now, you may be facing a new set of decisions that have to be made to launch your career. Consider which decisions have to be made now, are important for your future goals, and have helped you in your career already. Then, choose one to explore further in the Career Journal: Decisions to Make.

Academic Decisions

There are many decisions that involve your education. These decisions are critical for meeting deadlines and accomplishing goals, such as getting applications in on time or fulfilling the requirements for graduation. These decisions can include the following:

- choosing a school or academic program
- declaring a major
- transferring to a different school
- selecting a concentration, minor, or specialization
- selecting courses
- changing majors
- considering study abroad
- considering graduate school or further training

For decisions about your major or next steps in your education plan, consider enlisting the support of a professor or academic advisor.

iStockphoto.com/Chris Schmidt

Decisions During College

In addition to your academic decisions, you must choose how you spend your time while you are a student. You may not relate some of these decisions to your career, such as choosing your friends or participating in social activities, but every decision you make can impact your social network, your learning environments, your leadership skills, and your preparation for a job search. These decisions can include the following:

- Considering how to spend your summer
- Selecting leisure activities
- Choosing activities and student groups
- Choosing part-time or full-time work
- Joining clubs or sports teams
- Creating friendships with peers
- Selecting volunteer activities
- Identifying career interests
- Taking on leadership roles
- Choosing internships

Decisions Before Entering the Workforce

When you prepare to enter the workforce, you will have a number of decisions to make. Some must be made first, because they will impact the others. For instance, if you have a location in mind where you want to live, you will have to understand the job market in that area before you choose target organizations and positions. These decisions can include the following:

- Confirming career interests
- Determining exams, credentials, or licensure
- Considering alternatives, such as a gap year
- Identifying target jobs and organizations
- Deciding where and how to network
- Choosing where to live
- Determining living arrangements
- Deciding on a back-up plan
- Considering a paid internship
- Evaluating offers

Lifelong Learning and Ongoing Career Development

There are many other times in your life when you will be facing decisions. Some may involve a change in direction, while others will help you maintain or build your credentials. Some of the career decisions you may face throughout your lifetime include the following:

- Choosing professional associations
- Considering leadership roles
- Considering exams, credentials, or licensure
- Considering further education or training
- Deciding whether to reenter the workforce
- Choosing continuing education
- Considering work-life balance
- Planning for retirement
- Choosing to look for a new job
- Deciding on a career change

Identifying decisions you have to make can help you set priorities, plan your time, and seek support or further resources when they are needed.

Use the space below to write about your thoughts and feelings.

Describe a career decision that you need to make.

Consider why you need to make a decision. This is part of the first phase of the CASVE (pronounced ka SAH ve) cycle, a decision-making model you will learn about in this chapter. (Sampson et al., 2004; and Reardon et al., 2009). According to this theory, all of these areas below can impact your awareness that a decision is needed. What tells you that this decision is necessary to make at this time?

Events. Are there any events that occurred or will occur soon, such as an impending academic deadline, a job offer, or a layoff? Describe career-related events in your life that require a decision.

Comments from Friends or Relatives. Have you heard comments or questions that address a decision you need to make, such as those about your plans after graduation or how you will cover your expenses? What were the comments, and what is your reaction?

The Way You Feel. Do you have any strong emotions about career decisions, such as feeling anxious, scared, angry, bored, disinterested, or frustrated? What emotions are you feeling?

(Continues)

Avoiding Your Problems. Procrastinating can also be a signal that a decision is looming. Describe ways you may be putting off decisions and the decisions you are avoiding.

Physical Problems. Headaches, stomachaches, loss of appetite, or lethargy might be body signals that suggest the need for a decision to be made. Describe any body signals you have noticed.

Do you feel ready to make the career decision you described? Why or why not?

Journal Feedback . . . There can be many signals that a career decision is necessary. Becoming more aware of these external and internal signals can motivate you to start the steps toward addressing your concerns. The CASVE cycle suggests that one of the first steps of decision making involves recognizing a need and realizing that a decision can help (Sampson et al., 2004). Consider whether your exploration of these signals has inspired you to take steps toward making career decisions.

>> Improve Your Decision-Making Skills

To improve your decision-making skills, learn more about various approaches to making decisions and how you can use a model to help in your decision making. When you experience a challenging decision, a model can help you look at the decision you need to make in stages, and the parts may be easier to address than the whole.

Name: Jessica Burns
College Degree: BA in English and Journalism
Graduate Degree: MBA *(achieved through an evening program while working full time)*
Current Position: Label Advertising and Trademark Administrator
Employer: Reckitt Benckiser

Courtesy of Jessica Burns

Can you describe your career?

I have degrees in English and journalism, because I didn't know exactly what I wanted to do after graduation and I figured any job I wanted would require good communication and writing skills. However, when I graduated, the economy crashed. I would get to the third round of interviews, and then learn about a hiring freeze or something else. I spent one year without a career-related full-time job, but I didn't want gaps in my résumé so I wrote articles for the local newspaper and I worked as a substitute teacher. Then I landed a job at Reckitt Benckiser, a Fortune 500 consumer goods company, with global brands such as Finish, Airwick, Lysol, French's, Veet, and more. I expressed my excitement for working for a global company to Markus, my supervisor, and together we worked on a development plan. About four months into my experience, I had the opportunity to go to a global meeting in England. At the meeting I worked with directors and global experts to launch the company's new electronic system for the review and approval of labeling for the company's entire portfolio. This opportunity gave me a lot of responsibility and ownership.

What decisions are you facing?

I'm 25 now, and I know where I want to be in 10 years. I want to build my career and be in a leadership position. I'm very career oriented and this is what I want from life, but I was not sure which steps to take to get there. I went into this position, and I was not given a lot of training, which required working autonomously and learning on the job. Someone gave me the advice to take advantage of working at a global company and to learn different things, so I try to treat the office as a classroom. Markus encouraged me to get a master's degree in business administration (MBA) since the company would pay for it. I did a three-month back in mini MBA program at a state university. I enjoyed this experience, so I enrolled in a full-time MBA evening program and I'll graduate this spring. I've also been able to learn a lot about different departments and what they do. I shadowed people to learn more about marketing, brand management, and product management. I also joined the graduate recruitment team to learn about human resources, and, most importantly, I learned what they look for in candidates. I need to decide what steps to take next and which direction I want to go in. I'm in the legal department now, and I've been exploring sales and human resources, but I am passionate about marketing. I plan to take advantage of whatever opportunities come my way.

From Jessica's Mentor

Name: Markus Hartmann
Title: Vice President and General Counsel, Europe and North America, Reckitt Benckiser

Courtesy of Markus Hartmann

How has Jessica positioned herself to have so many good career options?

Jessica came to us at a time when we wanted someone who could grow in the role, and she's grown tremendously. She has project-management skills. She keeps the database up to date, on time, and she supervised our move to a paperless office. That was her capacity and her own motivation. I realized I had more than an administrative assistant; I had a budding project manager. She's expanded into trademark work, and, on a personal level, as a manager, I've encouraged her to get an MBA and pursue an MBA-level career. She got the MBA and put in the time. An MBA is not a prerequisite, but a lot of brand managers have them. If she wants to develop into a management level, this makes her more marketable. She's working for a global company and, by going back to school and taking on internal projects, she's made herself more marketable internally and in the larger job market.

What led you to become a mentor to Jessica?

She's coachable. She has a sense of urgency. She lights up a room, and she can make people excited about a project. As her mentor, sometimes I realize I can encourage her to take on too many responsibilities, but I see her energy as a real positive. With Jessica, I see that she has unlimited opportunities. She may think that I'm too demanding, but I try to be the kind of mentor I wish I had. She has leadership capacity, and we've exposed her to various functions in the organization.

What are some of the options Jessica is considering? Can you rank them according to her priorities?

_____

_____

_____

How has Jessica's mentor relationship helped expand her options?

_____

_____

_____

For additional questions, visit CourseMate.

Good career decisions can involve analyzing concrete information, assessing personal feelings, and considering ideas shared by people whose opinions you value, such as family members.

Mark Edward Atkinson/Blend/Jupiterimages

Decision-Making Approaches

There are many approaches that people take when faced with decisions. Consider which of these approaches are most natural for you and those you have used in the past. After considering how you most frequently approach decision-making, you will be introduced to strategies that can be used to improve your decisions.

Logical thinking. Logical, rational models for decision-making involve step-by-step approaches that include gathering facts and data, analyzing information, assessing potential outcomes, and taking action. With its focus on analyzing information, this approach can be extremely effective, but could fall short if you fail to consider unexpected events or how you feel. For example, if you are leaning toward continuing your education after considering such pros and cons as the cost, time, effort, social experience, and course offerings in several different academic programs, but your feelings tell you this is not the right time, then a good decision will involve a consideration of your feelings and concrete information.

Trusting your intuition. If you have ever made a decision because it "felt right," you were relying on your emotions or intuition. The success of this approach relies on the quality of the information you gathered and your ability to understand the impact of your choices. For instance, if you declare a major based on how much you're enjoying one class, your decision is based on intuition. However, preparing for this decision could include reading your school's course catalogue, identifying a few interesting majors, and learning about career opportunities that could follow.

Pleasing others. Decisions that are made to please others involve taking steps towards outcomes or goals that have been presented to you by others, and often these are people whom you respect, such as your parents, professors, advisors, or mentors. They may have great ideas, know you well, and be insightful about your talents and the job market. However, working toward other people's goals is no guarantee you will reach their goals, or be satisfied when you do. To use other people's suggestions or advice to your advantage, consider whether it is consistent with your skills, preferences, and values, rather than focusing only on pleasing the person who gave the recommendation.

Avoidance or procrastination. When you avoid a decision, you do not choose. When you procrastinate, you put off making a decision. At least initially, these can feel like good alternatives, especially when you don't have an answer. However, these have many drawbacks. Perhaps most importantly, you give up responsibility for your role in the process and you miss the opportunity to be in control of the outcome. For instance, imagine you are given a challenging assignment in an internship, and you start the project and find you are having trouble. If you avoid talking about it with a supervisor and put off the work involved, time will go by and you will not make progress. Your avoidance and procrastination may lead you to miss deadlines, as well as the chance to learn, and it can also sour your relationship.

Make Decisions Using the CASVE Cycle

The CASVE (pronounced ka SAH ve) cycle is a guide for career problem solving and decision making (Sampson et al., 2004). This approach can be used to make better decisions and help you move through challenging areas of decision making. Furthermore, the model is a cycle, suggesting that the process does not end. After you have moved through each stage, you will begin the process again, affirming or modifying your choices as needed and identifying new career problems that must be addressed.

There are five phases of the CASVE cycle: Communication, Analysis, Synthesis, Valuing, and Execution (Sampson et al., 2009). The model is illustrated in **Exhibit 7.1**, The CASVE Cycle.

To apply the CASVE cycle to a career decision that you are facing, complete **Task 7.3**, Consider a Career Decision.

≫ EXHIBIT 7.1 • The CASVE Cycle

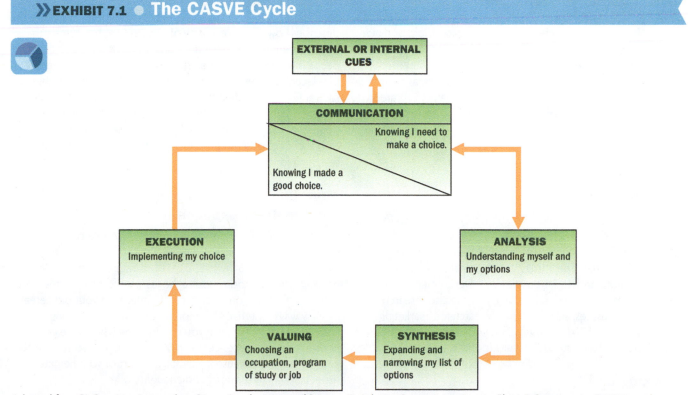

Adapted from *"A Cognitive Approach to Career Development and Services: Translating Concepts into Practice,"* by J. P. Sampson, Jr., G. W. Peterson, J. G. Lenz, and R. C. Reardon, 1992. The Career Development Quarterly, 41, p. 70. Copyright by the National Career Development Association. Copyright © 1992 by National Career Development Association. Reproduced by permission of John Wiley and Sons. Adapted from Peterson/Sampson, Jr./Reardon, Career Development and Services, 1E. © 1991 Cengage Learning.

(Continues)

C—Communication. The first phase involves your awareness that there is a problem, essentially a gap between your ideal and current situation. This is described as the "Knowing I Need to Make a Choice" phase. You may become aware of decisions to be made due to external signals, such as needing to choose a major or not getting any job offers in your field of interest; or internal signals, such as feeling overwhelmed or physically ill. In the Career Journal: Decisions to Make, you explored external and internal signals impacting the decisions you have to make.

A—Analysis. In the second phase, you analyze the problem using the information you know about yourself, such as your skills, interests, and values, and your knowledge of occupations, career preparation, and the world of work. This is described as the "Understanding Myself and My Options" phase.

S—Synthesis. In the third phase, you will use your analysis to identify steps that will help solve your problem. For instance, you might list all of your career options that satisfy your skills,

interests, and values. Or you might try brainstorming, to come up with unedited ideas about alternatives. This is the "Expanding and Narrowing My List of Options" phase.

V—Valuing. The fourth phase involves two parts. The first part requires you to evaluate how the decision will affect you and others. The second part involves ranking or prioritizing options according to how effectively they solve the problem. According to this theory, a good problem solver will then make an emotional commitment to implementing the decision, and also keep other options in mind as a back-up plan. This is the "Choosing an Occupation, Job, or College Major" phase.

E—Execution. This phase involves turning thoughts into action. This involves developing goals and engaging in specific action steps to reach them. This is the "Implementing My Choice" phase. After this phase, return to the Communication phase to evaluate your decision, and assess if you have solved the problem.

In today's world, choosing an occupation, job, or major is complicated by an array of choices. There are far more specialty areas for academic study, numerous choices for higher learning, including brick-and-mortar and online settings, seemingly endless options for gathering career information, and millions of online resources for job openings. All of this information should be helpful to individuals planning their careers, but it can be overwhelming.

TMI . . . Too Much Information about Everything!

What is too much information? In 2011, a Google search for "job boards" resulted in 5,950,000 results; "career information" resulted in 6,430,000 results; and, simply, "career" returned a list of 977,000,000 entries. The Bureau of Labor Statistics lists over 800 occupations and 400 industries (U.S. Department of Labor, Bureau of Labor Statistics). Obviously, you can also research companies, industries, and positions. A search for "marketing firm" resulted in 5,530,000 results. Are you ready for the job search? Google has 7,800,000 results for "interview tips."

How Do You Choose?

This overload of information is not unique to the field of career development. In *The Paradox of Choice*, Barry Schwartz

describes how an endless array of choices (e.g., the numerous boxes of cereal in the supermarket aisle) can lead you to poor decision-making approaches, such as facing the impossible task of selecting the very best cereal or simply choosing something familiar (2006). He identified two types of people: those who seek only the best, searching to maximize their outcomes by considering all the information available; and a second type, those who accept good-enough choices and are satisfied without searching for better options.

More Choices, Higher Expectations, and Greater Disappointment

Studies have shown that the more options people consider, the higher their expectations and greater their potential for regret (Iyengar Wells and Schwartz, 2006). For instance, with all the enticing claims on today's cereal boxes, an effort to find the best choice might lead you to one that is better than your old cereal in many ways—perhaps it is more nutritious, better tasting, and less expensive. However, if you consider the whole aisle of options, choosing a better cereal may make you *feel* worse than you did before, because it may still fall short of your heightened expectations. It is still not good *enough*.

Your Choices Can Feel Better

These suggestions are based on Schwartz's recommendations to optimize your satisfaction with the outcomes of your decisions (2006, p. 224):

Save time for decisions that matter to you. Spend less time on decisions that don't matter. If you have to make a decision, but the result is not very important to you, don't spend a lot of time debating alternatives. Save your energy for decisions that matter to you.

Spend time on the big questions. If you saved time by not belaboring the unimportant decisions, use that time for the tough decisions that need your attention. Which friend to sit with at lunch is not a big deal; which social club to join may involve a little more thought; and which major you choose should involve close examination.

Create your own alternatives. If you have considered all of your options, and you are not pleased with your choices, create new ones. Later in this chapter you will explore how to create opportunities in your career, and practice creating your own opportunity in **Task 7.4**, Create Opportunity.

Aim to choose a career, a job, or a work environment that makes you feel good, without considering so many options that the process is stressful or the outcome cannot possibly meet your expectations. If you find yourself having information overload, follow Schwartz's advice, and consider if the options you are considering are worth the time you are spending on them and if they will meet your needs.

» Create Opportunity from Unexpected Events

To make your choices fit your needs, sometimes you will need to create your own alternatives. However, you may not yet know what alternatives are best for you in some of the areas where you need to make decisions. As you have seen in the CASVE cycle, events and feelings can both be powerful instigators for decision making. You may still be left to wonder what planned and unplanned events will also influence your career, and in what way.

For instance, if you are a college student, you expect to choose a major. Factors that can influence your choice may be less predictable. A friend could invite you to a party where you meet several students who tell you about a course they are taking. The course sounds interesting to you and you enroll. You find yourself engaged and you opt for that major. An unplanned event, going to a party, impacted your planned event, the need to choose a major. Taking advantage of unplanned events is a skill in career development, and it can create many new possibilities for your decisions.

Being Open-Minded

Understanding the role of planned and unplanned events can significantly impact how you approach career development. Theory and tools that focus on unplanned events in career development suggest that planning is not even possible (Krumboltz, 2009; Krumboltz and Levin, 2010; Mitchell, 2003; and Pryor and Bright, 2011). Barack Obama could not have planned to become president; Martha Stewart could not have planned to go from a career as a model to a stockbroker to a lifestyle guru (Bright, 2009, September 13). Learning to make career decisions in an uncertain world requires you to prepare through education and experiential learning, then seek out and recognize opportunities, taking advantage of them when they arise.

Choosing activities you enjoy can lead to unexpected events that positively impact your career.

According to the Happenstance Learning Theory (HLT) (Krumboltz, 2009), there are many decisions about your future that may be unreasonable or inappropriate to make in advance. "What I want to be when I grow up," or "What I want to achieve in five years" cannot be planned because they are likely to be influenced by unexpected events that can impact your choices in ways you cannot predict. Embracing this theory suggests learning to adapt to new information and reframing undecidedness as open-mindedness.

Chance Events and Your Career

Many people attribute some of their greatest career opportunities to luck. Chance meetings, unexpected job offers, and pivotal project assignments are often described as "lucky breaks," "perfect timing," or "being in the right place at the right time."

There are many types of unexpected events that can impact your career. These could include meeting someone who has information about a job, discovering a skill that leads to a career change, or participating in a project that leads to a leadership opportunity. However, these events can occur when you least expect them. The person you meet could be sitting next to you in an airplane; the skill you gain could come from a parenting activity; the project could have been volunteer work that reflected a personal passion. Applying the HLT in your life can help you increase the likelihood of beneficial unplanned events, and help you take advantage of these events when they occur (2009).

Choose to Be Engaged

There are many self-directed activities that can increase your likelihood of having beneficial unplanned events according to the HLT, including the following (Krumboltz, 2009, p. 144):

- Taking up a new hobby
- Applying for an internship
- Getting involved in a school project
- Taking the initiative to meet new people
- Taking the lead on a class activity or project

Identify and Take Advantage of Opportunities

According to the HLT, here are three steps to help you take advantage of the unplanned events that occur (Krumboltz, 2009, p. 144):

- "Before the unplanned event, you take actions that position you to experience it."
  If you meet someone who can help you in your career, remember that you have been preparing through your coursework, and you have learned about the industry.
- "During the event, you remain alert and sensitive to recognize potential opportunities."
  Listen to the contact, and ask for clarification of key names, suggestions, or resources.
- "After the event, you initiate actions that enable you to benefit from it."
  Complete any suggested steps, say thank you, and follow up to let the contact know how the advice was helpful.

Apply the Happenstance Learning Theory (HLT) in Your Own Life

To apply this theory in your own life, get involved in the world around you, join clubs and committees, attend social events with friends or colleagues, try a new sport or hobby, meet people, develop authentic relationships based on shared interests, and learn from others. Build skills that you want to use, even if they do not match your current position or career path. Follow up with the people you meet, and maintain your connections. The opportunities that present themselves may not be direct, such as a job offer. However, how you choose to be engaged in the world around you, and how you choose to use the insights you gain, will affect your career decisions.

Some of the opportunities you may be able to create are the following:

- Receiving an introduction to someone with helpful information
- Gaining insight into key organizations or industry trends
- Learning about a job opening
- Increasing your knowledge about developments in the field

Any of these opportunities can help you develop your career in ways you had not anticipated. Use **Task 7.4**, Create Opportunity, to identify ways you can increase your opportunities for beneficial unplanned events. While you can't plan for these occurrences, you can increase their likelihood and prepare to take advantage of them when they happen. Others might describe this as "luck," but you can create your own luck.

>> EMBRACING DIFFERENCES ● Role Models and Career Choice

Your role models inspire you to pursue your dreams and take career risks because they offer real-world examples that show what your life could be like. When you think about the kind of luck you want in your life, or look for insight into options that are available, role models can often be a great source of inspiration. Role models shape childhood aspirations and adult career goals.

A belief in one's own capability is called "self-efficacy," and it is influenced by many factors (Bandura, 1977). Research has shown that your belief in your ability can also have measurable effects. For instance, if you believe you can become a nurse, or achieve any other occupation, you may find it easier to overcome challenges, remain motivated, and feel less stressed or anxious during the process of completing the steps towards that career.

However, research has also shown that self-efficacy can be diminished for those who lack role models. Many careers do not have an equal representation of ethnic groups, people of color, women, members of the LGBT community, or others, and it can be hard to see yourself in a career or find a role model when you don't see anyone like yourself in a specific job, organization, or career field. Consider this list of occupations and what these people look like in your mind. Notice the assumptions you make for each occupation, including your thoughts about the worker's race, ethnicity, and gender.

Teacher	Nurse	Investment banker	Social worker
Police officer	CEO	Construction worker	Principal
Scientist	Sculptor	Interior decorator	Chef
Fashion designer	Actor	Video game designer	Doctor

Whether you can see yourself in a given occupation can influence your beliefs about your likelihood to succeed. This can influence your willingness to take steps that involve time, effort, and persistence. Preparation for certain occupations, such as those in science, engineering, technology, and mathematics (STEM) fields, may require years of cumulative learning. Careers that use reading and writing skills require practice and training. Jobs that require physical and mental exams require people who are confident about their testing capacity.

To increase your self-efficacy, participate in mentor programs in school or through professional associations, attend networking events for careers that interest you, and build your network with people who can serve as role models. Role models will help you see career possibilities, find it easier to commit to decisions, and provide support as you take the steps to turn your dreams into reality.

» Choose a Major, Further Education, or Training

Choosing a major, further education, or training involves decisions that will contribute to your qualifications and credentials. If you are facing these decisions, there are many resources to assist you. Once you have explored available resources, certain questions can help you to analyze the information you have gathered and move forward toward making decisions.

Choosing a Major

Your major will impact the subject area you study, the people with whom you attend classes, and your career preparation. Your major can also impact your career options after graduation, especially if you choose a major that leads to certification or specialized skills. However, your major does not dictate your career options.

In many cases, your career options are influenced by a combination of factors, including your courses, internships, activities, and networking. Choosing a major that interests you will motivate you to succeed in your courses, and your ability to maintain a strong GPA is very important to employers, according to the 2012 Job Outlook Survey from the National Association of Colleges and Employers (NACE) (Koc and Koncz, 2011). Therefore, one approach is to choose a subject area where you think you will excel, will prepare skills you want to use, and will gain access to experiences that will increase your opportunities.

Some of the questions that can help you decide if a major is a good match for you are the following:

- What majors are common for people with my interests, personality type, skills, and values?
- What courses are required for this major?
- Do the courses for this major interest me?
- Do I feel I can succeed or excel in the courses?
- What internships and experiential learning will be available to me in this major?
- What options have students in this major chosen for the year after graduation?
- What are typical career paths of graduates of the major(s) I am considering?
- What are the salary ranges of graduates of the major(s) I am considering?
- Will this major prepare me for my future career interests or academic goals?
- Do I feel that I can learn with the students and faculty in the major I am considering?

Choosing Further Education or Training

There are many times in your career when you might consider further education or training, especially given the need for skill development throughout the lifetime. You might be looking to complete a bachelor's degree, apply for graduate study, participate in a certification program, or take professional development courses. If you are considering a degree or other form of education, identifying your goals and

If you are considering further education, a campus visit can help you evaluate your options as you learn about the steps for admission.

expected outcomes can help you determine if the program you are considering will be worth the investment of time, money, and effort.

Some of the questions you might want to answer before committing to an educational program include the following:

- Do I feel ready to commit to further education or training?
- Am I prepared for the costs involved?
- Can I manage the schedule or workload involved in further study?
- How will this education or training impact my career opportunities?
- How important is this credential to employers?
- What options become available if I complete this education or training?
- Are there any limits to my future options if I pursue this route; for instance, do I become very specialized, and, if so, does this fit my goals?
- What are the career paths of graduates of the program(s) I am considering?
- What are the salary ranges of graduates of the program(s) I am considering?
- Do I feel that I can learn with the students and faculty in the programs I am considering?
- Can I balance the demands of the program with my other commitments, such as work or family?

Making Educational Decisions

Given the range of questions you may have about your major or future study, you may be hesitant to declare your major or commit to further education or training. Transferable skills are learned in every major, so you can be assured that your major will not determine the course of your career or entire life. Majoring in a subject that interests you, and in which you can excel, can help you learn a unique set of skills that you will be motivated to incorporate into your career.

If you are considering further study, look to your skills, preferences, and values for insight. In some cases, education may be a requirement for work options that interest you. Reflecting on your exploration of the world of work can help you determine if further education will help you prepare for the tasks and positions that interest you. A career goal does not offer security, but it can help you assess the skills and credentials that may be useful for tasks you wish to perform in the future.

≫ WORK WITH AWARENESS ● The Gap Year

For students who want to build skills or gain experience in ways that do not fit directly into their career plans, a gap year offers an alternative to continuous study or directly entering the workforce. A gap year often refers to time off from academic studies after high school. However, it can also involve a break between an associate's degree and a bachelor's degree, a break before graduate study, or employment that may seem incongruent with career goals. For example, a college graduate interested in finance could spend a year teaching overseas, building transferable skills for a job in international finance. A student interested in a career in hospitality could spend time working on a farm to better understand different parts of the consumer food cycle, or volunteering in a soup kitchen to understand service and meal preparation from a different perspective. A student interested in law may choose to work on a political campaign.

A Gap Year Is Becoming More Common
In Britain, students are offered the option to defer college plans for one year, and almost a quarter million students take this option each year (Settersten and Ray, 2010). Although a gap year has been more common outside the United States, many Americans have opted for this alternative to going to school without a break. A gap year gives a person the chance to prepare for further study, build skills, explore interests, gain experience, and possibly earn money. The time period of a gap year does not have to be an actual year, but it does represent a break from seemingly continual plans.

Understanding the Gap Year
In an article in the *Occupational Outlook Quarterly, Bureau of Labor Statistics,* economist Elka Maria Torpey discusses the pros and cons of a gap year (2009). She notes that it can help people gain personal insights, offer a break from academic pressures, offer real-world learning, and increase enthusiasm for further study. On the downside, a change in focus away from academics can make it more difficult for some people to return to school, and a poorly planned or unplanned gap year can lead to disappointment or frustration, especially if the time feels underutilized. A gap year involves planning and organization skills; for instance, costs must be planned. A gap year can be funded by personal resources, scholarships, fellowships, grants, or can include paid employment.

Benefits of a Gap Year
Options for a gap year include service learning, part-time or full-time work, travel, volunteerism, and political work. Such experiences can increase maturity, generate relationships, and build transferable skills. In *Not Quite Adults: Why 20-Somethings Are Choosing a Slower Path to Adulthood and Why It's Good for Everyone,* researchers Settersten and Ray (2010) share examples of students who took a gap year and how it impacted their career development. In one example, Eduardo worked several jobs before returning to a community college in San Diego. He made friends with a group of phlebotomy students and completed a medical assistant certificate in six months. He then went to work, but soon decided to become a nurse and returned to school in a licensed vocational nursing program. Settersten and Ray describe how Eduardo's gap year helped him build a professional support network, learn about the job, and become familiar with requirements before making a commitment to further education.

Avoid the Downside of a Gap Year
For those considering a gap year, Torpey recommends several steps to ensure the experience is a success (2009):

1. **Tasks before leaving school.** If you plan to attend college or graduate study after the gap year, prepare before you leave school. Applying to schools, obtaining references, and deferring enrollment will all prepare you for your return.

2. **Expenses.** Assess the costs of a gap year before it begins, and resolve how you will maintain health insurance and cover other needs such as living expenses.

3. **Activities and goals.** Choose activities that help you to prepare for your career or to develop skills, such as volunteer opportunities, internships, part-time work, or service learning.

If you are making a decision about a gap year, consider your goals for the year and your commitment to take the action steps that will help you meet them.

Katie Clarke: Making Decisions

Katie enjoyed talking to people and had always been friendly and upbeat, but was never very interested in school. When a friend suggested leaving school, completing their GEDs, and getting an apartment together, Katie was eager. Soon she found a job as a bartender where she was making enough money to support herself. She could sleep late, spend time with her friends, and enjoyed her independence. After a year she met Owen, and soon they moved in together. They shared the same schedule, with Owen working nights as a DJ in a popular club. They had a fun, busy lifestyle that she enjoyed. The following year they got married. Within a month of their wedding, she was surprised to discover she was pregnant.

At work, she had become responsible for training new hires as well as managing schedules. Her personality helped her easily promote new drinks and specials, and she was regarded as a talent and asset at work. When her manager left for a large restaurant, she recommended Katie interview there for an assistant manager position. The position had not interested her much at the time, but she went to the interview out of respect for her former boss. The job involved working days instead of nights, and she would receive benefits and have a salaried position instead of relying primarily on tips, as in her current job. When they called with an offer, she decided that with a baby on the way, this seemed perfect. She envisioned day care for the baby in the day, and she would be home at night when Owen worked. However, as her pregnancy progressed, she was diagnosed with a pregnancy-related condition, and time on her feet was restricted. Katie and Owen were not prepared to survive on one income, so although Katie was entitled to eight weeks of unpaid maternity leave according to the Massachusetts Maternity Leave Act, she made arrangements to work less time and shorter shifts, taking only a short break after delivering. She had

a significant reduction in pay, but a promise that her full-time job would be secure.

Fortunately, the baby was born healthy and she recovered quickly, but now she and Owen were in debt, and struggling to keep up with the bills. Returning to full-time work was a must for Katie, but the costs of day care and motherhood took their toll. She was tired and overworked, found no time for leisure, and noticed that college graduates held most of the higher-level management positions. On New Year's Eve, she made a decision to make changes in her life in the hopes of a more secure future. She researched career fields and learned that medical billing was a growing occupation that would allow her to work from home. With a scholarship for working mothers and financial aid, she enrolled in a community college for an associate's degree in office technology. By arranging her work schedule to accommodate her courses, she was able to work full time while enrolled as a full-time student. She spent little time with her daughter or husband, and kept telling herself it would be over soon. By the end of her first semester, she started getting severe headaches and her husband told her that maybe she should quit school. Not sure what to do, she made an appointment with her academic advisor.

How would you describe Katie's approach to decision making?

What decisions is she facing now?

How can Katie use the strategies you have learned to improve her decision making?

Describe other decisions she could consider, other than dropping out.

To learn more about Katie's career development, visit CourseMate 🔲. View her résumé and job search materials in **Chapter 8: Tools.**

>> From Decisions to Action

In order to move toward action, you must make decisions. However, a decision does not need to be a commitment to a long-term career goal. In fact, according to several theories about careers (Krumboltz, 2009; Bright and Pryor, 2005), you cannot plan with certainty for a future career, because there are too many possibilities that can impact your life experience. Instead, consider how your career interests, major, or further study will help you develop assets that are consistent with your skills, preferences, and values and will reflect your knowledge of the world around you.

Taking action can involve developing skills that prepare you for a range of opportunities.

The Importance of Career Decisions

Career decisions that help you commit to your professional development will help you prepare for any opportunities you encounter. A career choice, in the traditional sense, is a commitment to a job in a given field and its linear path. But now, a career decision is often a temporary commitment to a profession, followed by a nonlinear path. Nevertheless, to receive a higher salary, more responsibility, and greater autonomy, it is critical to build skills that allow you to advance in your current industry or change careers without starting at the bottom. Therefore, good career decisions enable you to increase your skills and level of responsibility while still allowing you to remain flexible and mobile.

Career Decisions Require Action

Because it is necessary to make decisions, your ability to select appropriate options, learn to make good decisions, and understand how your decisions prepare you for future possibilities are key components to developing your career. Areas to consider before action are the following:

Define your career interests. Choosing career interests allows you to identify the key skills, experiences, leadership roles, and credentials that are necessary for advancement. Decisions about skills to develop and training that is useful will help you position yourself for opportunity.

Choose appropriate decisions. When external or internal signals make it clear that you cannot avoid a decision, consider your options or create new ones. Decisions that involve a commitment to education or training may be critical as you build your career. Choices about experiences and activities will help you select the environments and tasks that help you develop assets. Looking ahead to career paths and choosing steps that will keep those options open are also appropriate decisions.

Narrow your choices. Choosing between a few good alternatives is always much easier than choosing from everything. As you gather information, you may be able to narrow your selection further. Choose a first choice, a second choice, and possibly a third. As you develop a list of action steps, you might see that some careers involve steps that are more attractive to you. There are many parts of the career decision-making process in which your choices can become more focused, or you can rule out or rank less attractive options.

Select target jobs, organizations, and industries. Although you cannot map out a predictable future with certainty, choosing target opportunities is important when you look for work or evaluate your educational options. If, along the way, you learn of opportunities you did not foresee, your earlier decisions will have armed you with a valuable knowledge base. For instance, if your education prepared you for a very specific position, such as a physical-therapist assistant, and you are looking primarily for job openings with physical therapists in private practice, you might be surprised when a networking contact tells you about a job in an assisted-living facility, especially if you are less experienced in working with an aging population, but feel it interests you. Your knowledge of the requirements for other settings will help you research the new position and market your relevant assets.

Move Toward Action Steps

If you are finding it challenging to make specific decisions throughout your career, consider how the approaches in this chapter can help you narrow your choices and move forward. For example, **Exhibit 7.1**, The CASVE Cycle, can help you identify parts of the decision-making process that require further attention. Once you have identified a decision to make, assess information in the Analysis phase. Refer to the tools you used for self-assessment in **PART I: Know Yourself**. Reflect on the occupational interests you identified using Holland's RIASEC theory in **Chapter 2: Preferences**. After you have narrowed your options to a few good choices, brainstorm or rank priorities in the Synthesis phase of the CASVE cycle.

When you have made a decision, you are ready to create an action plan to implement your choice in the Execution phase, the fifth stage of the CASVE cycle. Your Flexible Plan: Commit to Your Next Step will help you create a Plan of Action for your decisions. After you have listed your action steps, you can begin to test your choice by recycling into the Communication phase. Ask yourself if it feels right and if your choice has addressed your key concerns. When new information makes you question the decisions that once seemed right, return to the Analysis and Synthesis phases. By recycling through the stages, you can consider all the information you have and also adapt to new information or events.

Making effective and appropriate decisions and turning them into action will be important at many different stages of your career. These skills can be applied whenever you need to make choices, and they also will help you commit more fully to key components of your professional development at any given moment in time.

Your Flexible Plan

Commit to Your Next Step

PLAN OF ACTION

Step 1: Set Broad Objectives

What decisions do you need to make? List the decisions you need to make at this time, and the dates of any deadlines you have, whether external (e.g., the need to declare a major) or self-imposed (e.g., a date for sending out your first batch of résumés).

Decisions that need to be made:	What is my deadline for this decision?
1)	
2)	
3)	
4)	
5)	

Step 2: Identify Specific Goals

The next step is to look at your prioritized list, and determine which decisions you are ready to make. For these, prepare a list of specific goals. Choose one decision for this task.

I am ready to make this decision:

_____

Example: To decide which internships to pursue for the summer (broad objective)

To make this decision, I have these specific goals:

Example: (1) learn about internships (2) network with alumni

1. _____

2. _____

3. _____

Step 3: Define Action Steps

Choose one goal and list the steps you will take to achieve it:

action steps, the tasks involved, and deadlines for completing each step. *Example: To decide which internships to pursue for the summer (broad objective), I will learn about internships (goal) and network with alumni (goal). To achieve these goals, I must:*

(1) Review listings on the website for the career center at my school. (2) Learn about alumni networking events. (3) Attend alumni networking events.

List the action steps you will take.

Goal: _____

1. _____

2. _____

3. _____

4. _____

5. _____

Performance Appraisal

Now that you have read the chapter, answer the questions below and complete the Tasks.

1. Which of the following improve your decision making?
   a. Listening to your intuition
   b. Gathering important facts and data
   c. Realizing that avoidance (not making a decision) is a decision, too
   d. All of the above

2. The following are the five phases of the CASVE cycle:
   a. Communication, Analysis, Synthesis, Valuing, and Execution
   b. Collaborating, Agreeing, Synthesis, Vetoing, and Evaluating
   c. Communication, Agreeing, Synchronizing, Valuing, and Elaborating
   d. Collaborating, Analysis, Synchronizing, Valuing, and Elaborating

3. Which of the following is true about information overload?
   a. More choices make decision making easier.
   b. The more choices a person considers, the happier they are with their decision.
   c. A greater number of choices can lead to higher expectations, and the potential for greater disappointment.
   d. a and c.

4. Which of the following increase(s) the likelihood of unexpected events that positively impact your career?
   a. Trying a new hobby
   b. Taking on a role in a school project
   c. Getting to know a professor
   d. All of the above

5. Why are role models important in career development?
   a. They will tell you what to do, and always know best.
   b. They can help you see yourself in a career, and this can help you overcome challenges as you work toward your goals.
   c. They are your only hope of getting a referral for a job.
   d. None of the above

6. If you are debating about going back to school, which of the following should you consider?
   a. Your budget
   b. Your commitment
   c. Your career goals
   d. All of the above

7. A good career decision
   a. Limits your choices and locks you into one job for your entire life;
   b. Allows you to move ahead and can give you job security;
   c. Can expand your options, and help you build new skills;
   d. Is none of the above.

Performance Appraisal Answer Key

1. d   2. a   3. c   4. d   5. b   6. d   7. c

Thought Questions

1. Have you identified the decisions you need to make next? What are they?

2. Do you feel prepared to start making decisions in your career?

3. Can you identify the decisions that seem most difficult to you? What are they?

Notes:

_____

_____

_____

_____

_____

_____

TASK 7.1:

What Decisions Are Next?

In this chapter, a lot of career-related decisions were addressed, and in Your Flexible Plan and the Career Journal you had the chance to explore individual decisions. However, you may be in the midst of many decisions, depending on your stage of career development.

Use the space below to list all of the career-related decisions you have to make, and then try to number them, according to which you feel should receive the most attention, or must be addressed first due to deadlines.

_____   _____

_____   _____

_____   _____

_____   _____

_____   _____

_____   _____

TASK 7.2:

Consider a Career Direction

In this exercise, your career interests will be considered. First, list up to three career fields you are considering. Under each career field, list all the skills you expect to build and use in that field. If you are not exploring three careers, but are considering different majors or different types of summer internships or job types, replace "career" with the decision you are facing.

Career # 1   **Career # 2**   **Career # 3**

_____   _____   _____

Skills

_____   _____   _____

_____   _____   _____

_____   _____   _____

_____   _____   _____

Looking at the list above, evaluate each career based on the skills you will use. Which list has the most skills you enjoy using? Which list has the least? Do you feel informed enough about the fields to list skills used in this way? Why or why not?

_____

_____

Now, follow this exercise through by considering interests and personality, and values.

Career # 1   **Career # 2**   **Career # 3**

_____   _____   _____

Interests and Personality Characteristics

_____   _____   _____

_____   _____   _____

_____   _____   _____

_____   _____   _____

_____   _____   _____

Career # 1   **Career # 2**   **Career # 3**

_____   _____   _____

Values

_____   _____   _____

_____   _____   _____

_____   _____   _____

_____   _____   _____

_____   _____   _____

What career stands out as the most appealing to you based on your intuition? Why? Use the model in **Task 7.3**, Consider a Career Decision, to see if an approach that uses logical thinking led you to the same conclusions.

TASK 7.3:
Consider a Career Decision

Consider each phase of the CASVE cycle, and answer the questions below to Consider a Career Decision about which of the three career directions above are right for you. As with **Task 7.2**, Consider a Career Direction, if you are not considering different careers, but are considering different majors or different types of summer internships or job types, replace "career" with the decision you are facing.

The following topics represent the phases of the CASVE cycle, and can also be found in **Exhibit 7.1,** The CASVE Cycle (Sampson et al., 2009).

Knowing I Need to Make a Choice. Why do you need to make a career choice?

_____

_____

Understanding Myself and My Options. What are your career options? Here you can list any options you are considering.

_____

_____

Expanding and Narrowing My List of Options. Use techniques such as brainstorming to expand and narrow your career options until you have a small list. Write your reduced list of options here.

_____

_____

Choosing an Occupation, Job, or College Major. Using techniques such as rank ordering and prioritizing, make a top choice that you are ready to pursue, and list two or three back-up choices.

_____

_____

Implementing My Choice. Now that you have made a choice, take a step forward. If you chose a major, visit the department's website, declare your choice to family or friends. Next, ask yourself how you feel about your decision. Do you feel that you made a good choice?

_____

_____

TASK 7.4:
Create Opportunity

In the book, _Luck is No Accident,_ Krumboltz and Levin (2009) offer these suggestions for creating opportunity. List at least one action you can take in each category to help increase your own opportunities and unexpected events.

Ways to Create Opportunity (Krumboltz and Levin 2009)	What I Can Do to Accomplish This Objective and Create Opportunities for Myself
1. Meet people in industries that interest me	
2. Learn more about career fields that I am exploring	
3. Gain experience that will help me build related or transferable skills	
4. Engage in nonwork activities that interest me	
5. Make a greater contribution to society	

TASK 7.5:
Overcome Obstacles to Decision Making

Consider decisions with which you are still struggling. The CASVE cycle (Sampson et al., 2004 and Reardon et al., 2009) helps you recognize what is important to you. What obstacles make it difficult to make these decisions at this time?

Possible obstacles:	Which of your decisions have these obstacles? For each decision you need to make, how will you overcome these obstacles?
I need to gather more information.	
I need to listen to my intuition and internal signals.	
I need to evaluate the information I have from my self-assessment, career research, and intuition.	
I need to narrow my choices.	
I need to prioritize my choices.	

Link to CourseMate

On CourseMate, you can find documents to help you update your Career Portfolio as well as additional resources and activities. Here is some of the information you can find online for **Chapter 7: Decision Making**.

Career Portfolio
Your Flexible Plan

Resources
Career Profile: Jessica Burns

SECTION

III

Market Yourself

West Coast Surfer/age fotostock

Tools

> Your premium brand had better be delivering something special, or it's not going to get the business.
> —*Warren Buffett*

Prepare to . . .

- Understand the purpose of job search tools in your career development
- Explore ways to define and build a personal brand
- Learn about the sections and content of a résumé
- Improve your ability to communicate your accomplishments
- Understand how to write cover letters and other job search tools that get results

Job search tools include the résumé, cover letter, and thank you letters. These concrete tools show employers how your assets fulfill their needs. Preparing job search tools is also a chance to identify a clear and consistent message about your assets, also called a personal brand. Job search tools are useful for a job or internship search as well as for networking, and can help you become aware of skill areas you want to develop to increase your marketability.

» Job Search Tools and Your Career Development

To market yourself successfully in a job search, internship search, or for any experience that requires a résumé, you will want to create a clear and consistent message about your assets. Job search tools also provide an at-a-glance look at your assets, which can help you notice skills gaps and areas you want to develop. This can help you choose targeted experiences in the future that will increase your marketability for career paths that interest you or for a specific opportunity.

What are Job Search Tools?

The job search tools you will use most throughout your lifetime are the résumé, cover letter, and thank you letter. In addition, a reference page, networking letter, and online profile can act as supporting materials. Depending on your career interests, industry-specific materials might be important to maintain, such as writing samples, a portfolio of your art or design work, or a list of publications or presentations. The first step is to assess which documents are typically requested by employers in your industry, and then learn how to prepare the most effective materials.

A Clear and Consistent Message

To create strong job search tools, you need a clear message. In this chapter, you will reflect on the qualities you represent or want to develop, as well as the assets you want to highlight. It can be difficult to connect your skills and assets into a succinct message at the beginning of your career, but over time you will begin to see themes emerge. These themes will be reflected in your personal brand, characterized by the qualities and behaviors others expect of you. At this time, consider who you are and who you want to become. Your experiences, choices, and opportunities will help you build your brand for the future.

Your job search tools will take time to create, but they will be useful to you for multiple purposes, including a job or internship search, networking, and self-assessment.

Learn from Your Job Search Tools

By thinking about your personal brand, and identifying specific target opportunities that interest you, you can assess how well your skills, experiences, and credentials match the assets employers are seeking. When all of your job search tools are prepared and stored in your Career Portfolio, you will notice the strength of your message. You may also notice some gaps in skills areas that employers are seeking. Even if you are not ready for a job search or already have a job lined up, preparing job search tools is a relevant exercise because they can be used for ongoing self-assessment as well as a future job search. Your ability to recognize and build relevant assets that help you market yourself in the world of work is a skill that you will use throughout your career.

As you begin this next step in your career development, you will start by preparing documents that reflect all your accomplishments, while highlighting those that are most relevant for the positions and industry experiences that interest you now.

Tetra Images/Jupiterimages

Create a cluster map of your assets by listing your valuable qualities, traits, experiences, and skills. Write your list quickly and spontaneously, with an effort to include every asset that comes to mind. Use the example below for inspiration, then complete your own cluster map.

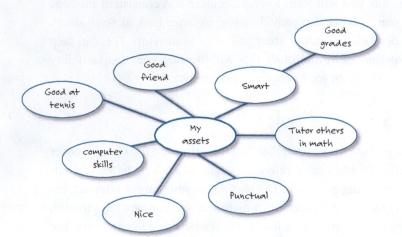

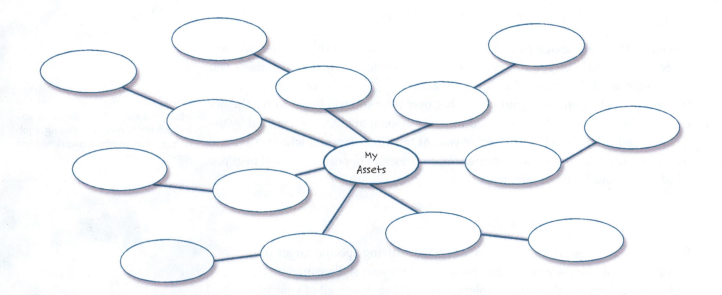

Journal Feedback . . . Considering all of your assets can help you prepare to market yourself in the world of work. Your unique combination of assets also contributes to your personal brand. Because employers are seeking individuals who can be creative, innovate, and also add value, seemingly unrelated assets may be important to include on your résumé. These can be suited to such sections as activities, community service, or accomplishments. This exercise can also help you identify or recall experiences or activities in which you developed or used the assets you listed.

Name: AJ Sabath
College Degree: BA in Social Work
Current Position: Business Owner, Lobbyist
Chair, Board of Trustees, Ramapo College of New Jersey (*volunteer position*)
Industry: Business Consulting

Courtesy of AJ Sabath

Tell us about your transition from college to the world of work.

My career really started while I was in undergrad. I have a degree in social work, and I was interested in the macro side of social work—social policy and community organizing. We needed 2000 hours of fieldwork similar to an internship. I worked for a professor, Mitch Kahn, at the School of Social Work at Ramapo College. He was Executive Director of the Bergen County Housing Coalition and he was involved in the New Jersey Tenants Organization. I was there for four years, working as a Housing Organizer and a Paralegal. Tenants would call—maybe there was no heat in the winter or infestations of rodents. We'd go in, have a big meeting, tell them their rights, and help them organize. The tenants movement in NJ was filled with activists from the labor and the civil rights movements. I was inspired. From there, I moved around a lot. Every two years, my resume had a new position. I always sought out opportunities for growth.

What were some of the early experiences that shaped your career?

When I was 22 years old, I had the opportunity to run a campaign. The candidate won, and I was offered a job in communications—writing press releases, speeches. These are great skills, but I knew I wasn't going to be a speechwriter. So I began poking around. I ended up working on a number of races. I would work in government, take a leave of absence, and work on a race. I worked on state, congressional, US Senate, and gubernatorial campaigns. Then I wanted to do something different. I thought about the Peace Corps, but they didn't need political organizers, and somebody suggested the National Democratic Institute for International Affairs, which is sometimes referred to as the 'Political Peace Corps.' I worked in Azerbaijan. I ran the office, and it was an amazing experience. But, after a few years, I realized people would forget who I was in NJ. I came back to NJ and got a job for a large lobbying firm. That was a big league opportunity. My political background and communication skills were assets. I had 12-hour days, and I traveled all over the country. I had just gotten married, and the travel and long hours took its toll. I made a quality of life decision. It was bittersweet, but my family was important. I went back to working in government then taking leaves of absence to work on campaigns. I had a lot of success on the campaigns, and I worked on a lot of races.

From AJ's Network

Name: Beth Barnett, EdD
Title: Provost and Academic Vice President, Ramapo College of New Jersey

Courtesy of Beth Barnett

We understand that AJ is currently the Chair of the Board of Trustees for Ramapo College. Can you tell us about his professional reputation and the contribution he offers?

AJ is an individual who really cares about New Jersey, and knows what's going on in the state. He has always been involved politically, and is able to offer insight. He has his finger on the pulse and can pull together a lot of information into a few short sentences. Rather than thinking very linearly, he has the flexibility to look at a problem from many different perspectives to create a solution. He has had to do that to be successful in politics, and you see that here, as well.

Can you discuss how his education and career preparation are reflected in the reputation he has developed?

AJ majored in social work, which is an interdisciplinary major, bringing together ideas from such fields as psychology, anthropology, and political science. He approaches problems from an interdisciplinary point of view. A cornerstone of Ramapo College is its four pillars of academic excellence—interdisciplinary curriculum, intercultural understanding, international education, and experiential opportunities. These are all clearly applied in his career. He's even had international experience that rounds out his perspective. We also encourage service learning and civic engagement. First, you are a member of your family; then your closest community; then, you connect with the broader state level. He is involved, and he gives back. He embodies each of these pillars, which is also why he can understand what we aim to achieve, and help us reach our goals.

How did AJ develop a reputation that helped him become a "go-to" person for the ideas and activities he enjoys most?

_____

_____

_____

How would you define AJ's personal brand?

_____

_____

_____

For additional questions, visit CourseMate.

(Continues)

How did you build your professional reputation?
Early on I learned that loyalty was important. There were al-ways people who were respected by others—not a popularity contest, but qualities that were important to me. They were loyal, not vindictive. They were able to make positive changes. They were aligned with me ideologically. To me, these were honorable men and women. I realized that there was a lot I didn't know. I listened. I respected authority. I recognized that I needed to have a strong sense of humility. Everything that I learned was slow, incremental. I had to be teachable. I remem-ber there came a point where I went from being a junior staffer, a policy person, to being regarded as an advisor, a strategist. I can't say when that was, but after that my advice and counsel mattered. That's when I really understood the influence and power I had earned.

» Build Your Brand

As you prepare to market yourself and develop job search tools, consider your assets and how others perceive you. When you build your career intentionally, you choose ex-periences that help you develop the skills you are motivated to use and that are relevant to employers. You create your own personal brand, and make yourself a "go-to" person for the tasks and activities you enjoy. In fact, you have already completed the first step in identifying your brand by listing your assets in this chapter's Career Journal.

I'm a Person, Not a Brand!

Of course, you're not a "brand" in the corporate sense, but the concept suggests that we all carry recognizable characteristics that make us unique and memorable (Peters, 1997). Successful athletes are known for their physical ability, their commitment to the team, and their ability to show up. A trendsetter is known for her taste in clothes and other products, her knowledge of online sites for shopping or following trends, and her personal style.

Personal branding enthusiasts argue that whether you make intentional decisions to develop your image and actions, we are all branded. Personal style, performance, ability, reliability, and many more characteristics, choices, and behaviors all contrib-ute to the development of each person's unique brand.

Identify Your Brand

You may not be sure how you are unique, or if you are unique enough to "brand" your personal qualities. If your friends go to you when they have a dating dilemma or want

You will build your personal brand through the choices you make and the reputation you develop at work, school, and in your leisure time.

iStockphoto.com/Raul Rodriguez

help solving a problem, it is because they expect something. Perhaps you are known as a good listener, helper, or confidant. You have been branded, and this gives them the expectation that you will be helpful. Similarly, if you are good at math, savvy on the computer, or always know the best parties, you may find your friends and others have begun to contact you when these talents are useful. Are you the person in your office to whom others turn when they need help with the copier, software, or online communication? The information others seek from you is a good indicator of how you have already been branded.

Demonstrate Your Personal Brand in Your Job Search Tools

Your tools can reflect the consistent message of your brand by showing evidence of the skills that have made you a "go-to" person for certain skills or tasks. The résumé is a chance to highlight these assets. In this chapter, you will learn to create a targeted résumé that connects your assets to those sought by employers. A targeted résumé tells the story of your experience and assets, and how they fit the needs for certain opportunities. Your self-marketing effort is a chance to communicate your brand by delivering a clear, focused message that is supported by evidence of your skills with references who endorse your best qualities with their recommendations.

Skill, Preferences, Values, and Your Brand

By developing your personal brand around the skills, preferences, and values that are important to you, you will have a brand that is consistent with you. However, it may not clearly connect with a job or career path right now. In fact, the career path that fits your self-assessment may not even have been invented yet, since careers are growing and changing so fast.

Your task is to choose activities, leadership roles, and experiences that help you build the assets you want to use in the world of work. In time, some experiences may connect more with your leisure or volunteer activities, while others will contribute to your professional growth. However, everything you do becomes connected with your brand. Consider the Career Profile with AJ Sabath, who became a "go-to" person for political insights—honing his skills and expertise while changing jobs frequently, spending time overseas, taking breaks from employment for political campaigns, and switching a job to increase his work-life balance.

It may be challenging to differentiate yourself from others when you are not yet certain of your career path, or just starting out in your career, but defining what is important to you will help you make choices that make you proud. Over time, as was described already, you will notice themes emerge, and you will become branded for the qualities and skills you have developed.

Every time you create a blog post, "like" or "pin" something online, or share a thought on Facebook, LinkedIn, or Twitter, you are developing your brand. Your online activities do not have to be related to your career interests to impact your brand. Have you commented on products you've bought, events you've attended, or posted comments on websites? A large majority of online activity is public, easily searchable, and instantly accessible to employers, potential mentors, and others who might evaluate you just by Googling your name.

Make a plan and choose your resources. Although there are many ways to develop your brand online, a personal blog, Facebook, Twitter, and LinkedIn are by far the most popular and effective tools at the time this book is being written. A LinkedIn profile with résumé-related details can serve as a professional tool, as can a Twitter or Facebook account with a professional bio or profile.

Get involved. Add connections and keep in touch, "like" companies that interest you, and post or tweet articles, news, and information that are relevant to your core interests and values. Create a Twitter feed, write a blog, and respond to blog posts that interest you. You don't need to be an expert to develop a brand; part of your brand can be your interest in growing within the industry. Discussions on LinkedIn frequently include questions from students or recent graduates asking for tips about breaking into various fields. Read these discussions for insider tips or start your own and build insider contacts.

Online participation impacts your brand. What you "like" on Facebook and who you "follow" on Twitter can affect your brand. These often reflect your interests and views on politics, social awareness, hobbies, interests, current events, and more. As you develop your professional identity, your interests may shift. Old posts, tagged photos, or activities that do not reflect your current career objectives may seem less desirable. Determine your goals and make decisions that you think will work for the long-term. Use privacy settings, but realize that aspects of your online participation may be accessible to employers, so make your choices with this consideration in mind. Check into your own "digital dirt" by Googling yourself and developing a strategy to remove inappropriate postings.

Avoid confusion. Given the global reach of the Internet, even if your name is fairly obscure, employers and others who search for you online might find another person with your name. Consider Curtis Jackson, a software engineer, who posted his résumé with his contact information on his personal website (Charnock, 2010). Despite having definitive interests and experience in the field of engineering, fans of another Curtis Jackson, better known as "50 Cent," began calling, sending letters, and e-mailing. Maintaining a consistent image in your social media and using the same photograph can help employers and others know it is the real digital you.

》 Résumés for the Real World

Effective résumés present a story of an individual's experience, skills, and assets, set up in an easy to read format, and are targeted for a specific position. Selecting a format, layout, design, and appropriate sections are important aspects of crafting a great résumé.

Choose a Résumé Format

There are numerous ways to set up your résumé, and there are differences in how each format is prepared as well as its purpose. Explore the descriptions of each, and determine which will best highlight your key assets. In this section you will learn about these résumé formats: reverse chronological, functional, combination, curriculum vitae, and biography.

 © ONOKY - Photononstop/Alamy

Your résumé is the story of your career development. To make sure it conveys the message you intend, review it with someone before sending it to employers.

Reverse chronological. The reverse chronological résumé is the most common résumé format for recent graduates and experienced professionals with a linear career path. This format typically includes experience sections with detailed descriptions, as well as sections for education and skills. Employers generally prefer this format because the timeline design makes it very easy to follow. (See **Exhibit 8.7**, Alex Moreno, **Exhibit 8.13**, Leticia Beason, **Exhibit 8.18**, Mason Wolff, for examples of reverse chronological résumés.)

Functional. Functional résumés separate tasks, skills gained, and job "functions" from the positions themselves. This is accomplished by featuring a section highlighting skills gained during experiences as well as a separate section with employers. This résumé style is more common for inexperienced candidates with minimal employment or internships, or career changers seeking to illustrate how their experiences are relevant when recent job titles or activities do not directly relate to the job's requirements. (See **Exhibit 8.11**, Daniel Chee, for an example of a functional résumé.)

Combination. These résumés combine a summary of skills, similar to the skills section of a functional résumé, with an experience section that offers details as they are listed in the reverse chronological format. This résumé style offers an opportunity to highlight key assets, while also listing experiences with descriptions in an easy-to-follow order. This format is useful for experienced professionals or recent graduates with extensive school and work activities who wish to highlight key points that may otherwise be hard to find in the various sections of the résumé. (See **Exhibit 8.16**, Katie Clarke, for an example of a combination résumé.)

Curriculum vitae (CV). This type of résumé is similar to a reverse chronological format but is far more comprehensive, listing all degrees, awards, credentials, experiences, publications, conferences, research, teaching, and professional affiliations. While sections may vary by field, this format is generally reserved for academics and scientists, but may be used by medical doctors and professionals with advanced degrees whose publications and presentations are key assets. This type of résumé does not involve the dynamic formatting and style of typical résumés; instead, it lists all data with a standard font in a consistent size. (See **Exhibit 8.10**, Alex Moreno, for an example of a CV.)

Biography. Celebrities, artists, public figures, senior-level executives, and others who are in the public eye will likely use a biography or brief bio. The "bio" or "brief bio" is a story that details the highlights of an individual's career. Usually bouncing from present to past and back to present, the bio is written as a short story and may include references to past experiences, major accomplishments, degrees and awards received, as well as mentions of press coverage. Bios are commonly found in "About Us" sections of company websites and can also provide an overview of key assets on social media pages, such as LinkedIn. (See **Exhibit 8.20**, Mason Wolff, for an example of a brief biography.)

The Basics of Résumé Writing

Content. Expect to include your contact information, education, experience, and best assets and accomplishments on your résumé. Note that employers will expect you to be honest on your résumé, and not to embellish your experiences or credentials. If you present false or misleading information, employers have the legal right to rescind an offer or terminate employment.

Résumé length. Typically, the résumé is one page in length. Certain résumé formats, such as a CV or bio might be longer, and for experienced professionals a one-and-a-half- or two-page résumé is acceptable. Recent graduates often struggle to pull all of their skills and experiences into this limited page length, but once you are familiar with the variations in layout and design, it will be easier to identify and include the most important content.

Layout and design. The purpose of a strong layout and design is to present information in a way that is easy and meaningful to employers. Adding lines to separate sections, making sure there is enough white space on the page, using lists (with round or square bullets), tabs, and choosing the best location for dates and titles will all help you personalize the design of your résumé. If you lack graphic-design skills and find yourself, for example, using the space bar rather than the tabs tool, consider developing basic, graphic-design skills by learning to use advanced functions of word-processing programs. Explore whether your school's career center or computer center offer expert assistance.

Fonts. Choose one font for your entire résumé that is easy to read and has a style you prefer, then use bold, Italics, or capital letters to make the sections and details stand out. Some common résumé fonts, all in 11 point, are shown below.

Arial	Century Gothic	Helvetica
Arial Narrow	Garamond	Times New Roman

Naming your document. The filename for your résumé should include your name and the word "résumé." While some employers prefer ".pdf" files, since they ensure consistency, others prefer ".doc" files. If you have questions about what employers prefer in your industry or region, simply ask your career center, or contact target employers directly. Several examples of good choices for résumé filenames follow, and they are all correct.

> Leticia Beason's résumé → leticia beason resume.pdf
>
> Alex Moreno's résumé → Alex Moreno - resume.doc
>
> Mason Wolff → wolff_ mason_resume.doc

Sharing your résumé. In most cases, you will e-mail or upload your résumé, rather than physically send it via snail mail or fax. However, in addition to an electronic version, you will need printed copies to bring to interviews. It is acceptable to bring copies on plain, white paper, but it is preferred that you use a heavier-stock paper with a watermark (an imprint that is visible when the paper is held up in front of a light), typically in cream, ivory, or white. Although you can expect most employers to review your résumé in its electronic format, some may print a copy for note taking. Try a practice run. First, print it. Does all of your text fit within the margins? Is the font large enough to read clearly? Are you pleased with the overall look? Next, e-mail it to yourself and open it to confirm that it sends properly. (For additional tips, see Tech Savvy: Sending Your Résumé and Cover Letter Online.)

Prepare a Targeted Résumé

A targeted résumé is designed to highlight the assets and accomplishments that are most relevant to the needs of the reader. A successful targeted résumé makes the reader think, "Wow! These are exactly the requirements that meet our needs!"

Most recruiters will spend 20–30 seconds or less reviewing résumés in the initial screening process. Try glancing at one of the sample résumés in this text for less than a minute. What did you learn? You might notice the school or degree, the most recent employer, and a few other details, particularly those in bold or italics or with clear white space above or below. In such a short time it is difficult to learn much about a candidate, but it is often enough time to know what they are most qualified to do and what they have been doing. (See **Exhibit 8.2**, How to Get Your Résumé Past a Recruiter's Screening Process, for ideas about overcoming some of the obstacles that employers might see on a résumé in less than a minute.) By preparing a targeted résumé, you ensure that your résumé will meet the needs of the employer directly, making it far more likely that yours will pass the half-minute review.

Start with a master résumé. A master résumé will include everything you have done, with details and accomplishments from all of your experiences, as well as all of your education courses and activities. Free of formatting, it will likely be too long to be used as is, and far harder to find those sought-after, targeted details that relate to job requirements. By starting with a master résumé, however, you have one source for all of your potential résumé content.

Choose a sample target position. Start with four or five job listings for positions that interest you. You can find these through your college's job listings or in an on-line job board. Select *one* for your target position that includes a detailed list of job requirements. By beginning with several listings for your target position, you can be sure your sample covers the key requirements, and that your résumé will, too.

Select a résumé format. Select the best format for your experience: reverse chronological, functional, or combination.

Open a new document that will become your résumé. Start with your name and contact information and then add section headings. Although there are templates available through some word-processing programs, we recommend against using these, because they embed formatting within the document that is difficult to change. Instead, type your information directly into a new document, with a filename that includes your name and the word "résumé."

Start by entering contact information. Enter your education, assets, and experiences into each section, or cut and paste from your master résumé.

Determine the most appropriate sections and the best order. How you organize your résumé is an important factor in how you present your assets. Choose sections that highlight your best assets and put the most important sections at the top of the page (see **Exhibit 8.1**, Résumé Sections). Include a profile or summary section if your career objective is not clearly evident by your most recent experiences. Using your master résumé, cut and paste information into each section.

Determine the look. The next step is choosing a font style and size, plus determining the layout and design. Choose your desired font, with a size that is easy to read. Use bold, italics, underlining, and line rules to highlight information. Refer to résumé samples in this book, online, or in your career center to choose a "look" for your résumé.

Evaluate your finished product. Finally, look at your résumé side-by-side with the sample target position. Does your résumé cover all of the key requirements of the position? Are your primary assets easy to find on your résumé? Are other valuable points present on the résumé, even if they are not prominently featured? Have you devoted the most space to the most important details? Is it an appropriate length? If your résumé goes beyond one page, consider what you can cut, shorten, or if there is a layout you can use that will help you include more on the page (see Career Profile—Case Studies in this chapter for examples).

Get feedback. For a résumé critique, visit a career counselor in your school or ask for feedback from a networking contact, mentor, or faculty member. The purpose of a résumé is to get an interview, and, later, to guide the interviewer towards questions that will help you describe your best assets and land the position. To get the best feedback, share your sample job description and your résumé with the person giving feedback, and ask whether your résumé meets the requirements in the listing and whether it leads toward questions regarding your most relevant qualifications.

>>**EXHIBIT 8.1** ● **Résumé Sections**

Name and Contact Information	This can include your full name, address, e-mail, and telephone number. Confirm that your e-mail address is professional, and that any voice message is brief and appropriate for employers. In cases where you would prefer to leave off your address (e.g., public job boards), but want employers to know your geographic location, include only your city and state.
Online Profile, Blog, or Personal Website	If you maintain a personal website, blog, or online portfolio that is relevant to your career goal, you may wish to include the URL alongside your phone number and e-mail address. A LinkedIn or Google Profile can also be listed. Make sure that any links you provide lead to information that is current and professional, and that each link opens properly.
Objective	This optional section is an opportunity to convey to the reader your current career focus (see **Exhibit 8.18**, Mason Wolff), or a target position (see **Exhibit 8.13**, Leticia Beason, and the bold-faced, top line of **Exhibit 8.16**, Katie Clarke). This is especially helpful when applying to large organizations, where they sort an extensive number of resumes.
Profile or Summary	A short profile or summary can highlight experience, specific skills, or credentials that will help you to stand out (see the bold-faced, top line of **Exhibit 8.11**, Daniel Chee, and the paragraph below the objective in **Exhibit 8.16**, Katie Clarke). This section is especially helpful if your experience is varied, making it difficult for employers to see a focus, or if you are a mid-career professional with extensive experience.
Education	This required section is a summary of your higher education. Usually high school is not included, unless you have a specific reason such as a desire to highlight a relationship to a geographic area.
	Include the full name of your college with the city and state, your graduation date, the degree you received or expect, or the dates you attended if you did not graduate. List any other institutions you attended. If outside the United States, list the country where your school is located. Include any international study or summer educational programs.
	Include your major, minor, dean's list, scholarships, or departmental awards. Your GPA should be listed, especially if it is 3.5 or higher, and for some industries such as finance and STEM fields, any GPA over 3.0 should be listed. Include "Awards," "Honors," and "Coursework" in this section or in separate sections.
Experience	List past or current employers, city, and state, title, dates of employment, and, if using a reverse chronological or combination format, include details about your responsibilities and accomplishments.
	You can choose to have more than one section for your experience or experiential learning, such as a separate section for "Internships" or "Volunteer Experience," or you may wish to separate "Related (or Industry) Experience" from "Additional Experience." "Coursework" can also be highlighted in a "Project Experience" section (see **Exhibit 8.18**, Mason Wolff).
Activities	Activities are great examples of your interests and dedication; in addition, your participation can demonstrate leadership skills. This can include activities on and off campus, such as sports, volunteer work, travel, fraternities or sororities, student groups, professional associations, service learning, involvement in campus or local politics, and more (see **Exhibit 8.5**, Jasmine Nouri, and **Exhibit 8.13**, Leticia Beason).
	Alternative sections might be titled "Professional Associations" (See **Exhibit 8.18**, Mason Wolff), "Memberships," "Extracurricular" (see **Exhibit 8.7**, Alex Moreno, and **Exhibit 8.11**, Daniel Chee), "Volunteer Activities" or "Community Service" (see **Exhibit 8.5**, Jasmine Nouri).
Skills	While not required, this section is highly recommended. The two most common are computer and language skills. Others include technical (e.g., design or equipment and lighting) or laboratory skills. Skills can be listed on the bottom of the resume (see **Exhibit 8.5**, Jasmine Nouri, **Exhibit 8.11**, Daniel Chee, and **Exhibit 8.13**, Leticia Beason), toward the top of the resume (see **Exhibit 8.7**, Alex Moreno, and **Exhibit 8.18**, Mason Wolff), or as part of a combination resume (see **Exhibit 8.16**, Katie Clarke).
Certification	Some professions require you to be certified in key skills areas, such as CPR, first aid, teaching, financial planning, or social work. To save space, it is also appropriate to combine headings, such as "Professional Affiliations and Certification."
Specialty Headings	Depending on the field you are going into, you may wish to include additional sections, for example, "Exhibitions and Grants" for artists, "Publications" for writers, or "Social Media."
Interests	This optional section can be used to show interests that are relevant to your career or show personal interests that do not appear elsewhere on the resume. It can also be a conversation starter (see **Exhibit 8.18**, Mason Wolff).
Additional	This heading can be used for information that does not fit into any other section. For example, this is an appropriate section for optional information such as your citizenship or permanent resident status, that you have a driver's license or other non-education job-related credential, or other data that shows how you are qualified for a position.
References or Portfolio	These sections are no longer common on the resume and should not be listed. Employers expect a separate page for references and will ask to see your portfolio if applicable.

While college recruiters are generally more open to variations in a candidate's preparation for positions than other recruiters, understanding how recruiters screen candidates can help you prepare a targeted resume that gets attention. Review this chart for solutions to some of the flags that lead recruiters to reject candidates quickly (see also Remillard, 2010).

Reason for Rejection	Description	How to Overcome This Obstacle
Geographic Location Is Not Local	You are applying for a position in an area where you do not live	Include experiences that tie you to the area, and mention your desire and intent to relocate in the cover letter, and possibly in an objective or summary on the résumé. If you are returning to an area where you grew up, include a permanent address (such as your parent's address) or include high school in the education section.
Industry, Major, or Position Is Different	Your background, experience, or training is in a different industry than the position	Highlight courses, volunteer work, experience, or activities that prepared you for the scope of that industry. Consider a profile statement or combination résumé to highlight relevant skills and accomplishments.
Experience, Skills, or Areas of Study Are Unrelated	Your work tasks, or the tasks you are prepared to do based on education, training, or experiences must relate to the required functions of the positions	List your most relevant activities or experience before unrelated experience. As a student, your paid employment might be unrelated to your career goals, while coursework or student activities are more relevant. Consider moving these experiences above "Work Experience" in sections such as "Coursework," "Project Experience," "Activities" (with leadership roles), or "Internships." Another choice is to create a section titled "Related Experience."
Level of Education Does Not Meet Minimum Requirements	The level of education must be consistent with the position's requirements.	Try to seek out opportunities that ask for a level of education that corresponds to yours. You will be a better match, and your résumé will get more attention. If you have less education than requested, you can also draw attention to your relevant credentials, including years of industry experience, internships, and coursework. A profile or summary can also be helpful.
Mistakes or Errors	Errors in grammar or spelling; the résumé is too long, information seems to be left off; dates are unclear, etc.	Proofread for typos, grammatical errors, dates, titles, and other possible errors or mistakes. Make sure your résumé is an appropriate length, and that tabs, fonts, and formatting are consistent. Check that links are up-to-date, and that the résumé prints properly on the page, even if you are sending it via e-mail.

There are many different ways you will be sending your résumé online. Understanding the basics will help you prepare a résumé that is compatible with current technology. While these are some of the new and current tools in the job search, they may not be the most common in your industry, region, or in use by the time you are reading this text. Check with your career center to make sure your approach is current and relevant.

E-mail résumés. Your résumé can easily be e-mailed as an attachment, giving you the opportunity to send a detailed cover letter in the body of the e-mail. The advantage to submitting a formatted résumé via e-mail, versus an unformatted electronic résumé, is that your résumé can serve the double purpose of being easy to read and understood by a recruiter as well as easily read by most databases.

Electronic résumés. Electronic résumés, also called "scannable résumés," are unformatted, "text-only" résumés that are flush left and no more than 65 characters across. To prepare an electronic résumé, use your original résumé, then remove all bullets, underlining, italics, line rule, and other formatting. All text should be the same size (10 point is fine), in a font such as Courier or Arial. One option is to save your file in a program like Notepad to remove all formatting. Save your "text only" résumé with the suffix ".txt" so that it is easily opened in any program on any platform.

Which should you send: text only or formatted? With technology developing so rapidly and changing the job search process dramatically, there is conflicting advice on methods for sending résumés. As résumé-reading software becomes more sophisticated and can read formatted résumés without errors, fewer employers are requesting electronic résumés. As a general rule, include your résumé as an attachment with a ".pdf" or ".doc" extension, and only send an electronic résumé in the body of an e-mail and as a ".txt" attachment in cases where this is requested by an employer. Whenever possible, confirm what is required by checking with employers, your career center, or anyone else to whom you will be sending a résumé.

Applicant Tracking Software (ATS). Applicant Tracking Software is used by companies to search through résumés and identify applicants by keywords in their résumé. For your résumé to be effective in this environment, it must include the terms and language that human resource personnel will use as search terms or keywords. By using job listings in your résumé preparation, you can confirm employers' terms are present in your résumé.

Job boards. When uploading your résumé to a job board, you can expect it will be reviewed using ATS and searched by keywords. Another issue to consider with job boards is privacy, as this information is available to the public.

Online profiles. Online profiles, such as those on LinkedIn, are a great resource for employers and job seekers. Combined with ATS, these also offer new opportunities for employers and recruiters to find candidates who have not applied for positions (Zielinski, 2011). You can upload your résumé to your online profile or type in only the details you wish to include. Your profile will often include a photo, heading, and details of your education, employment, certifications, and activities. It is very much like a résumé, but all of your data is stored in searchable fields. Furthermore, with your data come recommendations by the site for jobs, networking contacts, and groups that might interest you. This is an interactive tool that uses social networks for your job search after you upload your résumé information.

≫ Just Say It! Action Verbs

Action verbs are the verbs that precede the detailed descriptions in your résumé and help explain what you have done. Action verbs should be written in the correct tense—past or present. Alternatives to action verbs include such phrases as "duties included" and "was responsible for," but such phrases are long, taking up valuable space on the résumé, and do little to add to the descriptions of your activities. Instead, action verbs can demonstrate your level of responsibility, accomplishments, and the role you played throughout your experiences. Consider the list in **Exhibit 8.3**, Action Verbs, and how they can add to your descriptions within your résumé.

Leadership/Management Skills

Accomplished Achieved Acted Addressed Advocated Appointed Approved Assessed Briefed Controlled Delegated Directed Earned Effected Elected Emphasized Employed Enacted Enforced Established Governed Handled Headed Justified Led Maintained Managed Maximized Motivated Orchestrated Oversaw Piloted Ran Restructured Spearheaded Supervised Transitioned

Administrative/Organizational Skills

Acquired Allocated Arranged Assisted Checked Clarified Classified Collected Combined Completed Composed Coordinated Delivered Designated Determined Distributed Eliminated Generated Hired Implemented Interviewed Inventoried Kept Merged Moderated Monitored Operated Ordered Organized Outsourced Prepared Printed Prioritized Processed Procured Purchased Received Reconciled Recorded Recruited Reorganized Scheduled Sorted Staffed Streamlined Summarized Supplied Supported Standardized Structured Systematized Tracked Transferred Undertook Updated Upgraded Utilized Worked

Communication/Interpersonal Skills

Answered Collaborated Communicated Consulted Contacted Cooperated Corresponded Critiqued Cultivated Demonstrated Discussed Displayed Documented Edited Entertained Explained Facilitated Hosted Interacted Introduced Judged Launched Marketed Mediated Mentored Negotiated Participated Presented Promoted Proofread Publicized Raised Renegotiated Represented Reported Resolved Responded Sold Trained Translated Transmitted Wrote United

Analytical/Research/Financial Skills

Administered Analyzed Applied Appraised Balanced Budgeted Calculated categorized Charted Compared Compiled Computed Debugged Diagnosed Engineered Estimated Evaluated Examined Financed Fixed Focused Forecasted Formulated Gathered Hypothesized Identified Increased Inspected Installed Interpreted Invented Investigated Measured Observed Outlined Planned Prescribed Projected Proposed Questioned Recycled Reduced Researched Reviewed Revised Screened Solved Studied Synthesized Troubleshot Totaled Uncovered Validated Verified

Creative/Innovative Skills

Adapted Conceived Conceptualized Constructed Crafted Created Customized Designed Developed Drafted Drew Enhanced Formalized Improved Incorporated Innovated Instituted Integrated Joined Manufactured Modeled Modified Performed Photographed Produced Rendered Sketched Started Strengthened Transformed

Counseling/Helping/Teaching Skills

Advised Aided Coached Contributed Corrected Counseled Educated Enabled Encouraged Enriched Fulfilled Guided Helped Illustrated Instructed Learned Lectured Programmed Provided Recommended Referred Rehabilitated Served Shared Suggested Taught Tested Tutored Volunteered

© Cengage Learning 2014

Using action verb phrases can help you demonstrate transferable skills. A camp counselor could include phrases starting with "supervise," "help," "instruct," or "motivate."

© Jeff Greenberg/Alamy

Consider one of the case studies in this chapter. In this excerpt from **Exhibit 8.13**, Leticia Beason, her experience at the Marriott Hotel is described using action-verb phrases. For more examples, refer to the résumé samples in this chapter.

Marriot International, Tucson, AZ

Intern, Event Planning, Summer 2012

· Assisted with coordination of corporate meetings and events.
· Acted as point person between events coordinator and hourly associates.

Do your job search materials reflect your community involvement, volunteer work, and the social causes that concern you? These experiences benefit society and are personally fulfilling. For many, this drives their motivation to participate. However, to employers, your social awareness can reflect your core values, help you illustrate many important qualities, and reflect applicable, transferable skills.

Listing volunteer experiences on your résumé, following up with people you meet through community service activities, and identifying connections between your target employers' social causes and your own personal activities are all examples of including your social awareness in your self-marketing. Some examples of participation in social causes are the following:

- Participation in a fundraising walk for breast cancer as part of a team
- Staffing a booth at a fundraising carnival at your local church, temple, or mosque
- Serving food at a homeless shelter or soup kitchen
- Sorting contributions to the animal shelter
- Reading to senior citizens
- Attending a fundraising event
- Organizing a clothing drive for victims of a natural disaster
- Gathering care packages for troops overseas
- Distributing information for a political campaign
- Collecting garbage and recyclables in a public park or beach

Consider just a few of the transferable skills gained in such experiences.

- Teamwork
- Customer service
- Project management
- Sales
- Research
- Organization
- Marketing
- Administrative

For many volunteers, the skills used in community service activities differ from skills they gained deliberately through coursework or work experience. The result is that you build skills that you may not have used in other formal experiences, *plus* evidence of these skills, *plus* professional references that can attest to your skills. This is often because the desire to help out or get involved superseded any intentional efforts to build skills. As you consider the message you wish to convey to employers, reflect on activities in your free time as well as formal activities. Community involvement can help convey a detailed picture of what you offer employers and the skills you can and will contribute, both at work and in the world. This can help distinguish you from other candidates, and give you an opportunity to discuss additional assets that are unique to your interests, skills, and talents.

If the skills, experience, and training from your volunteer work apply directly to your career interests, consider highlighting them in your résumé and cover letter. Depending on their relevance, these experiences can be listed with dates and locations, or detailed in the same way you would describe a job or internship, including the organization, dates, location, your title, and a description of your tasks. Volunteer experiences can be included in a variety of sections in your résumé. They can be included in a section titled "Activities" or "Community Service," or they can be integrated into a section on "Experience" or "Related Experience."

» Prepare Winning Cover Letters

The purpose of the cover letter is to serve as an introduction. Like the résumé, it will not land you a position, but it can cost you one. In certain industries, where writing, communication, and marketing skills are highly valued, the cover letter is also the first writing sample you are submitting, and will be examined for style, tone, content, and grammar.

A winning cover letter can serve as a sample of your writing, elaborate on key assets listed in your résumé, and describe your skills using terms from the employer's listing. Cover letters should be written in your own words, rather than copied from samples, and should reflect a business writing style.

A cover letter is expected to accompany your résumé every time you send one—unless there is no opportunity to submit one, such as in some college-recruiting programs, at a career fair, or when uploading a résumé to a job board.

In most cases, a simple formula can be applied to write effective cover letters in three to four paragraphs. According to résumé and cover-letter-writing experts Wendy Enelow and Louise Kursmark, the cover letter presents the "skills, qualifications, achievements, and credentials that you want to bring to a specific reader's immediate attention" (Enelow and Kursmark, 2010).

Cover Letter Sections

The greeting. First, address your résumé to a person. While it is not always possible to find the name of the key decision maker, in most cases you will be able to find an appropriate person to whom to address your letter. If no name is given, see if you can learn the name of the person responsible for making the hiring decision using online tools like LinkedIn or Hoovers, or direct your cover letter to the human resources director or the senior officer in the department you are targeting. If you are sending your résumé to someone other than the person whose e-mail address is listed in the job posting, always copy ("cc") your résumé and cover letter to that e-mail address as well.

Your introduction. The introduction is the first paragraph of your cover letter. It tells the reader why you are writing, highlights one or two of your most relevant assets, and mentions any names of those who referred you to the listing. Be sure to include the name of the position to which you are applying and how you heard about it. If you have been referred by someone, ask if you can use his or her name in the letter.

The body. The body of the letter consists of the middle paragraph (or two), and is the most significant component of the letter. This is your opportunity to market yourself to the potential employer. Use this section to detail the skills, qualities, and requirements they have described in their job listing. If the job listing is very brief, use another job listing for a similar position as a guideline for points to address. Instead of repeating the content of your résumé, describe your key skills or qualities and connect them to the needs of the position. Show your industry or company knowledge with a sentence outlining your passion for the position or company.

The closing. The last paragraph is the closing and tells the reader what action you expect to happen next. Unless you have been expressly instructed not to contact the employer, you can describe how you intend to follow up. At the end of the letter, use a professional closing such as "Sincerely," and type your full name. If you are printing and mailing or faxing the letter, you will want to sign the page above your printed name. However, there are few instances where you would submit a printed cover letter.

Create a Targeted Cover Letter

Like your résumés, cover letters need to be targeted for the specific employer and position. This helps the employer understand how your assets are relevant, and also demonstrates your awareness of the skills that you plan to use on the job. To create a targeted cover letter, review the job listing for specifics, as you did with a general listing when preparing your targeted résumé, and decide which points you plan to highlight in your letter. Consider which of your knowledge, skills, and abilities (KSAs) match the specific requirements in each job listing (Gaw, 2011). Choose three areas to address; then create one sentence for each main point, connecting your assets to the employer's needs. Each cover letter sample in this chapter is targeted for the specific job listing connected to that case.

Sending the Cover Letter

Currently, the most common method of sending your résumé and cover letter is via e-mail. It is generally acceptable to send the cover letter as the body of the e-mail and attach the résumé. Large organizations or corporations may prefer a very brief email cover letter with your résumé and cover letter as separate attachments. (See the many examples in this chapter; for instance, **Exhibit 8.8**, Alex Moreno, shows an e-mail cover letter and **Exhibit 8.9**, Alex Moreno, is a traditional cover letter to use as an attachment or if you are faxing or mailing your résumé.) If you are required to apply via a website, follow the instructions given on the site. Of course, before you send your cover letters, be sure to proofread and correct grammatical errors or typos.

≫ EMBRACING DIFFERENCES ● Where in the World Will Your Career Take You? Cultural Differences in Job Search Materials

Networking, interviews, résumés, cover letters, and other job search materials can look a lot different depending on where you are—or where you want to work. In this text, you are primarily focusing on learning how to market yourself in the United States. However, if you are an international student or an American student who plans to look for work in a different country, then you will benefit from an understanding of the culture and business customs of the country where you are interested in working. Keep in mind, even regional differences within the United States are useful to note. For instance, if you are on the East Coast, but looking for work on the West Coast, you may need to learn about differences in formality, style of dress, or communication in the workplace.

Cultural Differences

Cultural norms strongly influence how people do business and search for jobs. In order to blend more seamlessly into the culture where you would like to work, learn more about it! Your cover letters and résumé will reflect an understanding of cultural norms only if you know them. Read books, set up networking meetings with people from that country, and, if you are overseas, ask for information on job search techniques from a local university. If you can, visit offices and work settings that interest you, even if they are satellite offices based in the United States. Speak to people familiar with the hiring process to learn variations. For instance, in some countries, a handwritten cover letter is preferred instead of a printed one, even in our computer era. Your school's career center may have alumni-networking contacts in the countries where you would like to work or an advisor for the international job search.

Variations on the Résumé

In the United States, the résumé is the most common tool used to illustrate your past experiences and strongest assets. In many

European countries, a curriculum vitae or "CV" is commonly used instead of the American style résumé. This is different from an American CV, which is used primarily for academic or science positions. The CV you prepare for countries outside the United States will include personal information such as date of birth, place of birth, and marital status, which is considered inappropriate to include on a résumé in the United States. In Europe, the CV is usually much longer than the standard one-page American résumé. In some countries (e.g., Germany), a photograph may also be required with the CV, whereas in the United States a photograph is inappropriate, except when submitted as a headshot for such positions as model or actor where appearance is directly related to the requirements of the job. Copies of your diploma or other documentation may be required as well.

Communication for Your International Job Search

In many countries, English is a widely accepted language. However, unless you are participating in a recruiting program targeting U.S. students, companies may expect you to submit your application in the country's official language. To find out the expectations of an organization, contact the human resources department and ask these and any other basic questions you may have. Learning which languages are commonly spoken in locations you are targeting can also help you prepare. For instance, German and French are both common languages in Switzerland and Luxembourg, and, in Canada, speaking French may be a requirement of the job. In addition, if you list any level of foreign language knowledge on your résumé, you may be put to the test with interview questions in that language—whether you are looking for a job in the United States or abroad.

» Additional Job Search Tools

In addition to résumés and cover letters, additional materials, such as references, thank you letters, and job search applications, are critical tools for your job search preparation.

References

Often, references will be requested with a résumé for a job opening. When this occurs, employers are referring to a page with a list of three or four references, each with current contact information (see **Exhibit 8.15**, Leticia Beason). To prepare your list, contact your references in advance to ensure they are available and will be able to speak about your current interests. If necessary, set up a phone or in-person meeting to review your current needs. Always thank references with thank you letters—e-mail or handwritten notes can be appropriate.

Thank You Letters

Whether handwritten or sent via e-mail, personal thank you notes for your references show your appreciation and helps maintain your relationships for the future.

Thank you letters are not just a chance to thank an employer for an interview: they are an opportunity to restate your interest in the organization and position, add information that relates to the interview, and review some of your key selling points (see **Exhibit 8.6**, Jasmine Nouri). They are more than a courtesy; employers expect them. Thank you letters give you a chance to follow up and further develop the relationship that was established within the interview. They may also be used by employers to compare two candidates who are being considered for the same position. As a rule, thank you letters should always be sent within 24–48 hours after an interview, and should be written for anyone who took the time to speak with you during your interview.

To write an effective thank you letter that adds to your candidacy, thank the interviewer and highlight one or two points that reflect your strongest assets, especially if they were not highlighted during your meeting. Then, feel free to address one or two additional points that you wish to reiterate from your résumé or discussion. By noting only a few key points in your thank you letter, you will add to your case, show that you are focused, and reflect your understanding of the position and the employer's needs.

Job Applications

Many jobs require candidates to complete job applications. The application is a legal document. Your signature at the end tells employers that the information on the form is accurate and truthful (see **Exhibit 8.21**, Job Search Applications). If you have been convicted of a crime, you must answer honestly, although it is perfectly appropriate to list that you will describe the circumstances during an interview. In a job application, far more detail is often required than in your résumé. For instance, you may be asked to list all the schools you attended, rather than only those from which you received a degree. Keeping clear records can help you complete job search applications when they are needed.

While you may find yourself using networking letters, talking points, transcripts, and other resources in your job search, the tools discussed in this chapter are some of the most common for any job search.

Throughout this text, you have been introduced to six students in the Career Profile—Case Studies. Now, these students are ready to market themselves. They have each chosen a sample target job listing to use to create targeted, job search materials. Their job search tools have been proofread and reviewed, and are all good examples, but, remember, there is no one, right way to write a résumé or cover letter.

In these case study examples, consider the following questions:

How does each résumé and cover letter respond to the needs of the employer?

What résumé sections are used to separate and highlight each candidate's most relevant assets?

Do you notice any similarities or differences in the résumés or cover letters? What are they?

Do you respond to one font, or layout and design, more than others? Can you describe why?

>> **CAREER PROFILE** ● Case Study 1: Mike Pollan (see Chapter 2: Skills)

Mike recently passed his certification as a personal trainer. He found a part-time position in a gym, but he is now considering other settings where he could work as a personal trainer, or to build a career in physical therapy. He is exploring jobs as a physical therapy aide, and also wondering whether he wants to pursue an associate's degree toward a position as a physical therapist assistant, or possibly continue his education and become a physical therapist. He would like to explore his options and learn about the jobs, requirements, and opportunities in the job market. See Exhibit 8.4.

>> **EXHIBIT 8.4** ● Elevator Pitch/Mike Pollan/Physical Therapy

Mike's Elevator Pitch, to be adapted for e-mails, phone calls, and in-person conversations. (To learn more how to create your own elevator pitch, see **Chapter 9: Launch**, Networking for Job Opportunities.)

For people in the field of physical therapy, including sports and orthopedic physical therapists:
My name is Mike Pollan. I received your name from Jim Rose, my personal-training instructor at Pembroke University Continuing Education. I am a certified personal trainer and am now considering a career in physical therapy, either as an aide or as a physical therapist assistant. I was hoping I could set up an informational interview with you to learn more about your experience and ask you some questions about the field.

For people in the field of health care and wellness, including assisted living or sports medicine:
My name is Mike Pollan. I received your name from Jim Rose, my personal-training instructor at Pembroke University Continuing Education. I am a certified personal trainer and am interested in working with seniors (or former athletes) and possibly pursuing a career in physical therapy. I was hoping I could set up an informational interview with you to learn more about your experience.

If asked about his interests or questions, Mike has identified a list of topics to explore when and if they are appropriate.

Interests
- *Working with seniors or the elderly*
- *Working with former athletes*
- *Assisting in rehabilitation*
- *Assisting after surgeries*
- *Helping people maintain an active lifestyle*
- *Helping people make exercise and/or movement a part of life*
- *Motivating others*
- *Possible interest in running my own business or maintaining private clients*

Concerns and Questions
- *The job market*
- *The educational requirements—how hard are they?*
- *Exams or certifications—what is expected of me?*
- *Professional associations—which should I consider or join?*
- *Job opportunities—where are they listed?*

Jasmine will be receiving a Bachelor of Science degree in business in a year and a half, and is participating in on-campus recruiting for internships for the upcoming summer. As part of on-campus recruiting, she was required to take an internship course in which she has begun to reevaluate some of her career goals. However, she has determined that a finance internship will be a strong asset for many of the directions that interest her, especially finance positions that combine knowledge of business, law, and science. She has also determined that to integrate them with her love of science, she will have to add activities in that area during her senior year. She has selected a listing for a finance internship to serve as her sample to create a targeted résumé. See Exhibit 8.5 and Exhibit 8.6.

Target Job Listing:

Stevens International - Finance Internship

Stevens International is a worldwide financial institution, providing investment management for individuals, corporations, and not-for-profits.

The Summer Internship Program at Stevens International is a 10-week program. Interns will be required to work 20 hours/week, will receive school credit, if applicable, and receive a monthly transportation and lunch stipend.

Interns will contribute to project-based tasks in various departments. Interested students should submit résumé only through on-campus recruiting. Attendance at on-campus information session is expected. Check with your career center for more information on information session and interview dates.

Qualifications:

- Professionally mature and able to thrive in a corporate environment
- Basic analytical and research skills; ability to create a spreadsheet with basic calculations and formulas
- Able to work effectively on a cross-functional team with members throughout the organization
- Experience working with team members remotely, using phone, e-mail and online collaboration tools
- Able to work with changing priorities and business objectives
- Excellent organizational, written, and oral communication skills
- Excellent analytical skills
- Must be extremely detail oriented
- Computer Skills: Microsoft Office, Word, Excel, Knowledge of Accounting 1 & 2
- Ability to multitask/prioritize and meet deadlines

Responsibilities:

- Typical duties may include: reviewing performance measurements, performing ad hoc analysis, analysis of account balances, journal entry and analysis, A/P invoice coding, system input, check production and mailing, bank, A/R & Verisign (CC payments) reconciliations, various expenses account analysis, and update operational metrics to assess and drive performance and achievement of business objectives.
- Administrative tasks, including file maintenance, creating worksheets
- May contribute to special projects, including internal audits and accumulation of data for analysis

At the request of the employer, only résumés (no cover letters) were accepted through on-campus recruiting. For on-campus recruiting, submit as requested. In almost all other cases, you will be able to submit a cover letter.

JASMINE NOURI   Jasmine.Nouri@yahoo.com • www.linkedin.com/in/jasminenouri

SCHOOL	32 GRACE AVENUE, GENESEO, NY 14454	(585) 555-5533
PERMANENT	14 OAK STREET, HOBOKEN, NJ 07046	(201) 555-3333

EDUCATION

STATE UNIVERSITY OF NEW YORK AT GENESEO   **Geneseo, NY**
School of Business – AACSB Accredited   Expected May 2014
Bachelor of Science in Business Administration, Minor: Entrepreneurship. GPA: 3.54

HONORS & AWARDS

Dean's List, Women in Business Scholarship Recipient, Beta Gamma Sigma Honor Society

WORK EXPERIENCE

U.S. CUSTOMS AND BORDER PROTECTION   **Buffalo, NY**
Student Intern   Summer 2012
• Provided administrative support to the CBP Officers
• Answered and transferred telephone calls to appropriate personnel
• Sorted and distributed all incoming mail to various offices

OPPENHEIMER & CO.   **Corners, NY**
Volunteer Intern   Spring 2012
• Assisted managers with contacting potential clients
• Completed managerial tasks for office staff

COMMODITY FUTURES TRADING COMMISSION (CFTC)   **New York, NY**
Paralegal   Summer 2011
• Entered statistical data for various cases for attorneys
• Analyzed bank statements and other financial documents
• Prepared financial data on spreadsheets used by attorneys in preparation
  for conclusions of their cases
Office Automation Clerk   Summer 2010
• Utilized Excel, Word, and PowerPoint to prepare materials

ACTIVITIES

THETA PHI ALPHA FRATERNITY, SUNY GENESEO   Spring 2009 - Present
Vice President of the College Panhellenic, Fall 2011 - Present
Recruitment Chair, Fall 2010 - Spring 2011
Philanthropy Chair, Fall 2009 - Fall 2010

COMMUNITY SERVICE

Member, **Relay for Life**   Fall 2003 - Present
Breast Cancer Walk, **American Cancer Society,** Various Locations   Spring 2009 - Present
Basketball Coach, **Boys & Girls Club,** Hoboken, NJ   Fall 2003 - Spring 2007

SKILLS

Word, Excel, PowerPoint, Outlook, QuickBooks, Lexis-Nexis, SPSS, SAS, STATA.

>> **EXHIBIT 8.6** ● **Thank You Letter/Jasmine Nouri/Finance Internship**

Ms. Angela Strauss, HR College Relations Coordinator
Stevens International
2 Broadway
New York, NY 10028

December 4, 2012

Dear Ms. Strauss:

Thank you for the opportunity to interview with you today for the research internship opportunity at Stevens International for summer 2013. I was very excited to discuss my education and qualifications with you and to learn more about the opportunity in New York. After speaking with you, I am even more enthusiastic and feel I can make a positive contribution while gaining important and relevant experience at a top 10 firm.

At this time, I would like to reiterate my interest in the green securities market. I have become increasingly interested in this growing sector, and focused one of my research papers on Socially Responsible Investments, as I mentioned. Our discussion inspired me to conduct further research and I learned that recent compliance regulations may provide additional opportunities for investors. I would be very excited to join your team and participate in this area of research. In addition to my enthusiasm, I bring strong research and analytical skills and I am adept at using technology to locate information and manage data.

Again, thank you for meeting with me today. Feel free to contact me at (585) 555-5533 or jasmine.nouri@yahoo.com if you require any additional information to support my candidacy. I eagerly await the opportunity to speak with you again.

Sincerely,

Jasmine Nouri

Alex will be receiving a Bachelor of Science degree in biology this year. He has decided that he is most interested in conducting research and possibly practicing medicine, but he does not know which setting he would prefer: working in a hospital, working in private practice or a clinic, or working as a researcher. He is considering medical school or a doctorate, or both, as possible future options. However, he is not ready to commit to either path in the next year, and has decided to target research positions in hospitals, university settings, and medical centers. He has selected a listing for a *research assistant* position to serve as his sample to create a targeted résumé and cover letter. He has created a networking-style letter because he has been able to gain the names of referrals in many of the organizations to which he will apply. He has also created a curriculum vitae, or CV, for those positions that request one, and also for use in networking, given his interest in research and the relevance of his publication record. See Exhibit 8.7, Exhibit 8.8, Exhibit 8.9, and Exhibit 8.10.

Target Job Listing:

Research Study Assistant I, Radiation Oncology
Added 02/12/2013
Miami, FL

Research Support

Miami Cancer Center is a world class facility dedicated to the progressive control and cure of cancer through programs of patient care, research, and education. The incumbent will work as an integral member of the research team and in compliance with all regulatory, institutional, and departmental requirements, perform data collection and data entry, and participate in data analysis for various studies within MCC. The Research Study Assistant will provide project supervision to ensure data quality and integrity during each phase of the cycle. Minimum requirements that must be met include a bachelor's degree with no prior experience or a high school diploma with research experience. Medical terminology and interest in science are helpful. This position requires that the incumbent must complete tasks of moderate to standard difficulty with limited supervision and/or assist more senior research staff in working on more complex assignments.

Apply by sending cover letter and resume to Matthew Kidd, Human Resource Manager, at matthew.kidd@miamicancercenter.org.

ALEX MORENO
6788 Archer Road • Gainesville, FL 33411
(352) 555-5533 • akm523@ufl.edu

EDUCATION

UNIVERSITY OF FLORIDA   **Gainesville, FL**
Bachelor of Science   Expected May 2013
Major: Biology, GPA: 4.0, Dean's List, Provost Scholarship

Relevant Coursework:

Fundamentals of Biology Lecture/Lab 1 & 2   Fundamentals of Chemistry Lecture/Lab 1 & 2
Fundamentals of Physics Lecture/Lab 1 & 2   General Ecology

SKILLS

Technical Skills: General laboratory maintenance, solid phase peptide synthesis, SDS-PAGE, NMR, IR, pH testing, sterilization, bacterial culturing

Computer Skills: Microsoft Word, Microsoft Excel, Microsoft PowerPoint, Microsoft Front Page, Photoshop, Logger Pro, CAD, Autodesk Inventor Professional, 3D Studio Max, Windows Movie Maker

Language Skills: Fluent in written and spoken Spanish. Familiar with Italian and Portuguese.

WORK EXPERIENCE

NORTH FLORIDA REGIONAL MEDICAL CENTER   **Gainesville, FL**
Medical Intern, Summer 2012
- Shadowed doctors and assisted them with acquiring medicine and equipment.
- Attended conferences and learned about the latest medical research.
- Researched information on nutrients associated with preventing cognitive decline and prepared a report and a poster for the public.

Junior Volunteer, Summers 2010 & 2011
- Transported patients from one clinic to another and discharged patients.
- Answered phones and delivered packages and papers from one place to another.

CHILDREN'S THERAPY CENTER   **Gainesville, FL**
Receptionist, October 2010 - May 2011
- Acted as a liaison between the principal, faculty, and parents.
- Answered and transferred calls from teachers, parents, and faculty.
- Delivered packages of school supplies to teachers.
- Made copies for the principal and teachers for upcoming faculty meetings.
- Constructed bookmarks out of finger paintings made by students with disabilities to be distributed to parents and visitors.

MEMBERSHIPS

Golden Key International Honor Society	2011 - Present
Phi Delta Epsilon	2011 - Present
Alpha Lambda Delta	2010 - Present
Pre-Med/Pre-Health Club	2009 - Present
Chon-Ji Academy of Martial Arts	2006 - Present

The referral is the "to:" address; the human resources e-mail is copied in the "cc." Note that the same letter, in a traditional cover-letter style with a return address, is being sent as an attachment with the résumé. (See Exhibit 8.12 for the attached cover letter.)

To: gregory.allen@miamicancercenter.org
Cc: matthew.kidd@miamicancercenter.org
Bcc:
Subject: Alex Moreno Application_Research Study Assistant I
Attachment: Alex Moreno_Resume.doc, Alex Moreno_Cover Letter.doc

This is a networking-style cover letter, in which a referral is mentioned.

Dear Dr. Allen:

I was referred to you by Dr. Francis Jagger at Miami Cancer Center, who is familiar with my work as a medical intern at North Florida Medical Center in Gainesville, FL. I will be graduating from University of Florida with a 4.0 in biology this May, and am eager to apply my technical and laboratory skills in a research position. I am writing to express my interest in the position of Research Study Assistant I - Radiation Oncology currently listed on Miami Cancer Center's website. I also submitted a resume and cover letter to the Department of Human Resources.

My experience includes a long commitment to working in a medical setting. Most recently, I completed a medical internship at North Florida Medical Center, where I participated in research projects under the guidance of senior researchers. While there, I also attended conferences and managed an independent research project. Prior to that, I served as a junior volunteer at North Florida Medical Center for two summers and as a receptionist at Children's Therapy Center in Gainesville, where I learned to provide excellent customer service while working with doctors, nurses, occupational therapists, and physical therapists. Gaining the skills to work independently and as part of a team in a research setting has been a focus of my education and training. I would look forward to applying my enthusiasm for research and broad skill set to this position.

Thank you very much for your consideration. I will follow up with your office to ensure you have received my resume and cover letter, as well as with the Department of Human Resources, as instructed by the job posting. I hope to have the chance to speak with you directly to learn more about your work and to explore this or any other research positions that might become available.

Sincerely,

Alex Moreno

>> **EXHIBIT 8.9** ● **Cover Letter (as Attachment)/Alex Moreno/Research Position**

6788 Archer Road
Gainesville, FL 33411
(352) 555-5533
akm523@ufl.edu

Dr. Gregory Allen
Senior Research Associate
Radiation Oncology
Miami Cancer Center
1020 Northeast 125th Street
North Miami, FL 33161

October 14, 2012

Dear Dr. Allen:

I was referred to you by Dr. Francis Jagger at Miami Cancer Center, who is familiar with my work as a medical intern at North Florida Medical Center in Gainesville, FL. I will be graduating from the University of Florida with a 4.0 in biology this May, and am eager to apply my technical and laboratory skills in a research position. I am writing to express my interest in the position of Research Study Assistant I, Radiation Oncology currently listed on Miami Cancer Center's website. I also submitted my resume and cover letter to the Department of Human Resources.

My experience includes a long commitment to working in a medical setting. Most recently, I completed a medical internship at North Florida Medical Center, where I participated in research projects under the guidance of senior researchers. While there, I also attended conferences and managed an independent research project. Prior to that, I served as a junior volunteer at North Florida Medical Center for two summers. I also served as a receptionist at Children's Therapy Center in Gainesville, where I learned to provide excellent customer service while working with doctors, nurses, occupational therapists, and physical therapists. Gaining the skills to work independently and as part of a team in a research setting has been a focus of my education and training. I look forward to applying my enthusiasm for research and broad skill set to this position.

Thank you very much for your consideration. I will follow up with your office to ensure you have received my resume and cover letter, as well as with the Department of Human Resources as instructed by the job posting. I hope to have the chance to speak with you directly to learn more about your work and to explore this or any other research positions that might become available.

Sincerely,

Alex Moreno

ALEX MORENO
6788 Archer Road • Gainesville, FL 33411
(352) 555-5533 • akm523@ufl.edu

EDUCATION

University of Florida   **Gainesville, FL**
Bachelor of Science   Expected May 2013
Major: Biology, GPA: 4.0, Dean's List, Provost Scholarship

SKILLS

Technical Skills: General laboratory maintenance, Solid phase peptide synthesis, SDS-PAGE, NMR, IR, pH testing, Sterilization, Bacterial culturing

Computer Skills: Microsoft Word, Microsoft Excel, Microsoft PowerPoint, Microsoft Front Page, Photoshop, Logger Pro, CAD, Autodesk Inventor Professional, 3D Studio Max, Windows Movie Maker

Language Skills: Fluent in written and spoken Spanish. Familiar with Italian and Portuguese.

RESEARCH EXPERIENCE

University of Florida, Dept. of Biology   **Gainesville, FL**
Advisor: Dr. Felix Arthur
Undergraduate Research Assistant   September 2011 - present
Conducted analysis of Developmental and Molecular Effects of Aspartame on *Lumbriculus variegates*. Presented at 9th Student Research Symposium and at the Florida Academy of Science.

Theoretical and Applied Sciences Team Research Program   Summer 2010
Awarded college support to work on the synthesis of potassium channel blocker, kalkitoxin. Chosen to present research at the Regional Murdock Conference at Duke University in 2012.

MEDICAL EXPERIENCE

North Florida Regional Medical Center   **Gainesville, FL**
Medical Intern   Summer 2012
Researched information on nutrients associated with preventing cognitive decline and prepared a report and a poster for the public. Attended conferences and worked under the supervision of senior researchers.

Junior Volunteer   Summers 2010 & 2011
Transported patients from one clinic to another and discharged patients. Answered phones and delivered packages.

AWARDS

Sept. 14, 2011: Flag Bearer for College of Science at Convocation
April 27, 2011: Provost Award for Outstanding Achievement in Biology
April 20, 2011: Co-Chair, 10th Annual Science Research Symposium
Spring 2009: CRC Press Freshman Biology Award

(Continues)

PUBLICATIONS

Arthur, F., Miller, V., & Moreno, A. (2011) Developmental and Molecular Effects of Aspartame on Lumbriculus variegates. Journal of Cell Biology, 10, 89-98.

Arthur, F., Miller, V., & Moreno, A. (2012) Studies in Potassium Channel Blockers. Biology International, 41, 111-125.

Daniel followed the suggestion of his career counselor who recommended he apply to AmeriCorps. Having taken a year off (a gap year) to participate in AmeriCorps, after completing his associate's degree, Daniel returned to college to complete a bachelor's degree. After returning from AmeriCorps, he took courses over the summer while maintaining a part-time office position in which he could earn money and build skills he needs for a career in a not-for-profit setting.

However, he realized he needed a full-time position for the extra income, and now feels ready to handle school and full-time work. Daniel decided to be selective and target not-for-profits where he felt he would have a passion for the work. He has selected a listing for a nonprofit receptionist/office assistant to serve as his sample to create a targeted résumé and cover letter. See Exhibit 8.11 and Exhibit 8.12.

Target Job Listing:

Non profit – Receptionist/Office Assistant

JOB SUMMARY: The Receptionist will take telephone calls and receive visitors in a courteous and professional manner at all times, and provide clerical support to staff whenever needed. The policy of confidentiality regarding client information must be strictly adhered to. Reply to Ms. Elaine Turnbull, Director, Hope's Village at hr@hopesvillage.org.

Essential Duties:
- Provide administrative support in all aspects of the day-to-day operations
- Provide information and assistance to parents, staff, and children, as well as to the public
- Operate a variety of office equipment, including computer and copier
- Provide operations team with administrative support
- Draft office documents such as letters, reports, and presentations as needed
- Coordinate / schedule meetings and maintain calendars
- Perform clerical tasks such as data entry, filing, typing, photocopying, and collating
- Receive and help distribute office supplies and packages; distribute mail to staff members
- Greet and announce participants and guests upon arrival
- Answer and direct all incoming calls to appropriate staff
- Assist in gathering data and compile statistical information for program reports

Qualifications:
- Extensive experience in telephone and reception techniques; modern office procedures
- Ability to establish and maintain effective and cooperative working relationships
- Ability to deal pleasantly, tactfully, and courteously with the public; have an understanding and appreciation of human diversity, organization, and community
- Ability to operate standard office machines and basic computer programs including Microsoft Office Suite, calculator, fax, and copy machine
- Ability to maintain confidentiality; understand and carry out oral and written instructions
- Ability to give verbal directions clearly and concisely
- Flexibility in regards to schedules, sharing tasks, changes in routines or plans
- Positive attitude, helpful to others, and able to work cooperatively
- Ability to interact in a positive and courteous manner with all visitors and callers
- Ability to multitask and work in a fast-paced environment
- Patience and flexibility
- Sense of humor!

EXHIBIT 8.11 ● Functional Résumé/Daniel Chee/Not-for-Profit

DANIEL CHEE

10329 S.W. Cascade Blvd. ♦ Beaverton, OR 34555
(445) 678-0909 ♦ dpc531@pcc.edu

SERVICE ORIENTED – MULTI-TASKER – ATTENTION TO DETAIL

EDUCATION	University of Oregon	Eugene, OR
	Bachelor of Arts, Major: Communications, *expected May 2014*	
	Portland Community College	Portland, OR
	Associate of Arts, Major: Communications, *May 2011*	

PROFESSIONAL EXPERIENCE

INTERPERSONAL

- Certified in crisis-intervention counseling
- Trained children and youth in basic fire safety, preparedness, and first aid
- Open, personable demeanor, with genuine respect for individuals
- Experience working on team projects in many different settings

ADMINISTRATIVE

- Scheduled vendor and shelter agreements with 40 community organizations
- Reorganized and improved filing system and CRC guidelines
- Planned, coordinated, and facilitated campus advocacy workshops and campaigns
- Organized holiday food basket collection resulting in a 50% increase in donations

COMMUNICATION

- Designed and wrote *Guide to Disaster Services* for use by Red Cross volunteers
- Chaired committee meetings
- Answered phone calls for the CRC Helpline
- Delivered disaster preparedness program to the public at community events

---

EMPLOYMENT HISTORY

Community Resource Council	Rock Creek, OR
Office Assistant (part-time)	June 2012 - Present
AmeriCorps, National Preparedness and Response Corps	Philadelphia, PA
Corps Member	August 2011 - May 2012
Karp Construction	Portland, OR
Laborer	June 2009 - August 2011

EXTRACURRICULAR

Community Parks Committee	Portland, OR
Volunteer	January 2008 - Present

COMPUTER SKILLS

Microsoft Office Suite, Adobe Photoshop, HTML, WordPress, Blogspot, Twitter, Facebook

To: hr@hopesvillage.org
Cc:
Bcc:
Subject: Daniel Chee - Receptionist Applicant
Attachment: Daniel_Chee_Resume.doc

Another option for the cover letter is to include bullet points. This is an alternative to using a three or four-paragraph approach, and is best applied if you can use the bullets to highlight specific accomplishments or quantifiable results from your contributions.

Dear Ms. Turnbull:

I am writing to you to apply for the position of part-time receptionist/office assistant at Hope's Village which was listed on idealist.org. I am currently a student at the University of Oregon after spending a year as a Corps member with the AmeriCorps, National Preparedness and Response Team in Philadelphia, PA. I am available to work immediately.

I am a team player, patient and flexible, and always willing to help others. I believe my experience with AmeriCorps will be an asset in handling the diverse clients served through Hope's Village. As a Corps member, I developed greater insights into the issues of poverty and homelessness that your organization confronts. Throughout my experience at AmeriCorps and my office assistant position at a busy community resource center, I also gained strong administrative experience.

- Scheduled vendor and shelter agreements with 40 community organizations servicing more than a dozen staff members and thousands of clients annually.
- Reorganized and improved the filing system and guidelines for client intake and day-to-day operations that created greater staff efficiencies and time management.
- Handled 30 incoming calls daily at the National Preparedness and Response Center.

I have enclosed my resume for your review. You may contact me by phone at (445) 678-0909 or reach me via e-mail. I look forward to an opportunity to meet with you in person.

Sincerely,

Daniel Chee

Leticia will be receiving a Bachelor of Arts degree in sociology this year, and has identified positions in event planning as her target. She has decided that the internship in event planning she completed last summer was a very good fit for her interests. She has found that entry-level titles vary, but often are called "event coordinator" or "event planning assistant." She has selected a listing for event coordinator to serve as her sample to create a targeted résumé and cover letter. See Exhibit 8.13, Exhibit 8.14 and Exhibit 8.15.

Target Job Listing:
Event Coordinator

This exciting position will coordinate logistics for events, sponsor materials, copy-editing, proofing, and database creation and updates. This person will be the main contact person for three annual events. To apply, e-mail resume and references to Kendra Lopez, Marketing Manager, Nichols Harrison, at kglopez@nnhmarketingfirm.com. No calls, please.

Responsibilities:
- Organize and execute charity events and fundraising activities
- Receive and handle all company-wide donation requests
- Lead internal activities committee
- Plan corporate events
- Select site location and contract with external vendors as needed
- Utilize Corporate Activities Committee to plan and execute the details of each event
- Lead multi-team meetings and delegate appropriate tasks
- Assist with communication/marketing of conference
- On-site set-up, registration, attendee and sponsor assistance, tear down of event
- Create, deploy, and tabulate attendee surveys
- Prepare post event reports and sponsorship packets
- Set up website event page/basic HTML
- Create database and maintain updates, using the phone and Internet
- Manage online event calendar, communications, and review promotion materials

Professional Qualifications:
- Strong relationship skills—internal, including executives, and external
- Strong organizational and multitasking skills
- Ability to solve a variety of problems in situations where only limited standardization exists
- Event planning, coordinating and executing experience
- Excellent verbal and written communication skills; detail-oriented; well-organized; able to set priorities under pressure
- Self-starter
- Professionally minded and hard-working

Leticia Beason

15544 South Hidden Springs Drive
Oro Valley, Arizona 54859
(520) 555-8792 • leticiajbeason@gmail.com

OBJECTIVE

Event Coordinator

EDUCATION

University of Arizona, Tucson, AZ
Bachelor of Arts in Sociology, Expected May 2013

University of Westminster, London, United Kingdom
Study Abroad: British Theatre, Literature, and Women Studies, Fall 2011

EXPERIENCE

Marriot International, Tucson, AZ
Intern, Event Planning, Summer 2012
- Assisted with coordination of corporate meetings and events.
- Acted as point person between Events Coordinator and hourly associates, ensuring that associates understood expectations and parameters for event.
- Provided administrative support for staff of 10 senior event planners.
- Worked with social media tools to distribute weekly newsletter.
- Scheduled new clients and participated in customer meetings to plan details for events.
- Performed post-event follow-up with clients.

YMCA, Tucson, AZ
Lifeguard and Swim Instructor, Summers 2009, 2010, 2011
- Maintained certifications and supervised pool area.
- Taught weekly swim lessons; assisted with special-needs children.

ACTIVITIES

Public Relations Student Society of America, Member, Spring 2012 - Present

University Dance Team, Member, Fall 2010 - Present
Captain, Spring 2012 - Present

Alpha Epsilon Phi, Member, Fall 2010 - Present
Public Relations Representative, Spring 2012 - Present

SKILLS

Computer: Microsoft Office (Word, Excel, Outlook, PowerPoint), FileMaker Pro, InDesign, HTML, and Photoshop.
Social Media: Facebook, LinkedIn, Twitter.
Language: Working knowledge of French.

>> **EXHIBIT 8.14** ● **E-mail Cover Letter/Leticia Beason/Event Coordinator**

To: kglopez@nhmarketingfirm.com
Cc:
Bcc:
Subject: Leticia Beason - Event Coordinator Resume & Cover Letter
Attachment: Leticia Beason_Resume.doc, Leticia Beason_References.doc

Dear Ms. Lopez:

Please accept my resume and cover letter as an application for the event coordinator position currently listed with the University of Arizona career center. I will be receiving my Bachelor of Arts degree in sociology from the University of Arizona in May 2013. Having developed strong project coordination, organization, and problem-solving skills, I believe I could make an immediate contribution at Nichols Harrison.

As an event-planning intern at Marriott International, I assisted in organizing and executing corporate events, including setup, registration, teardown, and post event follow-up. Furthermore, I have been involved with event planning throughout campus as an active member of numerous student groups and clubs. I am extremely self-motivated and hard working, and would be excited to contribute my skills to Nichols Harrison. I am particularly interested in the opportunity to work with a marketing firm, such as Nichols Harrison, that specializes in the arts. As a dancer for more than 12 years, and the current captain of the University of Arizona Dance Team, I am committed to the arts and would be eager to develop a specialization in reaching others in this market.

Thank you very much for your time and consideration. Attached please find my resume and list of references, as requested in your job posting. I will follow up by e-mail within two weeks to ensure that you have received my application and look forward to speaking with you further.

Sincerely,

Leticia Beason

The format of a References page should match the format of the resume. Notice the centered heading and similar page layout.

Leticia Beason
15544 South Hidden Springs Drive
Oro Valley, Arizona 54859
(520) 555-8792 • leticiajbeason@gmail.com

REFERENCES

Mr. Owen Strand
Event Coordinator
Marriot International
770 West Third Street
Tucson, AZ 85719
(520) 555-3333
o.strand@marriott.com

Katherine O'Rielly, Ph.D.
Professor of Sociology
Department of Sociology
University of Arizona
P.O. Box 76345
Tucson, AZ 85859
(520) 555-8888
katherineoreilly@arizona.edu

Mr. Carson James
Camp Merrimac
P.O. Box 8910
Tucson, AZ 85859
(520) 555-6666
cjames@merrimac.com
(Former Director of Youth
Programs, YMCA;
served as supervisor for
all pool staff)

Writing your own References page

√ Contact all references prior to providing their names to any employers and ask permission to use them as references. Confirm the means by which the person wishes to be contacted: mailing address, phone (office or mobile) and e-mail.

√ Include 3 or 4 references.

√ Offer a brief description of references that do not list employers on your resume.

√ List references in order of their helpfulness to your current search.

√ Include job titles.

√ Alert your references whenever an employer may be contacting them to ensure they are in town and available!

√ Thank your references with thank you notes and personal calls.

With several years of full-time work experience before returning to school for her associate degree, Katie continued working while pursuing her degree. Although she started her education as an office technology major, she switched majors and decided to build on her experience toward a career in hospitality. She is now ready to graduate. She plans to market her combination of experience and education toward a hotel-management position with career potential. She has selected a listing for assistant general manager to serve as a sample for her targeted résumé and cover letter. See Exhibit 8.16 and Exhibit 8.17.

Target Job Listing:

Hotel Management—Assistant General Manager

Job Description: The Assistant General Manager is responsible for overseeing all front office operations to insure profitability, control costs and quality standards ensuring total guest satisfaction. A combination of education, training or experience that provides the required knowledge, skills and abilities is required. A minimum of two years experience as an assistant front office manager, or equivalent, and a college degree, or equivalent, is preferred. Submit resume and cover letter to Lee Moran, General Manager: lmoran@courtyard.com

Technical Requirements:
- Ability to coordinate various departments on behalf of General Manager.
- Experience in front office, housekeeping, engineering, and/or related departments.
- Ability to assimilate operational statistics quickly and to enhance position of property.
- Experience in developing standards and operating procedures, and responding to complaints/problems.

Leadership and Managerial Requirements:
- Ability to manage change effectively.
- Ability to conceptualize the mission.
- Provide leadership to various departments to achieve goals and objectives.
- Develop and implement business plan.
- Clear, concise written and verbal communication skills including presentations to groups.
- Maintain a good working relationship with guests, groups, and personnel
- Track record promoting an atmosphere of teamwork.
- Demonstrate ability to lead by example and team building experience, build morale and spirit.
- Participative management style, "hands-on" approach to management.
- A mentor who has inspired, trained, and developed people for promotion.
- Instill a calm, organized approach in all situations.

Business Skills:
- Excellent skills required: time management/organizational/customer service orientation/problem solving/scheduling/listening/cost control/safety and sanitation/computer.
- Exceptional detail in follow-up.
- Assume responsibility/accountability.
- Understand security requirements.
- Create courteous, friendly, professional work environment.
- Provide overall direction, coordination, and ongoing evaluation of operations.
- Understand basic asset management.
- Involved with local community to develop business.

EXHIBIT 8.16 • **Combination Résumé/Katie Clarke/Hospitality**

KATHRYN "KATIE" CLARKE

88A Macarthur Avenue • Natick, MA 07026 • (828) 218-7769 • katieclarke@yahoo.com

Hospitality Manager • Training Facilitator

Conscientious individual with solid-food and beverage-service experience seeking an entry-level management position in the hospitality industry. Strong work ethic as evidenced by holding full-time positions while attending school and maintaining a 3.0 or better GPA for three semesters.

PROFESSIONAL SKILLS

Management and Leadership Skills:
Hire, train, supervise, and motivate floor staff, including servers and bartenders
Provide support for higher management, resolving staff complaints and scheduling conflicts
Recognized for being on-time, reliable, and able to manage time effectively

Customer Service, Sales and Marketing Skills:
Build rapport with customers, and provide entertaining and engaging service as bartender
Develop repeat customer business, with specific customer requests to be seated in section
Promote beverage and food offers, engaging customers with corporate-driven promotions

Interpersonal Skills:
Selected by management and co-workers as Employee of the Month repeatedly
Chosen to serve as "shadow" for new hires, responsible for modeling highest performance standards

Technical Skills:
Operate a cash register, POS system (Aloha Insight)
Work directly with technical team and account managers to resolve technical issues
Provided training to new hires on POS system

EDUCATION

Charles River Community College, Boston, MA
Associate of Science Degree, Hospitality/Hotel Management, expected December 2013
Current GPA 3.3/4.0

WORK EXPERIENCE

Thurston's Restaurant, Boston, MA   **2009 to Present**
Assistant Manager/Trainer
- Oversee the quality and accuracy of station workers
- Train newly hired employees (4–6 monthly) in food products, menu, table service and customer focus
- Manage cash and credit card transactions for the shift
- Act as bartender and server 30–40 hours weekly
- Model the job duties for new hires through shadowing

On The Border, Natick, MA
Trainer/Bartender – Shift Leader   **2006 to 2009**
- Trained employees to deliver quality service
- Developed a strategy to accomplish tasks and achieve goals for product promotions
- Created teamwork atmosphere through open communication

>> **EXHIBIT 8.17** ● **E-mail Cover Letter/Katie Clarke/Hospitality**

Katie is sending a traditional-style cover letter in the body of her e-mail, and the same letter in a font that coordinates with her résumé, as an e-mail attachment.

To: lmoran@courtyard.com
Cc:
Bcc:
Subject: Katie Clarke – Assistant General Manager application
Attachment: Lee Moran_Resume.doc, Lee Moran_Cover Letter.doc

Lee Moran, General Manager
Courtyard Hotel Corporation
3000 Market St.
Portsmouth, MA   33801

The subject of the letter "Lee" is a name that could belong to a man or woman. Calling the company and listening to this person's voicemail, or looking Lee Moran up on a company website, will help you determine whether Ms. or Mr. is appropriate.

January 17, 2012

Dear Ms. Moran:

Please accept my resume in consideration of the position of Assistant General Manager of the Courtyard Hotel located in Portsmouth, MA. I found this opportunity listed on CareerBuilder and am very excited to submit my application. I will be graduating in December with a degree in hospitality/hotel management and 7 years experience in the industry. With a commitment to service and community, I believe I am a good fit with Courtyard Hotel's expressed value of "serving the associates, the customer, and the community."

My experience, combined with my academic credentials, has prepared me for this opportunity. Throughout my experience and education, I have taken on leadership roles and made an impact. In my role as a trainer at Thurston's restaurant, I developed a model that positively impacted the retention of new employees and received accolades in the company newsletter. As team leader of a hotel management competition that involved an 18-month management simulation, my team received the highest award for quality and standards for 6 consecutive inspections, an achievement not reached before. I am detail-oriented and have strong time-management skills as evidenced by my ability to manage a 35+ hour a week job while attending school, earning a 3.3 GPA overall.

Enclosed please find my resume and references as requested. I believe you will see that I am highly qualified for the position of Assistant General Manager. I will follow up within two weeks to confirm that you have received my application. Thank you very much for your time and consideration.

Sincerely,

Katie Clarke

Mason will be graduating with an Associate of Arts degree this year, and has identified multiple targets, including positions in Web design, graphic design, and multimedia design. He has had success working with the business community and has created an online portfolio (personal web-site) showcasing samples of his work and links to online projects, including logos and websites. Due to the different job areas, he must create cover letters for all three, and has elected to create one résumé that can be modified slightly, if necessary. He has selected a listing for Web designer to serve as a sample for a targeted résumé and cover letter, as well as for a brief biography, which he will share on his online portfolio. See Exhibit 8.18, Exhibit 8.19, and Exhibit 8.20.

Target Job Listing:

Web Designer

The Web Designer is a key member of the E-commerce team who will contribute inspired, original compositions to projects and be focused on detail-oriented design to make sure the interface is stylistically consistent and accurate. The right candidate is a talented designer, ambitious, and passionate about Web/interface design.

Summary

The Web Designer will possess exceptional design skills, working with the E-commerce team and outside creative agency to design key website pages based on project objectives, creative briefs, user experience design documentation, and corporate standards. To apply, submit resume and salary requirements to hr@rtgs.com

Essential Duties and Responsibilities include the following:

- Works with E-commerce team and outside agencies to create truly inspired compositions
- Executes website comps, assets, and templates
- Ensures all designs meet usability standards
- Develops existing concepts established by the E-commerce team into templates
- Executes final adjustments and assists delivery of sliced/optimized assets for HTML production
- Works with E-commerce team to correct performance problems

Job Specifications:

- A talented designer with good verbal and communication skills
- Excellent knowledge of Photoshop and ImageReady
- Basic or advanced skills in Flash/ActionScript is preferable
- Experience and knowledge of typography, page layout, information design, interactive design
- Associate's degree or equivalent, specializing in design, or equivalent on-the-job experience
- A clear communicator with ability to present ideas to team members with confidence
- Accept and process constructive criticism
- Reasoning Ability—able to grasp the brand and business and explain why a particular design decision supports the company's needs
- Web-design experience with an apparel brand is a plus

»EXHIBIT 8.18 ● **Reverse Chronological Résumé/Mason Wolff/Web Design**

As a Web-design candidate, it is appropriate for an online portfolio to be listed that would show samples from design projects and work experiences.

MASON WOLFF

57 Breezewood Lane, Menasha, WI 54952
555.555.5555 ▪ masonwolff1@yahoo.com ▪ www.masonwolffdesigner.com

OBJECTIVE
A position utilizing my skills in website and multimedia design

EDUCATION
Appleton Community College, Appleton, WI
AA in Multimedia Design, Expected May 2013

COURSEWORK
Web Design, Graphic Design, Typography, Idea Development, Studio Painting & Drawing.

SKILLS
Computer: Adobe Photoshop, Illustrator, InDesign, Dreamweaver, Microsoft PowerPoint, Microsoft Publisher, Final Cut Pro X, Flash, HTML, and CSS.
Design: Typography, Layout & Design, Information Design, Multimedia, Graphics, Template Preparation, Storyboards.

PROJECT EXPERIENCE

Coursework can be written in a format similar to past employment.

"Idea Development," **Appleton Community College**, Appleton, WI
Course Member, Spring 2012
- Participated in a group project to redesign a website utilizing e-commerce for local retail business.
- Initiated design ideas and worked as a team to prepare visually exciting layout that would appeal to target market.
- Created storyboard design solutions to illustrate ideas.
- Presented ideas to class members, professor, store owners, marketing coordinator, and sales team members.

WORK EXPERIENCE
CopyWrite Center, Greenville, WI
Associate, December 2011 - Present
- Tasked with creating a new store logo and website that involved programming code and creating a brand image.
- Assist customers with graphic design material to market products and events.
- Provide customer service at design shop servicing small business community.
- Design advertisements, business cards and stationery, and provide professional quality product markups.

College Experiential Learning Office, Appleton, WI
Student Aide, January 2010 - May 2011
- Assisted with the development and implementation of creative and relevant marketing campaigns for more than 20 events, including work shops, career fairs, and recruiting programs.
- Conceptualized solutions to capture the attention of over 400 students, 50 faculty, and local employers.

Harris Daniels, Graphic Designer, San Francisco, CA
Summer Apprenticeship, Summer 2010
- Honed graphic-design skills as part of a competitive summer internship; only high school student selected.

Interests
Travel, Basketball, Running, Science Fiction, Video Games.

Professional Association
Member, SIGGRAPH, 2010 - Present

>> **EXHIBIT 8.19** ● **E-mail Cover Letter/Mason Wolff/Web Design**

Since human resources was listed as the contact, this candidate looked up the company name (via the Web address given in the ad) and the name of the director of human resources. This gives him the chance to address the letter to a person, while copying the address that was listed in the job posting.

To: akessler@rtgs.com
Cc: hr@rtgs.com
Bcc:
Subject: wolff_mason - web designer resume & cover letter
Attachment: wolff_ mason_resume.doc

Dear Mr. Kessler:

I am writing in response to the recent listing on Monster.com for a web designer. I will be graduating in May with an associate's degree in multimedia design from Appleton Community College where I have studied web design and various other mediums. Having developed websites in course projects and in my work experience, I believe I would be an asset to Right Talent Graphic Solutions.

Having conceptualized and redesigned the customer-oriented website for CopyWrite in Greenville, I am accustomed to web design projects that are collaborative, involving input from marketing, advertising, and management executives. In fact, all of these groups contributed to the website redesign at CopyWrite, and the finished product was the result of design aimed to meet various goals, such as initiating sales, integrating e-commerce, and reinforcing the company's brand through colors, images, and text. (That website and other samples of my work can be viewed from a link in my online portfolio at www.masonwolffdesigner.com.)

In addition to the website I designed for CopyWrite, I participated in a student project that allowed us to serve as design consultants to a local retail store selling women's apparel and accessories. After researching the apparel industry and the store's needs, my team developed a web design solution that we presented to the store's owners, marketing coordinator, and several sales team members. We received a top grade for the project, but, more significantly, we were told that several of our ideas would be integrated into the store's website.

Thank you very much for your time and consideration. In regards to salary requirements, I am flexible depending on the opportunity, given that salary is not my main consideration. I will follow up within two weeks to confirm that you have received my resume. I look forward to speaking with you then.

Sincerely,

Mason Wolff

When salary requirements are requested in the job application, employers prefer that you address this topic. There are numerous approaches, and here is one option. If you wish to include salary, listing a range is an alternative. You can learn these ranges through online salary calculators and confirm their accuracy through networking.

»EXHIBIT 8.20 ● **Brief Biography/Mason Wolff/Web Design**

Mason Wolff, Multimedia Designer
A Brief Biography

Mason Wolff is a multimedia designer who has focused his skills toward creative, solution-driven designs for the business community, having developed websites, logos, and corporate literature through student projects and employment. During his teen years, his art talent led to a coveted summer apprenticeship and training in San Francisco where he studied under his mentor, graphic designer Harris Daniels. The opportunity to work in this region, where technology and business intersect so powerfully, inspired Wolff to connect powerful design techniques, using technology to help solve common business problems, such as creating graphic design that is memorable for consumers and e-commerce interfaces that are visually interesting and easy to navigate. Returning to his home of Wisconsin, and completing his HS Diploma, he began studies in Multimedia Design at Appleton Community College, from which he will receive his AA in May 2013. Working on campus and in a local business, he combined his design aesthetic and technological know-how to create functional and successful design projects. He is an active member of SIGGRAPH.

>> EXHIBIT 8.21 ● Job Search Application

Employment Application

Please write clearly and complete all sections. Write N/A (Not Applicable) if necessary. You may attach a resume, but we still request that you list previous employers and related information. Please do not leave any questions unanswered.

Applicant Information

Last Name	First		M.I.	Date

Street Address	Apartment/Unit #

City	State	ZIP

Home Phone ( )	Cell Phone ( )	E-mail Address

Date Available	Social Security No.	Desired Salary

Position of Interest

Are you a citizen of the United States?   YES ☐ NO ☐   If no, are you authorized to work in the U.S.?   YES ☐ NO ☐

Have you ever worked for this company?   YES ☐ NO ☐   If so, when?

Have you ever been convicted of a felony? YES ☐ NO ☐   If yes, explain

Education

High School	Address
From To	Did you graduate? YES ☐ NO ☐	Degree
College	Address
From To	Did you graduate? YES ☐ NO ☐	Degree
Other	Address
From To	Did you graduate? YES ☐ NO ☐	Degree

References

Please list three professional references.

Full Name	Relationship
Company	Phone ( )
Address	
Full Name	Relationship
Company	Phone ( )
Address	
Full Name	Relationship
Company	Phone ( )
Address	

(Continues)

»EXHIBIT 8.21 ● Job Search Application *Continued*

Previous Employment

Company		Phone ( )
Address		Supervisor

Job Title	Starting Salary $	Ending Salary $

Responsibilities		

From To	Reason for Leaving	

May we contact your previous supervisor for a reference?	YES ☐ NO ☐	

Company		Phone ( )
Address		Supervisor

Job Title	Starting Salary $	Ending Salary $

Responsibilities		

From To	Reason for Leaving	

May we contact your previous supervisor for a reference?	YES ☐ NO ☐	

Company		Phone ( )
Address		Supervisor

Job Title	Starting Salary $	Ending Salary $

Responsibilities		

From To	Reason for Leaving	

May we contact your previous supervisor for a reference?	YES ☐ NO ☐	

Military Service

Branch	From To
Rank at Discharge	Type of Discharge
If other than honorable, explain	

Disclaimer and Signature

I certify that my answers are true and complete to the best of my knowledge.

If this application leads to employment, I understand that false or misleading information in my application or interview may result in a termination of my employment.

Signature	Date

Your Flexible Plan

Create Your Job Search Tools

PLAN OF ACTION
Step 1: Set Broad Objectives

Which documents are you ready to prepare?

	Are you ready to prepare this document? (Y/N)	**If not, what must you do next?**
Résumé		
Cover Letter		
Thank You Letter		
Page of References		
Social Media Presence		
1.		
2.		
3.		

Step 2: Identify Specific Goals

To prepare these documents, what do you need to do? State the goals that will help you with your broad objectives.

Example: To prepare my résumé (broad objective), I must gather material including: (1) information about my past experiences and accomplishments (goal), (2) job search listings (goal), and (3) choice of a format, layout, and design (goal).

1. _____

2. _____

3. _____

Step 3: Define Action Steps

Choose one goal and list the steps you will take to achieve it.

Example: To prepare my résumé (broad objective), I must gather job search listings (goal). Action steps: (1) Review job listings on the website for the career center at my school. (2) Select three listings that interest me. (3) Choose one as a target position so I can prepare a targeted résumé.

List your goal you have chosen to address, and the specific action steps you will take.

Goal: _____

1. _____

2. _____

3. _____

4. _____

5. _____

Performance Appraisal

Now that you have read the chapter, answer the questions below and complete the Tasks.

1. For which of the following are job search tools useful?
   a. A job or internship search
   b. Determining if you lack relevant skills
   c. Making career-related decisions, such as choosing courses or activities
   d. All of the above

2. What is a targeted résumé?
   a. A résumé that can be used only on an online résumé board
   b. A résumé written for a specific career or industry
   c. A résumé that can be used for networking but not for a job search.
   d. None of the above

3. Which of the following is an example of an action-verb phrase?
   a. Maintained data for monthly reports
   b. Duties including serving as supervisor for a one-week period
   c. Responsibilities included programming code, Web design, and preparing logos
   d. b and c

4. Which of the following is true?
   a. Personal branding is useful only for celebrities.
   b. Personal branding is always inauthentic, because it requires you to constantly promote yourself.
   c. Personal branding is a way to connect your assets with your unique characteristics.
   d. Students cannot create a personal brand because they do not have enough experience.

5. Which of the following is true of volunteer activities?
   a. They are a great way to meet friends.
   b. They are a great way to help others.
   c. They are a great way to learn about careers.
   d. All of the above.

6. Which of the following is true about cover letters?
   a. Employers do not assess your writing skills by the quality of your cover letter.
   b. Each cover letter you send should be targeted for a specific position.
   c. If your cover letter has typos, no one will notice.
   d. A generic cover letter addressed "Dear Sir:" is always fine.

7. Which of the following is true if you decide to apply for an international job?
   a. You must be able to speak the national language.
   b. You should always send the same job search tools as you would in a domestic job search.
   c. You might be asked for a photo with your résumé.
   d. b and c.

Performance Appraisal Answer Key

1. d   2. b   3. a   4. c   5. d   6. b   7. c

Thought Questions

1. Do you feel prepared to sum up your assets in a résumé?

2. Do you feel that your experiences reflect your best assets? Do your activities and involvement reflect your leadership potential?

3. Do you feel your reputation and personal choices present a consistent brand that makes you proud? Why or why not?

Notes:

_____

_____

_____

_____

_____

_____

A strong brand is clear and consistent. Developing a strong message through your reputation can help you market yourself, and also help in many other aspects of career development.

TASK 8.1:
Your Personal Brand

Everyone is a destination for some kind of insight, support, or expertise. What do people "go to" you for? In this exercise, you will explore aspects of your personal brand and consider how well your overall brand represents the "real" you.

Relationships. Are you known as a helper? A leader? A trend setter? Are you the one they turn to when they need to figure out the bill at the end of a group dinner? Do people want you around when they need a laugh? Do others look to you for information on certain topics, and, if so, which ones? Describe how your relationships impact your reputation.

_____

_____

_____

Activities. What are your favorite activities? Do you spend your time reading, writing, playing computer games, training for a sport, participating in social events, or other activities? Describe how your activities impact your reputation.

_____

_____

_____

Lifestyle. What kind of lifestyle have you adopted? Consider if these terms describe you or if there are other descriptors you would choose: studious, well-organized, a procrastinator, a social butterfly. When you think about your lifestyle, consider how you spend your time as well as how you would *prefer* to spend your time. Describe how your lifestyle choices impact your reputation.

_____

_____

_____

Appearance. What is your style? What do you wear? How do you style your hair? Do you wear jewelry, piercings, or body art? Are you neat or messy? Do you describe your style as tailored and conservative, dramatic and flamboyant, or would you use other terms? Describe how your choices regarding your personal appearance impact your reputation.

_____

_____

_____

Overall Brand. Do you feel your relationships, lifestyle, activities, and appearance reflect an accurate representation of the "real" you? Is this reflected in your reputation? How is this reflected in your résumé, job search materials, and career interests?

_____

_____

_____

What stand out as being key aspects of the qualities you represent? And, in contrast, what are the strongest inconsistencies you have noticed?

_____

_____

_____

Finish this sentence: When people think of me, I think they are most likely to recognize me for _____
_____

Now, finish this sentence: If people could think of only one thing when they think of me, I want them to recognize me for _____
Consider what actions you can take to make both statements reflect the brand you want to represent.

TASK 8.2:
Create a Description Using Action Verbs

Select a job, internship, volunteer project, or student group in which you are an active member. What did you do? Prepare three phrases that describe your participation and contributions to any projects. Begin each phrase with an action verb in the past or present tense, and then describe your role and the actions you took. Refer to the list of action verbs and résumé samples for inspiration.

1. _____

2. _____

3. _____

TASK 8.3:
Summarize Your Assets

What are your best assets? At this point in your career development, you are ready to consider how your transferable skills meet the needs sought by employers. Do you write well? Do you have strong technical abilities? Have you held relevant work or training positions that prepared you for your field? Did you demonstrate an ability to be responsible and reliable by working while you were in school? Prepare phrases, starting with action verbs, to describe three to five of your most valuable assets. Asset statements can be useful in numerous job search materials. They can be used in a summary section of your résumé, shortened for a profile statement, included in cover letters, or referred to as talking points. Here is an example to get you started: Held several leadership roles within award-winning, student-run publication, serving as features editor, copy editor, and sports writer.

_____

_____

_____

_____

_____

TASK 8.4:

Are Your Career Interests Represented in Your Experience?

Employers want to see how you are qualified for the job you are seeking. This requires you to demonstrate skills and experience in relevant areas. Now that you can articulate your career interests, ask yourself if they are represented in your past or part-time employment. You might find that your career interests are most closely related to your coursework, internships, student clubs, or leisure activities. In the left-hand column, list your career interests. In the right-hand column, list any related clubs, courses, or activities where you were introduced to and practiced skills that relate to these areas of interest. For this exercise, you will see these are referred to as related experiences. Consider whether any of these can be highlighted on your résumé, even if they are through informal activities.

Career Interests	Related Experience
Marketing/Social Media	_Updated sorority Facebook page to include photos from fundraising event_
Sports .	_Play ultimate Frisbee on weekends; follow sports media, played field hockey in high school._

TASK 8.5

Your Social Media: Asset or Liability?

Your Facebook page represents you to friends and family, but is it a professional asset or a liability? In this exercise, list all the social media you currently use (e.g., Facebook, Twitter, LinkedIn, Google+, Pinterest, Foursquare, Meetup). Now, add notes regarding your participation in these sites. What message are you sending through your participation? If someone views your page, your image, or your updates, what are they learning about you?

My Social Media	Images, Discussions, and Links
Example:	
Pinterest	_Contribute fashion photographs to personal Pinterest page; add links to related articles and blog entries_
1.	
2.	
3.	

Now that you have evaluated the content of your social media presence, evaluate your online activity. What are you telling others about yourself? Is this consistent with your intended brand?

_____

_____

_____

Link to CourseMate

On CourseMate, you can find documents to help you update your Career Portfolio as well as additional resources and activities. Here is some of the information you can find online for **Chapter 8: Tools**.

CAREER PORTFOLIO

Your Flexible Plan
Master Résumé
Résumé
Cover Letter
Thank You Letter
Social Media Presence

RESOURCES

Case Study Career Portfolios
Sample Master Résumés
Additional Sample Job Search Correspondence
Sample Online Profiles/Social Media Presence
Career Profile: AJ Sabath

Launch

AP Photo/Republican-Herald, Nick Meyer

You have to trust in something—your gut, destiny, life, karma, whatever. This approach has never let me down, and it has made all the difference in my life.

—*Steve Jobs*

Your career launch is the time when your activity shifts towards securing career-related work that interests you. You will learn how to use numerous resources and job search approaches, while adopting strategies for staying organized and motivated throughout your search. Learning to network, interview, and negotiate will help you create more options and make a selection that works well for you.

What's Inside

Conduct a Successful Job Search

A New Beginning: Resources for Career Change and Reentry

Networking for Job Opportunities

Strategies for Successful Interviewing

Professional Attire and Your Job Search

Evaluating Next Steps and Negotiating

Prepare to . . .

● Develop a strategy for a job or internship search

● Consider what is necessary if you are preparing to relaunch your career

● Learn common interview questions and explore how you will answer them

● Understand appropriate interview attire for networking and interviewing

● Make decisions about job offers and alternatives

» Conduct A Successful Job Search

A career-related job will help you define who you are in the world of work as you continue to assess and develop your skills, experiences, interests, and values. Essentially, your next job will be a platform, or a launch pad, for you to build upon. To create the best foundation for your career success, consider this an opportunity to find the best environment to obtain experience and training for your future while you develop relationships within your chosen field.

Finding a job can be challenging, but if you start early and use all of your available resources, you will position yourself for the best results. Here are four suggestions that outline a job search strategy and guide you to the resources available to help in your search.

Reflect on Your Target Industries, Organizations, and Positions

To conduct a successful job search, clarify what you want. Identify target industries, organizations, and positions, and prepare to make a case for how you add value. To market yourself effectively, you must be able to show employers how your skills and assets are relevant to their needs. Connecting your self-assessment with your career exploration is the foundation of self-marketing. This will provide direction for your

Your job search should include a variety of activities including campus events such as job fairs.

job search, drive the content for your résumé and cover letters, and provide insight for your interviews and networking conversations.

Search for Job Leads

To locate job leads, plan to review advertised jobs, network for jobs that are not listed, and expand your search through networking to include jobs that are listed, but not easily found. **Exhibit 9.1**, Search for Job Leads, offers many suggestions to help you find your next job. Job boards, company websites, professional associations, recruiting programs, campus career fairs, and employment agencies are common resources for finding listed or advertised positions.

Most jobs are found through networking. These "hidden" jobs may represent 75 percent or more of jobs available at any time, and, although they are not advertised, you can learn about them through word-of-mouth. Therefore, close to 75 percent of your time should involve building and nurturing relationships that can lead to information about job openings, additional contacts, or support and referrals. **Exhibit 9.4**, Networking Letter, will help you contact people you have met in order to expand your network.

Create a Job Search Plan

Unlike the flexible plan you have been developing throughout this text, your job search plan is goal-oriented and short-term; your objective is to get a job. **Task 9.1**, Create a Job Search Plan, will help you organize and plan. Once you have found target positions, a job search plan will help you track where you have sent your résumés and cover letters, whom you plan to contact for further networking, what upcoming events and commitments relate to your job search, which upcoming interviews you have scheduled, and whether thank you notes were sent. Results and success will come more quickly when you put in the time upfront and target your job leads.

Stay Active and Engaged

Because a job search takes time, it is important to stay active and engaged. This involves taking steps to improve your job search while continually expanding your network.

Take action. At every stage of a job search, there are actions you can take to improve your results. For example, if you are not getting called for interviews, your résumé or cover letters may need to be reworked. Revisit **Chapter 8: Tools** to review résumé and cover letter preparation. If you are sending out your résumé and getting called for interviews, but the interviews are not leading to offers, review your interviewing skills. **Exhibit 9.6**, Interview Questions, offers a list of common interview questions that you can practice with a networking contact or in a practice interview at your career center. If your interview skills, résumé, and correspondence are strong, but offers still elude you, it may be worthwhile to consider your fit for the industry or position you are seeking. However, it is reasonable to expect that job offers may take time, even for strong candidates who are doing everything right. Consider the example of Jessica in the Career Profile in **Chapter 7: Decision Making**, who is now succeeding in a Fortune 500 company, but spent a full year after college searching for a full-time career-related position—while working in other positions and staying active the entire time.

Stay engaged. Being engaged during the job search can involve volunteer work, leisure activities, physical fitness, and part-time or temporary work. Activities such as these help you stay motivated, involved, build new connections, and offer current activities for your résumés and interview conversations. Employers are aware of the impact of the economy, and they take notice of activities that reflect your desire to work hard during a challenging period.

≫ CAREER JOURNAL ● Career Success

 Use the space below to write about your thoughts and feelings.

Describe what career success means to you. This question is intentionally open-ended to invite any thoughts that come to mind.

How will you feel when you have achieved career success?

What do you have to do to create this type of career success for yourself? List three action steps you can take toward creating career success.

Journal Feedback . . . Creating your own personal career success will help you reach goals that are meaningful to you, rather than set by others or personally unfulfilling. Exploring how career success will improve your life and the steps it will take to reach your goals can help you put your plan into action.

Name: Sarah Moltzen
College Degree: BS in Environmental Science, Minor in Biology
Current Position: Field Technician
Employer: Environmental Compliance Services

Courtesy of Sarah Moltzen

How did you choose your career direction?

I knew that I wanted a career where I could be outdoors. I love doing things like hiking and camping. I worked as a lifeguard for almost 10 years, played soccer in college, and I do a lot of sports and outdoor activities. I am outdoors whenever I have free time. In college, I started off with a major in biology. In my sophomore year, I took a class in environmental science and then switched my major to environmental science and my minor to biology. I found that when I was in my classes, studying, or working, I would look down at what I was learning and I would ask myself if I could see doing this as my job.

Can you describe your job search?

I would say my #1 goal was to network and talk to people. Not in the sense of always just asking people for jobs, but actually learning as much as I could about what they do in order to narrow down what I thought I wanted to do. I used career services for résumé building, practice interviews, and I went to job fairs. Before each job fair, I researched all the companies and changed my résumé to fit the descriptions of the jobs or employers that were coming. I saw these as a chance to get my résumé out to a lot of people, and I spent a lot of time preparing. I also went on a lot of interviews and tried to learn from each one. I sent e-mails to thank everyone.

How did you get your current job, which I understand is also your first job?

Yes, it's my first job, since I just graduated. My last couple of years at school I took a lot of upper-level classes that had a small number of students. I tried to get to know my professors and their research. It gave me some really awesome ideas—real-world examples of what is out there. I took one 500-level course that was incredibly specific and focused directly on environmental consulting. I really enjoyed it, and when you enjoy something, you're more engaged. The class was taught by the CEO of my company. He put me in touch with human resources. I'm in an entry-level position, and I'm being trained in all areas—geothermal heating and cooling systems for homes, remediation of environmental conditions, learning about the guidelines set by the EPA and state government, and more. For instance, my company was hired to clean up the southern part of Vermont after Hurricane Irene. I was cleaning the oil leaks in people's basements when the oil tanks became dislodged. I'm out in the field. It's really satisfying, because I get to clean up the environment in a very tangible way.

From Sarah's Supervisor

Name: Alicia Flammia
Title: Environmental Scientist, Environmental Compliance Services

Courtesy of Alicia Flammia

How do you hire for entry-level candidates?

We put out requests to area schools and on our website internally. Our branch manager will go through the résumés and create a smaller subset of potential candidates who will get passed to different supervisors in the office. In Sarah's case, the CEO had recommended her. He already had the opportunity to review her technical writing, including conclusions and recommendations she developed based on the data that she reviewed in the course.

How did Sarah demonstrate her interest?

She came in very excited to learn everything that we do here. The excitement is a good motivating factor and she was engaged right away and wanted to talk about all the decision-making processes we use. She took the initiative to gather data as best she could without a lot of oversight. She asks questions when she can't answer them herself. This work is not glamorous, but it can be as exciting as you make it. Her eagerness to always learn new things really stands out.

What steps did Sarah take to prepare for her career launch?

_____

_____

_____

What activities helped Sarah find employment?

_____

_____

_____

For additional questions, visit CourseMate.

EXHIBIT 9.1 ● **Search for Job Leads**

To find your next job, use all the resources available to you. Your networking contacts and school's career center can help you find the places where jobs for your industry are listed, as well as assist you in locating hidden jobs, creating your own job, or starting a business. These suggestions are only some of the many ways to locate or create jobs related to your career interests.

Sources for Leads	Where to Search
Advertised jobs	Search newspapers, online job banks, company websites, industry resources, campus career center listings, social media such as Twitter or LinkedIn, and for more information see:
	● **Exhibit 9.2:** Job-Listing Websites
	● **Exhibit 5.2:** Online Resources for Career Exploration
	● **Exhibit 5.3:** Professional Associations
"Hidden" jobs	Searching for jobs that are not listed is more challenging, but worth the effort. To learn about hidden jobs, seek out:
	● *Job openings* that are not listed to the public but are shared by word-of-mouth.
	● *Insider information* about anticipated openings.
	● *Referrals* to others who may know of openings.
Campus resources that may help you find "hidden jobs"	There are many opportunities for networking on campus.
	● *Professors* can be valuable networking contacts.
	● *Career counselors* can assist you in navigating career services.
	● *Career fairs* allow you to meet employers directly and can be great for networking.
	● *Job shadowing* are experiential programs that allow you to visit employer sites and follow someone on the job.
	● *Organized employer site visits* are a chance to visit employers with your peers.
	● *Mentor programs* pair you with someone who has more experience.
	● *Alumni events* help you meet alumni and build your network.
	● *Industry events* can be an opportunity for employers and alumni to visit campus, allowing you to build your network, gain insight, and possibly learn about job openings.
Campus resources	Check your campus career center, academic department, student activities, and office of alumni affairs for dates and deadlines. Campus resources may include the following:
	● *Job listings* specifically targeted for your school.
	● *Career fairs* targeted for specific industries or majors, depending on the size of your school. (These can include full-time, part-time, or internship opportunities.)
	● *Résumé help*—walk-in, brief, résumé critiques.
	● *On-campus recruiting*—employers schedule interviews with students.
	● *Employer visits on campus*—employers come to campus to speak about their openings, their culture, and more. (If these are part of on-campus recruiting, employers will expect you to attend.)
Employment agencies	Employment agencies, or third-party recruiters, may offer opportunities to prove yourself to an employer.
	● *Job listings* for permanent or temporary jobs.
	● *Temporary office work* or *"temp to perm"* positions.
	● *Networking opportunities.*

Sources for Leads	Where to Search
Create a job	If a particular organization interests you, and you feel you can add value and are willing to work hard to prove your worth, consider using your networking resources to explore creating a position. To create a position: ● *Connect* with a decision-maker. ● *Describe* your relevant skills and assets. ● *Connect* your assets to their needs. ● *Address* how your contribution will increase sales or save costs, if applicable. ● *Share* your ideas and invite them to use them, even if they do not have a position for you.
Create your own job as an entrepreneur	Another alternative is to create your own business or start a small business on the side while working for an employer. There are many responsibilities as an entrepreneur, as well as perks. You are responsible for your own taxes, bookkeeping, and health insurance, and you need to manage your own time and be self-motivated.
Alternatives to a full-time career job	Although you might prefer a full-time, career-related job as your next step, in a competitive and downturn economy it is not always possible to find your ideal next position. Here are options that build skills and relationships while adding to your résumé: ● *Two part-time positions* relating to your career interests ● *Full-time internship* after graduation (paid or unpaid) ● *Part-time internship* or *volunteer work combined with noncareer-related work* to cover expenses ● *Any job in your industry,* even in another position or with less responsibilities ● *Service-learning* or *not-for-profit experiences* that build related or transferable skills in a different industry ● *Further training* or *graduate school*

» A New Beginning: Resources for Career Change and Reentry

Launching your career or reentering after time off can be challenging in ways that differ from the experiences of students who have not yet graduated, but there are many resources to assist you. If you have returned to school to prepare for a new career, you are not alone. For many adults, a return to school is prompted by career issues (Aslanian, 2001).

iStockphoto.com/Alina Solovyova-Vincent

Networking for Experienced Adults

In addition to all of your campus resources, your life experience may also provide you with contacts for your new career. However, you may feel uncomfortable because of dual relationships. For instance, if your son's coach is in your field of interest, he may know of job openings; however, you may hesitate to ask him because you feel uneasy,

There are many people on campus to assist in your job search. A librarian can help you identify resources for your first job search, a career change, or to relaunch your career.

embarrassed, or think it is the wrong thing to do. There are many ways to network with courtesy and respect, such as asking for an e-mail address and following up during routine business hours.

As an experienced adult, networking will play a very important role in your job search. Your network may be larger and easier to access than you think, and you may be able to expand it quickly through campus resources.

The Most Challenging Job Search Topics

If you are reentering the workforce or making a career change, you may have specific concerns. Preparing your response to questions or conversations that address difficult topics can help you prepare for interviews and networking. Some of the topics that may challenge you are the following:

- Taking a pay cut
- Reporting to someone who is younger than you
- Reporting to someone who has less experience than you
- Your knowledge of technology or current trends
- Starting at entry-level
- Learning independently or training during nonbusiness hours
- Being required to be available 24/7, work overtime, or travel
- Shifting gears from having control of your time to "being on the clock" (if you are returning to work)
- Your family's ability to adapt to your return-to-work, if you are a stay-at-home parent.

Networking contacts and campus resources can help you identify and practice addressing difficult topics that may arise during your interview or networking (e.g., your experience out of the workforce, current motivation, and work history). Career counselors can also help you address your individual concerns.

Use All of Your Available Resources

You may not think of campus as your first resource if you are an older student, especially if you do not live on campus and are not involved in campus activities. However, you may have access to a career center, alumni association, career counseling, and many other campus resources that offer job search support, from job and internship listings to mentor programs to opportunities to practice interview and networking skills. In addition, community resources and industry activities can help you in your job search.

To make the most of your time, create a plan. Make appointments with counselors or advisors, prepare questions in advance, learn dates and deadlines for important events such as career fairs on campus or in your community, and set aside regular time each day for networking e-mails and follow-up calls. While your time may be limited, if you create a strategic approach, you can utilize many helpful resources to make the most of the time you have.

> > **EXHIBIT 9.2** ● **Job-Listing Websites**

There are many job search resources online, and new sites are added regularly while older sites may be eliminated. Although the sites listed here were useful at the time this text was written, familiarizing yourself with current job search websites for your industry is always recommended.

Online Resources	Examples of Websites
Metasearch engines	careerjet.com
	glassdoor.com
	indeed.com
	jobbind.com
	Justjobs.com
	Simplyhired.com
General job boards	CareerBuilder.com
	craigslist.org
	jobmonkey.com
	Monster.com
	NationJob.com
	LinkedIn.com
	tweetmyjobs.com
	twitjobsearch.com
	tweetajob.com
Sites for recent college grads	AfterCollege.com
	CampusCareerCenter.com
	college.monster.com
	CollegeCentral.com
	CollegeGrad.com
	CollegeJobConnect.com
	CollegeRecruiter.com
Publications with listings	EmploymentGuide.com
	jobmarket.nytimes.com
	online.wsj.com/public/page/news-career-jobs.html
Accounting/finance	accounting.com
	AccountingJobsToday.com
	afponline.org/pub/cs/online_job_center.html
Advertising/marketing/sales	jobs.adweek.com
	marketingpower.com/Careers
	prsa.org/jobcenter
Art/design	asid.org/career
	coroflot.com
	creativeheads.net
	designjobs.aiga.org
	NYFA.org
	siggraph.org/jobs

(Continues)

EXHIBIT 9.2 ● **Job-Listing Websites** *Continued*

Online Resources	Examples of Websites
Education	academic360.com
	chronicle.com/section/Jobs/61
	higheredjobs.com
	k12jobs.com
	isminc.com
Engineering	engineer.info
	engineerjobs.com
	engcen.com
Fashion/retail	careers.apparelandfootwear.org
	stylecareers.com
	wwd.com/wwdcareers
Government job listing sites	americasjobexchange.com
	governmentjobs.com
	usajobs.gov
Green/socially responsible	cleantechies.com/cleantech-job-search-career-services
	csrjobs.nl
	greenbiz.com
	grist.com
	justmeans.com/alljobs
Healthcare	healthecareers.com
	healthjobsusa.com
	healthcarejobs.org
	medzilla.com
Hospitality	allcruisejobs.com
	hcareers.com
	restaurant.org/careers/jobcenter/
	starchefsjobfinder.com
Human resource management	jobs4hr.com
	jobsinhr.org
	jobs.shrm.org
International	GigaJob.com
	jobbank.com
	JobServe.us
Law	911hotjobs.com
	alternativelawyerjobs.com
	americanbar.org/careercenter
	officer.com/careers
Nongovernmental organizations	devnetjobs.org
	jobs.un.org
	unjobs.org
Nonprofit job sites	idealist.org
	opportunityknocks.org
	philanthropy.com/section/Jobs/224

Online Resources	Examples of Websites
Publishing/media	bookcareers.com
	jobs.mashable.com
	mediabistro.com/joblistings
	newspapercareerbank.com
Recruiters/employment agencies	adecco.com
	futurestep.com
	kellyservices.com
	manpowergroup.com
	us.randstad.com
	us.hudson.com
Sports and recreation	fitnessjobs.com
	outdoorindustryjobs.com
	teamusa.org/jobs
Technology	computerjobs.com
	devbistro.com
	justtechjobs.com
	odinjobs.com

≫ WORK WITH AWARENESS ● Wellness

Searching for a job and preparing for interviews can be stressful. Maintaining emotional and physical wellness is important. Your work is only one aspect of your life, and no matter how fulfilling and rewarding it is, there are other life dimensions that contribute to how you feel and to your overall health.

Recognizing what went well and why good things have happened each day has been shown to positively impact overall well-being (Seligman, 2011). This can help you become more aware of what is going well in your job search, your life, your family, or elsewhere. It can help you identify small moments as well as significant accomplishments. It can help you feel good right away, and help you become more aware of positive experiences throughout each day.

To try this exercise, spend 10 minutes writing down "what went well" at the end of each day (Seligman, 2011). Next to what went well, write why it happened. For instance, if you have a good networking meeting with someone and you choose that for "what went well," then you might write that it was "because I asked for a contact from the career center," or "my mom asked her friend's cousin to help me." This assignment has been used in schools, businesses, and with individuals, and it can help increase your awareness of the good things in your life and why they happen.

Consider these areas that contribute to overall wellness, and the suggestions for building yourself up (Hettler, 1976). You might begin to notice what went well each day in more areas of your life, too.

- To improve your *emotional wellness*, listen actively to others and try to understand them. Ask questions when you feel you do not understand others, and value their ideas. Learn to manage your own emotions, express yourself, and tolerate a range of feelings.

- To achieve *occupational wellness*, be active and involved in your work and profession, understand your values, and seek out opportunities for work that is meaningful and rewarding to you.

- To improve your *physical wellness*, integrate physical activities and healthy choices into your life. Take a walk, join a fitness class, and enjoy healthy food. Pursue medical attention for minor illnesses when needed.

- To improve your *social wellness*, look for ways to better your world, connect to nature, and contribute to your community.

- To achieve *intellectual wellness*, aim to stretch your mind through learning activities. Read books, stay current on events, and engage in activities that allow you to learn more about your personal interests.

- To improve your *spiritual wellness*, learn to tolerate and appreciate people's differences while you search for your own meaning and purpose in life. Spiritual wellness can help you manage difficult times or emotional hardships.

During your job search or other times of career transition, your focus may be on getting a job, and you may find it hard to focus on a bigger picture. Remind yourself that a job search is part of a greater whole, your occupational wellness. Then, explore how improving all the areas of wellness can positively impact your experience. Seek help or support if any area of wellness seems difficult to manage on your own.

Technology is now used in all aspects of the job search, including job listings, career exploration, résumés and cover letters, applicant screening, and even the interview itself with real-time and video interviews online.

Your tech savvy can help you stand out from other applicants, or create new opportunities for your career. One approach is to use social media to connect your tech savvy with your branding and self-marketing skills. Consider examples of people using technology in innovative ways throughout the job search:

- Christa Keizer received her offer to intern at Cone, a strategy and communications firm, after posting daily tweets about her industry. Her thoughtful comment on one of Cone's blogs led to a post from an executive at Cone, followed by a discussion about her summer plans, and ultimately an interview and an offer for an internship (Swallow, 2010).

- Brian Freedman responded with a YouTube video after reading a job posting for financial articles or videos for the site iGrad.com. Although the site was primarily seeking articles, Freedman's video got their attention and he was offered a position (Sniderman, 2010).

- When Eric Romer's dream employer listed his dream job in marketing, he opted for an all-out approach, creating a full online marketing campaign with a dedicated website, Twitter page, Facebook page, and YouTube account that highlighted his skills as well as his interest in the company. Within 48 hours after submitting his first blog, he was contacted by the company, invited to interview, and eventually hired. (Swallow, 2010). You can explore his online campaign from his Twitter ID, @hiremeheadblade.

To add your own tech savvy twist to the job search, consider these ideas:

Develop Your Online Presence

Set up a Twitter account with an image and brief bio. Create a LinkedIn page with a complete profile that includes recommendations and a brief summary. Do not simply repost your résumé. Consider requesting recommendations from a former internship supervisor, professor, advisor, or mentor. Ask for feedback on the professionalism of your profiles from trusted mentors. Build your professional connections and followers by requesting referrals from people you know.

Make Your Online Presence More Personal

Consider creating a personal webpage or online résumé. Use YouTube to add a video résumé that reflects your personality and demonstrates your presentation and interpersonal skills. Connect your webpage to your Twitter and LinkedIn accounts as well. Use your online presence to demonstrate your tech skills as part of your overall package, regardless of the industry or job you are seeking.

Learn More and Join the Discussion

Follow companies of interest on Twitter and Facebook, learn about their current activities, and participate in discussions if you have something valuable to contribute. Read blogs concerning your industry. Learn what industry leaders are talking about. Share important articles, blog entries, or tweets with your connections on Twitter or LinkedIn. Consider developing your own blog if you like to write and have time. Do not send messages unless they are relevant, and include a small introduction that helps your followers understand why it is relevant to them. Ask networking contacts about industry news you learned about online, and gain further insight from your real-world connections.

» Networking for Job Opportunities

Friends, family friends, colleagues, mentors, and professors are all members of your network. When you ask them about their careers, tips for your job search, details about their employers, or if they know about openings, you are turning your relationships into a professional network.

"Networking" is a set of behaviors aimed at developing and maintaining informal relationships that have the potential to benefit you in your work or career (Forret and Dougherty, 2004). Networking has tangible benefits, and has been linked to increased salary and career satisfaction (Wolff and Moser, 2009). While networking may be the most important tool in your career toolbox, it can also be the most difficult to master. Approaching networking with a clear strategy that focuses on connecting with others can increase your effectiveness.

Think of Others First

When you start networking, think about what others know, what their interests are, or what you might have in common. If you think only of yourself, you may find you learn very little about your contacts. Online or in the real world, connecting involves a two-way dialogue.

At the beginning, avoid asking about jobs. Perhaps you are given the name of an industry insider. Your first instinct might be to e-mail your résumé and inquire about job openings. However, no matter how professional or well-written your e-mail, you run the risk of missing an opportunity by not initiating a two-way dialogue. Your networking contact:

- May know of job openings, and tell you about them;
- May know there are job openings, and tell you where they are listed;
- May forward your résumé to human resources;
- May not know about openings;
- May take another action, but will be *unlikely to engage you just to get to know you.*

Networking involves give and take. Whatever the outcome, you did not learn more about this contact, the organization, or how you could help him. Approaching networking as a two-way street requires you to seek out learning opportunities all the time. When you get to know others, you both share more relevant information. When they get to know you, they often think of opportunities that would not have come to mind without knowing your specific skills, talents, and interests.

Plan to learn. Whether you are at a networking event or in an informational interview, plan to learn more about the other person, as well as information that could help you in your job search. This will help you build a connection. It is okay to request an informational interview or networking meeting. At some point, you may also want to bring up job opportunities at the person's company that you know about and that interest you. However, talking only about your job search will make it hard to connect with others. You can be transparent about your interests and goals, as long as your primary focus involves learning about your contact.

Break the Ice before You Ask for Anything

There are certain questions that can break the ice and lead to a conversation. These are questions that your connection will be able to answer, because the information is based on his or her own experiences and insight.

> *Can you tell me more about your experience as a _____?*
> *How do you like working in _____?*
> *What would you recommend for someone looking to enter the field of _____?*

Review the list of questions in **Chapter 6: Relationships, Exhibit 6.1,** Networking Questions, for additional questions that can help you learn more about the people

Using your elevator pitch when you meet new networking contacts will help you make the most of every opportunity.

you meet as well as help you prepare for your job search. This way, you gain insider information through a natural conversation in which you can also share information about your goals and interests.

Use an Elevator Pitch

Whenever you are networking, your introduction must be clear and concise, and an elevator pitch can help you do that. Imagine yourself in an elevator with a recruiter for your ideal employer. In this short amount of time, what would you say? This is the thinking behind developing an "elevator pitch", which is a brief introduction that is targeted for the person who is listening.

The content of an elevator pitch. Harvard Business School offers these five tips to help you develop an elevator pitch in an online tool at alumni.hbs.edu/careers/pitch/ designed to help business owners or others seeking to brand themselves (HBS Elevator Pitch Builder, 2007).

1. Who: Describe who you are.
2. What: Describe what you do.
3. Why: Describe why you are unique.
4. Goal: Describe your immediate goals.
5. Analyze: Analyze your pitch.

To use their tool as a graduating student, you can try an introduction with punch, or try creating an elevator pitch that lacks some pizzazz, but still gets your point across. This might not offer the "wow" that will bring in business, but it will help you communicate with employers in the networking process.

I'm Kayla Jenson and I'm completing my BS in communications [*Who*]. I have strong skills in writing, research, and art history from my courses and an internship at the Boston Art Museum. I also volunteered in communications at the American Red Cross and Habitat for Humanity [*What*], where I helped write press releases and contact media for upcoming events [*Why*]. I believe I could make a strong contribution in communications at a museum, school, or community center [*Goal*].

The style of an elevator pitch. If you are seeking to promote your small business or business services, you have to actively promote your assets. Telling others how you can help them is a lot more effective than simply saying what you do. Dale Kurow, an executive coach, gives this example of how an introduction can be reworked into an elevator pitch that can make your introduction more memorable; it includes several other catchy introductions (2012).

Trust me, no one is going to be riveted if you say:

"Hi, I'm Sally Hopeful, and I'm an executive recruiter."

Two big yawns. . . .

"Hi, I'm Sally Hopeful. I partner with companies that need to find talented people to help their business grow and become more profitable."

Now, you've got my attention! . . .

I know an Avon representative who says:

"I help women look beautiful."

Or a business coach who says:

"I help you get more clients than you know what to do with."

And here's my favorite, one that is used by an IRS agent:

"I'm a government fund-raiser."

Your introduction, whether it is a short summary or a promotional elevator pitch, should sound natural, feel comfortable when said out loud, and focus on what you can offer the other person rather than what you want. Ideally, your introduction will lead to a conversation in which you learn more about the other person and have the opportunity to share more about yourself.

Add a question. When you introduce yourself, add a question at the end. The question you add should be open-ended, which is a question that cannot be answered with a yes or no. If you are in an informal networking setting, you may not want to use your entire introduction, but could offer a brief summary of key points. With your open-ended question at the end, you can begin to engage your contact. This will help turn your "pitch" or "introduction" into a conversation starter.

> I'm graduating this year, and I interned at the Boston Art Museum last summer. I am looking at entry-level positions in communications, possibly at a museum. *I heard you mention that you work at the Lawrence Children's Museum. Can you tell me more about your experience there?*

The Goal of Networking

Even when your personal goal is to find a job, the goal for networking is to learn, not to ask for a job. Open-ended questions that cannot be answered with a simple yes or no engage your contacts and encourage them to speak about a topic with which they are familiar. For example, at a career fair, while meeting with the recruiter for a museum, a candidate could introduce herself by saying:

> Thank you for taking the time to speak with me. I'm Kayla Jenson and I'm completing my BS in communications [*Who*]. I have strong skills in writing, research, and art history from my courses and work experience [*What*]. I held an internship at the Boston Art Museum and volunteer positions in communications at the American Red Cross and Habitat for Humanity. I researched your openings online, and noticed you are hiring for entry-level communications positions. *Can you tell me more about the application process and opportunities in communications within the museum?*

This introduction adds a request for information and is tailored to the context (a career fair) and individual (a recruiter). The information generated by this question will help the candidate prepare stronger cover letters and target an application because of the insider information she will have gained regarding the organization and open positions.

Connect First, and the Job Leads Will Follow

As you gain information and communicate your assets, job openings are shared through natural discourse. Here are several tips to help you learn about openings as well as gain information that will help in your job search.

Offer help to others. If you think you have something to offer—do! People appreciate your help, such as the offer to send the name of a book or article you read that seems to fit their interests, or the name of one of your contacts who can add value to their work.

Have authentic conversations. Conversations that reflect your genuine interests will result in real relationships. You will naturally connect with some people better than others. If you find you are having trouble connecting with people in your field, it could be an indicator that aspects of the field are a poor fit for you. Stay mindful of the relationships that develop easily.

Set up informational interviews. Informational interviews allow you to learn about others and gain information. They might tell you about their experiences, give suggestions for career-building activities, and share other information that can help you learn more and build more contacts. Insider information is always helpful.

Build your network. The larger your network, the more information you will have access to. Build your network by engaging in activities, following up with people you meet, and asking for the names of others in your field.

Communicate your assets. No employer will ever hesitate from offering information about job leads if they think you are a good fit. The key is to learn enough about others to share the information that will be most relevant to them.

Realize that your agenda is not theirs. When you are in a job search, you may feel pressure to get results or experience some anxiety about the job market. However, your feelings are not your contacts' concerns; in fact, they may have their own! Your respect for others' time and willingness to help you should be clear in every conversation. If a conversation seems awkward or no help is offered, thank your contact anyway, accept this, and move on.

Thank everyone. Thanking people is critical. Say thank you, write thank you notes, and follow up with e-mails to let your contacts know how you used their advice or information. Your appreciation shows your connections that their time and input is valuable, and this is an easy way for you to stay connected.

Career fairs, or job fairs, whether on campus or off, bring employers and companies together to recruit for open positions including internships, seasonal job opportunities, and full- and/or part-time employment. These events are opportunities to develop new contacts, expand your network, meet recruiters, set up interviews, and distribute résumés. They can also be used to gather information and conduct informal informational interviews.

Before the Job Fair
- Obtain a list of attending employers.
- Research the companies in which you are interested.
- Plan your professional attire.
- Prepare at least 25–30 copies of your résumé.
- Bring your portfolio, a notepad, and a pen.
- Develop a brief, personal introduction.

At the Job Fair
- Arrive early and check your appearance.
- Turn off your cell phone.
- Prioritize the list of organizations in which you are interested.
- Respect the privacy of other participants, and read brochures and company materials while waiting.
- Introduce yourself, make eye contact, and have a firm handshake.

- Ask for a business card, and take notes after you walk away to remember your conversation.
- Network, network, network.

Make a Positive First Impression
- Listen carefully.
- Avoid filler words "um," "like," or "you know"—aim to speak with confidence.
- Do not fidget or rock back and forth.
- Do not chew gum.
- Do not look around while a recruiter is speaking to you.
- Do not approach recruiters with a group of friends. Interview independently.

Questions to Ask Recruiters
- What full-time career opportunities are available in your organization?
- What is the employment outlook in the field right now?
- What opportunities do you have for my major?
- What types of assignments are given to new graduates?
- What type of training is available?
- What do you look for in candidates?

After the Job Fair
- Write thank you letters to all recruiters you met.

© Cengage Learning 2014

≫ CAREER PROFILE ● Case Study

Mason Wolff: Networking for a Job

Mason is completing his associate's degree in multimedia design this semester, and is looking for a job after he graduates. He has worked on website design and graphic design projects through his coursework, and has developed on-the-job skills as an associate at CopyWrite Center, a copy center where he has worked while in school. At his job, he became the "go-to" person for small business graphic-design solutions, helping numerous businesses with logos, business card design and layout, business stationery, and promotional flyers and mailings. His hard work also helped him land the opportunity to design the store's website.

Given the competitive economy and increased outsourcing for graphic design positions, he knows the key to obtaining a job will be his ability to network. He is flexible about job opportunities, as long as they will allow him to be creative and use his training. He is aware of an upcoming career fair at his community

college, but he reviewed the list of employers and opportunities and was disappointed to find that most jobs were in sales and business. In addition, he is so busy at work and with school that he is finding it hard to meet people or get information he can use in his job search.

What activities or events could Mason attend that could help him meet people for his job search?

What information could Mason include in his elevator pitch?

What questions could Mason ask people he meets that will help him in his job search?

To learn more about Mason's career development, visit CourseMate. ⊞ View his résumé and job search materials in **Chapter 8: Tools**.

© Cengage Learning 2014

>> **EXHIBIT 9.4** ● **Networking Letter**

To: pisaacs@productionsolutions.com
Cc:
Bcc:
Subject: Appleton Community College Career Fair
Attachment: mason wolff resume.pdf

Dear Ms. Isaacs,

It was so nice to meet you at yesterday's career fair at Appleton Community College, where I am completing my AA in multimedia design. I greatly appreciated the time you took discussing your Midwest division. I was able to review your website following our discussion, and found Production Solutions' recent expansion and wide range of clients to be very impressive. I was particularly interested in your production and graphic design work with small businesses, because I have developed websites and design solutions for small businesses through school projects and my experience as an associate at CopyWrite Center.

I understand you were not on campus to recruit for positions in graphic design; however, I enjoyed our conversation, and look forward to keeping in touch, as you suggested. It was very nice for you to offer to send my resume to Ronald James, Regional Manager of the Graphics Design team, whose name you mentioned. I have enclosed my resume, which includes links to my online portfolio. If he is not hiring at this time, please feel free to let him know that I would be interested in setting up an informational interview with him or someone else in the department, if possible. I am seeking to learn more about the field and would appreciate any opportunity to learn more.

Thank you very much. I will follow up within two weeks to confirm that you received this letter and to learn if I should follow up with anyone else at your company. I believe my skills and experience are a great match for the graphic design projects at Production Solutions, and I look forward to speaking with you in the future.

Sincerely,

Mason Wolff

» Strategies for Successful Interviewing

If you are invited for an interview, then your résumé and cover letter have successfully illustrated that you possess the skills and assets an employer is seeking. Interviews are your opportunity to further discuss your strengths while demonstrating your professionalism, as you learn more about the organization and position to determine if the opportunity is right for you.

Your interview experiences can vary, and may include telephone or online interviews.

Types of Interviews

There are many types of interviews, and understanding the formats you might encounter can help you put your best foot forward. Interviews may be conducted in person, over the telephone, online, or via video-based recorded interviews. Employers will let you know how you are going to be interviewed, and if you are unfamiliar with the approach, you can learn more about it and prepare in advance.

In-person. In this format, you will have the opportunity to engage in conversation with the employer in person. You will be evaluated on your professionalism as well as your ability to answer questions. Prepare answers to common questions and prepare several questions to ask as well.

Telephone. Often used for an initial screening, especially in a long distance job search, the telephone interview may involve more than one company representative on the other end of the line. Dress for the interview if possible, since you may be inclined to speak differently or listen more intently if you are prepared just as if you were in an in-person interview. Prepare by having a paper copy of your résumé in front of you for reference, because clicking on your computer can be a distraction to you and noisy to them. Smile while you speak; surprisingly, it can make you sound more upbeat and interested.

Online or video. Companies are increasingly using Web-based tools to interview, such as Skype or Oovoo. Wear interview attire, as you will be seen by the employer, and practice to be aware of your facial expressions and hand movements, as these may seem more pronounced on the screen. Video interviews may offer the opportunity for you to record and rerecord. Realize that a taped interview may be viewed my many individuals.

Group or panel. A group interview involves an interview with more than one person at the same time. When responding to a question, address the person who asked the question, but realize that everyone is interested in your answer.

Series. This format involves interviewing with a series of individuals, one after the other. Even though you are interviewing separately with each person, try to use different examples in each interview, as the interviewers will likely compare notes regarding your responses.

Lunch or dinner. If you are interviewed during a meal, you will be evaluated on your professionalism, responses, and dining etiquette skills. This type of interview may involve an opportunity to get to know the interviewers better, as conversation may become more informal, or you may be given more opportunities to ask your questions. Prepare your questions in advance, and order food that is easy for you to eat without a mess, following the cues as to the number of courses from your interviewers.

Interview Formats

General questions. Many interviews, and at least part of most interviews, involve general questions. These are meant to help the interviewer learn more about you. Sample questions can be found in **Exhibit 9.6**, Interview Questions.

Presentation. For some positions, you may be asked to do a presentation. Your presentation should highlight your assets, and be relevant to the position. If you will need to use technology provided by the employer, let them know in advance, and prepare with a back-up plan in case the technology fails to work properly, such as a poor wifi connection.

Structured. A structured interview involves a series of the same questions that will be asked of all applicants. This offers the employer an opportunity to compare all interviewees on the same dimensions.

Behavioral. A behavioral interview involves questions that require you to describe a situation and its outcome. You can answer these questions using the STAR Technique (QuintCareers.com n.d), which is described in **Exhibit 9.6**, Interview Questions.

Case Study. Case study or case model questions were once reserved for certain types of interviews, such as those for consulting, but have grown in popularity. They can involve a case that requires critical thinking, math skills, and reasoning. You will be presented with a situation and asked how you would address it, usually to solve a particular challenge. To learn more about case study questions, consider reading sample questions and responses on a website like Wetfeet. Be aware that the interviewer is interested in understanding how you arrive at your answer, not just the answer itself.

Prepare through Career Exploration

To be successful in your interviews, you must first understand the value of your skills and experience in the marketplace. Your preparation should include a basic knowledge of the industry and company, answers to common interview questions, and an understanding of professional attire for the industry, so that you will be dressed appropriately for the interview. The good news is that you may have already begun your preparation long before your interviews, by learning about careers, gaining exposure to work settings, and assessing how your skills, experiences, interests, and values connect with career fields.

Employers expect you to know about the world of work, and your knowledge will be tested in your interviews. If you still need to learn more about the industry or type of job for which you are interviewing, **Chapter 5: Explore** offers many resources to help you learn more. **Exhibit 5.1**, Career Exploration Questions, can help you assess the information you may want to learn before your interview. **Exhibit 5.2**, Online Resources for Career Exploration, offers suggested websites, and **Exhibit 5.3**, Professional Associations, can help you learn more from industry insiders.

Improve Your Interviewing Skills

Once you have a basic understanding of the industry, organization, key competitors, and position for which you will be interviewing, then you can shift your focus from general knowledge to specific interview preparation.

Practice interview questions. Preparing answers to common interview questions and practicing your responses out loud are two of the best ways to prepare for your interviews. You can start preparing even before your first interview. You may find this preparation improves your networking as well. Use **Exhibit 9.6**, Interview Questions, to learn common questions and how to answer them.

Understand illegal questions. It is also important to know that there are some questions that are illegal for employers to ask. (For information about discrimination, see the Embracing Differences section in this chapter.) Illegal questions can make you uncomfortable and can be used to discriminate against you. In some cases, employers may be unaware that they are asking illegal questions, but you still have the option not to answer any questions that could violate your rights. See **Exhibit 9.7**, Illegal Interview Questions, to learn a range of specific responses to various illegal questions. In addition to these responses, you may wish to use one of these approaches from Michelle Tullier, author of *The Unofficial Guide to Acing the Interview* (1999):

(1) Answering it if you feel fine about sharing the information
(2) Evading the question with humor or another question
(3) Avoiding an answer or refusing to answer, by responding with a question that
    asks about its relevance to the position

Learn about interviewing. Understanding the structure of an interview—including what to do before, during, and after—can help you plan your time, know what to expect, and understand how to follow up appropriately. For example, after your interview, plan to send a thank you note, and possibly a follow-up letter, to express your gratitude and interest. Sample letters and tips are offered in **Chapter 8: Tools. Exhibit 9.5**, Before, During, and After an Interview, will help you understand the interview process.

≫EXHIBIT 9.5 ● Before, During, and After the Interview

 In order to make each interview a success, consider the following tips for before, during, and after your interview.

Before the Interview
- Confirm that your voicemail is not full, and that it reflects a professional tone and wording.

- Research the company to understand its mission, structure, history, recent events, product lines, and competitors.
- Research the position to know common salaries and job details. Evaluate your knowledge, skills, and abilities and how you qualify for the opportunity.
- Call to confirm the date, time, and place of your appointment on the day prior to the interview.

(Continues)

»EXHIBIT 9.5 ● **Before, During, and After the Interview** *Continued*

- Confirm directions and how long it will take you to get to the interview. Consider a practice run to avoid unexpected travel delays.
- Know the names of those people with whom you will be meeting, if possible, and any names of people who recommended you.
- Have answers prepared for common and tough interview questions.
- Know what interview attire is appropriate, and have it ready for the interview—clothes clean and pressed, shoes shined.
- Have an appropriate bag or briefcase, a pad of paper and pen for notes, and copies of your résumé and other necessary materials (such as a portfolio).
- Review your questions for the interviewer.
- Avoid foods the night before that might have a lingering odor, such as garlic.
- Arrange for reliable others to be available for personal "emergency-type" tasks that may come up (such as back-up care for family members).
- Get a good night's sleep.

The Day of the Interview

- Plan to arrive 15 minutes before your scheduled appointment. You may need to wait, or you may be asked to complete an application or other forms when you arrive.
- Turn off your cell phone before you check in.
- Odors linger and can be distracting, or an interviewer may have allergies. Do not smoke beforehand and choose unscented lotion or none at all.
- Decline any food or beverage offers. Do not chew gum.
- Make a quick stop in the restroom to look in a full-length mirror. Check your hair, teeth, clothes, and makeup. Is your tie straight, your hair neat, and your teeth free of food?
- Be polite and friendly to every person you meet from the moment you arrive, whether it is a person in the elevator, a security guard, a senior-level or mid-level executive, a receptionist, or an administrative assistant. Everyone within the organization should be treated with respect, as they will all be your colleagues if you are hired, and anyone you meet that day may have the chance to evaluate you.
- Bring a mint, but eat it on the way to the interview, so you are finished by the time you get there!

During the Interview

- Be confident. Project interest and enthusiasm.
- Greet the interviewer with a firm handshake.

- Smile and maintain appropriate eye contact. Never look at your watch.
- Be aware of hand and facial movements.
- Wait for the interviewer to ask you to be seated.
- Be aware of your posture and body language.
- Avoid using the interviewer's first name unless invited to do so.
- Do not take notes unless you are asked something for which you must follow-up. If you wish to write something, as a form of courtesy, consider asking the interviewer first.
- Listen to the questions, and answer what is really being asked.
- Pause briefly before answering to indicate that your response is not rehearsed.
- Respond to questions with examples from your professional or academic experiences, while avoiding long, rambling answers and descriptions of personal stories.
- If you are leaving your current job, explain why succinctly before the interviewer asks.
- Back up your skills and strengths with relevant, clear, concise examples.
- Answer questions carefully and noncontroversially, avoiding political or religious references, as well as examples that reveal details that could be used to discriminate, such as references to family activities or children.
- If an interview takes place over a meal, review dining etiquette prior to the meeting.
- When the interview is over, shake the interviewer's hand and express your gratitude.
- Ask when a decision will be made, if it has not already been indicated.
- If you have multiple interviews, think of new things to present in each conversation.

After the Interview

- Send a thank you note to each person you met within 24–48 hours.
- Follow up in any ways that you discussed.
- Keep an interview journal. Take the time to make notes immediately after the interview.
- Write down any difficult moments or questions, so you can prepare for them in the future.
- Consider a follow-up note after two weeks, if appropriate.
- Congratulate yourself for a job well done!

© Cengage Learning 2014

»EXHIBIT 9.6 ● Interview Questions

 There are several types of interview questions, and each requires a slightly different approach. Understanding the structure of an interview, what to expect, and how you might answer common questions will help you focus on communicating your assets and building rapport.

Icebreaker Questions

Experienced recruiters understand you might be nervous during an interview. They conduct hundreds of interviews and screen many applicants for each position. They will usually open with questions to break the ice and help you relax. Answer briefly and positively so that the interviewer can move on to more detailed questions.

- How did you learn about our organization?
- Did you have any difficulty finding our office?

Getting Started

Certain questions can set the tone for the interview based on your response, as these will help the interviewer learn more about you. This is your opportunity to give a brief overview of what you have done and how your experiences and skills have prepared you for this position.

- Tell me about yourself.
- Walk me through your résumé.

General Questions

The interviewer will then move into more general questions to gain an overall sense of who you are. These are often general and open-ended. While you may be able to speak endlessly, it is more effective to limit your response and keep your answer connected to the position. This provides the interviewer with a brief sketch of your assets and their relevance to the position.

- What kind of leadership positions have you held?
- Why do you think you would be a good fit for our organization?
- What motivates you in your work?
- What are your strengths? Weaknesses?
- Why are you interested in this field?
- What experiences have you had which you believe qualify you for this position?

Behavioral Questions

You may also be asked behavioral questions to determine how well you meet the requirements of the job and if your skill set is a good match for the position. This involves details about a particular task, experience, or responsibility, allowing the interviewer to learn how you approach situations, and how you deal with them. You may draw on your work, academic, volunteer, and extracurricular experience to answer these questions.

To answer behavioral questions, try breaking them down in the STAR format (also see QuintCareers.com (n.d.):

1. State the **S**ituation . . .
2. . . . or **T**ask you are going to describe, in specific, not general, terms.
3. Describe the **A**ctions you took, and your role in the situation.
4. State the **R**esults of your action and the outcome of the situation—as it relates to the question.

Here are examples of behavioral questions.

- Tell me about a time when you worked in a team and there was disagreement in the group.
- Tell me about a time when you had to go above and beyond the call of duty in order to complete a project or get the job done.
- Give me an example of a time when you faced obstacles in achieving a goal.
- Give me an example of when you showed initiative and took the lead.
- Tell me about a time when you made a mistake at work, and how you dealt with the situation.
- Describe a time when you had to make a fast decision with limited information.
- Describe a time when you had to persuade a person to do something he or she did not want to do.
- Give me an example of when you worked with a group to complete a project, and describe your role.
- Give me an example of a time when you tried to accomplish something and failed.
- Tell me about a time when you had to build rapport quickly with someone under difficult conditions.
- Describe a time when you had to analyze information and make a recommendation. What was the thought process for your decision?
- Give me an example of a time when you motivated others.

Questions You Can Ask During the Interview

The interview is a two-way process. It is an opportunity for you to learn more about the company and position to see if it is a good fit for you. You are expected to have questions, and it is fine to ask them during the interview if you choose, or at the end, when they invite you to ask questions. Plan two to five questions you want to ask.

- What could I expect a typical day to be like?
- Who will be working with me on a regular basis?
- What will be the candidate's first priorities in this position?
- What will be the measurements of my success in this position?
- Do you have management training or mentorship programs?
- How would you describe your company culture?
- When and how should I follow up with you?

(Continues)

Questions *Not* To Ask During the Interview

Finally, there are questions you should never ask during an interview. Employers will review benefits, salary, compensation packages, and pertinent information with you at the appropriate time. In addition, information pertaining to policies and benefits may be available on the company website or can be discussed after an offer is presented.

- What exactly does your company do?
- What salary will I earn?

- What bonus do you offer?
- Do you offer a relocation package to help with my moving expenses?
- What type of benefits package will you offer me?
- How much vacation/sick time can I expect?
- How quickly will I be promoted?
- Will the company pay for my graduate degree?
- Can I bring my children to work?

》EMBRACING DIFFERENCES ● Discrimination and Affirmative Action

During your job search and when you are working, you are protected against discrimination by federal laws. The U.S. Equal Employment Opportunity Commission (EEOC) is responsible for enforcing these laws, which are designed to make sure that employees are hired, trained, and treated fairly. In addition, affirmative action policies were created to address and overcome past discrimination by involving efforts to recruit, train, and promote those who are members of protected groups, including women, minorities, veterans, and individuals with disabilities. In some cases, affirmative action policies may be court ordered; in other cases, they may be adopted voluntarily in an effort to increase diversity. It is illegal to discriminate against applicants or employees, and understanding your rights can help you prepare for the interview process and experiences on the job.

According to the U.S. Equal Employment Opportunity Commission (2009), it is illegal to discriminate in any aspect of employment, including the following:

- Hiring and firing
- Compensation, assignment, or classification of employees
- Transfer, promotion, layoff, or recall
- Job advertisements
- Recruitment
- Testing
- Use of company facilities
- Training and apprenticeship programs
- Fringe benefits
- Pay, retirement plans, and disability leave
- Other terms and conditions of employment

Furthermore, the EEOC (2009) states that discriminatory practices under these laws include the following:

- Harassment on the basis of race, color, religion, sex, national origin, disability, genetic information, or age
- Retaliation against an individual for filing a charge of discrimination, participating in an investigation, or opposing discriminatory practices
- Employment decisions based on stereotypes or assumptions about the abilities, traits, or performance of individuals of a certain sex, race, age, religion, or ethnic group, or individuals with disabilities, or based on myths or assumptions about an individual's genetic information
- Denying employment opportunities to a person because of marriage to, or association with, an individual of a particular race, religion, national origin, or an individual with a disability (Title VII also prohibits discrimination because of participation in schools or places of worship associated with a particular racial, ethnic, or religious group.)

Knowledge of your rights can help you understand how your responses to interview questions may be used to discriminate against you. Large employers usually offer training programs to educate employees about discrimination and teach them how they can report such behavior if they believe it has occurred. However, small businesses may not offer training in such areas, and interviewers may even ask illegal interview questions unintentionally. Understanding your rights will help you in your job search, and empower you to address workplace discrimination if you believe it has occurred. Visit the U.S. Equal Employment Opportunity Commission at eeoc.gov for detailed information or to initiate a claim.

≫ EXHIBIT 9.7 ● Illegal Interview Questions

The table below provides alternatives for directly answering—or refusing to answer—a question that might elicit information that could be used to discriminate against you in the hiring process. Of course, how you decide to handle illegal interview questions is up to you, whether you want to answer the question, avoid the question, or redirect the question.

ILLEGAL QUESTIONS What you can't be asked	LEGAL QUESTIONS If you are asked an illegal question, consider answering as if you were asked a legal question.	POSSIBLE RESPONSES Options for responding to illegal questions
Race, Color, Religion, or Political Affiliation		
What is your religion?	Are there any days that you will be unavailble to work?	If you are asking about my religion because you are concerned about my work availability, I am available to work . . .
Can you tell me about your social activities (or clubs or organizations)?	Tell me about the activities listed on your resume. Are you involved in any related professional activities?	I serve as the _____ for the _____ group, in which I _____ (list responsibiltiies or skills). or I am a student member of the _____ professional association in which I . . .
Nationality		
Are you American? or Are you a U.S. citizen?	Are you legally authorized to work in the U.S.?	If you are asking about my ability to work, yes, I am authorized to work in the U.S.
What is your native language? or In English your first language?	Do you speak, read or write any languages fluently other than English?	If you are asking about my translating ability, I am fluent in written and spoken Russian and also familiar with German.
Where are you from? or Where do you live?	Are you able to start work on time, which is at _____? Are you willing to relocate?	I am from ___ (state of residence from where you will be commuting). or I currently live on campus, and I am looking forward to moving somewhere that will be convenient for my work schedule after graduation.
Age		
How old were you when you graduated from ____?	What year did you graduate from _____?	I graduated from _____ in _____, or . . .
How old are you?	Are you 18 years old or older?	*If you are very young:* I am over the age of 18 and looking forward to applying my skills as well as my level of energy and enthusiasm. *If you are mature:* I have experience, certainly, and I've also engaged in lifelong learning that makes me current and competitive in my field.
Are you planning to retire soon?	What are your career plans?	I plan to work for the foreseeable future and do not have any plans to retire at this time. I enjoy my work, and it's such an important part of who I am.
Sara will be your supoervisor. She is 26. Is she younger than you?	Are you able to work well with others in a team?	It doesn't matter to me if my supervisor is older or younger, I am eager to learn from everyone.
Marital and Family Status		
Are you married? Is this your maiden / married name?	Have you been employed or earned a degree using another name?	If you are asking about my personal commitments, please know my personal life will not interfere with my work (or travel / overtime). or This is the only name I have used. or You may find in my records that I was previously known as _____ .
Do you have children? Are you planning to start a family? Who will care for your children when you are at work? If you get pregnant, will you come back after maternity leave?	Are you available to fullfill the job requirements, such as working evenings, weekends, or travel? Tell me about your experience working with children?	If you are asking if I am available to work for the foreseeable future, I am. or My family life will not interfere with my ability to work overtime or travel. or If you are asking about my experience with children, I have been a _____ (list relevant experience), where I learned _____ .

(Continues)

ILLEGAL QUESTIONS What you can't be asked	LEGAL QUESTIONS If you are asked an illegal question, consider answering as if you were asked a legal question.	POSSIBLE RESPONSES Options for responding to illegal questions
What do your parents do?	*Tell me how you became interested in this industry.*	Interestingly, I am taking a different / similar path from my parents. I became interested in this field because of an inspirational teacher / employer / relative . . .
Gender		
As a woman, do you think you can do this job?	*Are you able to perform the job?*	I feel that I have the qualifications and experience you seek and I am confident that I will be an excellent addition to your team.
How do you feel about dating a coworker?	*Are you willing to follow our workplace policies regarding harassment?*	If that's a policy here, I would, of course, be willing to follow it.
How do you feel about having a male/female supervisor?	*Are you able to work well with others in a team?*	It doesn't matter to me if my supervisor is male or female, I am eager to learn from everyone.
Health and Physical Abilities		
Do you smoke or drink?	*Have you ever been disciplined for violating company policies regarding the use of alcohol or tobacco products?*	No. or I do not abuse any substances.
Do you take drugs?	*Do you use illegal drugs?*	I do not take any illegal drugs.
Do you have any disabilities?	*Are you able to perform the specific duties of this position?*	I will be able to perform all of the duties of this position. With reasonable accommodations, I will be able to perform the duties of this position. I will be happy to explain these.
Military Service		
Are you a member of the National Guard or Reserves?	*Do you have any upcoming events that would require extensive time away from work?*	I do not have any commitments that will require me to be unavailable for work. or Yes, as a member of the national guard/reserves I serve my country one weekend per month and two weeks per year.
Arrests		
Were you ever arrested (or accused) of a crime?	*Have you ever been convicted of a crime?*	No. or I have never been convicted of a crime. Yes, and I appreciate this opportunity to discuss . . . (Share limited information, focus on work readiness.)

Sources: US Equal Employment opportunity Commission (200); HR World editors/http://www.focus.com/fyi/30-interview-questions-you-cant-ask-and-30-sneaky-legal-get/

≫ Professional Attire and Your Job Search

There is no right way to dress for all interviews. However, there are guidelines and suggestions that vary by industry. To learn the norms for your industry, be aware of the dress and style of your networking contacts, and any employees who come to campus for recruiting events or career fairs. Your networking contacts and campus career center can provide feedback on your choices for interview attire. A list of the aspects of professional attire that you should consider when putting together your look is in **Exhibit 9.8**, Professional Attire.

Interview Attire

Your interview attire should be appropriate for the most dressed-up day on the job when you would meet senior executives or industry leaders. In some industries, a navy or black suit is still the norm, while in others, a fashion-forward suit, a skirt with a blouse for women, or pants and a blazer for men would be appropriate. In some fields or with certain employers, dressing in traditional interview attire could be as inappropriate as dressing too casually in others. However, some clothing would be inappropriate for most interviews. This includes skirts that fall more than two inches above the knee, shorts and tank tops, and clothing that reveals undergarments such as underwear showing above low, baggy pants, or exposed bra straps. **Exhibit 9.8**, Professional Attire, can help you better understand employers' expectations.

A Professional Wardrobe

During your job search, you will have numerous occasions to wear professional attire, such as networking events, informational interviews, employer visits, and, of course, interviews. Purchasing a few basic items that can mix and match is often a good approach if you do not yet own these items. Consider your industry, and then look for appropriate items that can be worn repeatedly. Your career center may have suggestions for local stores that have discounted suits and business casual items. There are also some colleges and local charitable organizations that provide suits or other work clothing, to keep or to borrow, for the interview process or your first days or weeks on the job. If you are uncertain about how to dress, you may wish to request a practice interview with a career counselor in which you dress in professional attire.

Appropriate interview attire may vary by industry, but all interview attire should be neat, clean, and professional.

❯❯ EXHIBIT 9.8 ● Professional Attire

Topic	Suggestions
Clothing	• Interview attire is expected to be professional attire.
	• A matching navy or black suit is considered appropriate for corporate interviews.
	• Business casual attire or a fashion-forward suit may be appropriate for other settings such as jobs in early education, art, or design, where hands-on projects are the focus of work tasks.
	• Even if you find yourself interviewing with someone wearing jeans, you should be dressed professionally.
	• Daily attire may be common for everyday work, but is still not right for an interview. This can include "dress down" or "casual attire."
Shoes	• Shoes should be clean and polished.
	• Style should be consistent with the approach you took to clothing (i.e., low, simple heels in a color to match your suit for women in corporate interviews).
	• Shoes that are difficult to walk in should be avoided.
Hair	• Hairstyles also can vary by industry, but should be neat for the interview.
	• Review images of professionals in your career field to see the ways people wear their hair.
	• If your hair is very long, consider wearing it back or styling it off your face for the interview.

(Continues)

Topic	Suggestions
Makeup and Nails	• In general, makeup for the interview will be less dramatic than evening or social occasions, and nails should be groomed. • Determining the right makeup for your interview can be aided by reviewing images of professionals in your career field. • Typically, creative fields will offer more latitude, while conservative industries will typically prefer less makeup.
Jewelry	• Jewelry should also be considered when planning your professional attire. • From body piercings to necklaces to rings, some topics to consider are the type of jewelry you are choosing. • Consider the statement you are making, and its consistency with your industry. Is it conservative and traditional, such as one stud earring in each ear and a single strand of pearls; fashion conscious, such as a striking necklace or oversized cocktail ring; or unconventional and nonconformist, such as an eyebrow piercing? • Choose jewelry that is consistent with your overall image and appropriate for your industry, while remaining slightly more conservative for the day of the interview.
Body Art	• While body art and tattoos are increasingly common, many industries still prefer they be hidden, either by makeup or clothes. • Of course, if you are interviewing at a tattoo shop, you will likely want to show your body art. Your target job and industry should determine your approach.
Purse/Portfolio	• Limit items you carry to those that are completely necessary. • Purses/portfolios should not be overstuffed, should match your overall style, and should hold the items you need to bring, such as a pen and pad.
Other	• If the weather is inclement and you need to wear snow or rain boots, wear them with your professional outfit. • If necessary, bring shoes and a bag in which to store your wet items.

▶▶ Evaluating Next Steps and Negotiating

Evaluating your next steps may involve accepting a position, planning for job alternatives while continuing your search, and negotiating. Managing this last step of the job search process is important, and can be challenging. Your patience and willingness to see the big picture are critical skills for this important time.

When an Offer Is Made

Congratulations! Your hard work has paid off and you have been rewarded with an offer.

Before you accept or reject the offer. Immediately thank the person who delivered the good news, even if you are not fully pleased with the offer or would like to negotiate. Then, take time to review the offer before making a decision. You may decide it is exactly what you want; you may have further questions; you may prefer to negotiate one or more points that could include your title, salary, benefits, or schedule; or you may decide to decline the offer.

Focus on your skills and the value you will add to the position when negotiating a job offer.

Set a timeframe. If there is no set timeline for your review of an offer, it is respectful to ask the employer when they would like you to get back in touch so that you can discuss their offer. Set up a phone meeting if you have questions. It is also appropriate to ask when they would like to know if you will accept the offer.

Drug testing. For some employers, drug testing for illegal substances is a standard part of the hiring process. There are real costs to employers when employees use illegal drugs, abuse or misuse alcohol or legal substances, including prescription medication. This is the reason for drug screening. According to research by the Substance Abuse and Mental Health Services Administration, employment by those with alcohol or drug abuse disorders were responsible for estimated losses of $80.9 billion in lost productivity, with $66.7 billion from alcohol problems, and $14.2 billion from drug issues (2011).

In most cases, drug screening will be done after an offer is made, and the offer will be rescinded if tests are positive. Know your rights regarding testing by checking the Department of Labor's website. If you are to be screened, check with your doctor to find out if any prescription drugs you take will impact your results. Policies vary from one employer to the next and screening may be a requirement in some industries. For example, an occupation in transportation with federal oversight will not only require applicants to be screened for drug testing, but may require random drug tests throughout employment.

Negotiating Your Compensation Package: Salary, Benefits, and More

Understand your compensation package. Your overall compensation package may include such benefits as health insurance, sick days, vacation days, commuting costs, and bonuses. In addition, some companies offer workplace amenities or other benefits that can offset some of your other expenses and add to your quality of life. These may include a gym, tuition reimbursement, professional development, free snacks, soda, coffee bars, cafeterias, car service when overtime is expected, daycare, pet sitting, dry cleaning, or other perks.

Prepare to negotiate. Knowing your worth can help you negotiate more effectively, especially if an offer is far below typical salaries for your industry, position, and part of the country. Therefore, it is appropriate to negotiate by stating the range of typical salaries if your offer is lower. A resource like the NACE Job Seekers Salary Calculator, which you can access online, can help you learn salary ranges in your region. In addition, your negotiation should reflect an understanding of the unique skills and assets you possess and what value they can add. If an employer is unwilling to adjust the salary, consider if there are other aspects of the offer that would make salary less important, such as your title or benefits. If you truly want the position, consider requesting a three-month review with an opportunity for a salary increase.

Negotiate your offer. Here are a few ideas for scripts that address different negotiating tactics. However, whenever you negotiate, realize that you may not get what you want. If you truly cannot accept an offer because of your budget, but can find another way to add income or cut your expenses, you may be able to make the offer work for you. Negotiating is a conversation, and is an opportunity to set up a professional and courteous rapport with any potential employer.

If an employer asks you what you expect to earn, here is an example of an appropriate response that addresses the salary range, and your industry knowledge and preparation.

> *I have researched comparable positions as a film editor in Denver, Colorado, and I am aware that salaries range widely. However, I feel that with my education in film and media studies, internships, and summer work at Goal Studios, I believe I am competitive for a salary between $45 and $55,000.*

When you negotiate, it is appropriate to compare your salary goals with the marketplace.

> *I would be thrilled by the opportunity to work with you. Given the current market and my strong qualifications, I would be ready to accept an offer at $32,000.*

It is also appropriate to negotiate based on your skills.

> *I am very excited about this position. Based on my skills and experience, I know I will add tremendous value to this position and am prepared to hit the ground running. I believe that $40 to $45,000 is a competitive salary for someone with my background.*

Ask how much time is acceptable before you answer.

> *Can you let me know how long I could consider the offer you have made? As I said, although I was anticipating a higher starting salary, I'd like to give it some thought, because the opportunity to work here is very appealing to me and I think I could make a strong contribution.*

Evaluating Offers and Making Decisions

Now that you have considered your options, negotiated to the best of your ability, and discussed any points that concerned you, you will likely have the best offer in front of you. If the salary is lower than expected, but the offer as a whole, including your title, reputation of the organization, training and mentoring, or your overall compensation make the offer more enticing, consider how important each aspect of the offer is to you, and weigh the state of the economy as well as other factors, such as local concerns, that may impact competition.

Now it is up to you to make a decision. Keep in mind that every job is an opportunity to learn and grow, apply your training, gain experience, and build connections. When you consider whether the offer measures up, be sure to evaluate all of the components that are most important to you, as well as the offer in its entirety. Sometimes it is possible to get caught on one point (e.g., salary) when the offer as a whole meets or exceeds your career goals.

If You Do Not Receive an Offer

During the job search, you may interview for positions for which you do not receive offers, or find that your résumé and cover letters are not leading to interviews. Stay positive, and consider how you can maintain balance in other areas of your life during this potentially stressful time. Refer to the suggestions for maintaining your wellness discussed earlier in this chapter. Another technique is to reframe setbacks in the job search as learning opportunities. This can help you use the information you gather to improve your applications and job search skills. Also keep in mind that you cannot expect to be a match for all employers, that the job search takes time, especially in a difficult economy, and that you can accept only one option, no matter how many offers are ultimately presented.

First, review your job search materials. Each résumé should be targeted to reflect the key points that are relevant for a given job, so learning to connect your résumé to job requirements will improve the likelihood that you are called for interviews, and that you are asked about relevant topics during your interviews. Review **Chapter 8: Tools** for suggestions about creating targeted résumés and job search correspondence.

Second, broaden your search. In addition to working on your job search materials and interview skills, aim to broaden your job leads through networking. If your networking is not leading to job leads, improve your skills and widen your networking circle. Consider revisiting **Chapter 6: Relationships** to improve the depth and breadth of your network.

Finally, stay active and involved. Attend networking events, campus activities, professional association meetings, and additional opportunities to engage with people in your field. Participate online and read about your industry. If you have time on your hands, consider engaging in volunteer activities that will further expand your network, connect you with a cause you value, and keep you occupied. Selecting career-related volunteer work can also add to your résumé. **Chapter 5: Explore** offers suggestions for professional associations that may host industry events, and Work with Awareness, Connect Around Causes, in **Chapter 6: Relationships** offers suggestions for identifying volunteer activities. You can also find ideas and inspiration for the job search in the Career Profiles in this text.

Your Flexible Plan

Initiate a Job or Internship Search

PLAN OF ACTION

Step 1: Set Broad Objectives

Are you prepared for your job or internship search? Complete this checklist to assess your readiness for a search. All information in the table reflects "broad objectives."

	Are you prepared? (Y/N)	If not, what must you do next?
Interviews		
Networking Meetings		
Online Discussions		
Schedule of Job Search Events		
1.		
2.		
3.		

Step 2: Identify Specific Goals

To move forward, state the goals that will help you with your broad objectives.

To practice my interviewing skills (*broad objective*), I will schedule a practice interview (*goal*) and practice interviewing questions with a career counselor who can offer me feedback (*goal*).

1. _____

2. _____

3. _____

Step 3: Define Action Steps

Choose one goal and list the steps you will take to achieve it.

To practice my interviewing skills (*broad objective*), I will do a practice interview (*goal*). I will call the career center (*step*) ask them if they can interview me and have interview suggestions (*step*), and ask what I should do to prepare before the practice interview (*step*).

List your goal you have chosen to address, and the specific action steps you will take.

Goal: _____

1. _____

2. _____

3. _____

4. _____

5. _____

Performance Appraisal

Now that you have read the chapter, answer the questions below and complete the Tasks.

1. Which of the following is true of a job search plan?
   a. It is goal-oriented and short-term.
   b. It should focus on the job you want most because there is no need to consider alternatives.
   c. It is useful only if you are not using campus recruiting.
   d. All of the above

2. Where can job leads be found?
   a. On campus
   b. Online
   c. Through your network
   d. All of the above

3. Which of the following is true regarding improving your overall wellness?
   a. It is important only if you are physically ill.
   b. It involves listening to others.
   c. It will not impact your career.
   d. a and c

4. Which of the following is true?
   a. Technology is part of all aspects of the job search.
   b. Technology cannot help you stand out in your job search because everyone uses it.
   c. When you use technology in your job search, the only people who notice are techies.
   d. Students should use only conventional job search methods and avoid social media in the job search.

5. Which of the following is true of campus career resources?
   a. They are only helpful for graduating students.
   b. They are not useful for students in every major or career field.
   c. They are less valuable if you do not prepare in advance.
   d. They are only for job hunting, rather than information gathering or self-assessment.

6. Which of the following is true about networking in a job search?
   a. Networking is easy for everyone.
   b. You should not waste your time talking to someone if they do not know about job openings.
   c. It is okay to prepare a scripted introduction before a networking event.
   d. You cannot improve your networking skills.

7. Which of the following is true about an interview?
   a. An employer will not ask you about information on your résumé, because he or she can read about it instead.
   b. An employer might ask you about how you will deal with hypothetical situations.
   c. An employer will never unintentionally ask you illegal interview questions, such as whether you have children or your national origin, because all interviewers know what topics are illegal and have been well-trained and prepared.
   d. b and c

Performance Appraisal Answer Key

1. a
2. d
3. b
4. a
5. c
6. c
7. b

Thought Questions

1. Searching for a job is time consuming and can be stressful. How will you take care of yourself during this time?

2. Do you feel that you are prepared for the job search? Why or why not?

3. Networking and interviewing involve communication skills. How can you improve your communication skills for the job search? Where can you practice these skills?

Notes:

_____

_____

_____

_____

_____

_____

TASK 9.1:

Create a Job Search Plan

Once you have found target positions, a job search plan will help you track where you have sent your résumés and cover letters, whom you plan to contact for further networking, what events and commitments relate to your job search, which upcoming interviews you have scheduled, and whether thank you notes were sent. Use the table below as a guideline for mapping out your own job search plan and the action steps you need to take.

Target position	Employer	Where job lead was found	Materials sent	Date sent	Follow up?	Interview scheduled?	Thank you note sent?
Example: Pharmaceutical Sales Representative	Pfizer	Website, referred by Kaya Timmins	Résumé & cover letter to: Jane Phillips, HR exec Cc: Kaya Timmins, Account Manager	10/24/11–job app 10/24/11– thank you to Kaya for referral	E-mail/ Call in 2 weeks 11/7/2011		

TASK 9.2:

Create an Elevator Pitch

Using the HBS Elevator Pitch Builder (2007), consider who you are, what you do, why you are unique, and state your goals. This information will form the foundation of your introduction, or elevator pitch, which you can use in networking opportunities when you must introduce yourself quickly and succinctly. After you have addressed the who, what, why, and goals, craft your key points into a brief, 20-second-or-less introduction. Use the examples and suggestions in the section Networking for Job Opportunities in this chapter to help you make your introduction sound natural and to add an open-ended question at the end that helps start a conversation.

Name _____

Job Title(s) Sought _____

Industry Targeted _____

Requirements for Position(s) Sought

1. _____

2. _____

3. _____

4. _____

5. _____

Who: Describe who you are. _____

What: Describe what you do. _____

Why: Describe why you are unique. _____

Goal: Describe your immediate goals. _____

Analyze: Analyze your pitch. _____

Your 20-Second Summary, Elevator Pitch, or Introduction _____

Add a question to turn your Elevator Pitch into a conversation starter. _____

TASK 9.3:
Tell Me about Yourself

When you first sit down in the interview "hot seat," chances are you will be given some kind of lead-in, for example, "Walk me through your résumé" or "Tell me about yourself." Such open-ended questions could take the rest of the interview to answer completely, but this is not the expectation of the interviewer. Try a past, present, and future approach, with each portion represented in one or two sentences. This allows the interviewer to have at the very beginning a brief sketch of your assets and their relevance to the position. Your response can be used as an introduction as well.

Example:

Past: "I have always loved to draw, as well as babysit, and I was a camp counselor for seven years."

Present: "I decided to major in art and minor in education to combine my two primary interests."

Future: "I am seeking an opportunity that would allow me to combine my interests and teach art to children."

Now prepare your own brief answer to the invitation, "Tell me about yourself," using the past, present, and future approach.

Past:

_____

_____

Present:

_____

_____

Future:

_____

_____

TASK 9.4:

Prepare for a Practice Interview

This exercise involves scheduling a practice interview and preparing for it—and performing in it—as if it were a real interview.

1. Schedule a practice interview with a networking contact, faculty member, friend, or counselor from your campus career center.

2. Give a sample job listing (a real job that interests you) and a copy of your résumé and cover letter for that position to the person who will be conducting the practice interview.

3. Use the form Interview Details to include details to help you prepare for the interview, and as a reference for your review immediately before the interview.

This form is designed to be prepared in advance and reviewed on the day of the interview. Include any details that will help you remember key points and arrive at the interview on time, prepared, and ready to put your best foot forward.

INTERVIEW DETAILS

Day & Date:		Time:	Address:
Position:		Interviewer & Title:	
Details on locating office/Directions:			
Notes:			

EMPLOYER DETAILS

Name of Interviewer:		Organization/ Company:	Application Submitted (method/ date):
Position Title:		Learned of Position through:	Received Reply (date/time/whom):
Position Requirements:			
Employer Key Facts:			
Other:			

YOUR RELEVANT KEY ASSETS

Describe Key Points to Highlight:

TASK 9.5:

Prepare for a Career Fair

If you are aware of an upcoming career fair, consider how you can use this opportunity to learn about employers, find out about job openings, and practice your networking and interviewing skills. Career fairs may be held at your school, by local municipalities, or by the Department of Labor. They are often advertised in campus career centers, public libraries, or the Department of Labor's Career One Stop, with branch offices that can be located using servicelocator.org.

When is the next career fair that you can attend?

_____

Many career fairs offer a list of employers before the event. Review the list of employers who will be attending the next career fair, or a past fair. List all employers that interest you.

_____

_____

_____

Formulate three questions that will help you learn from employers to improve your knowledge of job openings, industry information, or details about the organization. What are your questions, and how will they help you launch your career?

1. _____

2. _____

3. _____

Link to CourseMate

On CourseMate, you can find documents to help you update your Career Portfolio as well as additional resources and activities. Here is some of the information you can find online for **Chapter 9: Launch**.

CAREER PORTFOLIO
Your Flexible Plan
Elevator Pitch

RESOURCES
Career Profile: Sarah Moltzen

iStockphoto.com/kristian sekulic

Career Management

> After climbing a great hill, one only finds that there are many more hills to climb. —*Nelson Mandela*

What's Inside

Professionalism in the Workplace

Succeeding with Mentors

Financial Planning Basics

The Life You Want Now . . . and in the Future

Prepare to . . .

- Develop the attitudes and behavior of professionalism that will help you in any career field

- Learn how to make the most of mentoring relationships

- Use your emotional intelligence in your career

- Understand the fundamentals of financial planning

- Build the life you want, and make career decisions with your future in mind

Managing your career involves an ongoing commitment to developing and maintaining your skills, talents, and self-knowledge. Many factors will contribute to your career success, such as developing a positive attitude, building mentoring relationships, and seeking out opportunities for lifelong learning. Your eagerness to learn, responsiveness to the world around you, and willingness to adapt your plan will help you manage your career throughout your lifetime.

» Professionalism in the Workplace

You are ready to get to work, perform the tasks you were hired to do, and hit the ground running. However, developing a career successfully involves more than learning to execute tasks well. It entails adapting to a new environment, understanding your role, learning organizational dynamics, and contributing as part of a team. Whether you are starting a new job, internship, or volunteer position, knowing what to expect can help you manage your career with a strong start.

According to David Maister, former Harvard Business School professor and author of *True Professionalism* (1997), "Professionalism is predominantly an attitude, not a sense of competencies" (p. 16). It is not just what you know; it is how you behave and participate.

Use these suggestions for your first day and first year on the job to show that you are hard-working, attentive, interested, and responsible. While many of these tips directly address your career launch, the strategies are relevant throughout your career.

The First Day

Your enthusiasm and professionalism will show your employer that you are ready and excited for work. On your first day you will learn more about your new job, meet new people, and become familiar with your surroundings. Your first day is a chance to demonstrate your eagerness to learn.

Your new routine. Get a good night's sleep, and start your day off right with a healthy breakfast and a schedule that will allow you to arrive 10–15 minutes early. This will give you time to get settled, put your things away, and learn where you will

Professionalism is reflected in everything you do in your work, including your level of interest and willingness to help.

iStockphoto.com/Lise Gagne

be stationed, and can also help if you have trouble with traffic, parking, or other delays. If you are not told about a lunch break or when the day ends, ask. Learn about breaks and other expectations that will impact your schedule. Understand when it is okay to interrupt your supervisor with questions. By making an effort to follow the schedule and the expected routine, you send the message that your job is important to you.

Time to learn. The first day is a chance to learn about your new job and work environment. You may receive a tour of the facilities or office. Initial projects may be described. For example, if you have to learn a computer system, you may be introduced to an online training program as an initial project. However, in some cases, your supervisor's plans to spend the day bringing you up to speed might be derailed by his or her own deadlines and projects. If you are not given many guidelines for your first day, take the initiative and ask if there is information you can read, or a project with which you can assist. This shows your willingness to get involved from the start.

Meet the team. Your first day may involve meeting others in the organization, including those with whom you will work and possibly people in other departments. Ask for business cards, and write details about each person so you can remember their names for your next interaction. In some jobs, it is common to report to more than one supervisor. Learn who will be evaluating your work, and greet everyone with enthusiasm.

To show that you are a team player, listen closely to instructions and ask questions that will help you perform your job.

Prepare your questions. Since the environment and job are both new, you will likely have questions. Some of these might be answered through the natural course of the day or the first week, and some will remain important and unanswered. Jot down your questions as they come up, and cross out those that are answered. If there are answers you need in order to complete an assignment or prepare for the next day, ask your supervisor when you can go over your questions. While you may have to hold off on finding answers until the end of the day, or end of the week, your list of questions will help you gather information to do your job well.

Appreciate your growth. Take a moment to congratulate yourself on all you have accomplished. At the same time, understand that the first year will involve new skills, experiences, and relationships. Your interests may evolve, your values may be challenged, and your ideas about your future may shift. However, growth is part of your career development, and your ability to respond and adapt your plan accordingly is a valuable asset.

Your First Year

Professionalism requires that you take responsibility for what you learn, how you perform, and the interest you bring to your job. Your first year on the job is the time to lay the groundwork for a strong, lasting impression as you build connections, learn, and grow. The pride and self-satisfaction you experience from your work can be increased by your effort. These strategies will help you manage the transition, and approach each task with a high level of engagement that employers appreciate.

Focus on the big picture. All projects contribute to the big picture. For instance, if you work in construction and are asked to go to the store to pick up wood trim for a project and you get the wrong size, you will be sent back, or someone else will have to go. This can slow down the work and lead to frustration and delays. In an office, if you are responsible for entering addresses into a database for a marketing project and you get the zip codes wrong, even the most beautiful and well-designed mailing kits will not be delivered properly, wasting time and money. Look at the big picture and realize that your contribution adds to the success of each project, even if you are not responsible for the most exciting parts of the project now. As you learn about the big picture and work hard to make every project a success, you will earn respect and credibility.

Use emotional intelligence at work. One can be "book smart" and also "people smart." Understanding your colleagues, listening to your emotions, managing negative thoughts, and demonstrating interest and engagement are all qualities that will help you succeed. Daniel Goleman (1995 and 1998) has popularized the importance of "Emotional Intelligence" with his many books on the subject, showing its relevance in the workplace and many other settings. Recognizing your own emotions and the emotions of others can help you understand various points of view and work with people more effectively. This can improve the quality of your interpersonal relationships and even affect your overall life satisfaction.

Manage from below. Stay on top of your projects and keep your supervisor informed of the status of your work. Consider weekly project updates, or daily updates if a project involves tight, time-sensitive deadlines. In some industries, your updates should be verbal; in others, e-mail them. If your boss can spend less time supervising your work and more time completing his or her own projects, you will be easier to manage, and this can help position you for more difficult projects.

Stay on task. Show your team that you are there to perform your job, and then do it with enthusiasm. Stay away from gossip, distractions, and personal interests during the work day. Avoid speaking negatively about others, complaining about projects or tasks, or chatting about topics unrelated to your work tasks. Turn off your phone, and do not text or use personal social media while you are expected to be working. Stay on task and be focused.

Take initiative. After you finish a project or task, ask what you can do next. A brief overview, in person or by e-mail, that includes a summary of the project you completed and how you wrapped up the details will help your supervisor know you can handle more.

Build strong relationships. You are building relationships that may affect your long-term professional career. Get to know people in your company and your industry. Participate in social outings with coworkers, professional associations, community service activities, or company sports leagues. If you would like to learn more about someone's career or experiences, ask for a chance to meet during lunch or before or after work hours. This can be fun and informal, and it is okay to offer to bring coffee, a snack, or lunch.

Develop a positive reputation. Consider how you want your work colleagues and professional connections to think of you. Remember that your brand develops out of your actions. Even when socializing with colleagues, it is not the time to act unprofessionally. Your actions will carry into the next day's conversation, so build a reputation that makes you feel proud. If you are not with colleagues, imagine how they might react to a disparaging photo posted on Facebook. Your brand will become stronger if you are consistent in all of your relationships.

Become a good team member. New graduates and career changers, especially student and club leaders or those who were successful in other industries, may need to adjust to playing a support role. As you contribute to the success of your entire team, you will see how a great team member will make everyone look good.

Understand your organization's culture. Every organization has a culture and set of norms that dictate policy. There is usually a formal and informal structure that exists in the workplace. Search for role models who are successful, regardless of age, time at the company, or title. Observe how your role models behave, dress, and interact. Ask questions and learn how to emulate positive examples.

Master your job, and build your career. As you start your career, there is much you will still need to learn in order to perform your job well. Look for opportunities to improve your skills on the job, participate in professional development opportunities, read about industry developments, and continue networking. Your formal training has prepared you to enter the field, but there is still much more to discover. Enjoy building your skills, expanding your career, and keep learning!

≫ CAREER JOURNAL ● On the Job

 Use the space below to write about your thoughts and feelings.

Demonstrating your professionalism can be part of your approach for on-the-job success. Choose one strategy for acting professionally such as taking the initiative, staying on task, or building strong relationships. Next, list three ideas about what you might do to turn that strategy into real-world actions that will help you succeed. For example, if your strategy is to take the initiative, you might plan to offer your help on projects to which you are not assigned, go beyond what is expected of you, and learn more about the company by looking at the company website.

Choose one strategy you will use.

What three, real-world actions will you take to make that strategy come to life?

1. _____

2. _____

3. _____

Describe how you expect this strategy to impact your work experience. For instance, do you anticipate that taking the initiative will help you add new projects, gain support of mentors, learn new skills,
prepare for more difficult assignments, or offer some other benefit? How?

Journal Feedback . . . As your focus shifts from the job hunt to on-the-job performance, consider
how your actions define who you are, impact what others expect of you, and contribute to how others
treat you. Learning to take control of your success by committing to action and understanding how your
actions will help you reach your goals can empower and motivate you.

≫ CAREER PROFILE ● Noemi S., Print and Web Publishing

Name: Noemi S.
College Degree: BA in
Hispanic Studies
Current Position: Associate
Editor
Employer: *Manhattan
Bride*

Courtesy of Rick Bard

Tell us a little about your academic experience and career preparation.

*I worked for a year and a half to save money before college.
I went to one four-year college first and then transferred to another with a full scholarship for the rest of my education. Even
though the scholarship covered my tuition, I needed money for
expenses, and so I started a full-time job while I was in school. It
was hard to leave work for my classes, and I got a lower grade
in one class and was off the dean's list for the first time. This motivated me to start my own business as a personal trainer while
I was still in school, to set my own hours.*

What led you to your current position?

*When I graduated, I kept working as a personal trainer while
I figured out what I wanted to do. One day, I was looking online
at a celebrity wedding and I told my sister what I liked and
what I would do differently for the wedding. She said, "You
should be in that industry. You love weddings." I went to the*

From Noemi's Employer
Name: Rick Bard
Title: Editor/Publisher, *Manhattan
Bride*

Courtesy of Rick Bard

How do you approach the hiring process?

*Our approach to hiring is closely
tied to our organizational values.
Over 25 years ago, while publish-
ing a different magazine, I started a foundation
to raise money for homeless children in New York and to help
fund breast cancer research. The first event was at the Plaza
Hotel, and it felt like a large, important wedding. I turned to the
bridal magazines and realized that a lot of my questions about
planning this event were not being answered. Fifteen years
later, after throwing more than 40 major charitable events, I
started Manhattan Bride. Our touchstone is the generous spirit
and ambiance we tried to create for each of those charitable
events. We want to offer our clients that same spirit of generosity, always giving more quality and service than they expect. We
want our new hires to appreciate this spirit of generosity and
to be aligned with that purpose. We want to train people, so
we're looking for people with a certain amount of—but not too
much—experience, and an eagerness to learn. Our candidates
also need to understand the importance of including a diverse*

(Continues)

career center at my college and I spoke with a career counselor. She directed me to the career resource center and I spent a lot of time reading about jobs and career fields. On my college's website, I saw the position at Manhattan Bride magazine, and I thought it was so perfect. I reworked my résumé and cover letter for the position, then I got an interview, but I had two weeks to wait. I spent the time going over their website, researching publishing and editorial writing online using Vault.com and other resources, and learning more about interviewing and practicing interview answers.

Describe your work.
Our days completely vary depending on where we are in the publishing cycle. There is no day where I am doing just one thing. Generally, we start with a meeting about what we're going to be doing that day. One day, it could be editing articles about real weddings, or styling a photo shoot. Right now, we're doing a strategic, social-media marketing effort using e-mail to tell advertisers how they can promote themselves using our website.

What is your career?
I can't really say; I feel I'm very early in my career. I would say it's gathering information and presenting it in a beautiful way.

group in our pages and on our website, and demonstrate multicultural awareness. We also look for strong language and communication skills and a good telephone rapport.

How does Noemi demonstrate her professionalism and contribute to your team?
Having started her own company, she was able to develop a higher level of professionalism than I would expect to see in a typical employee. She is conscientious about staying in contact with our clients, following up with them to make sure they are able to schedule times to get together, to review information, or to reschedule times as needed. We have to keep all the data organized to stay in touch with all these people. As simple as it seems, one can waste a lot of time if records are not kept or information is missing. For instance, for the real weddings, she has to follow up with details for about 35 brides per issue, plus their venues. We value people who can contribute, listen, comment, and evaluate. Most people come in ready to give their ideas but haven't yet learned to listen thoughtfully to others.

What unique combination of assets does Noemi use in her career?

_____

_____

_____

How do you think Noemi's professionalism on the job is helping her build her reputation?

_____

_____

_____

For additional questions, visit CourseMate. 🖥

❯❯ Succeeding with Mentors

A mentor relationship exists when a more senior person provides emotional and career-related support as well as role-modeling and advice over an extended period of time for a younger or junior person, sometimes called a "protégé." A mentor can teach you the ropes, take you under his or her wing, and help you learn the spoken and unspoken rules of the game.

Advisor, Teacher, Role Model, Friend reads the title of a guide written for teachers, faculty members, administrators, and others who mentor students in science and engineering (National Academy of Sciences, National Academy of Engineering, Institute of Medicine, 1997). In every industry, from science to education and fashion to finance, these four "hats" describe the multiple roles played by mentors.

The Benefits of Mentoring

Having a mentor, or numerous mentors, can offer significant benefits. A mentor can give you advice on transitioning to the workplace, help you learn the expectations of junior employees, and serve as a role model for appropriate participation in meetings, formality in e-mails, and workplace attire. Having a mentor has been shown to improve job placement and compensation (Carter and Silva, 2010) as well as increase promotions (Catalyst, 2002).

As you gain experience, your mentor's role within the organization and ability and willingness to advocate on your behalf becomes increasingly important. This form of advocacy by a mentor is called "sponsorship," and it has been shown to have a significant impact on whether employees ask for pay raises and request the stretch assignments that lead to advancement (Hewlett, 2011). Moreover, research has found that while women may have numerous mentors, men are more likely to have sponsors, the career advocates who may make the biggest difference in the long run (Hewlett, 2011; Carter and Silva, 2010).

A mentor acts as a sponsor by doing two or more of the following (Hewlett, 2011):

- Expand the perception of what the protégé can do
- Facilitate connections between the protégé and senior leaders
- Promote the protégé's visibility
- Open up career opportunities for the protégé
- Offer advice on the protégé's appearance and executive presence
- Make connections for the protégé outside the company
- Give advice to the protégé

Mentor and sponsor relationships are most effective when they are mutually beneficial.

As you develop your career, consider when and how your mentors act as sponsors. Be sure to recognize these significant efforts. For instance, if you are encouraged by a mentor to take on a project that is outside your job description, realize that this can raise your visibility within the organization or help you connect with senior leaders. If your mentor invites you to events or to join interdepartmental committees, appreciate that this is an opportunity to build additional contacts and increase your presence. You can also learn to model your behavior after a mentor or seek out your mentor's advice on such areas as performance, professionalism, reputation, and appearance. A trusted mentor will give you honest feedback that is designed to help you advance.

Find a Mentor

There are many ways to find a mentor. Sometimes, a relationship forms naturally with someone you meet at work or in your field. Your boss can be a mentor, as can a person on a project to which you are assigned, or someone you meet through a professional association or other industry event. A former professor with whom you maintain contact can be a mentor, as can an internship supervisor.

Within many industries, your early experience may involve an apprenticeship or on-the-job training with an assigned mentor. In addition, many large organizations have mentor programs to connect new hires or junior-level executives with older, more experienced workers who can guide them and help them in their early careers. Professional associations may also offer mentor programs and, if you are still in school, many colleges offer mentor programs to students to help them learn more about the fields they seek to enter. Your efforts to build the relationship and demonstrate your appreciation may make the difference in your ability to connect.

Be a Great Mentee

To improve your likelihood of receiving the benefits of mentoring, learn to be a great mentee.

Trust. Mutual trust is important for a strong relationship. Show your mentor that you are trustworthy by completing assignments on time, asking for help when needed, and coming through on projects.

Listen and follow through. Once trust is established, listen to the information that is shared by your mentor, and implement the advice and suggestions offered. John Parks, a plant manager for Gillette in Lancaster, South Carolina, suggested that to benefit from mentoring, the learner must have a "willingness to take to heart what is being shared." (Teicher, 2004) Let your mentor know when his or her advice has been useful and how you use it. For instance, if a mentor suggests you volunteer for a committee, follow up with information about the committee, including what you have learned and how you have contributed. Show that you listened and valued the suggestion.

Understand the role of culture. In such a close and personal relationship, mentors and mentees may rely on their instincts and preferred approaches to teaching and learning, but these may not reflect cultural understanding. For instance, when working in the United States, mentors might expect juniors to ask questions and seek clarification. However, mentees from other regions or cultures may have learned it is disrespectful to question someone who is older or to explain their own point of view if it differs from a more senior, or more experienced, mentor. Raising your awareness of your cultural orientation and understanding the differences between cultures can help you connect.

Do more than thank your mentor—give back. You should always thank your mentor for any assistance, including following up with details of how his or her advice or support has helped you. However, giving back involves one step more than just saying thank you and detailing the ideas you have implemented.

There are many ways to give back to a mentor, even if you feel inexperienced. In a work setting, offer to help with support tasks within your scope of skills. If you have additional skills that are not being tapped, such as the ability to set up or maintain social media, an ability to do hands-on work that can contribute to a project, or other specialized skills, and you see that these skills may be useful, propose your willingness to help. If you find an article that you think would be of interest, share it, and describe why it caught your attention and how it is relevant. If you have not seen your mentor in a while, ask if he or she will be at an upcoming industry event or conference you plan to attend. You may get the opportunity to meet up, or you can offer to report back with the insight you gain.

Name: Bhavika Mody
College Degree: AAS in Respiratory Therapy
Current Position: Respiratory Therapist
Employer: Saint Barnabas Medical Center

Courtesy of Bhavika Mody

Can you describe your career preparation and training?

I was working, but I had a five-month-old baby, and I was concerned with the economy. My sister-in-law is a respiratory therapist. She told me that it's a growing field. I went to community college and it took me two and a half years to complete a two-year program, but then I was done. I learned the clinical knowledge in school, and I started with a basic knowledge about equipment. I am registered and I obtained my license.

What steps are required to manage your career?

I need 30 CEUs [continuing-education units] every two years to maintain my license. Not all hospitals use as much new equipment, but here we receive frequent in-service training to introduce new equipment, and this provides CEUs. I have to attend these and other training sessions to stay licensed. I try to keep up with the market, and make an effort to use the new equipment. For my position, you have to learn the equipment, learn the patient, and troubleshoot. Also, you have to follow the protocol. The education is very important. I am thinking about whether to get my bachelor's degree and when would be a good time, if I decide to do it.

What do you like about your work?

I like to learn about the new equipment. Whatever skills I have, I use. If it helps the patient, they really appreciate it. The people I'm working with are all very helpful. I also have respect from the doctors. They always appreciate when we do something and the patient feels better. I work full-time, but that's a 12-hour shift, three days a week. This is very good with my kids. As a working mother, I still feel really connected in the house. The days I am home, I can take them to their afterschool activities—I take them swimming—and I can finish the laundry. I can do my job, and also be there for them.

From Bhavika's Supervisor
Name: Linda Melchor
Title: Respiratory Coordinator, Saint Barnabas Medical Center

Courtesy of Linda Melchor

What strengths make Bhavika successful in her career?

She's very straightforward, very matter-of-fact. She's very responsible and proactive. At times, we let her take charge. She's not limited to one area; she can take care of an infant in the NICU [neonatal intensive-care unit], a 100-year-old, or a patient in the burn intensive-care unit. You have to be in different parts of the hospital to maintain your clinical skills. If we don't put her in a certain area of the hospital for a while, she'll ask for that unit. She also communicates well with the physicians and with the nurses. If she thinks something is wrong, or potentially harmful to the patient, she acts as a patient advocate and she'll ask questions. Some people are afraid to ask questions. We also use Bhavika as a receptor, which is like a clinical instructor who orients new employees. When it comes to showing someone something new, she takes her time.

What other career opportunities can Bhavika explore?

With her associate's degree, she could make a very good charge therapist, which is like a junior supervisor. She would make assignments, help with equipment; the staff could go to her with problems. She would need to use critical-thinking skills and be able to stand on her own two feet, which she does. She can also prepare to provide expert instruction for various departments. For instance, she could become a CPR instructor, an advanced cardiac life-support (ACLS) instructor, a pediatric life-support instructor (PALS), or a neonatal resuscitation program (NRP) instructor. For these, the department pays you overtime. You're teaching, moderating, and having the students demonstrate knowledge. She can also work in a VA hospital, and for those positions you can become tenured. If she completes her bachelor's, she can become more of a professional and have the opportunity to apply for a specialty area.

What steps were necessary for Bhavika to succesfully launch her career?

_____

_____

_____

What minimum steps are required for her to maintain her career? What can she do to increase her marketability and create additional opportunities for her future?

_____

_____

_____

For additional questions, visit CourseMate.

The workplace is changing rapidly, and much of this change is due to technological innovation. As you aim to manage your career effectively, perform at your peak, and continue to build your professional reputation at work, you will need to use existing technology efficiently and effectively, while adapting as new technology is introduced.

Staying Up-to-Date on Technology

The technology you use today is likely to be replaced by something newer and different tomorrow. Look for opportunities to develop your technological skills by taking a class, engaging in independent learning, joining interdepartmental projects, and reading and learning from industry discussions in publications and social media. Pay attention to software and technological tools that are gaining in popularity, so that you can build skills that will help you market yourself in expanding areas. Speak with mentors and role models, and ask them what software, online tools, and technical skills will add value. Share your knowledge and offer to contribute your new skills.

E-Mail and Workplace Overload

While there may be many sources of work overload, e-mail may be the "cultural symbol" (Barley, Meyerson, and Grodal, 2010). In a recent study, workers described e-mail as the primary source of their long work hours, regardless of the actual amount of time spent on work tasks. This may explain why other sources of work overload go unaddressed, such as the structure of their work, work flow, or use of other technologies such as teleconferencing, phone calls, or simply time spent in meetings. Developing strategies for your e-mail use will benefit you and your colleagues.

These strategies for sending and reading e-mails can reduce stress, add to your level of professionalism, and provide more efficient results (see Barley Meyerson and Grodal, 2010).

- Write and send only coherent, clear messages that have been proofread.
- Use subject lines, and clearly state the point or request of your e-mail.
- Use bullet points and paragraphs in your e-mails to highlight key issues or requests in order to reduce reading time.
- State when you need an answer for your e-mails; all needs are not urgent.
- Learn whether (and to whom) you are expected to reply during nonwork hours, if you receive e-mails when you are not at work.
- If you are unclear what is being requested of you in an e-mail, reply with specific questions to clarify points.
- Scan e-mail headings, and read non-urgent e-mails in bulk when you are ready for a break rather than as they come in, interrupting your work.
- Reply to e-mails that are not urgent with details of when you will reply (e.g., this evening or tomorrow morning), if your full response will not be sent within two hours.

With technology developing so rapidly, it is hard to say what will change, when it will change, or how. Prepare yourself by staying on top of developments, looking toward the future to notice trends as they begin to impact your work experience, and develop skills to use today's technology effectively and to prepare for tomorrow.

There are many different workplace scenarios that may be experienced as harassment. These may involve sexual harassment, racial harassment, bullying, or other types of behavior. According to the U.S. Equal Employment Opportunity Commission (EEOC), "harassment is unwelcome conduct that is based on race, color, religion, sex (including pregnancy), national origin, age (40 or older), disability or genetic information" (n.d.). Harassment is illegal, and many organizations have clear policies for reporting harassment.

According to the EEOC, harassment becomes unlawful when (1) enduring the offensive conduct becomes a condition of continued employment, or (2) the conduct is severe or pervasive enough to create a work environment that a reasonable person would consider intimidating, hostile, or abusive.

At work, you will likely develop relationships and naturally connect more easily with some people than with others.

However, while many relationships are beneficial in the workplace, there are certain behaviors that are easily identified as unacceptable and illegal, and some that are harder to qualify. There are also circumstances where seemingly innocuous or good-intentioned behaviors reflect bias or racism based on stereotypes, such as a comment to a woman that she does not need a career because she is pretty, or telling a Latino that he is articulate.

Actions like these that perpetuate stereotypes have been labeled microaggressions: "brief, everyday exchanges that send denigrating messages to certain individuals because of their group membership" (Sue, 2010; see also Sue et al., 2007 for a discussion of racial microaggressions and how the concept can be expanded to include other groups). These actions can be seen as discriminatory, even if the person making the comment is unaware. In fact, it is this confusion about whether a microaggression has occurred and how to deal with it that further impacts the negative effect of such behaviors (Sue, 2007). Harassment can involve intentional or unintentional discrimination, and small acts that are persistent and pervasive can create a hostile workplace environment.

Consider the following scenarios:

A male supervisor and a female junior find themselves in the office late in the evening to complete a project. After their project is praised by the client, and she is acknowledged at a staff meeting, she passes a colleague's desk to find a group of her coworkers speculating that the source of praise at the meeting was not her hard work, but, instead, a sexual relationship with the supervisor. She is not involved in any romantic or sexual relationship with her supervisor, and feels her work has been devalued.

A male employee joins his supervisor for a beer at a local pub after work. At the other end of the bar, two men are holding hands while talking. The supervisor makes a remark about his disgust with homosexuality, using gay slurs. His supervisee, who is homosexual but is not out in the workplace, is extremely uncomfortable and offended.

After being relocated to another company office, an Asian American employee who has been in the same firm for three years and was born and raised in the United States, is asked by everyone he meets at the new site where he is from. When he answers, "Los Angeles," he is asked again, "No, where are you *from?*" and when he answers the same way a second time, he is asked again. He also notices that people speak slowly to him and explain things to him even though he has not given any indication that he does not understand. He wonders if he will be able to fit in at the new office.

A male employee asks a female coworker on a date. She says no. Later that week he shows a group of coworkers a picture posted on Facebook in which she is scantily dressed and dancing on a bar during nonwork hours. Soon the picture circulates in the office and beyond, accompanied by comments about the woman's outfit, body, and behavior. She is unaware.

A supervisor describes an upcoming industry event that requires work during a religious holiday that is observed by only one person on the team. When confirming who can attend, the employee does not volunteer. The supervisor turns to that employee and says, "I didn't see you raise your hand. Are you going to tell me this is on another religious holiday?" Everyone in the room laughs. The employee feels that her job is threatened.

A supervisor yells, rants, and curses at a junior employee when she notices a mistake on a task. The yelling is loud, goes on for a few minutes, and other workers are present in the room. Later, the supervisor acts as if the incident was a nonevent. The junior colleague feels hurt and humiliated.

Experiences at work can feel hurtful regardless of whether they meet the legal definition of harassment. Furthermore, it is up to you to decide whether you feel you have been the victim of harassment and how you want to proceed. Many organizations have educational programs as well as policies that address harassment, workplace behaviors and relationships, and possibly even dating in the workplace. The U.S. Equal Employment Opportunity Commission handles harassment grievances, and has extensive information about harassment on their website. This resource can help you learn more about harassment or report an incident.

» Financial Planning Basics

In the beginning of your career, or the relaunch of your career, your earnings may not put you in the position to save money; in fact, you may earn just enough—or possibly not enough—to cover your own expenses. It is increasingly likely that early career development may also be accompanied by student loans, credit card debt, and support by family members.

For many people, it is easy to adopt an "I'll do it later" approach to financial planning. However, regardless of your earnings, there is much you can do to set the stage for your financial future. Preparing for the future starts with learning the basics of financial planning.

Develop Financial Goals

Take inventory of short-term and long-term financial goals to plan for the future. This involves identifying what you want to do that will require saving money before you spend or accumulating debt that you must repay later. Setting financial goals that are realistic, and limiting your goals to those that you can achieve within your budget, will help you plan for a sound financial future.

Some examples of personal financial goals are the following:

- rent an apartment
- home ownership
- pay off student loans
- further education
- plan a wedding
- raise a child

- redecorate your home
- buy a car
- travel
- buy a work wardrobe
- donate to charity
- save money

Create a Budget

Create a budget to track and manage your spending. **Task 10.4,** Create a Budget, can help you assess the items in your weekly, monthly, and other expenses. Then, for greater accuracy, track what you spend over a two-week period. You can carry a notebook or use an online tool to help you. Once you have an understanding of your spending, you can begin to set a realistic monthly budget.

Your budget should include a monthly amount for savings, if possible, and, at the very least, allow you to make the minimal payments on your credit cards and other debt without adding new lines of credit. This may force you to cut out or limit certain expenses. You may be surprised to find that you can save a significant amount by making small changes, like taking lunch to work, taking public transportation or carpooling to work to save on gas. Consider your credit card bills as part of your budget; use credit cards to purchase items you can afford that month, and pay bills on time. By demonstrating your ability to manage financial decisions you will also improve your credit rating, which can become important for future plans, such as buying a home or a car. Setting up a realistic budget that you review and assess regularly will also help when unexpected expenses occur.

Financing Your Education

If you are considering continuing your education, or preparing to repay your loans, understand how your loans are designed. There are many options within financial

Learning about your benefits can help you make financial decisions, such as saving for the future.

Alistair Berg/Digital Vision/Jupiterimages

aid packages, and students should be aware of the differences. For instance, subsidized loans have deferred interest until repayment, while unsubsidized loans may accrue interest from the start of the loan. However, both of these types of loans offer lower interest rates than private bank loans. Nevertheless, they might not cover full expenses.

In addition to working in a part-time or full-time job off campus, work-study is a program that offers paid campus positions that can also help students build experience. Furthermore, many scholarships and grants are available for students; awards are given based on financial need, academic or real-world promise, or a combination of the two. Often, your school or financial aid office will have resources on private-funding sources, and the Internet can be another useful tool for such research. To learn more about financing your education, access The Student Guide published by the U.S. Department of Education at http://www.studentaid.ed.gov/students/publications/student_guide/index.html.

Debt and Investments, Assets, and Liabilities

Not all money you owe impacts your experiences the same way. Credit card debt, student loans, auto loans, a mortgage, and personal loans all describe money that can be owed, or debt, but they are not all the same.

Consider interest rates. Debt that is accompanied by very high interest rates may be more difficult to repay, and is usually common for credit cards or personal loans. On the other hand, auto and home loans may offer lower interest rates, and provide you with an asset, something you own and can sell in the future. If you still owe money on those items in the form of a mortgage or auto loan, the amount you must repay is a liability. You own the value of the home, minus the amount of the loan or mortgage.

The cost of education. Although education can be costly and all student loans require repayment, education is a different kind of asset than a home or car, namely, an investment in yourself. In *Not Quite Adults: Why 20 Somethings Are Choosing a Slower Path to Adulthood and Why It's Good for Everyone*, Settersten and Ray (2010) recommend education be considered an investment in the future, rather than a cost or liability. They argue that it is not college debt that is hurting young people, it is the cost of *not* attending college, or of having poor or too little academic preparation. However, they suggest evaluating the cost and relevance of educational choices so that they are a fit for the individual needs, rather than an effort for the "best" degree. The choices that are best for one person might not be best for another.

Understand Your Credit Rating

Your credit rating is more important than ever, as some companies may even request credit checks to evaluate candidates. Keep in mind they will need your written permission to do so and will generally ask for it at the time of your first interview.

When you apply for a loan or a line of credit, your FICO score will be checked to determine your credit rating, and whether you are likely to repay your loans. Your

FICO score is determined by several factors including your debt to income ratio and your record of paying on time. A record of paying your bills on time and in full will boost your credit score and save you money by avoiding late fees and providing lower interest rates.

To learn your FICO score and find out how your FICO score is determined, visit myfico.com and click "Financial Help Center" to learn more. You can learn more about credit reporting and access your credit report at no cost by visiting annualcreditreport .com. Begin reviewing your credit report annually and immediately address any inconsistencies or errors. If you notice a mistake, be sure to have it removed. If your financial history includes blemishes of your own doing, work to improve your credit history for the future, and follow up to be sure that your credit rating improves over time.

Company Benefits

Your benefits may include a 401K or another type of retirement or pension plan. Look over these materials carefully and speak with a financial counselor or planner to answer questions you might have on plans that include stocks and investments. Be aware of your tolerance for risk, and discuss this with your financial counselor. If you move to another job, learn about transferring your retirement plan. Also, learn more about your options. For instance, employers may permit you to supplement your contributions, offer a matching program, or provide free on-site or outsourced financial counseling and planning.

>> WORK WITH AWARENESS ● Lifelong Learning

Careers today require lifelong learning and growth in many areas. Learning to manage your career, your financial future, and maintain your skills and talents for on-the-job success all require you to learn throughout your lifetime. In addition, our global and increasingly diverse workforce requires greater cultural understanding and a wider array of communication skills for use in written, spoken, and online communication. Advances in technology require training and exposure. Advancement in one's career may require newly developed certification or specialized training. A career change may involve retraining or further education. Adults may also seek learning simply for the sake of learning with a desire to expand skills, knowledge, or interests through new subject areas.

Career-related learning. Lifelong learning is a must in every field. Hospital technicians must learn to use new equipment. Counselors must maintain their credentials through continuing education. Attorneys must be aware of changes in the law. Businesses marketing overseas must understand the customs and concerns of their potential customers. Even in our personal lives we must learn and adapt. Music enthusiasts have had to adapt to digital music.

Technological learning. New technology, such as next generation mobile devices including tablets and smart phones, social media (web 2.0), cloud computing, and big data, offer incredible opportunities for organizations to rethink how they store and communicate information and do business in general (Hinchcliffe, 2011). To harness the capabilities of our future world, it is critical to think, explore, innovate, and learn.

Creativity and problem solving. One advantage still offered by human capital is the ability to provide creative solutions wherever they can be offered (Pink, 2005). Areas that can be impacted by creativity are not just in the arts, but in such diverse fields as business, transportation, energy, politics, and communications. For workers, this requires ongoing learning and creativity, to understand new developments and integrate them into solutions. Developing right-brain creativity and innovative thinking add real value.

Expand your self-concept. Another way to grow is to expand your notion of who you are and what you can do. This can involve becoming more engaged with your family and friends, your community, government, politics, or human rights.

In your career, there may be times when you feel significant steps are warranted, such as whistle-blowing, physical risk, or risking your reputation. These types of behaviors involve heroism. However, according to social psychologist Philip Zimbardo, research and world events have shown that the majority of people are more inclined to do nothing than to take action (TEDTalk, 2010).

Zimbardo recommends these *Four Ds* to help you improve your ability to make a difference and become a hero (TEDTalk, 2010). His project is called "Heroic Imagination."

- **Democratized.** The new concept of heroism is that it is *democratized*; we can all become heroes.
- **Demystify.** It is important to *demystify* heroism by understanding that most heroes are simply everyday people doing extraordinary acts.
- **Diffuse.** Moving away from the notion of the hero working alone, it is necessary to *diffuse* heroism, because networks and teams are more effective than those who act alone, such as with the Underground Railroad or those who worked together to help Jews escape Nazi Germany.
- **Declare.** To become a hero, *declare* your intention and commit to taking action through deeds that make someone else feel good every day. These can be small deeds, such as helping someone with a homework assignment. Small, daily tasks build your heroic imagination and will help you take significant steps if they are needed.

Seek out learning opportunities. As you develop your career and your reputation over time, look for opportunities to use and develop the skills, assets, and personal traits that will positively contribute to your self-concept and personal brand.

To engage in lifelong learning and ongoing self-development, consider how one or more of these activities could add to your professional credentials, personal growth, and be part of your plan for ongoing development:

- Browse the library or bookstore for a recently published book in your field and read it.
- Ask your supervisor or colleagues about additional training they recommend.
- Learn about training or professional development offered by your organization.
- Register for continuing-education classes at a local university or professional school.
- Listen to speakers in subject areas that interest you.
- Attend an industry conference.
- Volunteer for a leadership role in a professional association.
- Volunteer for a charitable cause that exposes you to new people and tasks.
- Read trade journals or industry publications.
- Attend a workshop or seminar through a professional association.
- Learn a foreign language, computer program, or another new skill.
- Travel, and observe the cultures, customs, and other differences in your surroundings.

Lifelong learning is not simply about keeping up with technology, adding new skills, or becoming more culturally aware, although these areas are important. To manage your career successfully, aim to develop your creative side as well, because this may be the key for the innovations and solutions of the future.

» The Life You Want Now . . . And in the Future

iStockphoto.com/Get4Net

Creating a flexible career can allow you to have time for a satisfying work experience and other important activities.

Creating a career that is meaningful and satisfying is not just about creating work you enjoy. A successful career will help you create a life that works for you. Success is not just about getting ahead in your work. You can make money, receive promotions, and hold a high-level title and not be satisfied. Success is defined by your own terms. Ultimately, success is your ability to create the life you want now, and make changes and adjustments to create the life you want in the future.

Your Future Self

Imagine your future self. What is that person like? Whom does he or she meet? Where does he or she go? What is that person's day like? Would you enjoy spending time with this person?

In many ways, your work will help shape the person you become. Your career determines your lifestyle, establishes the people with whom you will interact, and guides you toward learning opportunities that will help you advance. These impact your professional skills as well as your values. Your career can help you develop into the person you want to be.

Work-Life Balance

Earning your degree and starting a new job is only the beginning of your career. While it is important and appropriate for your attention to be focused on developing your work identity at this time, it is by no means the only area of your life requiring your energy and attention.

Enjoy the journey. Your experience will be full of excitement, new experiences, new relationships, as well as ups and down. Engaging in activities that build your professional and personal identity will encourage the development of your whole self. Spending time with family and friends, participating in hobbies and fitness activities, and attending social and community activities can all provide important insight and growth.

Flexibility and work-life balance. Because it is now far easier to maintain flexibility by working at different times or locations, in different ways, and in multiple roles, spillover from work into personal time has led to fewer boundaries between work and home. To maintain work-life balance, determine what is important to you. You may be comfortable working long hours at the start of your career. What works for you at this time in your life may change, as you *and* the world both continue to change over time. Your goals and needs may change with your life decisions. Now, you may be eager to develop your career, earn an income, and enjoy personal time with friends and family. Some life events, like having and raising a child, or needing to care for a sick or elderly relative, may require flexibility that is not available at your workplace. As your needs evolve, your self-awareness can help you make changes to your career so that it continues to meet your needs.

Careers that balance work and life. Learning about options at your workplace or how others have managed their careers to allow for work-life balance can help you prepare and lay the groundwork for your evolving needs. For example, some career paths at your work may offer greater work-life flexibility but could require skills that you lack. Learn the skills and experiences that are valued by jobs or careers you want for the future. These may include technology skills that allow you to work from home, or skills that apply to work roles that are typically more family-friendly, such as teaching or writing. However, keep in mind that jobs are changing and evolving, and that it is also increasingly common to perform work as an independent contractor, performing service tasks such as programming, data entry, or design services at nontraditional hours or remote locations. Many careers now have options of part-time, flextime, flexplace, compressed work week, telecommuting, and many more possibilities than ever before.

Creating Ongoing Career Success

You prepared a self-directed, flexible, and responsive plan designed to change over time. You will personally define each goal, discover the tasks to help you reach it, and chart your course. Your commitment to evaluate and adapt as you learn new information along the way will help you make necessary adjustments to your goals and tasks, and hopes and dreams. Your future success, like your success in landing your first career-related job, is rooted in your ability to respond to your own cues and interpret real-world information in real time. There is no hidden secret to building lasting success. An approach that involves self-assessment, exploration, and self-marketing will allow you to cycle and recycle through these stages, learning and growing with every year. Successful career management is a lifelong commitment to listening and learning, living and growing, and engaging with others and the world.

Your Flexible Plan

Plan of Action and Analysis: Manage Your Career

PLAN OF ACTION
Step 1: Set Broad Objectives

What are your career objectives?

Having defined your career in terms of your jobs as well as your personal growth, what are your broad career objectives? What are you seeking to accomplish by developing your career?

Examples: To earn money (*broad objective*). To work in a safe environment (*broad objective*).

To work with people I respect (*broad objective*). To build a career that has longevity (*broad objective*).

1. _____

2. _____

3. _____

Step 2: Identify Specific Goals

To meet your broad objectives, what specific goals do you have for the present time, either this month, this year, or for a five year plan?

Example: To earn money (*broad objective*), I must find a job (*goal*). To build a career that has longevity (*broad objective*), I must look at what skills I want to build (*goal*), and what jobs will help me do that (*goal*).

1. _____

2. _____

3. _____

Step 3: Define Action Steps

Choose one goal. What are the steps you will take to achieve it?

Example: To build a career that has longevity (*broad objective*), I must look at what skills I want to build (*goal*), and what jobs will help me do that (*goal*). To determine which jobs use the skills I want to build (*goal*), I will (1) review my list of motivated skills, (2) apply to jobs and other opportunities that will help me build those skills, (3) participate in volunteer work where I can build those skills.

1. _____

2. _____

3. _____

4. _____

5. _____

PLAN OF ANALYSIS

Now that you are taking action to successfully manage your career, return to the process of analysis. Ask yourself these questions to determine if your plan still meets your needs or if it is ready to be modified. If there have been changes, revisit the steps of analysis and action in Your Flexible Plan.

- Have my skills, preferences, and/or values changed?
- Have changes in the world of work impacted my job, career, organization, or industry?
- Have I learned of new opportunities that I need to consider?
- Do changes in any other area make it necessary for me to revaluate my plans?

Performance Appraisal

Now that you have read the chapter, answer the questions below and complete the Tasks.

1. Which of the following is true about "professionalism"?
   a. It is less important after you get a job.
   b. It is more about your attitude, behavior, and enthusiasm than your work competencies.
   c. It is only for people who work in an office setting.
   d. It is none of the above.

2. Which of the following is true about managing your career?
   a. Employers do not want you to show your enthusiasm and eagerness to learn.
   b. Your team skills will help you contribute to work projects.
   c. Your learning stops when you graduate from college.
   d. All of the above.

3. Which of the following is true of "flexibility"?
   a. It describes opportunities for work to be done at different times and locations.
   b. It is leading to better work management, less work tasks, and decreased work overload.
   c. It means that workers can choose their hours and days of employment without having any arrangements with a supervisor.
   d. a and b.

4. To succeed with mentors, which of the following is true?
   a. Focus your efforts only on mentors who are very high up in the organization.
   b. Appreciate the range of activities that mentors can offer to help you build connections, become more visible within an organization, and expand your career options.
   c. Move on to a new mentor if yours does not take you to lunch and become your close friend.
   d. Avoid sending information or articles because your mentor will probably already know about everything going on in your field.

5. Bullying can occur at work, and may constitute a form of harassment.
   a. True
   b. False

6. Which of the following is true about financial planning?
   a. Financial planning should start when you make more money.
   b. You cannot learn about your credit rating unless you go to a bank.
   c. A budget can help you understand, manage, and plan your spending.
   d. Your current financial decisions cannot impact your future.

7. Which of the following is necessary to plan for the future you want?
   a. Make one-time decisions and stick with them even if they no longer work for you.
   b. Understand work-life balance and aim for goals that are personally relevant.
   c. Plan to cycle and recycle through the stages of career development throughout your career.
   d. b and c.

Performance Appraisal Answer Key

1. b
2. b
3. a
4. b
5. a
6. c
7. d

Thought Questions

1. How will you define career success now, and in the future?

2. What will you do to ensure your professionalism is evident?

3. How will you build and nurture relationships in your career?

4. What will you do to engage in lifelong learning?

5. How will you balance your personal and professional life?

Notes:

_____

_____

_____

_____

_____

TASK 10.1:
Skills That Demonstrate Professionalism

Review the suggestions for your first day and first year on the job. The recommendations reflect actions that demonstrate your professionalism. It is never too early to start practicing skills you will use on the job. Choose three of the recommended actions and give three ways you can exhibit each behavior now, in your experiences as a student, a member of a group, or in your current job or internship.

action that demonstrates professionalism

how you will practice this skill

1. _____

    1. _____

    2. _____

    3. _____

2. _____

    1. _____

    2. _____

    3. _____

3. _____

    1. _____

    2. _____

    3. _____

TASK 10.2:
Choose Your Mentors

Sometimes copying someone else can be a good thing. Copying your teacher's notes can help you learn important facts to remember. Copying your boss's style of dress can help you learn the unspoken rules of professional attire. Your mentors offer you a chance to learn more about the behaviors, skills, and experiences that will help you build career success. Some role models may be close confidants; others may be those you watch and follow from afar.

Who is a current role model? Whom would you like to emulate?

_____

_____

Why is this person an appealing role model? What does he or she say, do, or represent?

_____

_____

What actions or behaviors have you copied, or would like to copy, from this person?

_____

_____

How would copying this person help you succeed in your career?

_____

_____

TASK 10.3:
Lifelong Learning

You will have to keep learning throughout your life to stay current and aware of new developments, and to remain active in many professions.

What three actions can you take that will help you learn during your first year on the job?

1. _____

2. _____

3. _____

TASK 10.4:
Create a Budget

To create a budget, consider what you spend and what you earn. Include all expenses, such as meals out, food shopping, doctor copays, credit card or student loan payments, clothing, gym membership, gasoline for a car, rent, monthly savings, and so on. The more you are aware of your expenses, the easier it will be to understand how you are spending your money.

Weekly Expenses:		Monthly Expenses:		Additional Expenses:	
Item	Cost	Item	Cost	Item	Cost
Total Weekly Expenses:		Total Monthly Expenses:		Total Additional amount:	
Total overall Expenses:					

TASK 10.5:

Your Definition of Personal Success

Now that you have learned about career development and its interrelationship with personal and professional growth, take the time to write up a personal statement that reflects the measures you will use to judge your success. Identify measures that result from internal judgment (intrinsic measures), as well as those that depend on others' perspectives (extrinsic measures).

Intrinsic measures might include feeling good about the impact you make in your community or society through your work or other activities, connecting with others, finding personal meaning in your work, having time for family or personal interests, or enjoying your work tasks. Extrinsic measures might include your job title, the prestige of your organization or affiliations, your earnings, or the level of respect others have for you or your work.

What is your definition of career success?

_____

_____

_____

_____

_____

_____

_____

_____

Link to CourseMate

On CourseMate, you can find documents to help you update your Career Portfolio as well as additional resources and activities. Here is some of the information you can find online for **Chapter 10: Career Management.**

CAREER PORTFOLIO
Your Flexible Plan

RESOURCES
Exit Interview
Career Profile: Noemi S.
Career Profile: Bhavika Mody

Appendix

Your Career Portfolio can help you keep track of important items and prepare for your career. Use this checklist to add useful items as you complete each chapter. You can also find this checklist in CourseMate, and upload it to an online Career Portfolio to help you stay organized.

Career Portfolio Checklist

	Page Number in Creating Career Success	Item	Date Item Added	Check When Completed
CHAPTER 1: PREPARE	2	Career Development Calendar Career Portfolio Checklist Plan of Analysis: Prepare for Your Career		
CHAPTER 2: SKILLS	24	What Have You Done? Motivated Skills Matrix Worksheet Plan of Analysis: Assess Your Skills		
CHAPTER 3: PREFERENCES	46	Holland RIASEC Code / Personal Summary MBTI® Type / Personal Summary Plan of Analysis: Define Your Preferences		
CHAPTER 4: VALUES	73	Summary Sheet of Prioritized Values Career Options Worksheet Plan of Analysis: Discover Your Values		
CHAPTER 5: EXPLORE	96	Plan of Analysis: Explore Career Fields		
CHAPTER 6: RELATIONSHIPS	125	Informational Interview Request Networking E-mail Thank You Letter Plan of Action: Invest in Your Relationships		
CHAPTER 7: DECISION MAKING	148	Plan of Analysis: Commit to Your Next Step		
CHAPTER 8: TOOLS	174	Master Résumé Résumé Cover Letter Thank you Letter Additional Job-Search Materials • Credentials • Transcripts • Reference Letters • Other _____ Social Media Presence—list urls • LinkedIn_____ • Blog_____ • Facebook_____ • Twitter_____ • Other _____ Check those included: • Writing samples • Press clippings • Art portfolio • Other _____ Plan of Action: Create Your Job-Search Tools		
CHAPTER 9: LAUNCH	225	Elevator Pitch Plan of Action: Initiate a Job or Internship Search		
CHAPTER 10: CAREER MANAGEMENT	262	Plan of Action and Analysis: Manage Your Career		

Career Development Calendar

Resource (Include the location and contact information)	Services Offered and Upcoming Events	Sign-Up Date (Note if sign-up is recommended or required)	Requirements (e.g., Résumé drop, junior year status, prerequisite courses)	Date	Location	What to Bring
Career Center location: _____ phone number: _____ website: _____	Career Counseling Mentor Programs Workshops Courses Employer Visits Information Sessions Career Fairs Internships Recruiting Mentor Programs					
Academic Advising location: _____ phone number: _____ website: _____	Choose Courses Declare a Major Declare a Minor or Concentration					

Resource	Services Offered and Upcoming Events	Sign-Up Date (Recommended or required)	Requirements (e.g., Résumé drop, junior year status)	Date	Location	What to Bring
Student Activities location: _____ phone number: _____ website: _____	Activities Fair Leadership Training Workshop Student Government Elections Workshops					

Resource: _____
location: _____
phone number: _____
website: _____

Resource: _____
location: _____
phone number: _____
website: _____

References

Chapter 1

Borgen, W. A., and Amundson, N. E. (2001). *The portfolio project.* Vancouver, BC: Human Resources Development Canada.

Borgen, W. A., Amundson, N. E., and Reuter, J. (2004). Using portfolios to enhance career resilience. *Journal of Employment Counseling, 41,* 50–59.

Friedman, T. L. (2005). *The world is flat: A brief history of the 21st century.* New York, NY: Farrar, Straus and Giroux.

Holland, J. L. (1992). *Making vocational choice,* (2nd ed.). Odessa, FL: Psychological Assessment Resources.

Karpicke, J. (2010). Retrieval mode distinguishes the testing effect from the generation effect. *Journal of Memory and Language. 62*(3), 227–239.

Lancaster, L. C., and Stillman, D. (2002). *When generations collide: Who they are? Why they clash. How to solve the generational puzzle at work.* New York, NY: HarperCollins Publishers.

McLuhan, M. (1994). *Understanding media: The extensions of man.* Cambridge, MA: MIT Press.

Parsons, F. (1909). *Choosing a vocation.* Boston, MA: Houghton Mifflin.

Super, D. E. (1957). *The psychology of careers: An introduction to vocational development.* New York, NY: Harper.

Super, D. E. (1980). A life-span, life-space approach to career development. *Journal of Vocational Behavior, 13,* 282–298.

Super, D. (1990). The life-span, life-stage approach to counseling. In Brown, Brooks, and Associates (Eds.), *Career choice and development: Applying contemporary theories to practice,* (2nd ed.). San Francisco, CA: Jossey-Bass. 197–261.

Taylor, P., and Keeter, S. (Ed.). (2010). Millennials: A portrait of generation next. Pew Research Center. Retrieved from http://www.pewsocialtrends.org/files/2010/10/millennials-confident-connected-open-to-change.pdf

pubs/2128/social-media-teens-bullying-internet-privacy-email-cyberbullying-facebook-myspace-twitter

Morrison, T., Maciejewski, B., Giffi, C., DeRocco, E. S., McNelly, J., and Carrick, G. (2011). *Boiling point? The skills gap in U.S. manufacturing. A report on talent in the manufacturing industry sponsored by Deloitte and the Manufacturing Institute.* Retrieved from http://www.themanufacturinginstitute.org/Research/Skills-Gap-in-Manufacturing/2011-Skills-Gap-Report/2011-Skills-Gap-Report.aspx

National Association of Colleges and Employers (2011, November). Job outlook 2012. Retrieved from http://www.naceweb.org/Research/Job_Outlook/Job_Outlook.aspx

Pew Internet. (2011, May). Trend data. Pew Internet, Pew Internet and American Life Project. Retrieved from http://www.pewinternet.org/Trend-Data/Online-Activites-Total.aspx

Prensky, M. (2001). Digital natives, digital immigrants. *On the Horizon, 9* (5). Retrieved from http://www.marcprensky.com/writing/Prensky%20-%20Digital%20Natives,%20Digital%20Immigrants%20-%20Part1.pdf

Shuman, L. J., Besterfield-Sacre, M., and McGourty, J. (2005). The ABET "Professional Skills"—Can they be taught? Can they be assessed? *Journal of Engineering Education, 94*(1), 41–55.

The Partnership for 21st Century Skills (2009, December). *P21 framework definitions.* Retrieved from http://www.p21.org/storage/documents/P21_Framework_Definitions.pdf

Translating Military Experience to Civilian Employment. (2010, November 9). Retrieved from http://www.realwarriors.net/veterans/treatment/civilianresume.php

U.S. Department of Labor (2011, November 3). The veteran labor force in recovery. Retrieved from http://www.dol.gov/_sec/media/reports/VeteransLaborForce/VeteransLaborForce.pdf

U.S. Department of Labor (n.d.). Transition assistance program (TAP) participant manual Chapters 1 and 2. Retrieved from http://www.dol.gov/vets/programs/tap/tap1_2.pdf

Chapter 2

American Management Association (2010, April 15). *AMA 2010 critical skills survey.* Retrieved from http://www.amanet.org/news/AMA-2010-critcal-skills-survey.aspx

Baden, B. (2011, November 18) Are employers to blame for the skills gap? *U.S. News and World Report.* Retrieved from http://www.money.usnews.com/money/careers/articles/2011/11/18/are-employers-to-blame-for-the-skills-gap

Dweck, C. S. (2006). *Mindset: The new psychology of success.* New York, NY: Random House.

Knowdell, R. L. (2002). Motivated skills card sort. San Jose, CA: Career Research and Testing.

Lenhart, A., Madden, M., Smith, A., Purcell, K., Zickuhr, K., and Rainie, L. (2011, November 9). Teens, kindness and cruelty on social network sites. Pew Internet and American Life Project. Retrieved from http://www.pewresearch.org/

Chapter 3

Block, C. J., Koch, S. M., Liberman, B. E., Merriweather, T. J., and Roberson, L. (2011). Contending with stereotype threat at work: A model of long-term responses. *The Counseling Psychologist, 39*(4), 570–600.

Crant, J. M. (2000). Proactive behavior in organizations. *Journal of Management, 26,* 435–462.

Crant, J. M. (1995). The proactive personality scale and objective job performance among real estate agents. *Journal of Applied Psychology, 80,* 532–537.

Gottfredson, G. D., and Holland, J. L. (1996). *Dictionary of Holland occupational codes,* (3rd ed.). United States: PAR, Inc.

Grutter, J. (2006). Career exploration for college students. Using the Strong and MBTI® tools to chart your course. Palo Alto, CA: CPP, Inc.

Hammer, A. L. (2011). *Myers-Briggs type indicator® career report*. CPP, Inc.

Holland, J. L. (1994). *The self-directed search*. Odessa, FL: Psychological Assessment Resources.

Holland, J. L. (1997). *Making vocational choices: A theory of vocational personalities and work environments* (3rd ed.). Odessa, FL: Psychological Assessment Resources.

Ivester, M. (2011). *lol . . . OMG!: What every student needs to know about online reputation management, digital citizenship and cyberbullying*. Reno, NV: Serra Knight Publishing.

Ivester, M. (2011, November 10). Are you cyber-smart or cyber-screwed? Huffington Post. Retrieved from http://www.huffingtonpost.com/matt-ivester/are-you-cybersmart-or-cyb_b_1087028.html

Krumboltz, J. D. (2009). The happenstance learning theory. *Journal of Career Assessment, 17*(2), 135–154.

Li, N., Liang, J., and Crant, J. M. (2010). The role of proactive personality in job satisfaction and organizational citizenship behavior: A relational perspective. *Journal of Applied Psychology, 95*, 395–404.

Myers, I. B., Kirby, L. K., and Myers, K. D. (1998). *Introduction to type®*. (6th ed.). Palo Alto, CA: CPP, Inc.

Myers, P. B., and Myers, K. D. (1998). *MBTI® form M report form*. Palo Alto, CA: CPP, Inc.

Parker, S. K. (1998) Role breadth self-efficacy: Relationship with work enrichment and other organizational practices. *Journal of Applied Psychology, 83*, 835–852.

Pepitone, J. (2011, February 8). Facebook firing test case settled out of court, *CNN Money*, retrieved from http://www.money.cnn.com/2011/02/08/technology/facebook_firing_settlement/index.htm

Popkin, H. A. S., (2008, December 28). Evolution demands more Facebook drunkfail: Who among us has never called in sick to attend an awesome kegger? MSNBC.com, retrieved from http://www.msnbc.msn.com/id/28424059/ns/technology_and_science-tech_and_gadgets/t/evolution-demands-more-facebook-drunkfail/#.TvvyiJhOEUU

Prince, J. P. (2011, August 15). *Strong interest inventory profile with college profile*. Retrieved from https://www.cpp.com/Pdfs/smp284106.pdf

Schaubhut, N.A., and Thompson, R. C. (2011). *MBTI type tables for college majors*. Mountain View, CA: CPP, Inc.

Seibert, S. E., Crant, J. M., and Kraimer, M. L. (1999). Proactive personality and career success. *Journal of Applied Psychology, 84*, 416–427.

Smith, C. (2011, May 6). Top recruit's tweet leads to athletic director's firing. Rivals Yahoo. Retrieved from http://rivals.yahoo.com/highschool/blog/prep_rally/post/Top-recruit-8217-s-tweet-leads-to-athletic-dire?urn=highschool-wp1736

Steele, C. M. (1997). A threat in the air: How stereotypes shape intellectual identity and performance. *American Psychologist, 52*(6), 613–629.

Steele, C. M., and Aronson, J. (1995). Stereotype threat and the intellectual test performance of African-Americans. *Journal of Personality and Social Psychology, 69*, 797–811. doi:10.1177/0011000010382459

Stone, J., Lynch, C. I., Sjomeling, M., and Darley, J. M. (1999). Stereotype threat effects on black and white athletic performance. *Journal of Personality and Social Psychology, 77*(6), 1213–1227.

Chapter 4

Bowen, H. R. (1953). *Social responsibilities of the businessman*. New York, NY: Harper.

Crespin, R. (2011, December 15). Businesses continued investing in corporate responsibility and sustainability even as economy slowed. *Business Wire*. Retrieved from http://www.businesswire.com/news/home/20111215005147/en/Businesses-Continued-Investing-Corporate-Responsibility-Sustainability-Economy

Csikszentmihalyi, M. (2008). *Flow: The psychology of optimal experience*. New York, NY: Harper Perennial Modern Classics.

Csikszentmihalyi, M., and Nakamura, J. (2011). Positive psychology: Where did it come from? Where is it going? In Sheldon, K. M., Kashdan, T. B., and Steger, M. F. (Eds.) (2011). *Designing positive psychology: Taking stock and moving forward*. New York, NY: Oxford University Press.

Deci, E. L., Koestner, R., and Ryan, R. M. (2001). Extrinsic rewards and intrinsic motivation in education: Reconsidered once again. *Review of Educational Research, 71*(1), 1–27.

Flor. (n.d.). Our sustainability efforts. Retrieved from http://www.flor.com/sustainability

GE Citizenship. (n.d.). Our commitment areas. Retrieved from http://www.gecitizenship.com/our-commitment-areas/human-rights/

Kasser, T., and Ryan, R. M. (1996). Further examining the American dream: Differential correlates of intrinsic and extrinsic goals. *Personality and Social Psychology Bulletin, 22*(3), 280–287.

Knowdell, R. L. (2002). *Career values card sort*. San Jose, CA: Career Research and Testing.

Maslow, A. H. (1943). A theory of human motivation. *Psychological Review, 50*(4), 370–396. doi: 10.1037/h0054346

Maslow, A. (1987). *Motivation and personality*, (3rd ed.). Upper Saddle River, NJ: Pearson Learning.

Meister, J. C., and Willyerd, K. (2010). The 2020 workplace: How innovative companies attract, develop, and keep tomorrow's employees today. New York, NY: Harper-Collins.

Plato and Cranford, F. M. (Trans.) (1951). *The republic of Plato*. USA: Oxford University Press.

Sautter, E., and Crompton, D. (2008). *Seven days to online networking: Make connections to advance your career and business quickly (Help in a hurry)*. Indianapolis, IN: JIST Works.

Seligman, M. (2011). *Flourish: A visionary new understanding of happiness and well-being*. New York, NY: Free Press.

Stewart, E., and Bennett, M. (1991). *American cultural patterns: A cross-cultural perspective* (2nd ed.). Yarmouth, ME: Intercultural Press.

Target Volunteers. (n.d.). Retrieved from http://sites.target.com/site/en/company/page.jsp?contentId=WCMP04-031766

Toms. (n.d.). TOMS company overview. Retrieved from http://www.toms.com/corporate-info/

UNA-USA. (n.d.) Volunteer opportunities with global classrooms. Retrieved from http://www.unausa.org/globalclassrooms/volunteers

Chapter 5

About the Project, One Week Job, Discover Your Passion. Retrieved from http://oneweekjob.com/about-the-project/

Artim, M., Devlin, T., and Mackes, M. (2011, July). NACE message to the membership. A position statement on U.S. internships, a definition and criteria to assess opportunities and determine the implications for compensation. Retrieved from http://www.naceweb.org/about/membership/internship/

Belkin, L. (2007, November 29). What do I do? Depends on what week it is. *The New York Times*, Retrieved from http://www.nytimes.com/2007/11/29/fashion/29Work.html

Bureau of Labor Statistics. (2010, December 3). Occupational Outlook Handbook, 2010–11 Edition, Overview of the 2008–18 projections. Retrieved from http://www.bls.gov/bls/blswage.htm

Bureau of Labor Statistics. (n.d.). Employment projections programs. Retrieved from http://www.bls.gov/emp/

Coulter, S. (2011, August 10). Infographic: Where to get a green job. One block off the grid, Retrieved from http://1bog.org/blog/infographic-where-to-get-a-green-job/

Drucker, P. (1959). *Landmarks of tomorrow*. New York, NY: Harper and Row.

Florida, R. (2002). *The rise of the creative class: And how it's transforming work, leisure, community and everyday life*. New York, NY: Basic Books.

Gladwell, M. (2005). *Blink: The power of thinking without thinking*. New York, NY: Little, Brown and Company.

Kuang, C. (2011). Infographic of the day: Do green jobs really exist? *Fast Company's Co Design*, Retrieved from http://www.fastcodesign.com/1664826/infographic-of-the-day-do-green-jobs-really-exist

McClelland, C. (2011). Making sense of the new green career frontier: A framework of green industries. *Career Planning and Adult Development Journal*, Retrieved from http://findarticles.com/p/articles/mi_7494/is_200807/ai_n32305252/pg_2/?tag=mantle_skin;content

Neumayr, T. and Roth, J. (2008, April 3). iTunes store top music retailer in the US. Retrieved from http://www.apple.com/pr/library/2008/04/03iTunes-Store-Top-Music-Retailer-in-the-US.html

Osborn, D. S., Dikel, M. R., Sampson, J. P., and Harris-Bowlsbey, J. (2011). The Internet: A Tool for Career Planning, Third Edition. Broken Arrow, OK: National Career Development Association.

Pink, D. H. (2005). *A whole new mind: Why right brainers will rule the future*. New York, NY: Riverhead.

Roadtrip Nation. Retrieved from http://www.roadtripnation.org/

Settersten, R., and Ray, B. E. (2010). *Not quite adults: Why 20-somethings are choosing a slower path to adulthood, and why it's good for everyone*. New York, NY: Bantam Books.

Walshok, M., Munroe, T., DeVries, H., and Li, R. (Eds.) (2011). *Closing America's job gap*. W Business Books. El Monte, CA: New Win Publishing.

Chapter 6

Burt, R. S. (1992). *Structural holes: The social structure of competitions*. Cambridge, MA: Harvard University Press.

Dutton, J. E. (2003). *Energize your workplace*. San Francisco, CA: John Wiley & Sons.

Granovetter, M. S. (1973, May). The strength of weak ties. *American Journal of Sociology*, 78(6), 1360–1380.

Lin, N., Ensel, W. M., and Vaughn, J. C. (1981, August). Social resources and strength of ties: Structural factors in occupational status attainment, *American Sociological Review*, 46(4), 393–405.

Pollak, L. (2011, July 18). If you wouldn't do it in person, don't do it on LinkedIn! [Web log post]. Retrieved from http://blog.linkedin.com/2011/07/18/linkedin-etiquette-rules/

Subbaraman, N. (2011, September 7). Volunteering will save your career (Or put you in a new one). *Fast Company*. Retrieved from http://www.fastcompany.com/1778415/volunteering-will-save-your-career-or-be-a-path-into-a-new-one?partner=homepage_newsletter

U.S. Department of Justice (2009, June 15). Americans with Disabilities Act of 1990, As Amended. Retrieved from http://www.ada.gov/pubs/adastatute08.htm12102

U.S. Department of Labor, Office of Disability Employment Policy (n.d.). Diversity and inclusion. Retrieved from http://www.dol.gov/odep/topics/DiversityAndInclusion.htm

Chapter 7

Bandura, A. (1977) Self-efficacy: Toward a unifying theory of behavioral change, *Psychological Review*, 84(2), 191–215.

Bright, J. E. H., and Pryor, R. G. L. (2005). The chaos theory of careers: A user's guide. *Career Development Quarterly*, 53(4), 291–305.

Bright, J. (2009, September 13). Where will you be? Brightcareers [Video file]. Retrieved from http://www.youtube.com/watch?v=vrpC0pZHUe4

Iyengar, S. (2010). *The art of choosing*. New York, NY: Hachette Book Group.

Iyengar, S. S., Wells, R. E., and Schwartz, B. (2006). Doing better but feeling worse: Looking for the "best" job undermines satisfaction. *Psychological Science*, 17(2), 143–150.

Koc, E., and Koncz, A. (2011, November). *Job outlook 2012*. Bethlehem, PA: National Association of Colleges and Employers.

Krumboltz, J. D. (2009). The happenstance learning theory. *Journal of Career Assessment*, 17(2), 135–154.

Krumboltz, J. D., and Levin, A. S. (2004). *Luck is no accident: Making the most of happenstance in your life and career*. Atascadero, CA: Impact Publishers.

Mitchell, K. (2003). *The unplanned career: How to turn curiosity into opportunity: A guide and workbook*. Vancouver, CA: Raincoast Books.

Pryor, R., and Bright, J. (2011). *The chaos theory of careers: A new perspective on working in the twenty-first century*. New York, NY: Routledge.

Reardon, R., Lenz, J., Sampson, J., and Peterson, G. (2009). *Career development and planning: A comprehensive approach* (3rd. ed.). Mason, OH: Cengage Learning.

Sampson, J. P., Reardon, R. C., Peterson, G. W., and Lenz, J. G. (2004). *Career counseling and services: A cognitive information processing approach,* (3rd ed.). Cengage Learning.

Schwartz, B. (2004). *The paradox of choice: Why more is less. How the culture of abundance robs us of satisfaction*. New York, NY: Harper Perennial.

Settersten, R., and Ray, B. E. (2010). *Not quite adults: Why 20-somethings are choosing a slower path to adulthood, and why it's good for everyone*. New York, NY: Bantam Books.

Torpey, E. M. (2009, Fall). Gap year: Time off, with a plan. *Occupational Outlook Quarterly*. 26–33. Retrieved from http://www.bls.gov/opub/ooq/2009/fall/art04.pdf

U.S. Department of Labor, Bureau of Labor Statistics (2011). BLS information: Overview of BLS wage data by area and occupation. Retrieved from http://www.bls.gov/bls/blswage.htm

Chapter 8

Charnock, E. (2010). *E-Habits: What you must do to optimize your professional digital presence*. USA: McGraw-Hill.

Enelow, W., and Kursmark, L. (2010). *Cover letter magic*. Indianapolis, IN: JIST Publishing.

Gaw, K. (2011, August, 17). Measuring SLOs: Strategic cover letters, spotlight for career services professionals. NACE Knowledge Center. Retrieved from http://www.naceweb.org/s08172011/student_learning_outcome_cover_letter/

Peters, T. (1997, August 31). The brand called you. *Fast Company*.

Remillard, B. (2010, January 18). How recruiters read résumés in 10 seconds or less [Blog Post]. Retrieved from http://www.impacthiringsolutions.com/careerblog/2010/01/18/how-recruiters-read-resumes-in-10-seconds-or-less/

Zielinski, D. (2011). Applicant tracking systems evolve: Systems play new role in talent acquisition and other HR necessities. SHRM Online—Society for Human Resource Management. Retrieved from http://www.shrm.org/hrdisciplines/technology/Articles/Pages/ATSEvolves.aspx

Chapter 9

Aslanian, C. B. (2001). *Adult students today*. New York, NY: The College Board.

Forret, M. L., and Dougherty, T. W. (2004). Networking behaviors and career outcomes: Differences for men and women? *Journal of Organizational Behavior*, 25, 419–437.

Harvard Business School (2007). HBS elevator pitch builder. Retrieved from http://www.alumni.hbs.edu/careers/pitch/

Hettler, B. (1976). The six dimensions of wellness model. National Wellness Institute. Retrieved from http://www.nationalwellness.org/pdf/SixDimensionsFactSheet.pdf

HR World Editors (n.d.). 30 interview questions you can't ask and 30 sneaky legal alternatives to get the same info. Retrieved from http://www.focus.com/fyi/30-interview-questions-you-cant-ask-and-30-sneaky-legal-get/

Kurow, D. (2012). Preparing your elevator speech. Retrieved from http://www.dalekurow.com/elevator_speech

QuintCareers.com. (n.d.). STAR interviewing response technique for success in behavioral job interviews. QuintCareers.com. Retrieved from http://www.quintcareers.com/STAR_interviewing.html

Seligman, M. (2011). *Flourish: A visionary new understanding of happiness and well-being*. New York, NY: Free Press.

Sniderman, Z. (2010, October 23). 5 ways to get a job through YouTube. Mashable. Retrieved from http://www.mashable.com/2010/10/23/youtube-job/

Substance Abuse and Mental Health Services Administration (2011). *Results from the 2010 national survey on drug use and health: Summary of national findings*, NSDUH Series H-41, HHS Publication No. (SMA) 11–4658. Rockville, MD: Substance Abuse and Mental Health Services Administration.

Swallow, E. (2010, November 27). 6 ways to score a job through Twitter. Mashable. Retrieved from http://www.mashable.com/2010/11/27/twitter-job-tips/

Tullier, M. (1999). *The unofficial guide to acing the interview*. New York, NY: Macmillan.

U.S. Equal Employment Opportunity Commission. (2009, November 21). Federal laws prohibiting job discrimination questions and answers: Federal Equal Employment Opportunity (EEO) laws. Retrieved from http://www.eeoc.gov/facts/qanda.html

Wolff, H. G., and Moser, K. (2009). Effects of networking on career success: A longitudinal study. *Journal of Applied Psychology, 94*(1).

Chapter 10

Barley, S. R., Meyerson, D. E. and Grodal, S. (2010, September 30). E-mail as source and symbol of stress, *Organization Science*, 2010.

Carter, N. M. and Silva, C. (2010). Mentoring: Necessary but insufficient for advancement. Catalyst. *HBR Blog Network*. Retrieved from http://www.catalyst.org/file/415/mentoring_necessary_but_insufficient_for_advancement_final_120610.pdf

Catalyst. (2002). Creating successful mentoring programs: A Catalyst guide. Retrieved from http://www.catalyst.org/file/78/creating%20successful%20mentoring%20programs%20a%20catalyst%20guide.pdf

EEOC (n.d.). Harrassment. Retrieved from http://www.eeoc.gov/laws/practices/harassment.cfm

Goleman, D. (1995). *Emotional intelligence: Why it can matter more than IQ*. New York, NY: Random House.

Goleman, D. (1998). *Working with emotional intelligence*. New York, NY: Bantam.

Hewlett, S. A. (2011, January 26). The real benefit of finding a sponsor. *HBR Blog Network*. Retrieved from http://blogs.hbr.org/hbr/hewlett/2011/01/the_real_benefit_of_finding_a.html?cm_sp=blog_flyout-_-hbrhewlett-_-the_real_benefit_of_finding_a

Hinchcliffe, D. (2011, October 2). The "Big Five" IT trends of the next half decade: Mobile, social, cloud, consumerization, and big data. *ZDNet*. Retrieved from http://www.zdnet.com/blog/hinchcliffe/the-big-five-it-trends-of-the-next-half-decade-mobile-social-cloud-consumerization-and-big-data/1811

Maister, D. H. (1997). *True professionalism: The courage to care about your people. Your clients, and your career*. New York, NY: Touchstone.

National Academy of Sciences, National Academy of Engineering, Institute of Medicine (1997). *Adviser, teacher, role model, friend: On being a mentor to students in science and engineering*. Washington, D.C.: National Academy of Sciences.

Pink, D. H. (2005). *A whole new mind: Why right-brainers will rule the future*. New York, NY: Riverhead Books.

Settersten, R. and Ray, B. E. (2010). *Not quite adults, Why 20-somethings are choosing a slower path to adulthood, and why it's good for everyone*. New York, NY: Bantam Books.

Sue, D. W. (2010). *Microaggressions in everyday life: Race, gender, and sexual orientation*. John Wiley and Sons, Hoboken, NJ.

Sue, D., Capodilupo, C. M., Torino, G. C., Bucceri, J. M., Holder, A. B., Nadal, K. L., and Esquilin, M. (2007). Racial microaggressions in everyday life: Implications for clinical practice. *American Psychologist*, 62(4), 271–286.

TEDTalk. (2010). Dr. Philip Zimbardo's 2010 TED Talk: "Heroic Imagination Project" [podcast]. Retrieved from http://heroicimagination.org/2010/10/25/dr-philip-zimbardo's-2010-ted-talk/

Teicher, S., (2004, September 27). To make your career soar, get a mentor, Eager to retain employees, US firms are matching senior workers with newer hires. *The Christian Science Monitor*. Retrieved from http://www.csmonitor.com/2004/0927/p13s01-wmgn.html

U.S. Department of Education (n.d.) Funding your education 2012–2013 The Guide to federal student aid. Retrieved from http://studentaid.ed.gov/students/publications/student_guide/index.html

What's in your FICO® score? (n.d.). Fair Isaac Corporation. Retrieved from http://www.myfico.com/CreditEducation/WhatsInYourScore.aspx

Zimbardo, P. (n.d.). Understanding heroism. Heroic Imagination Project. Retrieved from http://heroicimagination.org/wp-content/uploads/2010/10/Understanding-Heroism.pdf

Index

Please note that f indicates a feature.

STEM. *See* Science, technology, engineering, and mathematics majors
Stereotype threat, 56–57
Super, Donald, 12
Super's five live stages, 12
Sustainablity, 109–110

T

Technology, 8–9
  job search and, 236f
Telephone interviews, 243
Temporary work, 118
Thank you letters, 191, 196
Traditionalists, 7

V

Values, 73–94
  activities, 84
  aiming to flourish, 87
  appearance, 84
  career, 80f–82f
  corporate social responsibility, 82f
  cultural values, 85
  environment, 79
  experience optimization, 86–87
  extrinsic motivation, 75

intrinsic motivation, 75
  lifestyle, 84
  needs hierarchy, 74–75
  personal, 80
  relationships, 79, 84
  reputation, 83
  tasks, 79
  work-life balance, 79–80
Veterans, 32
Volunteer, 25–26
  building connections, 133f
  career exploration, 117
  digital footprint, 84
  gap year, 162
  Happenstance Learning Theory and, 158
  networking and, 141–142
  relationships, 133
  skills, 25–29

W

Work-life balance, 278
Workplace diversity, 115

Z

Zimbardo, Philip, 277